James

THE CROSSWAY CLASSIC COMMENTARIES

James

by

Thomas Manton

Series Editors

Alister McGrath and J. I. Packer

CROSSWAY BOOKS

A DIVISION OF GOOD NEWS PUBLISHERS

WHEATON, ILLINOIS • NOTTINGHAM, ENGLAND

James

Copyright © 1995 by Watermark

Published by Crossway Books
   A division of Good News Publishers
   1300 Crescent Street
   Wheaton, Illinois 60187

Art Direction: Mark Schramm

First printing, 1995

Printed in the United States of America

Library of Congress Cataloging-in-Publication Data
Manton, Thomas, 1620-1677.
 James / by Thomas Manton.
   p. cm. — (Crossway classic commentaries)
  1. Bible. N.T. James—Commentaries. I. Title. II. Series.
BS2785.3.M36 1995   227'.91077—dc20   94-47149
ISBN 0-89107-832-0

VP		13	12	11	10	09	08	07	06	05	04
15	14	13	12	11	10	9	8	7	6	5	4	3

First British edition 1995

Production and Printing in the United States of America for
CROSSWAY BOOKS
Norton Street, Nottingham, England NG7 3HR

ISBN 0 85684 119-7

Contents

Series Preface

The purpose of the Crossway Classic Commentaries is to make some of the most valuable commentaries on the books of the Bible, by some of the greatest Bible teachers and theologians in the last five hundred years, available to a new generation. These books will help today's readers learn truth, wisdom, and devotion from such authors as J. C. Ryle, Martin Luther, John Calvin, J. B. Lightfoot, John Owen, Charles Spurgeon, Charles Hodge, and Matthew Henry.

We do not apologize for the age of some of the items chosen. In the realm of practical exposition promoting godliness, the old is often better than the new. Spiritual vision and authority, based on an accurate handling of the biblical text, are the qualities that have been primarily sought in deciding what to include.

So far as is possible, everything is tailored to the needs and enrichment of thoughtful readers—lay Christians, students, and those in the ministry. The originals, some of which were written at a high technical level, have been abridged as needed, simplified stylistically, and unburdened of foreign words. However, the intention of this series is never to change any thoughts of the original authors, but to faithfully convey them in an understandable fashion.

The publishers are grateful to Dr. Alister McGrath of Wycliffe Hall, Oxford, Dr. J. I. Packer of Regent College, Vancouver, and Watermark of Norfolk, England, for the work of selecting and editing that now brings this project to fruition.

THE PUBLISHERS
Crossway Books
Wheaton, Illinois

Introduction

Thomas Manton (1620-77) was a genial Devonian from Tiverton who, having distinguished himself at Oxford, was ordained at nineteen and fulfilled most of his ministry in and around London, taking a major role in public affairs and regularly preaching three or four times a week. He wrote a full manuscript of every sermon, which explains why his works, most of which were published posthumously, ran to five big folios, and in the 1870 reprint to twenty-three volumes of 450-plus pages each—all expositions of one kind or another, brisk, lucid, practical, experiential, and searching. "As an expositor of Scripture," wrote J. C. Ryle, no mean judge, "I regard Manton with unmingled admiration. Here, at any rate, he is *'facile princeps'* [easily the foremost] among the divines of the Puritan school."

Manton's Puritan contemporaries thought him outstanding. Richard Baxter celebrated him as "a man of great learning, judgment and integrity, and an excellent, most laborious, unwearied preacher." William Bates, preaching at Manton's funeral, spoke of his "unparalleled assiduity in preaching" with "fervour and earnestness . . . inflamed with holy zeal," and declared that "though so frequent in preaching, yet [he] was always superior to others, and equal to himself." Later, C. H. Spurgeon endorsed this verdict in his own expansive way: "His works . . . are a mighty mountain of sound theology. They mostly consist of sermons; but what sermons! . . . For solid, sensible instruction, forcefully delivered, they cannot be surpassed. Manton is not brilliant, but he is always clear; he is not oratorical, but he is powerful; he is not striking, but he is deep. There is not a poor discourse in the whole collection; they are evenly good, consistently excellent."

Ryle's sentiment is similar: "Manton's chief excellence as a writer, in my judgment, consists in the ease, perspicuousness, and clearness of his style. He sees his subject clearly, expresses himself clearly, and seldom fails in making you see clearly what he means. He has a happy faculty of simplifying the point he handles. . . . I find it easier to read fifty pages of

Manton's than ten of some of his brethren's; and after reading, I feel that I carry more away."

Manton's exposition of James, said William Harris, his early-eighteenth-century biographer, "has been thought by good judges to be one of the best models of expounding Scripture." One can only agree. James's rugged letter, in which the Old Testament styles of wisdom and prophecy blend as they do in the teaching of Jesus himself, is ideal raw material for Manton's no-nonsense, down-to-earth style of exposition; and the depth to which Manton digs in excavating the implications and applications of James's teaching on Christian reality makes this arguably the Mount Everest among expositions of the letter, both ancient and modern. Anyone who means business with God will find that Manton grabs, searches, humbles, and builds up in a quite breath-taking way. May this classic commentary find readers worthy of its quality.

J. I. PACKER

James
Chapter 1

Commentary on Verse 1

James, a servant of God and of the Lord Jesus Christ, To the twelve tribes scattered among the nations: Greetings.

James. There were two people of this name—the son of Zebedee, and the son of Alphaeus (James the Less); the latter is the author of this letter. Many of the ancients thought that there was a third person called James— James the brother of the Lord, also called Chobliham, or Oblias, or James the Just, who they thought was not an apostle but Bishop of Jerusalem. Jerome calls him the thirteenth apostle. But there were only two Jameses, this latter James being the same as the son of Alphaeus; for plainly the brother of the Lord is reckoned among the apostles in Galatians 1:19 and is called a pillar in Galatians 2:9; and he is called the brother of the Lord because he was in the family of which Christ was a member. Well, then, there being two, to which of these is the letter to be ascribed? The whole stream of antiquity carries it for the brother of the Lord, who, as I said, is the same as James the son of Alphaeus; and with good reason, the son of Zebedee being beheaded long before by Herod, from the very beginning of the preaching of the Gospel (Acts 12:2). But this letter must be of a later date, as it alludes to some passages already written and notes the degeneration of the church, which was not the condition of the church at the beginning.

James the Less is the person whom we have found to be the instrument whom the Spirit of God made use of to convey this treasure to the church. He was by his private calling a husbandman, by public office in the church an apostle, and was especially called to visit the church in and around Jerusalem, either because of his eminency and being a close relation of Christ, or for the great esteem he had gained among the Jews. And therefore, when the other apostles were going to and fro disseminating the Word of life, James was often found at Jerusalem. (See Galatians 1:18-19;

Acts 1:14, 21; 15; etc.) By disposition he was very strict and exceedingly just, and so was called James the Just. He drank neither wine nor strong drink and ate no meat. His knees were like a camel's hoof through frequent prayer. He died a martyr.

A servant of God. The word **servant** is sometimes used to imply an abject and vile condition, as that of a slave; thus the apostle Paul says, "neither . . . slave nor free . . . for you are all one in Christ Jesus" (Galatians 3:28); for "slave" he uses the word James uses for **servant.** This great apostle, James, thinks it an honor to be the **servant** of God. The lowest ministry and office for God is honorable.

But why not "apostle"? He does not mention his apostleship, first, because there was no need, as he was eminent in the opinion and reputation of the churches; therefore Paul says he was reputed to be a pillar of the Christian faith (Galatians 2:9). Paul, whose apostleship was openly questioned, often asserted it. Secondly, Paul himself does not call himself an apostle in every letter. Sometimes his style is, "Paul, a prisoner of Christ Jesus" (Philemon 1); sometimes "Paul and Timothy, servants of Christ Jesus" (Philippians 1:1); sometimes nothing but his name Paul is prefixed, as in 1 Thessalonians 1:1 and 2 Thessalonians 1:1.

And of the Lord Jesus Christ. Some people take both these clauses to apply to the same person and read it thus: "A servant of Jesus Christ who is God and Lord"; indeed this was one of the verses that the Greek fathers used when arguing, against the Arians, for the Godhead of Christ. But our reading, which separates the clauses, is to be preferred as less forced and more suitable to the apostolic inscriptions. Neither is the dignity of Christ impaired hereby, as he is the object of equal honor with the Father; as the Father is Lord, as well as Jesus Christ, so Jesus Christ is God, as well as the Father. Well, then, James is not only God's **servant** by the right of creation and providence, but Christ's **servant** by the right of redemption; yes, especially appointed by Christ as Lord—that is, as mediator and head of the church—to do him service as an apostle. I suppose there is some special reason for this distinction, **a servant of God and of . . . Christ,** to show his countrymen that in serving Christ he served the God of his fathers, as Paul pleaded in Acts 26:6-7.

To the twelve tribes. That is, to the Jews and people of Israel, chiefly those converted to the faith of Christ; to these James writes as the minister of the "circumcised" (Galatians 2:9) [see NIV footnote on Galatians 2:7— *Ed. note*]. And he writes not in Hebrew, their own language, but in Greek, as the language then most in use, just as the apostle Paul writes to the Romans in the same language, and not in Latin.

Scattered among the nations. In the original Greek, the word "dispersion" is used. But what scattering, or dispersion, is intended here? I answer:

(1) Either what happened in their ancient captivities and the frequent changes of nations; there were some Jews who still lived abroad, as John 7:35 shows.

(2) Or, more recently, by the persecution spoken of in Acts 8.

(3) Or by the hatred of Claudius, who commanded all the Jews to depart from Rome (Acts 18:2). And it is probable that the same was done in other great cities. The Jews, and among them the Christians, were thrown out everywhere, just as John was thrown out of Ephesus and others out of Alexandria.

(4) Or some voluntary dispersion, the Hebrews living here and there among the Gentiles a little before the decline and ruin of their state, some in Cilicia, some in Pontus, etc. Thus the apostle Peter writes "to . . . strangers . . . scattered throughout Pontus, Galatia, Cappadocia, Asia and Bithynia" (1 Peter 1:1).

Greetings. A usual salutation, but not so frequent in Scripture. Cajetan thinks it profane and pagan, and therefore questions the letter, but unworthily. We find the same salutation sometimes used in holy Scripture, for example to the Virgin Mary (Luke 1:28); see also Acts 15:23. Usually it is "grace, mercy, and peace," but sometimes it is "greetings."

Notes on Verse 1

Note 1. **James, a servant of God**. He was Christ's close relative and, therefore, in a Hebraism, is called "the Lord's brother" (Galatians 1:19)—not properly and strictly, as Joseph's son (though some of the ancients thought he was, by a former marriage), but his cousin. So James, the Lord's kinsman, calls himself the Lord's **servant**. Note that inward privileges are the best and most honorable, and spiritual relationship is preferred to physical. Mary was happier having Christ in her heart than in her womb, and James in being Christ's **servant** rather than his brother. Christ himself speaks about this in Matthew 12:47-50. The truest relationship to Christ is founded on grace, and we are far happier receiving him by faith than touching him by blood. Whoever endeavors to do his will may be as sure of Christ's love and esteem as if he were linked to him by the closest outward relationship.

Note 2. It is no dishonor for the highest to be Christ's servant. James, whom Paul calls " a pillar", calls himself **a servant of . . . Christ**; and David, a king, says, "I would rather be a doorkeeper in the house of my God than dwell in the tents of the wicked" (Psalm 84:10). The office of the Nethinim, or doorkeepers in the temple, was the lowest; and therefore when the question was proposed what they should do with the Levites who had moved away from God to idols, God says, "They must bear the shame"; that is, they shall be degraded and employed in the lowest offices and ministries of the temple, as porters and doorkeepers (see Ezekiel 44:10-13). Yet David says, "I would rather be a doorkeeper"; human honor and greatness is nothing compared with this. Paul was "a Hebrew of Hebrews" (Philippians 3:5)—that is, from an ancient Hebrew race and extraction, there being, to the memory of man, no proselyte in his family or among his ancestors, which was seen as a very great honor by that nation. Yet Paul says he counts everything dung and dogs' meat in comparison with an interest in Christ Jesus (see Philippians 3:8).

Note 3. The highest ranks in the church are still only servants: **James, a servant**. See 2 Corinthians 4:1. The sin of Corinth was man-worship, giving excessive honor and respect to those teachers whom they admired, setting them up as heads of factions and giving up their faith to their dictates. The apostle seeks to reclaim them from that error, by showing that they are not masters but ministers: give them the honor of a minister and steward, but not that dependence which is due only to the Master. See 2 Corinthians 1:24. We are not to prescribe articles of faith but explain them. So the apostle Peter bids the elders not to lord it over God's heritage (see 1 Peter 5:3), not to have mastery over their consciences. Our work is mere service, and we can but persuade; Christ must impose himself upon the conscience. This is Christ's own advice to his disciples in Matthew 23:10: "Nor are you to be called 'teacher,' for you have one Teacher, the Christ." All the authority and success of our teaching is from our Lord. We can prescribe nothing as necessary to be believed or done that is not according to his will or word. In short, we come not in our own name and must not act with respect to our own ends; we are servants.

Note 4. **A servant of God and of the Lord Jesus Christ.** In everything we do we must honor the Father, and also the Son: "all may honor the Son just as they honor the Father" (John 5:23); that is, God will be honored and worshiped only in Christ. "Trust in God; trust also in me" (John 14:1). Believing is the highest worship and respect of the creature; you must give it to the Son, to the second person as mediator, as well as to the Father. Do duties so as to honor Christ in them; and so:

First, look for their acceptance in Christ. It would be sad if we were only to look to God the Father in our work. Adam hid himself and did not dare to come into God's presence until the promise of Christ. The hypocrites cried, "Who of us can dwell with the consuming fire?" (Isaiah 33:14). Guilt can form no other thought about God when looking upon him apart from Christ; we can see nothing but majesty armed with wrath and power. But now it is said that "in him we may approach God with freedom and confidence" (Ephesians 3:12); for in Christ those attributes that are in themselves terrible become sweet and comforting, just as water, which is salt in the ocean, once strained through the earth, becomes sweet in the rivers.

Second, look for your assistance from him. You serve God in Christ:

a. When you serve God through Christ: "I can do everything through him who gives me strength" (Philippians 4:13). When your own hands are in God's work, your eyes must look to Christ's hands for support in it: see Psalm 123:2; you must go about God's work with his own tools.

b. When you have an eye for the concerns of Jesus Christ—in all your service of God (2 Corinthians 5:15). We must "live . . . for him who died for [us]"; not only for God in general, but for him, for God who died for us. You must see how you advance his kingdom, propagate his truth, further the glory of Christ as mediator.

c. When all is done for Christ's sake. In Christ God has a new claim on you, and you are bought with his blood, that you may be his servants. Under the law the great argument for obedience was God's sovereignty: do so-and-so, "I am the Lord"— as in Leviticus 19:37. Now the argument is gratitude, God's love in Christ: "For Christ's love compels us" (2 Corinthians 5:14). The apostle often persuades with that motive: be God's servants for Christ's sake.

Note 5. **To the twelve tribes scattered among the nations.** God looks after his afflicted servants; he moved James to write to the scattered tribes. Heaven's care flourishes toward you when you wither. One would have thought that people might have been driven away from God's care when they had been driven away from the sanctuary. "This is what the Sovereign LORD says: Although I have sent them far away among the nations and scattered them among the countries, yet for a little while I have been a sanctuary for them in the countries where they have gone" (Ezekiel 11:16). Though they lacked the temple, yet God would be a sanctuary. He looks after them, to watch their spirits, that he may comfort them, and to watch their adversaries, to go before them with his care. He looks after them to deliver them, that he may "assemble the exiles" (Micah 4:6) and make up his "treasured possession" (Malachi 3:17), those that seemed to be carelessly scattered and lost.

Note 6. God's own people may be dispersed and driven from their countries and habitations. God has his outcasts. He says to Moab, "be their shelter" (Isaiah 16:4). And the church complains, "Our inheritance has been turned over to aliens" (Lamentations 5:2). Christ himself had nowhere to lay his head; and the apostle tells us about some of whom "the world was not worthy. . . . They wandered in deserts and in mountains, and in caves and holes in the ground" (Hebrews 11:38). In Acts 8:4 we read of the first believers, who "had been scattered." Many of the children of God in these times have been driven from their homes; but you see we have no reason to think the case strange.

Note 7. **To the twelve tribes scattered among the nations.** There was something more in their scattering than usual: they were a people whom God for a long time had kept together under the wings of providence. What is notable in their scattering is:

(1) The severity of God's justice. The twelve tribes are scattered—his own people. It cuts out any privileges when God's Israel are made strangers. Israel is all for liberty; therefore God says he will "pasture them like lambs in a meadow" (Hosea 4:16). God would give them liberty and room enough. As a lamb out of the fold goes up and down bleating in the forest or wilderness, without comfort and companion, in the middle of wolves and the beasts of the desert—liberty enough, but danger enough!—so God would cast them out of the fold, and they should live a Jew here and a Jew there, thinly scattered and dispersed throughout the countries, among a people whose language they did not understand, and as a lamb in the middle of the beasts of prey. Consider the severity of God's justice; certainly it is a great sin that makes a loving father throw a child out of doors. Sin is always driving away and casting out; it drove the angels out of heaven, Adam out of paradise, Cain out of the church (see Genesis 4:12, 16), and the children of God out of their homes ("We must leave our land," Jeremiah 9:19).

Your houses will be tired of you when you dishonor God in them; and you will be driven from those comforts that you abuse to excess. You see in Amos 6:5 that when they were at ease in Zion, they would ruin David's music by using it for their banquets. For this, God threatened to scatter them and to remove them from their houses of luxury and pleasure. And when they were driven into a strange land they received the same treatment. The Babylonians wanted temple-music: see Psalm 137:3; nothing but a holy song would serve their unholy pleasure. Honor God in your houses, lest you become their burdens and they spew you out. **The twelve tribes** were **scattered**.

(2) The infallibility of his truth. In judicial dispensations, it is good to observe not only God's justice but God's truth. No calamity befell Israel except what was foretold to the letter in the books of Moses; one might have written their history out of the threatenings of the law. See Leviticus 26:33; God says, in effect, "if you do not listen to me, 'I will scatter you among the nations and will draw out my sword and pursue you.'" The same is threatened in Deuteronomy 28:64—"The Lord will scatter you among all nations, from one end of the earth to the other." See how the event fitted the prophecy; and therefore I conceive that James uses this expression **the twelve tribes** to show that they who were once twelve flourishing tribes were now, by the accompaniment of that prophecy, sadly scattered among the nations.

(3) The tenderness of his love to the believers among them. He has a James for the Christians of the scattered tribes. In the severest ways of his justice he does not forget his own, and he has special consolations for them when they

lie under the common judgment. When other Jews were banished, John, among the rest, was banished from Ephesus to Patmos, a barren, miserable island; but there he had those revelations (Revelation 1:9ff.). Well, then, wherever you are, you are near to God; he is a God close to hand, and a God afar off. When you lose your dwelling, you do not lose your interest in Christ.

Commentary on Verse 2

Consider it pure joy, my brothers, whenever you face trials of many kinds.

My brothers. A normal name in the Scriptures, and very frequent in this letter, partly because the Jews called all of their nation brothers, and partly because ancient Christians in courtesy used to call the men and women of their society and communion brothers and sisters, and partly from apostolical kindness, that the exhortation might be seasoned with more love and goodwill.

Consider it. That is, though sense will not find it so, yet in spiritual judgment you must so esteem it.

Pure joy. That is, a matter of chief joy. See 1 Timothy 1:5.

Whenever you face. This signifies such troubles as come upon us unawares, as sudden things upset the mind most. But, says the apostle, when you are suddenly attacked, you must look upon it as a trial and a matter of great joy; for though it seems to be chance to us, it is under God's control.

Many kinds. The Jewish nation was infamous and generally hated, especially the Christian Jews, who, besides the scorn of the pagans, were exercised with various injuries and attacks from their own people. This is clear from Peter's letter, where he speaks of suffering "grief in all kinds of trials" (1 Peter 1:6), and again from the letter to the Hebrews, written also to these dispersed tribes: "You . . . joyfully accepted the confiscation of your property" (Hebrews 10:34)—that is, by the fury of a crowd of base people, against whom the Christians could have no right.

Trials. This is what he calls afflictions that believers become used to.

Notes on Verse 2

Note 1. **My brothers.** Christians are linked to one another in the bond of brotherhood. It was an ancient use for Christians of the same communion to call one another brothers and sisters, which gave occasion of scorn to the pagans then. This is Christ's own argument: "You are all brothers" (Matthew 23:8). It also suggests love and mutual friendship. Who should love more than those who are united in the same head and hope? As Augustine said of himself and his friend Alipius, "We are cemented with the same blood of Christ." We are all traveling home and expect to meet in the same heaven; it would be sad that brothers should fall out by the way (see Genesis 45:24). It was once said, "See how the Christians love one another!" But alas, now we may say, "See how they hate one another!"

Note 2. **Consider it.** Miseries are sweet or bitter depending on how we view them. Seneca said, "Our grief lies in our own opinion and apprehension of miseries." Spiritual things are worthy in themselves; other things depend upon our opinion and valuation of them. So we must make a right judgment. In this lies our misery or comfort; things are as you **consider** them. Accept these rules so that your judgment in affliction may be rectified.

(1) Do not judge by sense. "No discipline seems pleasant at the time, but painful" (Hebrews 12:11). Christians live above the world because they do not judge according to the world. "I consider that our present sufferings are not worth comparing with the glory that will be revealed in us" ((Romans 8:18). Sense that is altogether for present things would judge quite otherwise; but the apostle says, "I consider (i.e., reason) in another way." See Hebrews 11:26.

(2) Judge by a supernatural light. Christ's eye-ointment must clear your sight, or else you cannot make a right judgment: there is no correct understanding of things until you get within the veil and see by the light of a sanctuary lamp: "No one knows the thoughts of God except the Spirit of God" (1 Corinthians 2:11). It is by God's Spirit that we come to discern and esteem the things that are of God, which is the main drift of the apostle in that chapter. See Psalm 36:9.

(3) Judge on supernatural grounds. Often common grounds help us discern the lightness of our grief—yes, human grounds; but your counting must be a holy counting. In Isaiah 9:10 the people say, "The bricks have fallen down, but we will rebuild with dressed stone"; it is a misery, but we know how to remedy it. So many despise their troubles. We can repair and make up this loss again; we know how to deal with this misery. God's corrections are sharp, but we have strong corruptions to be mortified; we are called to great trials, but we may count on great hopes.

Note 3. **Pure joy.** Afflictions to God's people do not only produce patience but great joy. The world has no reason to think that religion is a black and gloomy way. As the apostle says, "The weakness of God is stronger than man's strength" (1 Corinthians 1:25). So grace's *worst* is better than the world's *best*. A Christian is a bird that can sing in winter as well as in spring; he can live in the fire like Moses' bush—burn and not be consumed, even leap in the fire. The apostle writes, "In all our troubles my joy knows no bounds" (2 Corinthians 7:4). Paul in his worst state felt an exuberance of joy. In another passage he goes further still: "We also rejoice in our sufferings" (Romans 5:3). Certainly a Christian is not understood by the world; his whole life is a riddle. "Sorrowful, yet always rejoicing" (2 Corinthians 6:10)—this is Paul's riddle, and it may be every Christian's motto.

Objection 1. But you may object, does not the Scripture allow us a sense of our condition? How can we rejoice in what is evil? Christ's soul was "overwhelmed with sorrow to the point of death" (Matthew 26:38).

Solution. I answer: (1) Do not rejoice in evil: that is so far from being a fruit of grace that it is against nature. There is a natural abhorrence of what is painful, as we see in Christ himself: "My heart is troubled, and what shall I say? 'Father, save me from this hour'?" (John 12:27). As a private person, Christ would show the same affections that are in us, though as mediator he freely chose death and sufferings. In Christ's sufferings there was a concurrence of our guilt taken into his own person and of God's wrath. It is a known rule that no adversary except God can make us miserable; and it is his wrath that puts vinegar and gall into our sufferings, not man's wrath.

(2) Their joy is from the happy consequences of their sufferings. I will name some.

a. The honor done to us. We are singled out to bear witness to the truths of Christ: "it has been granted to you . . . to suffer for him" (Philippians 1:29). It is a gift and an act of free-grace. To be called to such special service is an act of God's special favor. Far from being a matter of discouragement, it is a ground for thanksgiving: "If you suffer as a Christian . . . praise God" (1 Peter 4:16). Do not accuse God with murmuring thoughts but glorify him. This influenced the first saints and martyrs. It is said that they went away "rejoicing because they had been counted worthy of suffering disgrace for the Name" (Acts 5:41); the Greek means that they were honored to be dishonored for Christ.

b. The benefit the church receives. Resolute defenses impress the world. The church is like an oak, which lives by its own wounds; and the more limbs that are cut off, the more new ones sprout. Tertullian says, "The heathen's cruelty was the great bait and motive by which men were drawn into the Christian religion." And Augustine writes, "They were bound, butchered, racked, stoned, burned, but still they were multiplied. The church was founded in blood, and it thrives best when it is moistened with blood; founded in the blood of Christ, and moistened or watered, as it were, with the blood of the martyrs."

c. Their own personal comforts. God has consolations for martyrs, and for his children under trials. Let me name a few. Sometimes it is a greater presence of the Word: see 1 Thessalonians 1:6. The sun shines many times when it rains. And they have sweet glimpses of God's favor when their outward condition is most gloomy and sad: see Matthew 5:10. Martyrs, in the act of suffering and troubles, not only have sight of their interest, but a sight of the glory of their interest. There are some thoughts stirred up in them that come close to ecstasy; a happy preview makes them almost insensible of their trials and sufferings. Their minds are so wholly swallowed up with the things that are not seen that they have little thought or sense of the things that are seen. The apostle seems to intimate this in 2 Corinthians 4:18.

Again, they rejoice because they pass into glory more swiftly. The enemies do them a favor by removing them from a troublesome world. This made the early Christians rejoice more when they were condemned than when they were absolved. They kissed the stake and thanked the executioner because of their earnest desires to be with Christ. So Justin Martyr writes, "We thank you for delivering us from hard taskmasters, that we may more sweetly enjoy the presence of Jesus Christ."

Objection 2. But some will say, "My sufferings are not like martyrdom; they do not come from the hand of men, but from providence, and result from my own sins."

Solution. I answer: it is true there is a difference between afflictions from the hand of God and persecutions from the violence of men. God's hand is just, and guilt will make the soul less cheerful. But remember the apostle's word is, **trials of many kinds**; and sickness, death of friends, and such things that come from providence are also trials to God's children. These afflictions require not only mourning and humbling, but a holy courage and confidence: "You will laugh at destruction and famine" (Job 5:22). Faith should be above everything that happens to us; it is its work to make a believer triumph over every temporary setback. In ordinary crosses there are many reasons for laughing and joy—such as Christ's companionship; if you do not suffer for Christ, Christ suffers in you, and with you. He is afflicted and touched with a sense of your afflictions. It is wrong for believers to think that Christ is altogether unconcerned by their sorrows unless they are endured for his name's sake, and that the comforts of the Gospel are only applicable to martyrdom.

Again, another ground for joy in ordinary crosses is that in them we may have much experience of grace, of the love of God, and of our own sincerity and patience; and this is a ground for rejoicing: "We also rejoice in our sufferings, because we know that suffering produces perseverance" (Romans 5:3). This rule holds good in all kinds of tribulations or sufferings; they bring sweet discoveries of God, and so are matters for joy. See also 2 Corinthians 12:9-10. They are happy occasions to discover more of

God. They give us a greater sense and feeling of the power of grace, and so we may take pleasure in them.

Lastly, all evils are the same to faith. You should walk so that the world may know you can live above every condition, and that all evils are much beneath your hopes. So, from all that has been said, we see that we should suffer the will of Christ with the same cheerfulness as we should suffer for the name of Christ.

Note 4. **Whenever you face.** Evils are borne better when they are undeserved and involuntary; that is, when we fall into them rather than draw them upon ourselves. It was Tertullian's error to say that afflictions were to be sought and desired. The creature never knows when it is well; sometimes we question God's love because we have no afflictions, and at other times because we have nothing but afflictions. In all these things we must refer ourselves to God's pleasure—not desiring troubles, but bearing them when he lays them on us. Christ has taught us to pray, "Lead us not into temptation"; it is only foolish pride to cast ourselves upon it. Philastrius speaks of some who would compel men to kill them out of an affectation of martyrdom; so does Theodoret. This was a mad ambition, not a true zeal: see 1 Peter 4:15. We derive no strength from our sufferings when there is guilt in them.

Note 5. **Many kinds.** God has several ways of exercising his people. Various miseries come on top of one another; thus God changes the dispensation, sometimes in this trouble, sometimes in that. Paul gives a catalog of his dangers and sufferings in 2 Corinthians 11:24-28. Crosses seldom come singly. Once God begins to test, he uses various methods of trial; and there is good reason for this. Different diseases must have different remedies. Pride, envy, covetousness, worldliness, wantonness, ambition are not all cured by the same remedy. One affliction pricks the bladder of pride, while another checks our desires. Do not murmur, then, if miseries come upon you like waves. Job's messengers came thick and fast one after another, telling of oxen, house, camels, sons, daughters, and all destroyed (see Job 1); messenger upon messenger, each with a sadder story. We have "all kinds of passions" (Titus 3:3), and therefore have many kinds of trials. In Revelation 6 one horse comes after another—the white, the red, the black, the pale. Once the floodgates are opened, several judgments follow in succession (see also Matthew 24:7). Learn also that God has several types of trial—confiscation, banishment, poverty, infamy, reproach; some trials test us more than others. We must leave it to his wisdom to make the choice.

Note 6. **Trials.** James does not call them afflictions or persecutions but trials, because of God's purpose in sending them. The same word is used in 2 Peter 2:9—"The Lord knows how to rescue godly men from trials." The afflictions of the saints are not judgments but corrections or trials—

God's discipline to mortify sin, or his means to discover grace, to prove our faith, love, patience, sincerity, constancy, etc. Watch over yourselves with great care so that no impatience, vanity, murmuring, or worldliness of spirit may appear in you.

Commentary on Verse 3

Because you know that the testing of your faith develops perseverance.

Here is the first argument to encourage them to be joyful in afflictions, taken partly from the trials' nature, partly from their effect. Their nature: they are a **testing of your faith**; their effect or fruit: they create or develop **perseverance**. Let us examine the words a little.

You know. This may imply that they ought to know, as Paul says elsewhere: "Brothers, we do not want you to be ignorant about those who fall asleep . . ." (1 Thessalonians 4:13). So some suppose that James is exhorting, **Because you know**—that is, I would have you know. Or else it is a report: **Because you know**; that is, you do know, being taught by the Spirit and experience. Or rather, lastly, it is a direction, in which the apostle tells them how the Spirit brings a joy into the hearts of persecuted Christians by a living knowledge or spiritual discourse, by acting their thoughts upon the nature and quality of their troubles.

That the testing of your faith. Here is a new word used for afflictions; before it was **trials**, which is more general. Here is a seeming contradiction between Paul and James. Paul says that patience produces perseverance or experience (Romans 5:4, KJV); James seems to invert the order, saying that trial or experience produces perseverance. But I answer: (1) There is a difference between the words ; they are correctly translated **testing** and "perseverance." (2) Paul is speaking about the effect of suffering, the experience of God's help, and the comforts of his Spirit, which produces perseverance. James is speaking about the suffering itself, which he calls **testing** because by it our faith and other graces are approved and tried.

Of your faith. That is, either of your constancy in the profession of the faith, or else the grace of faith, which is the chief thing exercised and approved in affliction.

Develops perseverance. The original Greek word means "perfecting patience." But this is a new paradox. How can affliction or trial, which is the cause of all murmuring or impatience, develop patience?

I answer: (1) Some explain this as natural patience, which indeed is caused by mere afflictions. When we become used to them, they are less of a weight. Passions are blunted by continual exercise, and grief becomes a

22

delight. But this is not in the apostle's mind. This is stupidity, not patience. (2) So the meaning is that our trials are an opportunity for perseverance. (3) God's blessing must not be excluded. Through trials God sanctifies affliction in us, and then they are a means to develop perseverance. (4) We must not forget the distinction between punishment and **testing**. The fruit of punishment is despair and murmuring, but of **testing** patience and sweet submission.

To the wicked every condition is a snare. They are corrupted by prosperity and dejected by adversity; but to the godly every situation is a blessing. Their prosperity produces thanksgiving, their adversity patience. Pharaoh and Joram became more angry from their afflictions, but God's people become more patient. See Psalm 11:5. To sum up, afflictions serve to examine and prove our faith and, by the blessing of God, to bring forth the fruit of patience, just as the quiet fruit of righteousness is ascribed to the rod (Hebrews 12:11), which is indeed the true work of the Spirit. "Discipline . . . produces a harvest of righteousness," and our apostle here says that **the testing of your faith develops perseverance.**

Notes on Verse 3

Note 1. **You know.** Ignorance is the cause of sorrow. When we do not rightly discern evils, we grieve because of them. Our strength, as humans, lies in reason; as Christians, it lies in spiritual discourse. See Proverbs 24:5, 10. Children are scared of every trifle. If we knew God and his dealings, we would not faint. So, labor for a right discerning. To help you, consider:

(1) General knowledge will not suffice. The heathen had excellent ideas concerning God (Romans 1:19); but "their thinking became futile" (Romans 1:21) when they applied their knowledge to particular things. They had a great deal of knowledge about general truths, but no wisdom to apply them to particular matters. Many people can talk well in general. Seneca, when he had rich gardens, could be patient, but fainted when he suffered. Eliphaz accused Job of being able to instruct and strengthen others; "but now trouble comes to you, and you are discouraged; it strikes you, and you are dismayed" (Job 4:5). Therefore, you not only need knowledge but the wisdom to apply general truths to particular cases.

(2) Our knowledge must be drawn from spiritual principles. This brings relief to the soul, and this is where our strength lies. You will always find that the Spirit works through right thinking. Christ had taught the apostles many comforting things, and then he promised, "The Counselor . . . will remind you of everything I have said to you" (John 14:26). That is the true work of the Counselor, to come in with powerful thinking that

relieves the soul. In many other places in the Bible we find that the Spirit helps us by waking us up and stirring up correct thinking in the mind.

(3) Those thoughts that usually create perseverance are these:

First, evils do not come by chance but are from God. So holy Job says: "The arrows of the Almighty are in me" (Job 6:4). Note that it is "the arrows of the Almighty," even though Satan had a great hand in them, as you may see from Job 2:7—God's arrows, though shot out of Satan's bow.

Second, where we see anything of God, we owe nothing but reverence and submission; he is too strong to be resisted, too just to be questioned, and too good to be suspected.

Note 2. **Testing.** Persecution is **testing** to God's people. God makes use of the worst instruments, just as fine gold is cast in the fire, the most consuming element. Innocence is tried best by iniquity. But why does God test us? Not for his own sake, for he is omniscient; rather, perhaps (1) for our sakes, that we may know ourselves. In trials we discern the sincerity of grace, and the liveliness of it; and so we know our weak hearts better. In times of trial God heats the furnace so hot that dross is totally removed. So that we may know ourselves, God uses severe trials. Sometimes we discover our own weakness: see Matthew 13:5, 20-21. We find that faith is weak in danger that out of danger we thought was strong. Peter thought his faith impregnable, until the sad trial in the high priest's hall (Matthew 26:69ff.). Trials help us to know either the sincerity or the weakness or the liveliness of the grace that is wrought in us.

(2) Or for the world's sake. And so, firstly, in our present lives we can convince others by our constancy, that they may be confirmed in the faith if weak and staggering, or converted if altogether uncalled. Note Luther's saying: "The church converts the whole world by blood and power." We are tested, and religion is tested, when we are called to suffer. Paul's chains led to the furtherance of the Gospel: see Philippians 1:12-13. In prosperous times religion is usually stained with the scandals of those who profess it; and then God brings great trials. Justin Martyr was converted by the constancy of the Christians. When he saw them willingly choose death, he reasoned thus within himself: surely these men must be honest, and there is something eminent in their principles.

Secondly, we are tried in connection with the day of judgment: see 1 Peter 1:7. God will justify faith before all the world, and the crown of patience is set on a believer's head on that solemn day of Christ. You see the reasons why God tries us.

Use. So, then, testing teaches us to bear afflictions with constancy and perseverance; God tries us through these things. For your comfort consider four things:

(1) God's aim in your afflictions is not destruction but testing, just as gold is put into the furnace to be purified, not consumed. Wicked men's

misery is a "disaster" (Ezekiel 7:5). But to godly men, miseries have another purpose: see Daniel 11:35.

(2) The time of trial is appointed: "at the appointed time" (Daniel 11:35). You are not in the furnace by chance or because of the will of your enemies; the time is appointed, set by God.

(3) God sits by the furnace looking after his metal: "He will sit as a refiner and purifier of silver" (Malachi 3:3). That the fire is not too hot, and that nothing is spilled and lost, notes his constant and assiduous care.

(4) Consider: this trial is not only to *approve* but to *improve*; we are tried as gold, and refined when tried; see 1 Peter 1:7, or, more clearly, Job 23:10, "When he has tried me, I will come forth as gold." The dross is burned away, and the sins that cling to us are purged away.

Note 3. **Your faith.** The chief grace that is tried in persecution is faith (1 Peter 1:7). Out of all graces, Satan especially hates faith; and out of all the graces God delights in, faith is the perfection. Faith is tried partly because it is the radical grace in the life of a Christian: "the righteous will live by his faith" (Habakkuk 2:4). We work by love but live by faith. Faith is also tested because it is the grace most exercised, sometimes in keeping the soul from evil actions. Believing makes the soul withstand a trial: see Hebrews 11:24ff. Sometimes faith is exercised to bring the soul to live on Gospel comforts in the absence of worldly comforts. There are many occasions to exercise faith.

Use 1. You who have faith, or profess to have faith, must expect trials. Graces are not crowned until they are exercised; nobody ever went to heaven without conflicts. Note that wherever God bestows the assurance of his favor, trials follow. See Hebrews 10:32. Some people are thrown into trials soon after their conversion. When Christ himself had received a testimony from heaven, Satan immediately tempted him. The Father proclaimed, "This is my Son . . . with him I am well pleased," and immediately Satan comes with an "If you are the Son of God . . ." (Matthew 3:17 and 4:3). See also Genesis 22:1. When the castle is well stocked with supplies, then look for a siege.

Use 2. You who are under trials, look to your faith. Christ knew what was most likely to be attacked and therefore told Peter, "I have prayed for you, Simon, that your faith may not fail" (Luke 22:32). When faith fails, we faint; therefore we should make it our main aim to maintain faith. Look after two things:

(1) Hold on to your assurance in the middle of the saddest trials. In the furnace call God Father: "I will bring [them] into the fire; I will refine them like silver and test them like gold . . . and they will say, 'The Lord is our God'" (Zechariah 13:9). Do not let any hard trial make you doubt your Father's affection. Christ had a bitter cup, but he said in effect, "My Father put it into my hands" (see John 18:11).

(2) Next, faith keeps your hopes fresh and lively. Let faith put your hopes in one balance when the devil has put the world in the other balance. Say with Paul, "I consider that our present sufferings are not worth comparing with the glory that will be revealed in us" (Romans 8:18).

Note 4. **Develops**. Many trials bring perseverance through God's blessing on them. Habits are strengthened by frequent acts; the more you act from grace, the stronger you become. The apostle says that discipline "produces a harvest of righteousness . . . for those who have been trained by it" (Hebrews 12:11). Perseverance is not found after one or two afflictions, but after we are exercised and acquainted with them. Trees often shaken are deeply rooted.

So, firstly, this shows how carefully you should exercise yourselves under every cross; in this way you acquire habits of grace and patience. Neglect causes decay, and God withdraws his hand from the idle. In spiritual matters as well as temporal matters, "diligent hands bring wealth" (Proverbs 10:4).

Secondly, this shows that if we complain about any providence, the fault is in our own hearts, not in our circumstances. Many blame providence and say they cannot do otherwise, as their troubles are so great and painful. But remember, many trials, where sanctified, work patience. There is no condition in the world that is not an opportunity for the exercise of grace.

Note 5. **Perseverance**. The apostle comforts them with this argument: fiery trials are nothing if you gain **perseverance**. Sickness, with **perseverance**, is better than health; loss, with **perseverance**, is better than gain. See 2 Corinthians 12:9. Certainly nothing makes afflictions a burden for us except our own human desires.

Note 6. **Perseverance**. We may observe more particularly that **perseverance** is a most valuable grace. We cannot be Christians without it; how else can we persevere in doing good when we meet burdensome crosses? Therefore the apostle Peter tells us, "add to your faith, goodness; and to goodness, knowledge; and to knowledge, self-control; and to self-control, perseverance . . ." (2 Peter 1:5-6). See also Luke 21:19.

Commentary on Verse 4

Perseverance must finish its work so that you may be mature and complete, not lacking anything.

Here James shows what **perseverance** is, by way of exhortation, encouraging them to move on to maturity. I start with a difficulty in the verse.

Finish its work [KJV, **have her perfect work**—*Ed. note*]. Remember that in the apostle's time there were various people who had a great deal of zeal and who bore the first attacks. But they tired, either because of the variety or the length of evils, and they yielded and fainted. Therefore, James wanted his readers to persevere and be **complete**. The best grace is maturity. We say of Abraham's faith that it was a perfect faith; so when **perseverance** is thoroughly tried by various lengthy afflictions, we say there is a perfect **perseverance**. Perfect **perseverance** is a resolute **perseverance**, holding no regard for the length, the acuteness, or the continual succession of various afflictions. One trial revealed Job's **perseverance**; but when evil upon evil came, and he bore everything with a humble and quiet spirit, that revealed a mature **perseverance**.

So that you may be mature and complete, not lacking anything. The apostle's purpose is not to assert a possibility of perfection in Christians: **We all stumble in many ways** (3:2). All that we have here in this life is incomplete: "We know in part and we prophesy in part, but when perfection comes, the imperfect disappears" (1 Corinthians 13:9-10). Here grace is imperfect, because the means are imperfect. So James means either that we should be sincere, for sincerity is called perfection in Scripture ("Walk before me, and be thou perfect," as Genesis 17:1 reads in the original; the NIV has, "be blameless"); or else it means the perfection of perseverance; or, lastly, the intended perfection is "the perfection of parts"—that we might be so perfect, or **complete**, that no necessary grace might be lacking—that, having other gifts, we might also have the gift of **perseverance** and the whole image of Christ might be completed in us—that nothing might be **lacking** that a Christian needs. Indeed, some make this a legal sentence, implying what God may justly require and what we should aim for—exact perfection, both in parts and degrees. It is true that this is beyond our power; but though we have lost our power, there is no reason why God should lose his right. God's right humbles us with the sense of our own weakness. God might require so much that we had power to perform, though we have lost it through our own fault. This is true, but the former interpretations are more simple and genuine.

Notes on Verse 4

Note 1. Our graces are not perfected until we go through many great trials. As a pilot's skill is discerned in a storm, so is a Christian's grace in many and great troubles. So in everything that happens to you say, "Patience has not yet been perfected." The apostle says, "In your struggle against sin, you have not yet resisted to the point of shedding your blood"

(Hebrews 12:4). Should we collapse in a lesser trial, before the perfect work is revealed? Job was in a sad state, yet said, "Though he slay me, yet will I hope in him" (Job 13:15); in a higher trial, I should not faint or murmur.

Note 2. Exercise grace until it is full and perfect—**that you may be mature.** The apostle chides the Galatians because their first enthusiasm quickly evaporated: "Are you so foolish? After beginning with the Spirit, are you now trying to attain your goal by human effort?" (Galatians 3:3). It is not enough to start. To falter shows that we are not "fit for service in the kingdom of God" (Luke 9:62). While you are in the world, go on to finish the work of patience; follow those who "through faith and patience inherit what has been promised" (Hebrews 6:12).

Note 3. Christians must aim at, and press on to, perfection. The apostle says, **so that you may be mature and complete, not lacking anything.**

(1) Christians aspire to absolute perfection. First, they go to God for justification, so that the damning power of sin may be taken away; then for sanctification, that the reigning power of sin may be destroyed; then for glorification, that its very being may be abolished. Those who have *true grace* will not be content with *little grace.* "I want . . . somehow, to attain to the resurrection from the dead," says Paul (Philippians 3:10-11)—that is, such a state of grace as we enjoy after the resurrection. Free grace makes a Christian press on and be earnest in his endeavors: see Hebrews 6:1.

(2) Christians must be perfect in all aspects of their Christian faith. Every part of life must be seasoned with grace (see 1 Peter 1:15 and 2 Corinthians 8:7). Hypocrites always lack something. The Corinthians had much knowledge but little charity. As Basil says, "I know many who fast, pray, sigh . . . but withhold from God and the poor." One negligence may be fatal. A Christian should not lack anything.

(3) They aim at a perfection that lasts. Subsequent acts of apostasy make our former crown wither (see 2 John 8 and Ezekiel 18:24). If a Nazirite defiled himself, he had to begin all over again (see Numbers 6:12). We have separated ourselves to Christ, and if we do not endure to the end, all the righteousness, zeal, and patience of our former profession is forgotten.

Commentary on Verse 5

If any of you lacks wisdom, he should ask God, who gives generously to all without finding fault, and it will be given to him.

The apostle says that to bear afflictions requires a great deal of spiritual skill and wisdom, but that God will help you if you ask him. In this verse James encourages us with God's nature and promise.

If any of you. This **if** does not imply doubt; it is only a supposition. But why does the apostle use a supposition? Who does not lack wisdom? May we not ask, in the prophet's question, "Who is wise? . . . Who is discerning?" (Hosea 14:9). In answer:

(1) Such expressions strongly support the argument under discussion. See Malachi 1:6, Romans 13:9, 2 Thessalonians 1:6, and James 5:15.

(2) Different people lack different things, so **if any of you lacks** includes everybody.

Wisdom. This is to be restricted to the text and not taken in a general way. This **wisdom** is for bearing afflictions. In the original the beginning of this verse clearly links on to the end of the previous verse—**lacking anything,** and then immediately **if any of you lacks.**

He should ask. That is, by serious and earnest prayer.

God—to whom our addresses must be directed.

Who gives generously to all. Some think this implies the natural bounty of God, which indeed is an argument in prayer; God, who gives to all, will not deny his saints. The psalmist takes God's common bounty to the creatures as a ground of hope and confidence for his people (see Psalm 145:16, 19). He who provides for every living creature will certainly provide for his own servants. But the context will not sustain this sense. **All** refers to all kinds of people—Jew, Greek, or barbarian; rich or poor. God gives to all people. Everyone who asks—all who seek him with earnestness and trust—will receive this wisdom.

Generously. In the original the word means "simply," but it is usually translated "bountifully." See Acts 2:46 and 2 Corinthians 8:2 and 9:11. This word "simplicity" is so often used for "bounty" to show (1) that it must come from the free desire of our hearts, for those who give sparingly give with a hand half closed; (2) that we must not give deceitfully, as serving our own ends. So God gives simply—that is, as David puts it, according to his will (2 Samuel 7:21).

Without finding fault. Here James reproves another common blemish on man's bounty, which is finding fault with what others have done for them. Courtesy requires that the receiver should remember and the giver forget. God does not find fault. But you will say, what is the meaning then of Matthew 11:20—"Then Jesus began to denounce the cities, in which most of his miracles had been performed"? Because of this objection, some expound this clause one way, some another. Some suppose it implies he does not give in a proud way, as men do, denouncing those who receive with their words or looks. God does not disdainfully reject anyone who asks, or confront him with his unworthiness, or reject him because of his present failings or former weaknesses. Rather, I think it shows God's indefatigability in doing good; ask as often as you wish, God will not tell you off for the frequency of your requests. God denounces us only to make us see our ingratitude.

And it will be given to him. In addition to the nature of God, here James emphasizes a promise: "Let him ask God, and it will be given to him." Descriptions of God help us think correctly about him. Promises help us hold on to him in trust.

Notes on Verse 5

Note 1. Everyone is needy: **If any of you**. This supposition is universal. God's wisdom allows creatures to lack, because dependence brings awareness. If we were not forced to live in continued dependence on God, we would not bother with him. We see this—the less people are aware of their condition, the less religious they are. Promises usually appeal to those who are in need, because they are most likely to take note of them: see Isaiah 55:1, Matthew 11:28, and Matthew 5:3 and 6. Those who are humbled by their own needs are most open to God's offers. Only God is self-sufficient; creatures have needs, so that their eyes are fixed on God. Certainly they lack most who lack nothing.

Note 2. **Lacks**. We pray about our own needs. The father would not have heard from the prodigal if he had not been "in need" (Luke 15:14). Note that the creature goes to God initially out of self-love. But remember, it is better to begin in the flesh and end in the spirit than to begin in the spirit and end in the flesh. The first motive is need.

Note 3. **Wisdom**. In this context, note the need for great wisdom to cope with afflictions. Cheerful patience is a holy skill that we learn from God: see Philippians 4:10. Such a difficult lesson needs much learning. Wisdom is needed in several respects: (1) to discern what God's purpose is in this; (2) to know the nature of the affliction, whether it is to build up or destroy; (3) to know what to do in every situation; (4) to check the desires of our own passions. So:

(1) Become wise if you want to become patient. People of understanding have the greatest control over their affections: see Proverbs 14:29.

(2) Become wise to confute the world's censure; they count patience as simplicity and meekness as folly.

(3) Become wise by patience and calmness of spirit. A person who has no command of his passions has no understanding.

Note 4. **Ask God**. In all our needs we must immediately turn to God. The Scriptures do not direct us to the shrines of saints but to the throne of grace. You need not use the saints' intercession; Christ has opened a way for you into the presence of the Father.

Note 5. More particularly, note that **wisdom** must be found in God. He is wise, the fountain of wisdom, an inexhaustible fountain. Men have the faculty, but God gives the light, just as the dial is capable of showing the time of the day when the sun shines on it. It is spiritual idolatry to lean on your own understanding (see Proverbs 3:5). The best way to proceed is not to go to nature but to Christ, "in whom are hidden all the treasures of wisdom and knowledge" (Colossians 2:3).

Note 6. **He should ask.** God gives nothing without our asking. This is one of the laws by which heaven's bounty is dispensed (see Ezekiel 36:37). Every audience with God increases love, thanks, and trust: see Psalm 116:1-2. Who does not want to be one of those whom God calls his worshipers (see Zephaniah 3:10)?

Note 7. Asking remedies our greatest needs. People sit down groaning under their discouragements because they do not look further than themselves. God humbles us with great weakness, that he may turn us to prayer. That is as easy for the Spirit as it is hard for nature. If God commands anything beyond our nature, it is to bring you to your knees for grace.

Note 8. **Who gives.** God's dispensations to his creatures are gifts. Usually God gives most to those who, in the eyes of the world, least deserve it and are last able to requite him. Does he not freely invite the worst? See Isaiah 55:1.

Note 9. **To all.** God's grace is universal. It is a great encouragement that none are excluded from the offer. Why should we, then, exclude ourselves? "Come to me, *all* you who are weary and burdened" (Matthew 11:28, italics added). Note, poor soul: Jesus Christ makes no exceptions.

Note 10. **Generously.** God's gifts are free. Often God gives more than we ask, and our prayers come far short of what his grace gives: see Ephesians 3:20. Examples of this are Solomon (1 Kings 3:13), Jacob (Genesis 28:20 with Genesis 32:10), Abraham (Genesis 15 with Genesis 22), and the prodigal (Luke 15:11-32). Certainly God's bounty is too large for our thoughts. So:

(1) Do not restrict God in your thinking: "Open wide your mouth and I will fill it" (Psalm 81:10). God's hand is open, but our hearts are not open. Note the expression of the virgin in Luke 1:46, "My soul praises the Lord"—that is, I make more room for God in my thoughts.

(2) Let us imitate our Heavenly Father and give **generously**. Some people give grudgingly, with a divided mind; this is not like God. Give like your Heavenly Father.

Note 11. **Without finding fault.** I am certain that nothing harms us as much as believing that God is "altogether like" us (Psalm 50:21).

Therefore God says, "My thoughts are not your thoughts, neither are your ways my ways. . . . As the heavens are higher than the earth, so are my ways higher than your ways and my thoughts than your thoughts" (Isaiah 55:8-9). See also Hosea 11:9. So when God gives, he will give according to his nature.

Note 12. **Without finding fault.** God never tires of doing his people good. It was Solomon's advice in Proverbs 25:17 to "Seldom set foot in your neighbor's house—too much of you, and he will hate you." But how different it is with our heavenly friend! The more frequently we come to God, the more welcome we are.

Well, then: (1) Whenever you receive mercy upon mercy, give the Lord the praise for his tireless love. (2) Since God is not tired of blessing you, do not become tired of serving him. See Galatians 6:9.

Note 13. **And it will be given to him.** God always answers prayer, though he does not always answer human desires: "Ask and it will be given to you; seek and you will find; knock and the door will be opened to you" (Matthew 7:7). If we do not receive through asking, let us go on to seeking; if we do not receive through seeking, let us go on to knocking. Prayers, when they come from a holy heart, in a holy manner, for a holy purpose, will be successful.

These are the limitations on prayer: (1) Concerning the person: God looks after not only the purpose of the prayer but the interest of the person. Prayer must come from a righteous person (see 5:16). (2) What we ask for must be good: see 1 John 5:14. It must be according to God's revealed will, not our own fancies. To ask according to our desires is blasphemous. But we must remember that God must judge what is good, not we ourselves. (3) We must ask in a right way, with faith. See Psalm 40:1. (4) You must pray with reference to the Lord's glory. There is a difference between an ungodly desire and a gracious supplication: see 4:3. Never let your requests terminate in self. "Give us water to drink" was a brutish request (Exodus 17:2).

Note 14. **It will be given.** James draws encouragement not only from God's nature but from God's promise. From God's promise we may reason thus: "You are good, and you will do good." This is God in covenant, God as ours.

Let the world think what it will about prayer. You have promises about prayer. Therefore when you pray for a promised blessing, God will answer you. "Ask and it will be given."

Commentary on Verse 6

But when he asks, he must believe and not doubt, because he who doubts is like a wave of the sea, blown and tossed by the wind.

Here James suggests caution, in order to avoid mistakes about what he has said. Every request will not be answered; you must ask in faith.

But when he asks, he must believe. Faith may be understood as follows: (1) As confidence in God, or an act of particular trust, as in Ephesians 3:12. (2) It may include confidence about the lawfulness of the things that we ask for; that is one accepted meaning of "faith" in Scripture (see Romans 14:23). (3) Faith is a state of believing. God only hears his own, those who have an interest in Jesus Christ. Here faith is contrasted with doubting and wavering, and so means a particular act of trust.

Not doubt. What is this **doubt?** The word does not mean disputing a matter but having doubtful thoughts. The same phrase is used in Acts 10:20, "Do not hesitate." The word is often used in connection with believing, as in Romans 4:20, "he did not waver through unbelief"; in the Greek this is, "he did not dispute," he did not debate the matter but settled his heart on God's power and promise. See Matthew 21:21: if they could remove the uncertainty of their thoughts, they would do miracles.

He who doubts is like a wave of the sea, blown and tossed by the wind. This simile is also used by the prophet Isaiah (see 57:20). James says here that the doubter is **like a wave of the sea**; and the prophet says about all wicked men that they are like "the tossing sea."

Notes on Verse 6

Note 1. The test of true prayer is its faith. Cursory requests are made out of habit, not in faith; so examine your prayers. Pray with hope and trust. See Matthew 15:28 and Mark 11:24; note the words "believe . . . and it will be yours." Through our trust God's power is engaged. But you will say, how do we pray in faith? I answer, this is what is required in every prayer:

(1) A reliance on the grace and merits of Jesus Christ: see Ephesians 2:18. We cannot have any trust in God except through him. You must realize that such worthless creatures as you are may be accepted in him: see Hebrews 4:16. Through Christ we may freely approach God. I am a sinner, but Jesus Christ, my intercessor, is righteous. Some people do not doubt God, but they doubt themselves. They ask, "I am a wretched sinner; will the Lord hear me?" I answer: this is Satan's strategy, for in effect it is doubting God and his mercy, as if he were unable to pardon and save. We

must come humbly, for we are sinners: but we must come in faith also. Christ is a Saviour; it is folly, under color of humbling ourselves, to have low thoughts of God. We may come humbly yet boldly in Christ.

(2) We must not pray except in faith. The apostle's words are relevant here: "This is the assurance we have in approaching God: that if we ask anything according to his will, he hears us" (1 John 5:14). Everything is to be asked in faith. Let prayer be according to the Word, and the success will be according to the prayer.

(3) The soul must magnify God's attributes in every prayer. To pray in faith, to have right thoughts about God in prayer, as we see in this verse, is enough to combat a particular doubt. See Matthew 9:28-29. Christ asked the two blind men if they had a correct estimate of his power, which he then called faith, and gave them the blessing. People who come to God need to view him correctly.

You may say, tell us what faith is required in every prayer. I answer: the question has already been answered for the most part.

Take these rules:

a. Where we have a definite promise, we must not doubt God's will. For the doubt can arise from a suspicion that this is not the word or will of God, which is atheism; or from thinking that God will not make good his word, which is blasphemy; or from fear that he is not able to accomplish his will, which is unbelief. So, where we have a clear view of his will in the promise, we may be confident toward him (1 John 5:14).

b. Where we have no certainty about his will, the work of faith is to glorify and apply his power. Difficulties terrify us so that we cannot pray out of faith in God's power. Search and you will find that God's power is the first ground for faith. Abraham believed because "God had power" (Romans 4:21). Unbelief shows itself in plain distrust of God's power: see Psalm 78:19 and 2 Kings 7:2. People deceive themselves when they think they doubt because they do not know God's will; they are mainly hesitating over God's power. Therefore the main work of your faith is to give God the glory of his power, leaving his will to himself.

In these cases, it is not only his power that is to be glorified but also his love. But you will say in an uncertain way, how must we glorify his love? I answer, in two ways. Faith has a double work:

First, to compose the soul to submit to God's pleasure. He is so good that you may give yourself to his goodness. He is a wise God and a loving Father and will do what is best; we must never dispute this: see Proverbs 16:3.

Second, to lift the soul to hope for the mercy prayed for. Hope is the fountain of endeavors, and we should neither pray nor wait on God unless we look up to him in hope.

Some people who have come close to God may have faith in some particular occurrence. By some special understanding in prayer from the Spirit of God they have said with David, "I will be confident" (Psalm 27:3). I do not say this is normal, but it sometimes happens. But remember, privileges do not make rules.

I have given you my thoughts about praying in faith.

Note 2. **Not doubt** or "dispute," as it is in the original. Man is given to doubting God's grace. Pride will not stoop to revelation. Ungodly reason is faith's worst enemy.

Note 3. **Not doubt.** The less we doubt, the more we show true faith. Grace settles the heart on God. So set aside your doubts, especially in prayer; strong belief in God's attributes, as revealed in Christ, removes all perplexities of spirit. So have a clear understanding of God's attributes. Ignorance perplexes us, but faith settles the soul and gives it a greater constancy.

Note 4. **Like a wave of the sea, blown and tossed by the wind.** Doubts are perplexing and torment the mind. An unbeliever is like the waves of the sea, always rolling; but a believer is like a tree, shaken but firm in its roots. We are in slavery so long as we are tossed by the waves of our own affections. There is no rest and peace in the soul until faith is strong: see Psalm 116:7. Go to God, and have your spirit settled.

Commentary on Verse 7

That man should not think he will receive anything from the Lord.

That man should not think. James does not say, "He shall receive nothing," but **That man should not think he will receive.** Whatever God's overflowing bounty may give them, they can expect nothing. Or else, **That man should not think,** in order to check his vain hopes. Man deceives himself and seduces his soul with ungodly hope. Therefore, the apostle says, **That man should not think**—that is, deceive himself with a vain hope.

He will receive anything. This kind of doubting does not spring from faith and only frustrates praying. God's people do have doubts but are victorious over them. Therefore, it should not be thought that any doubt makes us incapable of receiving any blessing. This only happens when doubt is allowed to persist.

From the Lord. That is, from Christ. In the New Testament, **Lord** most often applies to Christ, the mediator; and Christ the mediator commends our prayers to God and conveys all blessings from God. Therefore, the apostle says, "Yet for us there is but one God, the Father, from whom all things came and for whom we live; and there is but one Lord, Jesus Christ, through whom all things came and through whom we live" (1 Corinthians 8:6). The heathen had many gods, many intermediate powers who were agents between the gods and men. "Yet for us," says the apostle, "there is but one God," one sovereign God, "the Father," the first spring and fountain of blessings, and "one Lord"—that is, one mediator, "Jesus Christ, through whom all things came."

Notes on Verse 7

Note 1. Although unbelievers may receive something, they can expect nothing from God. **That man should not think**. They are under a double misery: (1) They can have no thoughts of hope and comfort, as they have no assurance of a promise. Oh, how miserable this is, to toil and still to be left in uncertainty—to pray, and to have no sure hope! When the task is over, they cannot look for acceptance or a blessing. The children of God have a more certain hope: see 1 Corinthians 9:26. So Solomon says, "The truly righteous man attains life" (Proverbs 11:19). The righteous have God's infallible promise and may expect a blessing. But the wicked, whether they run or sit, have no hope. Whether they run or sit still, they are in the same condition; if they run, they run uncertainly; if they pray, they pray uncertainly. They are like a slave who does his work not knowing whether he will give satisfaction; so, when they have done everything, they are still left in uncertainty. They pray and do not look for success in prayer; they perform duties but do not see the blessing of duties.

(2) If they receive anything, they cannot expect it to come as a promise or as a return for prayers. When the children are fed, the dogs may have the crumbs: all their comforts are just the crumbs of God's bounty. It is a great misery when blessings are given to us by chance rather than covenant. A person may be ashamed to ask of God, who is so slow to honor him.

Note 2. **That man should not think**. Men usually deceive themselves with vain hopes and thoughts: see Matthew 3:9. Ungodly confidence is rooted in some vain principle and thought; so men think God is not just, hell is not so hot, the devil is not so evil, nor the Scriptures so strict. The apostles meet with these ungodly thoughts everywhere: see 1 Corinthians 6:9-11. Men are persuaded that if they can offer any excuse, all will be well. But God is not deceived. So consider your private thoughts. All corrupt actions are based on some vain thought, and this vain thought is strengthened with some vain word. Therefore the apostle says, "Let no one deceive you with empty words" (Ephesians 5:6). In spiritual things we are happy when we have seduced our souls with a vain hope.

Note 3. **He will receive.** The reason we do not receive what we ask for lies in ourselves, not in God. He **gives generously**, but we **doubt** as we pray. He wants to give, but we cannot receive. Men are discouraged when they are distrusted; and certainly when we distrust God it is not reasonable we should expect anything from him. Christ said to Martha, ". . . if you believed, you would see the glory of God" (John 11:40)—that is, power, love, truth in their glory. Omnipotence knows no restraint but is discouraged by man's unbelief. Therefore Mark 6:5-6 says, "he could not do any miracles . . . he was amazed at their lack of faith"; he *could* not because he *would* not, not because of any lack of power in him, but because of the disposition of the people. When the father comes for a possessed child and says, "Teacher . . . if you can do anything . . . help us," Christ answers, "If you can? Everything is possible for him who believes" (Mark 9:17-23). The distressed father says, "If you can do anything"; our holy Lord says, "If you can?" as if he had said, do not doubt my power, but look to your own faith; I can if you can. If we were prepared to receive what God wants to give, we would not be long without an answer. God can do all things for the comfort of believers; faith is his immutable ordinance. So if we receive not, it is not because of any lack of God's power, but because we lack faith ourselves.

Note 4. **Anything.** God thinks the least mercy too good for unbelievers. In the days of Christ's life on earth he offered everything you could wish for: "You have great faith! Your request is granted" (Matthew 15:28). Ask what you will, and he will give it. But mercy shrinks at the sight of unbelief!

Note 5. **From the Lord.** The fruit of our prayers is given to us from the hands of Christ. He is the person through whom God blesses us: "I will do whatever you ask in my name, so that the Son may bring glory to the Father" (John 14:13). Note, "I will do it." Christ receives the power to convey the blessing; we must ask the Father, but it comes to us through Christ. We are unworthy to converse with the Father; therefore, Christ is the true mediator. God is glorified when we come to him through Christ. You must come to the Father in the Son's name and look for everything through the Spirit; and as the Spirit works as Christ's Spirit, to glorify the Son (John 16:14), so the Son gives glory to the Father. What an excellent ground of hope we have when we reflect on these three things in prayer—the Father's love, the Son's merit, and the Spirit's power! No one comes to the Son but by the Father (John 6:65); no one comes to the Father but by the Son (John 14:6); no one is united to the Son but by the Holy Spirit: therefore we read of "the unity of the Spirit" (Ephesians 4:3).

Commentary on Verse 8

He is a double-minded man, unstable in all he does.

James goes on to consider the unhappiness of unbelievers, and he says two things about them—that they are **double-minded** and **unstable**.

He is a double-minded man. The word signifies a person who has two souls, and so it may imply:

(1) A hypocrite, since the same word is used with that meaning in 4:8: "Purify your hearts, you double-minded." As he speaks to open sinners to cleanse their hands, so he speaks to secret hypocrites (whom he calls **double-minded** since they pretend one thing but mean another) to purify their hearts—that is, to grow more inwardly sincere. This word is similar to the Hebrew word for "deceive." "Their flattering lips speak with deception" (Psalm 12:2); in the Hebrew this is "with a heart and a heart," which is their way of expressing something that is double or deceitful (deceitful weights are "a weight and a weight" in the Hebrew of Proverbs 20:23). As Theophrastus says of the partridges of Paphlagonia that they had two hearts, so every hypocrite has two hearts or two souls.

(2) It implies a person who is distracted and divided in his thoughts, floating between two different opinions, as if he had two minds or two souls. In the apostle's time there were some Judaizing brethren who sometimes sided with the Jews, sometimes with the Christians. They were not settled in the truth. See also 2 Kings 17:33, "They worshiped the LORD, but they also served their own gods"; they were divided between God and idols. The prophet says this shows a double or divided heart: "Their heart is deceitful, and now they must bear their guilt" (Hosea 10:2). Thus Athanasius applied this description to the Eusebians, who sometimes held one thing and then another.

(3) In the context of James this may refer to those whose minds were tossed to and fro with various ideas: now lifted up with a wave of presumption, then cast down in a gulf of despair, being torn between hopes and fears concerning their acceptance with God. I prefer this latter sense, as it conveys the apostle's purpose best.

Unstable. An unstable man has no constancy of soul. He is sometimes ready to depart from God and sometimes to be close to him; he is not settled in his religious profession.

In all he does. Some apply this chiefly to prayer because those who are doubtful about its success often practice it intermittently; but I think it is a general maxim, and that prayer is only intended as a consequence, for the apostle says **in all he does**. Note the Hebraism (**in all his ways**, KJV), standing for any counsel, action, thought, or purpose.

Notes on Verse 8

Note 1. Unbelieving hypocrites have a double mind. They lack the Spirit and are led by their own affections and therefore cannot be settled; fear, love for the world, and ungodly hopes draw them here and there, for they have no certain guide and rule. It is said of the godly man that "He will have no fear of bad news; his heart is steadfast, trusting in the LORD" (Psalm 112:7). Such people walk by a sure rule and look to sure promises; and therefore, though their circumstances change, their hearts do not change, for the ground of their hopes is still the same. Ungodly men's hearts rise and fall with their news; and when affairs are doubtful, their hopes are uncertain, for they are fixed on uncertain objects.

(1) In their hopes they are distracted between expectation and jealousy, doubts and fears. One moment they are full of confidence in their prayers, and then later have nothing but sorrow and despair. Possibly this may be one reason why the psalmist compares the wicked to chaff (Psalm 1:4), because they are driven here and there, leading their lives by guesswork rather than any sure aim.

(2) In their opinions hypocrites usually waver, being distracted between conscience and ungodly desires. Their desires lead them to Baal, their consciences to God. As the prophet Elijah says about such people, "How long will you waver between two opinions?" (1 Kings 18:21). They are usually guilty of a promiscuous compliance that, though used by them in ungodly policy, yet often tends to their hurt; for this indifference is hateful to God and men. God hates this: "I know your deeds, that you are neither cold nor hot. I wish you were either one or the other! So, because you are lukewarm . . . I am about to spit you out of my mouth" (Revelation 3:15-16). Lukewarmness causes vomiting; so lukewarm Christians are spat out of God's mouth. His ways are not honored except by zealous earnestness.

Note 2. A doubting mind causes uncertainty in our lives and conversations. Their minds are double, and therefore their ways are **unstable**. A definite expectation of the hopes of the Gospel produces obedience, and a definite belief in the doctrines of the Gospel produces perseverance.

(1) Nobody walks so closely with God as those who are assured of the love of God. Faith is the mother of obedience. When people are apart from Christ, they are slack over their duties. We do not cheerfully engage in anything we have doubts over; therefore, when we do not know whether God will accept us or not, we serve God in fits and starts. It is the slander of the world to think assurance is an unimportant doctrine. Never is the soul so quickened as it is by "the joy of the Lord" (Nehemiah 8:10). Faith, filling the heart with spiritual joy, gives a strength for all our duties and labors.

(2) No one is so constant in any truth as he who is convinced of its

grounds. When we are only half convinced, we are usually **unstable**: see 2 Peter 3:17. Every believer should have some solid, rational grounds to support him. Believers are told to give "the reason for the hope that you have" (1 Peter 3:15)—that is, those inner motives that make them assent to the truth. See also 1 Thessalonians 5:21. So, work to understand the grounds of your religion. If you love a truth in ignorance, you cannot love it constantly.

Commentary on Verse 9

The brother in humble circumstances ought to take pride in his high position.

The apostle, having finished the digression about prayer, returns to the main matter in hand, which is bearing afflictions with joy. He gives another reason in this verse, because to be depressed by the world for righteousness' sake is to be exalted toward God. Let us look at the force of the words.

The brother. That is, a Christian. The people of God are called "brothers" because the truest friendship is among the good and godly. Groups of wicked men are more of a conspiracy than a brotherhood. Therefore, when you find in Scripture the words "a brother," you should understand "a saint." In the same way here James does not say "a Christian" but **the brother.** See also Paul in 1 Corinthians 16:20 and 1 Thessalonians 5:27.

In humble circumstances. The Greek word used here for **humble** signifies the condition, not the grace, and therefore we correctly translate it **in humble circumstances,** for it is contrasted with **rich** in the next verse. It is the same in Proverbs 16:19, "Better to be lowly in spirit and among the oppressed than to share plunder with the proud." "Lowly" refers to the lowly in condition, not in heart, for it is contrasted with "share plunder." So also in Luke 1:48, "He has been mindful of the humble state of his servant." The grace and the condition are expressed by the same word, because a humble state appeals to a humble heart. But remember, **in humble circumstances** does not just mean "poor," but being poor for Christ, as persecutions and afflictions are often expressed by the words "humility" and "humiliation." Thus in Psalm 9:12 we read, "He does not ignore the cry of the afflicted"; and in verse 13, "O Lord, see how my enemies persecute me!" The original has, "my humiliation." So here **the brother in humble circumstances** is one who is humbled or made low on account of opposition for being religious.

Take pride. The original is "boast" or "glory." It refers to the highest act of joy, even when joy begins to pass the limits of reason. I say it is the first step in the degeneration of joy and suggests that the soul is taken by surprise with excessive affection, for the next step beyond this is truly wicked. Joy begins to exceed when it exults over other people; but when it comes to insult them, it is nothing. Therefore, how should we boast or glory? I answer:

(1) It may be understood as a concession of the lesser evil. Rather than grumble under afflictions or faint under them or try to escape them through evil ways, you may boast about them. This is the lesser evil. Such concessions are frequent in Scripture, just as Proverbs 5:19 ("May you ever be captivated by her love") certainly implies excessive ecstasies. How then is this to be understood? Does Scripture allow any excess of affection? No; it is only the idea of the lesser evil. Rather than lose yourself in the embraces of a harlot, "May her breasts satisfy you."

(2) This may only imply our Christian privileges: let this brother view his privileges as something to boast about. However lowly your condition seems to the world, suffering for Christ is a thing you may boast in rather than be ashamed of.

(3) It may be that the word should be softened and be translated, "let him boast." But this is unnecessary, for the apostle Paul speaks in the same way in Romans 5:3: "We also rejoice in our sufferings."

In his high position. That is, in his sublimity. This may be understood in two ways: (1) More generally, that he is a brother or a member of Christ, and the honor of the spiritual state is often contrasted with the misery and obscurity of afflictions. Thus Revelation 2:9 says, "I know your afflictions and your poverty—yet you are rich!"—poor outwardly, but rich spiritually. (2) More particularly, it may refer to the honor of afflictions, that we are thought worthy to suffer for anything where Christ is concerned, which is certainly a privilege.

Notes on Verse 9

Note 1. The people of God are brothers. They are born by the same Spirit, by the same immortal seed of the Word. So, consider your relationship to each other. You are brothers, a relationship of the greatest endearment because it is natural—not founded on choice, as with friendship, but on nature [the natural working of God—*Ed. note*], and because it is between equals. So live and love as brothers.

Note 2. **The brother in humble circumstances.** He says **in humble circumstances** and yet still says **brother.** Despising the poor is called despising the church of God: see 1 Corinthians 11:22, "Don't you have homes to eat and drink in? Or do you despise the church of God and humiliate those who have nothing?" At their love-feasts they slighted the poor, and it is as if the apostle had said, "In your houses you have liberty to invite whom you please, but when you meet in a public assembly you must not exclude a considerable part of the church, which the poor are."

Note 3. **The brother.** Not a *man* in humble circumstances, but a **brother.** It is not poverty but being poor and a Christian that brings joy and comfort. Matthew 5:3 says, "Blessed are the poor in spirit"; note it is "in spirit," not "in purse."

Note 4. **In humble circumstances.** The poor have the greatest reason to be humble. A poor proud man is inexplicable; he has less temptation to be proud, and he has more reason to be humble. People often live in a way that is inappropriate to their circumstances, as if they can supply in pride what is lacking in their circumstances; whereas others who excel in abilities are most lowly in mind, just as the sun at its highest casts the least shadows.

Note 5. God may place his people among the lowest in society. A **brother** may be **in humble circumstances** in regard to his outward condition. The Captain of salvation, the Son of God himself, was "despised and rejected by men" (Isaiah 53:3); that is, he appeared in such a form and rank that he could hardly be said to be a man. So, in your greatest misery say, "I am not yet beneath the condition of a saint—a brother may be in very humble circumstances."

Note 6. **The brother in humble circumstances ought to take pride.** The most abject condition does not justify grumbling; you may yet rejoice and glory in the Lord. A man cannot sink so low as to be beyond the help of spiritual comforts. Do not blame your condition when you should blame yourself. It is not your misery but your passions that cause sin; wormwood is not poison. But, alas, the old Adam is found in us: "The woman you put here with me—she gave me . . . and I ate it" (Genesis 3:12). We blame providence when we should blame ourselves. Remember, **humble circumstances** have their comforts.

Note 7. **Take pride.** A Christian may glory in his privileges. To illustrate this, I shall show you:

(1) How he should not boast.

a. Do not boast about self, self-worth, self-merits. The apostle's reproof is justified: "And if you did receive it, why do you boast [the same word that is used here] as though you did not?" (1 Corinthians 4:7). That is a wrong way to boast—to glory in ourselves, as if our gifts and graces are bought by us. All such boasting is opposed to grace, as the apostle says in Romans 3:27, "Where, then, is boasting? It is excluded."

b. Do not boast over others; the Scripture never allows you to feel pride. It is the language of hypocrites to say, "Keep away; don't come near me, for I am too sacred for you" (Isaiah 65:5). To despise others, as men of the world, is a sign that we have forgotten who made the difference. The apostle rebukes such people: "Why do you judge your brother?" (Romans 14:10). Tertullian translates this as, "Why do you nothing him?" He who makes others nothing forgets that God is all in all to himself. Grace is totally different: "Show true humility toward all men. At one time we too were foolish, disobedient, deceived and enslaved by all kinds of passions and pleasures" (Titus 3:2-3). Think of what you *are* in such a way that you do not forget what you *were* before grace made the difference.

(2) How he may boast.

a. If it is for the glory of God, to exalt God, not yourselves. "My soul will boast in the Lord" (Psalm 34:2)—of his goodness, mercy, power. It is good when we see we have nothing to boast of but our God—not wealth or riches or wisdom, but the Lord alone: see Jeremiah 9:23-24, "Let not the wise man boast of his wisdom or the strong man boast of his strength . . . but let him who boasts boast about this: that he understands and knows me."

b. Recall the value of your privileges. The world thinks you have a bad deal to have a crucified Christ; glory in it. Remember Romans 5:3, "We also rejoice in our sufferings." The apostle does not say, "We must glory or boast *of* our sufferings," but glory *in* sufferings. This glorying lets the world know the honor we give to Christ, so that they may know we are not ashamed of our profession when we are persecuted. The apostle Paul is explained by the apostle Peter: "if you suffer as a Christian, do not be ashamed, but praise God that you bear that name" (1 Peter 4:16). They think it is a disgrace, and you think it glorious to suffer for Christ. Look forward to the reward. Christ scorned the shame in comparison with "the joy set before him" (Hebrews 12:2). For Moses, the treasures of Egypt were nothing in comparison with his reward (Hebrews 11:26). So here you may glory, counterbalancing the shame of the world with the dignity of your hopes. So then, you see how you may take pride in God and his ways.

Note 8. **In his high position.** Grace exalts a person; even people **in humble circumstances** may be exalted by it. All the comforts of Christianity are like riddles to a worldly outlook: poverty is promotion; servants are freedmen, the Lord's freedmen (1 Corinthians 7:22). The privileges of Christianity exceed all the ignominy of the world. Christian slaves are delivered from the tyranny of Satan and the slavery of sin; therefore they are "the Lord's freedmen." So James says, **Has not God chosen those who are poor in the eyes of the world to be rich in faith?** (2:5). Spiritual treasure and inward riches are the best. A Christian's life is full of mysteries: poor and yet rich; humbled and yet exalted; shut out of the world and yet admitted into the company of saints and angels; slighted, yet dear to God; the world's dirt but God's jewels. In one place it says, "We have become the scum of the earth" (1 Corinthians 4:13), and in another we are called God's "treasured possession" (Malachi 3:17). So then:

(1) Never quarrel with providence. Though you have nothing else, rejoice in this, that you have the best things. Never envy the world's pleasures. To complain like this is only disguised envy. Remember, God has called you to other privileges. You sin against the bounty of God if you do not value them above all the pomp and glory of the world. First Timothy 6:6 says, "Godliness with contentment is great gain"; or it may be read, "Godliness is great gain with contentment," in contrast with worldly gain. Men may gain much, but they are not satisfied; but godliness brings contentment with it. The apostle is saying the same as Solomon: "The blessing of the Lord brings wealth, and he adds no trouble to it" (Proverbs 10:22).

(2) Refresh your hearts with the sense of your privileges. As the people of God you are exalted in your greatest sufferings. Are you naked? You will be dressed in "fine linen," which is "the righteous acts of the saints" (Revelation 19:8).

Note 9. Observe more particularly that the greatest sufferings for Christ are an honor for us: see Acts 5:41. It was an act of God's grace to put this honor on them. So then, do not view as a judgment what is a favor. Reproaches for Christ are a matter for thanksgiving, not complaint. Oh, how happy are the people of God who can suffer nothing from God or men that does not bring comfort!

Commentary on Verse 10

But the one who is rich should take pride in his low position, because he will pass away like a wild flower.

Following on from the previous exhortation, James speaks about prosperity.

But the one who is rich. This includes the noble, the honorable, those who have outward excellence, and especially those who remain untouched by persecution. Some observe that James does not say "the rich brother," as before, **the brother in humble circumstances,** but only generally **the one who is rich.** Few of that rank give their names to Christ. But this may be too fanciful an interpretation.

In his low position. In the original a verb is lacking to make complete sense. What is to be understood? Oecumenius says, "Let him be ashamed," considering the uncertainty of his state; others understand it as,

"Let him be humbled," in that he is made low. So it would be a similar manner of speech to 1 Timothy 4:3 or 1 Timothy 2:12, where the opposite word is understood. But this seems somewhat to disturb the order of the words. I rather like the opinion of those who repeat the word used in the previous verse and read it as, "Let him rejoice, the poor man, in that he is spiritually exalted; the rich in that he is spiritually humbled." So grace makes them both alike to God. The poor who is too low is exalted, and the rich who is too high is humbled, which is a matter for glory or joy to both of them.

His low position. Some say outwardly and in providence, when his crown is laid in the dust and he is stripped of everything and brought to the state of the brother of low degree. But this is not accurate, for the apostle is speaking about a low position that goes with his being rich—made low while rich and high in rank and esteem. Some more particularly say the **low position** is because, being a Christian, he is no more esteemed than if he were poor. But this is inconsistent with the reason given at the end of the verse, **because he will pass away like a wild flower.** More correctly, then, it is to be understood of the disposition of the heart, a lowly mind; so it denotes either humility that arises from considering our own sinfulness or from considering the uncertainty of all worldly enjoyment. When we live in constant expectation of the cross, we may be said to be made **low**, however high we may be. This is consistent with the reason given and is parallel with 1 Timothy 6:17.

Because he will pass away like a wild flower. James gives a reason why they should have a lowly mind in the midst of their flourishing and plenty. The pomp of their situation is only like that of **a wild flower.** This simile is often used in Scripture: see Psalm 37:2 and Job 14:2 and Isaiah 40:6-7. Notice that the apostle does not say that *his riches* will pass away like a flower, but that *he* will pass away—he as well as his riches. Even if we had security over our possessions, we would not have security over our lives. We pass away and they pass away with a turn of providence as the flower of the field fades.

Notes on Verse 10

Note 1. **But the one who is rich**—that is, the rich brother. Riches are not altogether inconsistent with Christianity. But usually riches are a great snare. It is difficult to enjoy the world without being entangled in its pleasures. The moon is never eclipsed except when it is full, and it is usually in our fullness that we go wrong. That is why our Saviour says, "It is easier for a camel to go through the eye of a needle than for a rich man to enter the kingdom of God" (Matthew 19:24). This is a Jewish proverb indicating an impossibility. Rich men should often think of this. A camel can go through a needle's eye just as easily as you can enter into the kingdom of God. It would be a rare miracle of nature for a camel or an elephant to pass through a needle's eye; and it is as rare a miracle of grace for a rich man to find Christ. They least of all perceive spiritual excellences. The heathen Plato says almost the same as Christ, that it is impossible for someone to be eminently rich and eminently good. The way of grace is usually so narrow that there is no room for those who want to enter with their great burdens of riches and honor.

But you will say, what do you want Christians to do then? Throw away their estates? I answer, no. There are two passages that qualify our Lord's saying. One is: "With God all things are possible" (Matthew 19:26). Difficulties on the way to heaven bring us to despair of ourselves, not of God. God can so loosen the heart from the world that riches are no impediment. The other passage is Mark 10:23-24: "Jesus looked around and said to his disciples, 'How hard it is for the rich to enter the kingdom of God!' The disciples were amazed at his words. But Jesus said again, 'Children, how hard it is [for those who trust riches—*NIV* footnote] to enter the kingdom of God!'" It is not *having* riches but *trusting* in them that poses the danger. Riches are not a hindrance to Christianity, but our abuse of them is. To sum up, it is impossible to trust in riches and enter into the kingdom of God; and it is nearly impossible for us to have riches and not to trust in them.

Note 2. A rich person's humility is his glory. Humility is not only clothing but an ornament (see Colossians 3:12; 1 Peter 5:5). Augustine said, "He is a great man who is not lifted up because of his greatness." You are not better than others because of your possessions but because of your meekness. The apostles possessed all things though they had nothing. Others have more than you if they have a humble heart.

Note 3. The way to be humble is to ignore the world's advantages. The poor man must glory in that he is exalted, but the rich in that he is made low. Honors and riches put us beneath other men rather than above them. Riches will be your downfall if you do not watch out for them.

Note 4. If we want to be made low in the middle of worldly enjoyments, we should think how uncertain they are. We are worldly if we forget the world's vanity and our own transitoriness: see Psalm 49:11. Either we think that we shall live forever or we leave our riches to those who will continue our memory forever—that is, to our children, who are but the parents multiplied and continued. But this is all in vain, for we will perish, as do our possessions. It is mad to be proud about what may perish before we perish, just as it is the worst of miseries to outlive our own happiness. The apostle says, "Commend those who are rich in this present world not to be arrogant nor to put their hope in wealth, which is so uncertain" (1 Timothy 6:17). Riches are far from being the best things. Rather, they are not anything at all. Solomon calls them "that which is not" (Proverbs 23:5, KJV); and who ever loved nothing and would be proud of "that which is not"?

Note 5. The uncertainty of worldly enjoyment resembles a flower—beautiful but fading. This simile is used elsewhere: see Psalm 103:15-16 and 1 Peter 1:24. From this you may learn two things:

(1) The things of the world should not allure us, because they are fading. Flowers attract the eye, but their beauty is soon burned up; the soul lasts for eternity. An immortal soul cannot have total contentment in anything that fades. When you are tempted, say, here is a flower—glorious but fading; glass that is bright but brittle.

(2) The fairest things fade most. When plants flower, they begin to wither; compare Psalm 39:5. Be suspicious of outward things when you have them most. It is good to think of famine and want in the midst of plenty. The Lord knows how quickly your situation may change; when it seems to flourish most, it may be near to withering.

Commentary on Verse 11

For the sun rises with scorching heat and withers the plant; its blossom falls and its beauty is destroyed. In the same way, the rich man will fade away even while he goes about his business.

James continues the simile and at the end of the verse applies it. Nothing needs explaining except the latter clause.

Will fade. That is, *may* fade, for the passage is not absolutely definite about what always will be, but simply declares what may be; and therefore the future tense is used. We see many times that "the wicked live on, growing old" (see Job 21:7-10). So the apostle does not say what always happens but what may be, what usually happens, and what will eventually happen.

The rich man. This may either be taken generally to mean the rich, whether godly or ungodly, or more specifically for the ungodly person who trusts in riches.

Fade away. The word is used of plants when they lose their beauty.

While he goes about his business. Some read, as do Erasmus and Gagneus, "with his abundance," which Calvin also approves as fitting the context: "So shall the rich and all his abundance fade away." However, we follow the general and more commonly received meaning, "in his ways or journeys." The word is emphatic and refers to that earnest industry by which people travel on sea and land, running here and there in pursuit of wealth; and yet, when all is done, it fades like the flower of the field.

Notes on Verse 11

Note 1. From the continuation of the simile, note that the vanity of flowers should make us think about the vanity of our own comforts. We delight in pictures, for through them the soul, with the help of the imagination, has a double view of the object—a picture of it, and then the thing itself. This was God's former way of teaching his people through types; he still teaches us through similes taken from ordinary objects. When we think of them, spiritual thoughts may awake; every ordinary object is, as it were, hallowed and consecrated for a heavenly purpose. So let this be your field or garden meditation: when you see the plants full of splendor, remember that all this disappears in an instant when the sun rises. The text says, **the sun rises with scorching heat**. The Greek word used here is usually translated "scorching wind," which in the hot eastern countries came with the rising sun; see Jonah 4:8. It was a hot, piercing wind that blasted all things and was the usual symbol of God's judgments. When you walk in a garden or field to meditate, as Isaac did (see Genesis 24:63), think, "What a picture! But alas, these things last only for a season; they would fade away of their own accord, but more, the east wind will soon dry them up." In the same way, all worldly comforts are like spring flowers, good in their season but perishable.

Note 2. Our comforts fade away, especially when the hand of providence is stretched out against them. The flower fades by itself, but especially when it is scorched by the burning east wind. Our hearts should be detached from outward things. Do not make providence your enemy, for your comforts will perish more quickly. You cannot then expect a comfortable warmth from God but a burning heat. There are three sins in which you make providence your enemy:

(1) When you use your comforts to serve your lusts. Where there is pride and wantonness, you may expect a burning; certainly your flowers will be scorched and dried up. Salvian has said, "God will rain hell out of heaven rather than not visit for such sins."

(2) When you trust in those comforts. God can brook no rivals. If you make idols of creatures, God will destroy them. When you trust in your wealth, as if it will supply your family's needs, God will show that riches are useless when they are preferred to the living God (see 1 Timothy 6:17).

(3) When you obtain comforts in wrong ways. James 5:3 says, **Your**

gold and silver are corroded. Their corrosion will testify against you
and eat your flesh like fire. The fire of God's wrath falls on your family.

Note 3. **While he goes about his business.** Worldly men pursue wealth
with great care and industry. The rich have several ways of accomplishing
their ends. What pains people take for things that perish! Observe their
incessant care, earnest labor, and unwearied industry, and see how appropriate this would be for heavenly treasure! Secondly, observe such persons' work and care, and ask, shall an evil desire have more power over
them than God's love does over me? I have loftier motives and a more certain reward (Proverbs 11:18); they are more earnest for an earthly purchase
and to heap up treasure for themselves than I am to enrich my soul with
spiritual and heavenly excellences. Pambus, in ecclesiastical history, wept
when he saw a harlot dressed with great care and expense, partly because
she took such pains for her own undoing, and partly because he had not
been so keen to please God as she had been to please a wanton lover. We
should be ashamed that we do so little for Christ while others do so much
for wealth.

Note 4. **While he goes about his business.** All our endeavors will be
fruitless if God's hand is against us. As the flower is to burning heat, so is
the rich man in his ways; that is, despite all his industry and care, God may
quickly destroy him. "You earn wages, only to put them in a purse with
holes in it" (Haggai 1:6); that is, they did not benefit from their gains. Peter
"worked hard all night" but caught nothing until he took Christ into the
boat (see Luke 5:5). So you will catch nothing until you take God along
with you (see Psalm 127:1). So, acknowledge providence in order to come
under its blessing. Labor *without God* cannot prosper; labor *against God*,
and against his will, will end in disaster.

Commentary on Verse 12

*Blessed is the man who perseveres under trial, because when he has
stood the test, he will receive the crown of life that God has promised
to those who love him.*

Here the apostle concludes the previous teaching with a general sentence. I will deal with it very briefly.

Blessed. That is, already blessed. They are not miserable, as the world
views them. It is in contrast with the world's judgment that the apostle
says **Blessed.**

Is the man. The word used here usually only applies to males. Some
people, including Aquinas, have misinterpreted this Scripture.

Throughout the letter we will observe that our apostle delights to use this word for both sexes. In verse 23, **A man who looks at his face** ... means a man or a woman, for it corresponds to the Hebrew word, which includes women as well as men.

Who perseveres under trial. That is, a person who patiently and constantly endures. The wicked suffer but do not endure; they suffer unwillingly, with complaints and blasphemies. But the godly man perseveres; that is, he bears the affliction with patience and constancy—without complaining, fainting, or blaspheming. Enduring is meant in a good sense—as in Hebrews 12:7, "Endure hardship as discipline; God is treating you as sons."

Trial. Affliction is called a **trial**, as before. In itself it is a punishment for sin, but to the godly it is but a trial—just as death, the king of terrors, is in itself the payment for sin, but for those who endure it death is the gate to eternal life.

When he has stood the test. This word is often translated "approved": "approved by men" (Romans 14:18); "to show which of you have God's approval" (1 Corinthians 11:19). So here, he is made or found approved— that is, sound in the faith; this is a metaphor taken from the proving of metals by fire.

He will receive. That is, freely, for though no one is crowned *without* striving (see 2 Timothy 2:5), yet we are not crowned *as a result of* striving. In many places Scripture says that God will give every man *according to* his work, yet not *as a reward for* this work; for such passages only imply that as evil works will not remain unpunished, so neither will good works be unrewarded.

The crown of life. Often in Scripture the gifts of God are pictured as crowns, sometimes to show the honor that God puts on creatures (e.g., "You ... crowned him with glory and honor," Psalm 8:5) and sometimes to show the all-sufficiency of God's love. His love is like a crown; so Psalm 103:4 says, "He . . . crowns me with love and compassion." However, usually this applies to the heavenly state.

(1) This shows partly its honor, as a crown is an emblem of majesty; and so it shows that regal dignity which we have in Christ: "I confer on you a kingdom, just as my Father conferred one on me" (Luke 22:29). Christ, who left us the cross, also left us his crown. One of Christ's legacies to the church is his own cross; therefore Luther says, "The church is heir of the cross." So Christ says here, "I confer on you a kingdom." This is one reason why heavenly glory is expressed as a crown.

(2) This shows its complete fullness. A circular crown is an emblem of plenty and infinity. There is something on every side, and it has no end. So, Psalm 16:11 says, "You will fill me with joy in your presence, with eternal pleasures at your right hand."

(3) This shows that it is given after striving. It was a reward for conquest. There was a crown given to those who ran a race. The apostle alludes to this in 1 Corinthians 9:24-25, "Do you not know that in a race all the runners run, but only one gets the prize? Run in such a way as to get the prize. . . . They do it to get a crown that will not last; but we do it to get a crown that will last forever." In the races and games near Corinth, the reward was only a wreath made of flowers and plants that soon faded; but we run for a crown of glory that lasts. Or as another apostle states it, "the crown of glory that will never fade away" (1 Peter 5:4).

Now you see why heaven is pictured as a crown; sometimes it is called "a crown of glory," to show its splendor, and sometimes "the crown of righteousness" (2 Timothy 4:8); sometimes it is called "the crown of life," as in Revelation 2:10 ("Be faithful, even to the point of death, and I will give you the crown of life"), because it is a living crown that will flourish for all eternity.

That God has promised. This is added partly to show its certainty—we have the assurance of a promise—and partly to show the reasons for the expectation—not by virtue of our own merits, but God's promise. There is no particular promise mentioned, because it is the general drift of the whole Word of God. Even in the law, mercy is promised: see Exodus 20:6.

To those who love him. This is a usual description of the people of God. But why **those who love him** rather than those who serve or obey him or some other description?

(1) Because love is the sum of the whole law and the hinge on which all the commandments turn. The Decalogue is abridged into this one word. Therefore Paul says that "love is the fulfillment of the law" (Romans 13:10).

(2) Because love is the basis for our interest in Christ. Faith gives us a right to possess the promises, and love demonstrates this. Therefore love is often specified as the condition for the promises, as in 2:5—**the kingdom he promised those who love him**. He does not say, "fear him" or "trust in him," though these graces also are implied, but chiefly **to those who love him**. Similarly, Romans 8:28 says, "In all thing God works for the good of those who love him, who have been called according to his purpose." Here the love of God is made the consequence both of the effectual calling and of election.

(3) Because patience is the fruit of love. He who loves much will suffer much. Therefore, when the apostle speaks about enduring temptations, he encourages them with **the crown of life**, promised to those who love God; a man would not suffer for him unless he loved him.

Notes on Verse 12

Note 1. Afflictions do not make the people of God miserable. There is a great deal of difference between a Christian and a man of the world. The latter's best state is vanity (see Psalm 39:5); and a Christian's worst state is happiness. He who loves God is like a die; throw him high or low, he still lands on a solid square. Sometimes he may be afflicted, but he is always happy. There is a double reason for this:

(1) Outward misery cannot diminish his happiness. A man is never miserable until he has lost his happiness. Our comfort lies to a great extent in the choice of our main happiness. Those who say in effect, "Happy are the people who are in such a case" (see Psalm 144:12-15)—that is, where there is no complaining in their streets, sheep bringing forth thousands, barns full, oxen strong for labor, etc.—may soon be miserable. All these things may disappear at a change of providence, just as Job lost everything in an instant. But those who say, "Blessed [happy] is the people whose God is the Lord"—that is, who count enjoying God as their happiness—when they lose everything, they can still be happy because they have not lost God. Our afflictions reveal our state of mind; when we see outward crosses as the greatest evil, God is not our main happiness. There are great evils that are soon felt by an ungodly heart; yet the prophet, like all believers, says, "I will rejoice in the Lord, I will be joyful in God my Savior" (Habakkuk 3:18). In the greatest lack of earthly things there is happiness, and comfort enough in God's covenant.

(2) Sometimes afflictions increase as they bring more comfort and a further experience of grace. God seldom afflicts for no reason. Such dispensations leave us either better or worse. The children of God profit from them, for God recompenses outward losses with inner enjoyments: "For just as the sufferings of Christ flow over into our lives, so also through Christ our comfort overflows" (2 Corinthians 1:5). That is, inner comforts can increase with outward sufferings. Learn, then, that people may be happy whom men count miserable. The world judges according to outward appearances and therefore is often mistaken. Salvian says, "A godly man's happiness, or misery, is not to be judged by the world's sense, but by his own; his happiness and yours differ." The apostle Paul says, "If only for this life we have hope in Christ, we are to be pitied more than all men" (1 Corinthians 15:19).

Note 2. The sweetest afflictions are those that we endure for Christ's sake. James says, **Blessed is the man who perseveres under trial**—that is, persecution for religion's sake. There is comfort in corrections: "Blessed is the man you discipline, O Lord, the man you teach from your law" (Psalm 94:12). Note that when the discipline is from the Lord, there is comfort in it. Corrections aim at the mortifying of sin, and so are more humbling; but trials aim at the discovery of grace, and so are more comfortable. Corrections imply guilt; either we have sinned or are likely to sin, and then God takes up the rod. But trials come to us so that the world may know our willingness to choose the greatest affliction instead of the least sin; and so they bring us more joy. So then, when you are called to suffer for Christ, take comfort; it is a blessed thing to endure evil for that cause. Only be sure that your hearts are upright—that your suffering really is for Christ and that your hearts are right with Christ.

(1) That it is for Christ. It is not the blood and suffering that makes the martyr, but the cause. The glory of our sufferings is marred when there is evil in them (see 1 Peter 4:15).

(2) That your heart is right with Christ. There is no blessedness in sufferings that are born when our hearts are far from Christ. But you may suffer cheerfully when you appeal to God's omniscience for your uprightness, as in the Psalms: "God . . . knows the secrets of the heart. . . . Yet for your sake we face death all day long" (44:21-22). Can you appeal to God who knows our secrets and say, "For your sake we are exposed to such hazards in the world"?

Note 3. **When he has stood the test**. Note that before a crowning, there must be a trial. We derive no profit at all from the affliction—neither grace nor glory—until there is wrestling and exercise. For the sake of grace, the apostle teaches clearly, "discipline . . . produces a harvest of righteousness and peace for those who have been trained by it" (Hebrews 12:11). Trials do not earn us heaven, but they always precede it. Before we are brought to glory, God will first wean us from sin and the world: see Colossians 1:12.

Note 4. It is good to contrast the glory of our hopes with our sufferings. Here we have trials, but we look for a crown of glory. Paul says the inner man is strengthened when "we fix our eyes not on what is seen, but on what is unseen. For what is seen is temporary, but what is unseen is eternal" (2 Corinthians 4:18). A straight comparison of our hopes with our sufferings makes them seem light and easy. So our Saviour tells us, "Blessed are those who are persecuted because of righteousness, for theirs is the kingdom of heaven" (Matthew 5:10). So then, make use of this heavenly wisdom; consider your hopes—the glory of them, the truth of them.

(1) Their glory. Two things trouble men in their sufferings—disgrace and death. See what provision God has made against these fears: he has promised a crown against the ignomiy of your sufferings, and against temporal death a **crown of life**. A man can lose nothing for God that is not abundantly recompensed; the crown of thorns is turned into a crown of glory, and losing a life is the way to save it (Matthew 10:39). Thus, it is good to contrast our hopes with our sorrows, and not to look only to the

present dangers and sufferings, but to the crown—**the crown of life** that is laid up for us.

(2) Their truth. It is not only a crown of glory that you expect but "the crown of righteousness" (2 Timothy 4:8), which the righteous God will definitely bestow upon you. Although God makes the promise in grace, his truth, which is often called his righteousness in Scripture, makes him carry it out. Every promise is built upon four pillars: God's justice or holiness, which will not let him deceive; his grace or goodness, which will not let him forget; his truth, which will not let him change; his power, which makes him able to accomplish.

Note 5. Lastly, no enduring is acceptable to God that does not arise from love. The crown that God has promised, he does not say is "for those who suffer" but for **those who love him**. A man may suffer for Christ—that is, in his cause—without any love for him, but it is worth nothing (1 Corinthians 13:3). Vicious people who die in a good cause are like a dog's head cut off for sacrifice. So then, do not think that suffering will excuse a wicked life. Note that Christ says last of all, "Blessed are those who are persecuted because of righteousness" (Matthew 5:10), intimating that a martyr must have all the preceding graces. First, "Blessed are the poor in spirit," "blessed are the pure in heart," etc. and then "Blessed are those who are persecuted." First, grace is required, and then martyrdom. See also the notes on James 2:5.

Commentary on Verse 13

When tempted, no one should say, "God is tempting me." For God cannot be tempted by evil, nor does he tempt anyone.

James comes now to another kind of temptation. Having spoken about outward trials, he now speaks about inner temptations, so that he might correct a blasphemous error about their origin. Clearly, those outer trials are from God; but these inner trials, or temptations to sin, are altogether inconsistent with the purity and holiness of God's nature, as the apostle shows here and in the following verses.

When tempted, no one should say. That is, when tempted to sin, for this is how the word is used in Scripture. The Greek word used here means temptations to sin, just as the Greek word used in verse 2 means **trials**. Thus the devil is called "the tempter" in Matthew 4:3; and in the Lord's Prayer we pray that we may not be led "into temptation." So this verse means when one is tempted—that is, so enticed to sin that he is overcome by it.

Say. That is, either in word or thought, for a thought is the saying of the heart. Some who dare not whisper such a blasphemy certainly imagine it. The apostle implies that the creature is apt to **say**, to have some excuse or other.

"God is tempting me." That is, it was he who enticed or forced me into evil.

For God cannot be tempted by evil. The reason here is drawn from the unchangeable holiness of God; he cannot in any way be tempted into evil. Some read it actively—"he is not the tempter of evil"; but this would be a repetition of the last clause. Some translate it as, "God is not the tempter of evil people but only of the good, through afflictions"; but this does not agree with the original phrase, for it does not refer to evil people, but simply, without an article, to evil things. To sum up, God cannot by any thing external or internal be drawn into any evil.

Nor does he tempt anyone. That is, God does not seduce anyone. God wants everyone to conform to his holy nature.

Notes on Verse 13

Note 1. **No one should say.** Man is inclined to blame others for his own wrongs. Thus Aaron blamed the people for his evil action (see Exodus 32:23-24).

(1) Beware of these vain deceptions. Silence and owning up to being guilty is far better. God is glorified when people stop being deceitful. It is best to have nothing to say, nothing but confession of sin.

(2) Learn that excuses cut no ice with God. Ignorance is not excused by wrong teaching. When "a blind man leads a blind man," not one, but "both fall into a pit" (Matthew 15:14)—the blind guide and the blind follower. Saul was rejected as king for obeying the voice of the people rather than the Lord (see 1 Samuel 15:23).

Note 2. People, rather than admitting their guilt, blame God. They think, "It is foolish to blame Satan—to say, I was tempted by Satan." If there were no Satan to tempt us, we would tempt ourselves. It is useless to blame others—"I was tempted by others." But it is blasphemous to blame God and say, "I am tempted by God." People would do anything rather than think badly of themselves, for it is man's disposition to be "clean in his own eyes" (Proverbs 16:2, KJV). So beware of this wickedness of putting sin upon God. The more natural this is for us, the more we should heed James's exhortation. We blame God for our evils and sins in various ways:

(1) We do this when we blame his providence, the state of things, the

times, and the people around us. Adam said, "The woman you put here with me—she gave me some fruit from the tree, and I ate it" (Genesis 3:12). Note that this obliquely reflects on God: "The women you put here with me." So many plead their distractions. But God sends us miseries not to make us worse, but to make us better, as Paul seems to argue in 1 Corinthians 10:13-14.

(2) We blame God for our own evils when we ascribe sin to the defect in divine grace. People say they could do nothing else; God gave them no more grace (see Proverbs 19:3).

(3) People blame God for their own sins when they blame all their misfortunes on fate and their birth stars; these are mindless attacks on God himself, under the guise of reflections on his creation.

(4) People blame God for their own sins when they are angry without knowing why. Their conscience pricks them, and they fret and fume without knowing why. They want to blame God but dare not, as was the case with David himself: "David was angry because the Lord's wrath had broken out against Uzzah" (2 Samuel 6:8). He was angry but could not tell who he was angry with. He should have been angry with his own folly. Wicked men display anger: "they will become enraged and, looking upward, will curse their king and their God" (Isaiah 8:21).

(5) People blame God for their own sins most of all when they think he makes any suggestion to the soul to persuade it and incline it to evil. Satan may come and give evil counsel to the soul, but God does not.

(6) People blame God for their own sins when they misunderstand his decrees, as if they forced you to sin. Men will say, "Who can help it? God wanted it to be like this." God does not give you an evil nature or evil habits; these are from yourself.

Note 3. **For God cannot be tempted by evil**. God is so immutably good and holy that he is above the power of temptation. Men soon warp and vary, but he cannot be tempted. People foolishly compare God with the creature; because we can be tempted, they think God can also. But Habakkuk 1:13 says, "Your eyes are too pure to look on evil." We should tremble, as we are so easily tempted! How can you stand before the God who cannot be tempted? There are two applications of this note:

(1) It is an incentive for closer communion with God. A believer participates in the divine nature (see 2 Peter 1:4). The more of the divine nature you have, the more you can withstand temptations. We easily fall because we have more of man in us than of God. If all memory of sin and Satan were abolished, man himself would become his own devil.

(2) Use this thought in your temptations. When natural thoughts rise in us, thoughts against God's purity, say this: surely God cannot be the author of sin.

Note 4. **Nor does he tempt anyone**. The Lord is no tempter; the author of everything good cannot be the author of sin. God tempts no one; people tempt each other in many ways:

(1) When you add your authority to countenancing sin. Jeroboam made Israel sin (1 Kings 16:26); the guilt of a whole nation lay on his shoulders. Israel ruined him, and he ruined Israel. So also "Manasseh led Judah and the people of Jerusalem astray, so that they did more evil than the nations the Lord had destroyed before the Israelites" (2 Chronicles 33:9). Note that he "*led*" them.

(2) Through persuasion people pander to others' lusts: "With persuasive words she led him astray; she seduced him with her smooth talk" (Proverbs 7:21). Note that she led him astray and then seduced him; first he began to waver, and then he could no longer resist.

(3) People who encourage others in their evil ways, calling evil good and good evil, are like Ahab's prophets. They cry "Peace, peace!" to a soul utterly sunk in a pit of perdition. How far these are from the nature of God. God tempts no one; but these people are devils in the shape of men. Their work is to seduce and tempt. They are murderers of souls. So the apostle Peter says, "They mouth empty, boastful words and, by appealing to the lustful desires of sinful human nature, they entice people who are just escaping from those who live in error" (2 Peter 2:18).

Application. If God tempts no one, then God cannot be the author of sin. First I shall deal with those places that seem to imply this, then, secondly, show you God's dealing with sin.

(1) The teaching in Scripture. There are different levels; some places seem to say that God does tempt, as in Genesis 22:1, "God did tempt Abraham" [KJV; NIV, "God tested Abraham"—*Ed. note*]. But that was only a trial of his faith, not an inducement to sin. God tries our obedience but does not rouse us to sin.

But you will say, there are other places that seem to hint that God does incite to sin: "So the God of Israel stirred up the spirit of Pul king of Assyria . . . who took [Israel] into exile" (1 Chronicles 5:26). But his punishing a hypocritical nation was not evil but just and holy, part of his corrective discipline. God does not tempt the good that they may become evil, but only most justly punishes the evil with evil. The hardening and blinding of Psalm 105:25, Romans 1:24, and other places is not withdrawing good from men, but punishing them according to their wickedness.

(2) God's dealings with sin. All that God does here may be stated in these propositions:

a. Without God sin would never exist; without his prohibition, an action would not be sinful. The apostle says, "where there is no law there is no transgression" (Romans 4:15). But I mean without his permission and foreknowledge and, I may add, without his will and concurrence, without which nothing can happen. It cannot be outside the will of God, for then he would not be omniscient; and it cannot be against his will, for then he would not be omnipotent. Every action of ours needs the continued concurrence of God's providence; and if he did not uphold us, we could do nothing.

b. Yet God cannot be looked upon as the direct author of sin. In his providence he knows about sin without sin, as a sunbeam lights on a dunghill without being stained by it. This is best explained by a summary of all those actions in which providence is concerned in man's sin. Briefly, they are as follows:

Foreknowledge and preordination. God intended and appointed that it should be. Many people who allow prescience deny preordination, for fear of making God the author of sin; but these people fear where no fear is. The Scripture ascribes both to God: "This man was handed over to you by God's set purpose and foreknowledge" (Acts 2:23). Note that Peter says not only "foreknowledge" but "God's set purpose," which implies a positive decree. Now, that cannot infer any guilt or evil in God, for God appointed it, as he intended to bring good out of it. Wicked people have quite contrary intentions. Thus Joseph asked his brothers, when they feared his revenge, "Am I in the place of God?" (Genesis 50:19); that is, was it my design to bring these things to pass, or God's decree? Who am I that I should resist the will of God? And again in verse 20, "You intended to harm me, but God intended it for good to accomplish what is now being done, the saving of many lives." That is, God decreed it otherwise than you intended; your aim was wholly evil, but God's was good.

Permission. God's decrees imply that sin will exist, but they do not cause it. God leaves us the freedom of our own hearts and our own free choice; he is resolved not to hinder us (see Acts 14:16). Were grace a debt, it would be unjust to withhold it; but God is free and may do with his own as he pleases.

Concurrence in the action, though not in its sinfulness. It says in Acts 17:28, "In him we live and move and have our being." When God created mankind, he did not make them independent; we not only had our being *from* him, we still have it *in* him; we are in him, we live in him, and we move in him. Every action needs the support and concurrence of God.

Desertion of a sinner, and leaving him to himself. God may suspend or even withdraw grace in his sovereignty; that is, because he wills it. But he always does this either out of justice or wisdom. And when out of wisdom, it is for the trial of his children: "God left [Hezekiah] to test him and to know everything that was in his heart" (2 Chronicles 32:31). Sometimes God withdraws for the sake of justice, to punish the wicked, as in Psalm 81:12, "So I gave them over to their stubborn hearts to follow their own devices." When grace is withdrawn, which should moderate and govern the affections, man is left to the impulses of his own lusts. God cannot be blamed for any of this.

Concession. Wicked instruments such as evil acquaintances and false prophets are allowed to stir men up to evil: "The Lord has put a lying spirit in the mouth of all these prophets" (1 Kings 22:23). In God's providence, the evil spirit is brought in and uses wicked instruments. But the Lord is sovereign over all the instruments of deceit, so that they are restrained within limits.

Sometimes God's providence appears to be a trap. But this reflects no dishonor on God, because these events are good in themselves and are not temptations to sin. Wicked men abuse even the best things. God's Word irritates their corruption; sin draws strength from God's commandment: "Make the hearts of this people calloused"—that is, dull and heavy (Isaiah 6:10). The preaching of the Word, which should instruct them, makes them even more dull of hearing. Yet in all this God promises the glory of his justice.

A judicial handing over to the power of Satan and their own vile affections. "God gave them over to shameful lusts" (Romans 1:26). The truth is, we give ourselves over to evil. It is only because this serves God's ends that it is said, "God gave them over."

A limitation of sin. As God sets the bounds of grace according to his own good pleasure, so he sets the limits of sin. "Surely your wrath against men brings you praise, and the survivors of your wrath are restrained" (Psalm 76:10).

God turns it to his glory. God is so good that he would not allow evil if he could not bring good out of it. In the event of sin, it may be termed (as Gregory said of Adam's fall) "a happy fall," because it makes way for the glory of God. Note how many good attributes advance because of sin—mercy in pardoning, justice in punishing, wisdom in ordering, power in overruling it. The picture of providence would not be half so fair were it not for these black lines and darker shadows. So I must never blame God for allowing sin, as he offers so much mercy as he forgives sin.

Commentary on Verse 14

But each one is tempted when, by his own evil desire, he is dragged away and enticed.

James now shows the true cause of sin, having dealt with the false cause—namely, God's providence. The true cause of sin is in every man's soul; it is his **evil desire**.

But each one is tempted. James speaks universally, because no one is free except Christ.

When, by his own evil desire. He says **his own** because although we all have a corrupt nature, every one has a particular inclination to this or that sin rooted in his nature. **Own** excludes all attacks from outside. There is no greater enemy than our own nature.

His own evil desire. In order to show you what is meant by **evil desire,** I must make the following premises: (1) The human soul is mainly made up of desires. It is like a sponge, always thirsty and seeking something with which to fill itself. (2) This bias of the soul inclines toward desire. (3) Since the fall, people concentrate on their desires more than on anything else; so they are so corrupt that they influence all the rest. These reasons show why all sin is expressed by **evil desire.**

Lust may be considered in two ways:

(1) As a power, it is disposed towards evil, in all the faculties. "For the sinful nature desires what is contrary to the Spirit" (Galatians 5:17).

(2) As an act, the actual **evil desire** is nothing other than the first stirring of our human nature.

He is dragged away and enticed. Some think that in these two words the apostle gives two reasons for sin—one internal, which is lust, hinted at in the first word, **dragged;** the other external, a bait to entice the soul. As Plato said, "Pleasure is the bait of sin." Piscator and our translators seem to favor this and translate the words thus: **when, by his own evil desire, he is dragged away and enticed,** intimating that he is dragged away by his own evil desire and enticed by the object. However, the position of the words in the original shows that both refer to **evil desire:** "when he is dragged away and enticed by his own evil desire."

Notes on Verse 14

Note 1. The origin of evil is in man's own evil desires, the Adam and Eve in our own hearts. A man is never truly humble until he expresses indignation against himself. Do not say it was God's fault. He gave a pure soul. Suggestion can do nothing without **evil desire.** Nazianzen says, "The fire is in our wood, though it is the devil's flame." You cannot blame the world; there are allurements about, but it is your fault if you swallow the bait. Do not put all the blame on the sin of the times; good men are best in worst times, stars that shine brightest in the darkest nights. It is your venomous nature that turns everything to poison.

Note 2. Above everything else, a man should watch out for his desires. All sin is called **evil desire.** God requires the heart: "My son, give me your heart," which is the center of desires. The first thing through which sin makes itself known is **evil desire**. Before there is any consultation in the soul, there is a general tendency or bias in the soul. So look out for your evil desires; the whole person is swayed by them.

Note 3. **Evil desire** ensnares the soul by force and flattery. You are either **dragged away** or **enticed**.

First, **dragged away**. One way of knowing if desires are wrong is if they give too much pleasure. When affections are impetuous, you have good reason to be suspicious of them. Do not satisfy them. Greediness is an indication of uncleanness (Ephesians 4:19). When the heart burns or pants, it is not love but **evil desire**. When you cry out to God, "What a wretched man I am! Who will rescue me . . . ?" (Romans 7:24) you discern this power over your souls. This comes about:

(1) When your desires are irrational, but you are overtaken by brutish rage. "They are well-fed, lusty stallions, each neighing for another man's wife" (Jeremiah 5:8). They had no more control over themselves than a well-fed horse. This they proved with unbridled license against all reason and restraints.

(2) When your desires become uncontrollable. This is what the apostle calls "passionate lust" (1 Thessalonians 4:5). This violence is clearly seen in sensual appetite, as well as in other sins. "[They] were inflamed with lust for one another" (Romans 1:27).

(3) When **evil desire** troubles the soul so much that the person becomes ill. Thus Amnon was sick for Tamar (2 Samuel 13:2); that was a sickness of lust and uncleanness. Ahab was sick with covetousness (1 Kings 21:4), and Haman for honor (Esther 5).

The power of these evil desires tells us:

(1) Why wicked men are so set on sin and give themselves over to it and harm themselves. They "draw sin . . . as with cart ropes" (Isaiah 5:18). As beasts that are under the yoke put out all their strength to draw the load that is behind them, so these draw on wickedness to their disadvantage; they commit it even if it is difficult and inconvenient. So Jeremiah 9:5 says that they "weary themselves with sinning." Why is this? There is a power in sin that they cannot withstand.

(2) Why the children of God cannot do as they want in order to resolutely withstand temptation or perform duties acceptably. **Evil desire** may overpower them. Note that James said, **Each one is tempted**, which includes the godly. A wicked man does nothing but sin—his works are merely evil; but a godly man's deeds are not wholly good: "For what I do is not the good I want to do; no, the evil I do not want to do—this I keep on doing" (Romans 7:19). Although they do not plan to indulge in sin, they may become discouraged in the way of grace. "You do not do what you want" (Galatians 5:17). Resolutions are broken by this potent opposition.

Second, note that the next ploy of lust is flattery—**enticed**. That is one of the stumbling-blocks to conversion—**evil desire** promises delight and pleasure. Job 20:12 says, "though evil is sweet in his mouth and he hides it under his tongue." They are **enticed** by mischievous pleasure. So then:

(1) Learn to be suspicious about things that give you too much pleasure. Pleasures are only enticements, baits that have hooks under them.

(2) There is need for great care. Pleasure is one of the baits of evil desires. The truth is, all sins are rooted in a love of pleasure. Therefore, be watchful.

Commentary on Verse 15

Then, after desire has conceived, it gives birth to sin; and sin, when it is full-grown, gives birth to death.

Then, after desire. James goes on to describe the progress of sin: after birth comes death.

Has conceived—that is, as soon as sin begins to stimulate desires. Sin, or the corrupt nature, having inclined the soul to an ungodly object, works to set the soul in an evil frame of mind.

It gives birth to. That is, it completes sin and brings it to effect in us.

Sin. That is, actual sin. Our Saviour says that our first inclinations are sinful: see Matthew 5:28.

And sin, when it is full-grown. That is, settled into a habit. But why does the apostle say, **when it is full-grown**? (1) The apostle does not distinguish between sins. Every sin is mortal in its own nature and hands over the sinner to death and punishment. (2) Death is the result of all sin. Death may be laid not only at sin's door, but also at the door of evil desires.

Gives birth to. That is, hands the soul over to death. Evil desire is the mother of sin, but sin deserves death.

Death. This is but a euphemism for damnation; the first and second death are both implied. The apostle shows that the supreme cause of sin is lust, and its result is death.

Notes on Verse 15

Note 1. Sin takes over the spirit gradually. Evil desire leads to delightful thoughts, which lead the mind astray; then sin is born, disclosed, and strengthened; and then the person is destroyed. Sin is progressive, as

David noted: "Blessed is the main who does not walk in the counsel of the wicked or stand in the way of sinners or sit in the seat of mockers" (Psalm 1:1). Sin is never stationary: first, it is **wicked**, then **sinners**, then **mockers**; first **counsel**, then **way**, then **seat**.

Application 1. Oh, that we were wise enough to resist sin! A Christian's life should be spent watching out for evil desire. It is dangerous to give way to Satan (see Ephesians 4:27).

Application 2. This warns us about the danger of "small" sins. Consider how dangerous they are. It is not only great faults that ruin the soul, but small ones as well; dallying with temptations has serious consequences.

Note 2. Evil desires are fully conceived and formed in the soul when the will is drawn and gives its consent. So then, if evil desires have penetrated your thoughts, keep them from controlling your will.

Note 3. What is conceived in the heart usually comes out in life and conversation. That is the reason why the apostle Peter tells Christians to take care about the heart: "Abstain from sinful desires" (1 Peter 2:11).

(1) Learn that the hypocrite cannot always be hidden. God says that "his wickedness will be exposed in the assembly" (Proverbs 26:26).

(2) Learn the danger of neglecting evil desires and evil thoughts. If they are not suppressed, they will flower into sins. Permitted thoughts bring the mind and temptation together. David thought about Bathsheba's beauty, and so was all on fire. It is wrong to toy with thoughts.

(3) Learn what a mercy it is when sinful conceptions are stillborn. Restraints are a blessing. We are not as evil as we would have been otherwise. Take note of when your sinful ways are hedged around by providence (see Hosea 2:6).

Note 4. The result of sin is death; the apostle Paul says, "Those things result in death" (Romans 6:21). Sin comes with a pleasing and delightful sweetness, promising nothing but satisfaction and contentment; but the end is death. "The soul who sins is the one who will die" (Ezekiel 18:4). This is a principle stamped on nature. The godless were aware of it (Romans 1:32).

Application 1. This teaches us to halt the progress of evil desires that end in death and damnation. Place a flaming sword in the path of your ungodly delights (see Genesis 3:24). Wake up your soul; consider what Wisdom says: "All who hate me love death" (Proverbs 8:36).

Application 2. This shows us why we have to kill sin before it kills us. Either sin dies or the sinner dies. The life of sin and the life of a sinner are like two buckets in a well—if the one goes up, the other must come down. When sin lives, the sinner must die. There is an evil *in* sin and evil *after* sin. The evil in sin is breaking God's law, and the evil after sin is its just punishment. People who are not aware of the evil in sin will become aware of the evil after sin. For the regenerate, all God's dispensations save the person and destroy the sin: "You were to Israel a forgiving God, though you punished their misdeeds" (Psalm 99:8). God spared the sinner but punished the sin. The apostle Paul, speaking of himself when the power of the Word first came on him, says, "Sin sprang to life and I died" (Romans 7:9). So it is better that sin should be condemned than that *you* should be condemned. It is better that sin should die than that I should die; therefore, I should destroy my sin so that my soul escapes.

Application 3. Bless God who has delivered you from a state of sin; your soul has escaped a death-trap. Never look back on Sodom except with loathing; thank God that you have escaped. "I will praise the Lord, who counsels me" (Psalm 16:7). I might have been Satan's slave, and I deserved the reward of my own death; but God has called me to life and peace. In one place conversion is described as being called out of darkness into marvelous light; that is a great deal. But elsewhere it is described as being translated from death to life. I might have wasted my days in pleasure and vanity, and then gone to hell. Oh, blessed be the name of God forevermore, who has delivered me from so great a death!

Commentary on Verse 16

Don't be deceived, my dear brothers.

The apostle has argued with them about God being the author of sin; now he warns them against this blasphemy. There is no difficulty in this verse.

Don't be deceived. Do not wander. This metaphor is taken from straying sheep. Sometimes it indicates deviating from the Word as the yardstick of truth, which we most often express by the term "error."

My dear brothers. Speaking to them about an error, he is very meek with them, and therefore his request is loving and sweet.

Notes on Verse 16

Note 1. It is not good to brand things as errors until we have proved them to be so. After he had argued the matter with them, he said, **Don't be deceived.** (1) Loose slings do no good. Only fools are afraid of hot words. Facts do far better than invective. Our Saviour never denounced anyone without giving a reason for it. (2) This is an easy way to soil the holy truths of God. How often the Papists call us heretics. "These men speak abusively against whatever they do not understand" (Jude 10). If disputes were settled by argument rather than prejudice, there would be fewer differences.

Application. So we should be less passionate and more thoughtful. We should condemn things through reason rather than through abusive language. General invectives only make superficial impressions. Identify and name the error.

Note 2. We should be as careful to avoid errors as to avoid vices. A blind eye is worse than a lame foot. Indeed, a blind eye may cause lameness; without light, you are apt to stumble. Some opinions seem remote and theoretical, and yet they influence us; they make the heart foolish, and then life will not be right. There is a link between truth and truth, just as there is between grace and grace. So speculative errors do influence us. Some false teaching seems to encourage discipline; but when it is correctly evaluated, it greatly discourages discipline. So then, beware of false teachings in case your spirit is engulfed by them. People think nothing is to be avoided that is not an evil action and clearly wrong. But remember, there is contamination of the spirit as well as contamination of the body (2 Corinthians 7:1); a vain mind is as repugnant to God as an evil life. Error and idolatry are as dangerous as drunkenness and prostitution; therefore, you should carefully avoid everything that entices you into error, as well as those things that draw you into sin. Because error is the more plausible of the two, it is more deceptive. I am sure that many people toy with ideas because they do not know their danger. All false principles have a secret but pestilent influence on life.

Note 3. **Don't be deceived.** That is, do not be mistaken in this matter. It is a hard thing to see how God condones the act and not the evil motivation behind the act; however difficult this is to understand, **Don't be deceived.** Where truths are not plain to see, people tend to deviate from them. Many truths suffer a great deal because of their intricacy. False teachings may be so similar that it is hard to distinguish them. Human nature is prone to error; and, therefore, when truth is hard to discover, we content ourselves with our own prejudices. All truths are surrounded with such difficulties, so that those who want to doubt easily stumble: "This is a hard teaching. Who can accept it?" (that is, understand it) (John 6:60); and then (verse 66), "From this time many of his disciples turned back and no longer followed him." When there is something to justify our prejudices, we think we are safe enough. God leaves such difficulties as a stumbling-block for those who want to be offended.

Truth is presented in such a way that though it is clear enough for those who want to know, it is obscure enough to harden other people in their own unbelief. People want to be spared the trouble of prayer, study, and discussion. They are loath to "cry aloud for understanding" (Proverbs

2:3); they love an easy, short route to truth, and therefore run with those mistakes that come to hand, vainly imagining that God does not require belief about those things that are difficult to understand. They do not look for what is sound and solid but what is plausible and at first sight coincides with their thoughts and understanding.

Application 1. You see, then, how necessary it is to pray for gifts of interpretation for your ministers and an understanding heart for yourselves, that you may not be discouraged by the difficulties that surround the path of truth. Pray that God will give ministers a clear spirit and a plain expression and yourselves a right understanding. This is better than to grumble at the dispensation of God, that he should leave the world in such doubt and suspense. Chrysostom observes that saints do not pray, "Lord, make a plainer law," but, "Open my eyes that I may see wonderful things in your law," as David does (see Psalm 119:18). It is an unreasonable demand for blind people to desire God to make a sun so they can see. It is better to desire gifts of the Spirit for the minister, that the Scriptures might be opened; and the grace of the Spirit for ourselves, that our understanding might be opened, so that we may come to discern the mind of God.

Application 2. This shows how much people who make the things of God obscure are to blame. Many people have the ability to raise a cloud of dust with their own feet, and so darken the brightness and glory of the Scriptures.

Note 4. Note the importance of the matter. The mistake is so dangerous that James is all the more earnest. **Don't be deceived.** Note that errors about the nature of God are very dangerous. There is nothing more natural to us than to have wrong thoughts about God, and nothing is more dangerous. All behavior depends on keeping the glory of God unstained in your understanding. You see in Romans 1:23-24 that they "exchanged the glory of . . . God" and then "God gave them over in the sinful desires of their hearts." Idolatry is often expressed by prostitution; bodily and spiritual uncleanness usually go together. Wrong thoughts about God harm the spirit and make people lose their sense and their desire for piety. Do not let the glory of God be tarnished in your thoughts; abhor whatever comes into your mind or may be suggested by other people if it tends to eclipse the divine glory in your thinking.

Note 5. **My dear brothers.** A gentle approach best shows people their errors. It is said that we must speak to kings with silk words. Certainly we need to be very tender toward people who differ from us, speaking to them with silk words. Where the matter is likely to cause displeasure, the manner should not be harsh; pills should be sugared, so that they may be easily swallowed. Many people have been lost through harshness because you make them go over to the other party. Tertullian, when he had spoken favorably of the Montanists, was forced to join their fellowship through the harshness of the priests of Rome. Meekness may win over those who are not committed. Men from another party will think everything is spoken out of rage and anger against them. **Don't be deceived, my dear brothers.** I would to God we could learn this wisdom today: "Those who oppose him he must gently instruct, in the hope that God will grant them repentance leading them to a knowledge of the truth" (2 Timothy 2:25).

Commentary on Verse 17

Every good and perfect gift is from above, coming down from the Father of the heavenly lights, who does not change like shifting shadows.

James follows on from the former matter, which showed you that God was not the author of sin, to show you that God is the author of everything good, especially the spiritual gifts and graces bestowed on us. Here is a hidden argument: the author of everything good cannot be the author of evil. **Every good and perfect gift** is strengthened by an allusion to the sun as James represents God, in the latter part of the verse, as essentially and immutably good.

Every good . . . gift. The Vulgate has "the best gift," which fits the sense but not the original words. The gift is called **good** either (1) to exclude Satan's gifts, which are harmful: "blinded . . . minds" (2 Corinthians 4:4); these gifts from below are not good; or (2) to show the kind of gifts that he *is* speaking about—not common mercies but good gifts, which the apostle elsewhere calls "every spiritual blessing" (Ephesians 1:3). It is true that all common gifts come from God's bounty; but the apostle here intends special blessings, as is partly indicated by the attributes **good and perfect**. It is true that some people distinguish between the two words, making **good** imply earthly blessings and **perfect** imply heavenly or spiritual blessings. I think this is too fanciful. The two words indicate the same mercies.

And perfect gift. These gifts lead to our perfection. This includes initial grace, all progress in the spiritual life, and perfection and eternal life itself. All are the gift of God. Though eternal death is a reward, eternal life is a gift; and therefore the apostle varies the phrase when he compares them in Romans 6:23. So not only the start but all the gradual steps from grace to glory are gifts and from God's free mercy.

Is from above. That is, from heaven. Heaven stands for God, as in Luke 15:21—"I have sinned against heaven and against you"; that is, against God and his earthly father. I suppose there is some special reason why our blessings are said to be **from above**, because they were designed there, and heaven is their goal where they are perfectly enjoyed. Therefore, in Ephesians 1:3 we are said to be "blessed . . . in the heavenly realms with every spiritual blessing"; therefore James says, **from above** because blessings originate and are fulfilled there.

Coming down. Not "falling down"; this shows (says Aquinas) that we do not have blessings by chance, but through the normal channels.

From the Father of the heavenly lights. That is, from God. The word "father" is often used for the author or first cause, as in Genesis 4:20-21: "the father of those who live in tents," "the father of all who play the harp and flute"—that is, the author and founder. God is elsewhere called "the Father of our spirits" (Hebrews 12:9), because they are not from human descent but are created directly by God. So what is meant by **Father of the heavenly lights?** Some conceive that it means no more than "glorious Father," as it is usual in Hebrew to put the genitive for an epithet and the genitive plural for the superlative. But I think that God is likened to the sun, which gives out its light to all the planets; and so God, being the author of everything that is signified by light, is called here **the Father of the heavenly lights.** It is normal in the Scriptures to attribute light to God and darkness to the devil—as in Luke 22:53—"This is your [that is, Satan's] hour—when darkness reigns."

Who does not change. This is an astronomical term, taken from the heavenly bodies, which have many revolutions. The heavenly lights have their vicissitudes, eclipses, and decreases; but our sun always shines with the same brightness and glory.

Like shifting shadows. The allusion continues. Stars, according to their different light and position, have various shadowings. The nearer the sun is to us, the less shadow it casts; the farther off, the greater the shadow. So we know the sun's movements by its different shadows. But with the Father of spiritual lights there is no shadow of turning; that is, he does not change but always remains the same. This is a sun that does not set or rise and cannot be overcast or eclipsed.

Notes on Verse 17

Note 1. All **good** things are **from above**; they come to us from God. Evils do not come from God, because he is good. God delights in being the sole author of all our good, and therefore cannot endure that we should give that honor to another. When God was about to work miracles by Moses' hand, he first made it leprous (Exodus 4:6). Noting that God is the author of all the good that is in us prevents many corruptions, such as: (1) Glorying in ourselves. Who would glorify himself in what is **from**

above? We think it wrong for a person to take credit for another person's work; the apostle says in 2 Corinthians 10:16 that he would not boast about work already done in another man's territory. So all the good your hand accomplishes is heaven's bounty to you. It is not your work but God's.

(2) Lording it over others. Ungodly and weak spirits feed their evil desires with their enjoyments. The more you place on top of a straight pillar, the straighter it is; but a pillar that is bent bows under the weight it supports. So the more God puts on ungodly people, the more their spirit is perverted.

(3) Envying those who have received most. Our eye is evil when God's hand is good. Envy is a rebellion against God himself and the liberty and pleasure of his dispensations. God distributes gifts and blessings as he wills, not as we will. Out duty is to be content and to beg grace to make use of what we have received.

Note 2. Whatever we have **from above**, we have as a gift. We have nothing but what we have received, and what we have received we have received freely. There is nothing in us that could oblige God to bestow it; the favors of heaven are not for sale. When God invites us to his mercy, he does not invite us as a host but as a king—not to buy, but to take; the most welcome are those who have no money (Isaiah 55:1)—that is, no confidence in their own merits. Merit and desert are improper ideas to express the relationship between the work of a creature and the reward of a Creator; and they are even more incongruous since the fall. Sin, which indicates how undeserving we are, makes mercy even more of a gift, so that now in every *giving* there is some *forgiving*. Grace gives us even more, because in every blessing there is not only bounty but a pardon. Oh, that we were aware of this, that in all our actions we might have a sense of love and have God's glory as our goal.

Note 3. Out of all the gifts of God, spiritual blessings are the best. These are called here **good and perfect** because these make us good and perfect. "If you, then, though you are evil, know how to give good gifts to your children, how much more will your Father in heaven give good gifts to those who ask him!" (Matthew 7:11). The parallel passage in Luke 11:13 says, "give the Holy Spirit to those who ask him!" That is giving good gifts—to give the Holy Spirit. "There can be nothing good where there is not the Spirit of God" (Augustine). One may become tired of other gifts. An estate may be a trap; life itself may become a burden. But you have never heard of spiritual blessings being a burden. Ungodly spirits prefer soup to a birthright, vain delights before the good and perfect gifts. David makes a wiser choice in his prayer: "Remember me, O Lord, when you show favor to your people" (Psalm 106:4). Not every mercy satisfies David—only the mercy of God's own people; not every gift satisfies us—only the good and perfect gift. A similar prayer is in Psalm 119:132, "Turn to me and have mercy on me, as you always do to those who love your name." Note that these are not the mercies that he bestowed on the world, but the mercies he bestowed on his people. Nothing but the best mercy will satisfy the best hearts.

Note 4. God is **the Father of the heavenly lights**. Light is often used to indicate the essences and perfections of creatures as they come from God. The essence of God comes in 1 John 1:5, "God is light; in him there is no darkness at all." There light indicates the simplicity of the divine essence. It also shows the glory of God: "He lives in unapproachable light" (1 Timothy 6:16)—that is, in inconceivable glory. So Jesus Christ, in that he received his personality and subsistence from the Father, is called, in the Nicene Creed, "Light of light, and very God of very God." The creatures also, since they derive their perfection from God, are called lights. An angel is called an "angel of light" (2 Corinthians 11:14); the saints are called "the people of the light" (Luke 16:8). Rational creatures, as they have wisdom and understanding, are said to be lights; Christ is "the true light that gives light to every man" (John 1:9), and all the candles in the world are lighted from this torch. In short, reason, wisdom, holiness, and happiness are often expressed by light, and they are all from God.

As the stars shine with a borrowed luster, so do all the creatures; where you meet any brightness and excellency in them, remember it is only a ray of the divine glory. As the star brought the wise men to Christ, so should all the stars in the world bring your thoughts to God, who is "the Fountain and Father of lights." "Let your light shine before men, that they may see your good deeds and praise" not you but "your Father in heaven" (Matthew 5:16). If you see a candle burn brightly and purely, remember it was set alight by God. If there is any light in others, a sense of the mysteries of the Gospel, if they are burning and shining lights, if they give out the flame of godly conversation, remember that they are only revealing that luster and glory that they received from above.

If God is **the Father of the heavenly lights**:

(1) You must apply yourself to God. If you want the light of grace or knowledge or comfort, you must be set alight by his flame. We are dark bodies until the Lord fills us with his own glory. How devoid of comfort we would be without God! In the night there is nothing but terror and error; and so it is in the soul without the light of the divine presence. When the sun is gone, the plants wither; and when God, who is the sun of spirits, is withdrawn, there is nothing but discomfort and a sad languishing in the soul. Oh, pray then that God will shine on your soul not in flashes but with constant light. It is often like this with us in comfort and grace. Holy thoughts arise and, like a flash of lightning, make the room bright; but then the lightning is gone, and we are as dark as ever. But when God shines with a constant light, then shall we give out a holy luster: "Arise, shine, for

your light has come, and the glory of the Lord rises upon you" (Isaiah 60:1). We, like the moon, are dark bodies and have no light rooted within ourselves; the Lord must dawn on us before we can shine. It is the same with comfort: "Those who look to him are radiant; their faces are never covered with shame" (Psalm 34:5).

(2) This shows why wicked people hate God: "Light has come into the world, but men loved darkness instead of light" (John 3:19). Again, they "will not come into the light for fear that [their] deeds will be exposed" (verse 20). Those who delight in darkness cannot endure God, nor anything that represents God. Rachel could not endure Laban's search, nor can the wicked endure God's eye. He is **the Father of the heavenly lights**; he has a discerning eye and a searching beam.

(3) Children of God should walk in purity and innocence. "You are light in the Lord. Live as children of light" (Ephesians 5:8). Walk so that you reflect the glory of your Father; faults in you, like spots in the moon, soon show up. You who are the lights of the world should shine brightly; indeed, in the worst times you should shine brightest, like stars in the blackest night. Therefore the apostle says, "Shine like stars in the universe" (Philippians 2:15).

Note 5. The Lord is unchangeable in holiness and glory; he is a sun that always shines with the same brightness. God, and all that is in God, in unchangeable. This is an attribute that, like a silk thread in a chain of pearls, runs through them all. His mercy does not change—"his love endures forever" (Psalm 100:5). The same is true of his strength, and so he is called "the Rock eternal" (Isaiah 26:4). So his love is immutable. His heart is the same to us in all situations; we change, but God does not change. So then:

(1) The more changeable you are, the less you are like God. You should hate yourselves when you are so fickle! God is immutably holy, but you have a heart that loves to wander. God is always the same, but you quickly change (see Galatians 1:6). The more you "continue in what you have learned and have become convinced of" (2 Timothy 3:14), the more you resemble divine perfection.

(2) Go to him to establish and settle your spirits. God, who is unchangeable in himself, can bring you into an unchanging state of grace, against which all the gates of hell cannot prevail. Therefore, do not rest until you have received gifts from him that never alter—the fruits of eternal grace and the pledges of eternal glory.

(3) Go to God as one who is good and unchanging. In the midst of the greatest changes, see him as the same always; when there is little in the creature, there is as much in God as ever: "They will perish, but you remain; they will all wear out like a garment. . . . But you remain the same, and your years will never end" (Psalm 102:26-27). All creatures vanish not

only like a piece of cloth, but like a garment. Cloth would decay by itself or be eaten by moths; but a garment is worn every day. But God does not change. There is no wrinkle on the brow of eternity; the arm of mercy is not dried up, nor does his compassionate love ever end. This is the church's comfort in the saddest situation. No matter how the face of the creature changes, God will still be the same. It is said somewhere that "the name of God is as an ointment poured out." Certainly this matter of God's unchangingness is like an ointment poured out, the best cordial to refresh a fainting soul. When the Israelites were in distress, all the letters of recommendation that God would give Moses were those in Exodus 3:14, "'I am who I am. . . . "I AM has sent me to you."'" That was comfort enough for the Israelites; God could say, "I am." With God there is no change—no past or present; he remains in the same indivisible point of eternity and therefore says, "I am." So the prophet Malachi says, "I the Lord do not change [or am not changed]; so you, O descendants of Jacob, are not destroyed" (Malachi 3:6). Our safety lies in God's immutability; we cannot perish totally because God cannot change.

Commentary on Verse 18

He chose to give us birth through the word of truth, that we might be a kind of firstfruits of all he created.

The apostle shows that his main aim is to reveal God as the author of spiritual gifts, and therefore he mentions regeneration.

He chose. Because he wanted to, or being willing. The word is given here (1) to deny compulsion or necessity—God did not need to save anyone; and (2) to exclude merit—we could not force God to do it—it was merely his good pleasure. This **he chose** is equivalent to what Paul calls the natural inclination of God's heart to do his creatures good.

To give us birth. This word means natural birth, and sometimes it is used for creation. So we are said to be "his offspring" (Acts 17:28). Some people apply these words to God's creation of us, making people his firstfruits, or the most special part of the whole creation. But this is beside the point, for James speaks of this as birth that is **through the word of truth.** In the next verse he uses this to argue that we should be more aware of the duty of listening; therefore this **birth** implies the work of grace on our souls. The same metaphor is used elsewhere: "For you have been born again, not of perishable seed, but of imperishable, through the living and enduring word of God" (1 Peter 1:23). "He has given us new birth into a living hope" (1 Peter 1:3). These two quotations show you the two parts of the work of grace; in one we are begotten, in the other we are born again. In the one it is purely God's act; the other implies the manifestation of life in ourselves. This distinction clears up some controversies in religion.

Through the word of truth. Here the instrument is noted. Those who refer this verse to the creation apply it to Jesus Christ, who is the eternal, uncreated Word of the Father, through whom all things were made (see John 1:1-3; Hebrews 1:2). But clearly it means the Gospel, which is often called "the word of truth" and is the usual way in which God brings us to himself in birth.

That we might be a kind of firstfruits of all he created. Those who apply the verse to the creation say the apostle means that man was the chief part of it, for all things were subjected to him and put under his feet (Psalm 8). But I think it rather indicates the dignity and prerogative of the regenerate; for as it was the privilege of the firstfruits of all the sheaves to be consecrated, so believers and converts among all men were set aside for the purposes of God. The firstfruits of all things were the Lord's (1) partly to testify to his right in that people; (2) partly for a witness of their thankfulness—they had received everything from him and were to thank him for this ("Honor the Lord with your wealth, with the firstfruits of all your crops," Proverbs 3:9). This was the honor and homage they were to give to God.

Everywhere this is attributed to the people of God—to Israel—because they were God's special people, called out from all the nations. "Israel was holy to the LORD, the firstfruits of his harvest" (Jeremiah 2:3); that is, of all people, they were dedicated to God. So holy worshipers, represented by the virgins in Revelation 14:4, are said to be "purchased from among men and offered as firstfruits to God and the Lamb"; these were the most honored, Christ's own portion. So the church is called "the church of the firstborn" (Hebrews 12:23). The people in the world are ordinary people; the church is the Lord's.

Notes on Verse 18

Note 1. God engaged in the work of regeneration through his own will and good pleasure: **He chose to give us birth;** "God has mercy on whom he wants to have mercy, and he hardens whom he wants to harden" (Romans 9:18). God's will is the reason for all his actions, motivated by love and mercy. God can have no higher motive. "You did not choose me, but I chose you" (John 15:16); he begins with us first. When Moses speaks about the origin of God's love for Israel, he says, "The Lord . . . [chose] you . . . because the LORD loved you" (Deuteronomy 7:7-8); he had no other motive. "He rescued me because he delighted in me" (Psalm 18:19); that was the only reason he did it, because he wanted to. "I will . . . love them freely" (Hosea 14:4); there is the beginning of it all.

This is applicable in various ways:

(1) To stir us up to admire the mercy of God, that nothing should incline his heart except his own will. The same will gave us life and passed others by; whom he will he saves, and whom he will he hardens. Human thoughts are very unbalanced in the inquiry about why God should choose some and leave others. When all is said, you must rest in this supreme cause, God's will and pleasure: "Yes, Father, for this was your good pleasure" (Matthew 11:26). Christ himself could give no other reason, and there is the final answer to all disputes. Praise God, all his saints, for his mercy to you. This gives the purest understanding of the freeness of God's love, when you see that it was God's own will that brought you mercy and made the difference between you and others. In some ways it makes a difference between you and Christ. The goodwill of the Father kills one and saves others; he willed Christ's death and your salvation. In the same verse, Christ's bruises and our salvation are called God's pleasure: "It was the Lord's will to crush him, " and "the will of the Lord [in the salvation of the elect] will prosper in his hand" (Isaiah 53:10).

(2) This tells us why, in the work of regeneration, God acts with such freedom. God works according to his will; the Holy One of Israel must not be limited and confined to our thinking: "The wind blows wherever it pleases" (John 3:8). All is according to the will of the free Spirit; there are mighty deeds in Chorazin and Bethsaida when there are none in Tyre and Sidon. Israel had statutes and ordinances when all the world had nothing except the flickering candle of their own reason. It is the same with the work of the Spirit with the means; some have only the means, others the work of the Spirit with the means: "Why do you intend to show yourself to us and not to the world?" (John 14:22). Note Acts 9:7, where it is said of Paul's companions that "they heard the sound," and yet in Acts 22:9 it is said that "they did not understand the voice." Solomon Glassius comments that they heard a sound, but they did not hear it distinctly as Christ's voice. Some only hear the outward sound, the voice of man, but not of the Spirit in the Word.

It is the same with the amount of grace; to some more is given, to some less. "It is God who works in you to will and to act according to his good purpose" (Philippians 2:13). The manner is also very varied. God starts with some through love, with others through fear, snatching them from the fire (see Jude 22-23). Some are won through a cross and affliction, others through mercy. Therefore, we should not limit God to any one method, but must wait on him in the use of means for his good pleasure to our souls.

Note 2. The calling of a soul to God is, as it were, a new birth and regeneration. He gave us **birth**; there must be a new frame, for all is out of order. Therefore, grace is called "a new creation" (2 Corinthians 5:17); all was chaos and emptiness before. Elsewhere this is expressed as being "born again" (John 3:3); and so believers are called Christ's "offspring" (Isaiah 53:10).

This is useful:

(1) To show us the horrible defilement and depravation of our nature. Mending and repairing would not be enough; God must re-create us and give us birth again. Like the house infected with leprosy, scraping is not enough; it must be pulled down and rebuilt.

(2) This shows us that we are merely passive in our conversion. It is a begetting, and we (as the infant in the womb) contribute nothing to our own forming. "It is he who made us, and we are his" (Psalm 100:3); we had no hand in it.

(3) This shows us two aspects of conversion. First, there will be life; the effect of generation is life. Natural men are said to be "separated from the life of God" (Ephesians 4:18); they are complete strangers to the work of the Spirit. But when the soul is given life, there is spiritual feeling, and the soul is not dead toward God. Paul says, "I no longer live, but Christ lives in me" (Galatians 2:20). A man cannot be in Christ without receiving life from him. Second, there will be a change. God brings all the seeds of grace, and therefore there will be a change. Profane, godless hearts are made spiritual, heavenly, holy: "For you were once darkness, but now you are light in the Lord" (Ephesians 5:8). You see, there is a vast difference. If men remain the same, how can they be said to be born again? They are still ungodly and still worldly. There should be at least a desolation of the old frames of spirit.

Note 3. It is God's own work to **give us birth**. This is sometimes ascribed to God the Father, as here, and in other places to God the Son. Believers are "his offspring" (Isaiah 53:10). Sometimes it is ascribed to the Spirit, as in John 3:6, "the Spirit gives birth to spirit." We see God the Father's will: **He chose to give us birth**; God the Son's merit: through his obedience we have "the full rights of sons" (Galatians 4:5); God the Spirit's efficacy: he overshadows the soul, and the new creature is born. This is ascribed to all three persons of the Godhead together in one place: "He saved us . . . because of his mercy . . . through the washing of rebirth and renewal of the Holy Spirit, whom he poured out on us generously through Jesus Christ" (Titus 3:5-6). In another place you have two persons of the Godhead mentioned: "For we are his workmanship, created in Christ Jesus to do good works, which God prepared in advance for us to do" (Ephesians 2:10). It is true that the ministers of the Gospel are said to give birth, but it is as instruments in God's hands. So Paul says, "I became your father" (1 Corinthians 4:15); and about Onesimus he says, "who became my son while I was in chains" (Philemon 10). God loves to attribute his own honor to the instruments.

So then:

(1) Remove false reasoning. You cannot give birth to yourself—that would be monstrous; you must look beyond yourself, and beyond the means, to God who forms you after his own image. John 1:13 says that we were "born not of natural descent, nor of human decision or a husband's will, but born of God."

(2) This shows the wonderful relationship we have through the new birth. God is our Father; that brings his love and compassion and care and everything that can be dear and refreshing to the creature: "Your heavenly Father knows that you need them" (Matthew 6:32). This relationship is often called on by the children of God: "But you are our Father, though Abraham does not know us" (Isaiah 63:16). There is comfort in a father, and much more in a Heavenly Father. Evil men may be good fathers (see Matthew 7:11); they must follow their natural fatherly instincts. How much more will a good God be a good Father? As Tertullian said, "None can be so good and so much a father as he."

Note 4. The ordinary means whereby God gives birth is the Gospel. He gave us birth **through the word of truth**: "in Christ Jesus I became your father through the gospel" (1 Corinthians 4:15). There is the instrument, the author, the means: the instrument, Paul ("I became your father"); the means, "through the gospel"; the author, "in Christ Jesus." So 1 Peter 1:23 says, "born again, not of perishable seed, but of imperishable, through the living and enduring word of God." The Word is, as it were, the seed that is grafted into the heart and produces obedience. This is through the Word, and that part of the Word which is correctly called the Gospel. Moses may bring us to the borders, but Joshua leads us into the land of Canaan; the law may prepare the way, but the Gospel gives the grace of conversion.

Well, then, let us wait on God in the use of the Word; it is not good to balk the known and normal ways of grace. Wisdom is given at Wisdom's gates: "Blessed is the man who listens to me, watching daily at my doors, waiting at my doorway" (Proverbs 8:34). Remind your souls about the necessity of the means. "Faith comes from hearing the message, and the message is heard through the word of Christ" (Romans 10:17). Without grace I cannot be saved; without the Word I cannot have grace. Reason like this with yourselves, so that you may alert your soul to a greater sense of waiting on God in the Word. It is true that divine grace does everything; but remember, it is through the Word of truth. The influences of the heavens give fruitful seasons; yet plowing is necessary. It is one of the sophisms of this age to urge the Spirit's efficacy as a plea for the neglect of the means.

Note 5. The Gospel is a **word of truth**; it is called this not only here but in various other passages: see Ephesians 1:13; Colossians 1:5; 2 Timothy 2:15. The same expression is used in all these passages. You may constantly observe that in matters of the Gospel the Scriptures speak with the greatest certainty; their comfort is so rich, and their way so wonderful, that we are apt to doubt such matters the most, and so the Scriptures give us a more solemn assurance about them—as in 1 Timothy 1:15, "Here is a trustworthy saying that deserves full acceptance: Christ Jesus came into the world to save sinners." We tend to look on this as a doubtful thing, or at best as just a possibility; therefore Paul prefaces it with, "Here is a trustworthy saying." Similarly in Isaiah 53:4, "Surely he took up our infirmities and carried our sorrows." You say, surely I am a sinner. But it is just as certain that Christ is a Saviour; naturally we are more aware of our sin than of the comforts of Christ. The apostle Paul says about the heathen that they "know God's righteous decree" and that "those who do such things deserve death" (Romans 1:32).

Natural conscience will give us a sense of sin, but usually we look on Gospel comforts with a loose heart and doubtful mind; and therefore Scripture speaks in such a certain way. Is it certain that you are a sinner? It is just as certain that he "took up our infirmities and carried our sorrows." Similarly in Revelation 19:9, "'Blessed are those who are invited to the wedding supper of the Lamb!' . . . 'These are the true words of God.'" Similarly, in Revelation 22:6, after he had spoken about the glory of heaven, the apostle says, "These words are trustworthy and true."

Application. This makes us put our heart into these truths. How strange it is that our hearts should be so weak about those points that have a special note of truth and faithfulness linked to them! It may well be said, "Anyone who does not believe God has made him out to be a liar" (1 John 5:10). God has told you that these are trustworthy and true sayings; therefore you implicitly make God a liar when you think these things are too good to be true. This is to set your own sense and experience against God's oaths, which are everywhere in the Gospel. Assent to the greatest certainty there is; check those evil thoughts that secretly lurk in all our hearts, that the Gospel is some clever device that cheats the world.

Assents are of different kinds; some are very imperfect. There is conjecture, which is only a lighter inclination of the mind to what is only probable; it may or may not be true. Better than this is opinion, when the mind is strongly swayed to think something is true. However, there is a fear of the contrary, which is opposed to believing with all the heart. The next stage is "weak faith," where people look upon Christianity as true and good but cling to it feebly. Above this there is assurance. Here I mean the truths of the Gospel, not of our interest in its comforts. This is meant by the apostle when he says the Thessalonians received the Gospel "with deep conviction" (1 Thessalonians 1:5); they were persuaded of the truths of the Gospel. The same apostle, in Colossians 2:2, calls it "the full riches of complete understanding, in order that they may know the mystery of God"—that is, an understanding and experience of the truths of the Gospel and a resolution to live and die in this faith.

Question. You will say, how shall we attain such perfection? How is the soul assured that the Gospel is a **word of truth**?

Answer. This question is worthy of a reasoned answer, because atheism is so natural to us. In these times especially, the reigning sin is atheism and skepticism in matters of religion, brought about partly by corrupt and blasphemous doctrines, which agree with our thoughts, and partly by the sad divisions among the people of God. Everyone thinks he is in the right and suspects everyone else; therefore Christ prayed for unity in the church: "Let the world know that you sent me" (John 17:23). When there are divisions in the church, there is usually atheism in the world—partly through the scandals committed under a pretense of religion, through which Christ is, as it were, denied (see Titus 1:16, and also Hebrews 6:6, "they are crucifying the Son of God all over again"—that is, he is exposed to the derision and scorn of his enemies and portrayed as a criminal). Now more than ever, then, it is necessary to support the mind with solid arguments and to establish you in the holy faith. Many arguments are given by the Fathers and the schoolmen on behalf of the Gospel, but I have always preferred the arguments of the Fathers, such as Lactantius, Tertullian, Justin Martyr, Cyril, etc., rather than those of the schoolmen, as they are more practical and natural. The arguments of the schoolmen are more subtle and speculative, and so less easy to understand. Briefly, then, you may know that the Gospel is a **word of truth** because whatever is excellent in a religion is in an unparalleled manner found in our religion, or in the doctrine of the Gospel. The glory of a religion lies in three things—the excellency of rewards, the purity of precepts, and the sureness of principles of trust. Now examine the Gospel by these things and see if it can be matched elsewhere.

(1) The excellency of rewards. This is one of the most important aspects of a religion. Therefore the apostle proposes it as a principle and foundation of religion and worship to "believe that he [God] exists and that he rewards those who earnestly seek him" (Hebrews 11:6). Whoever comes to God—that is, to engage in his worship—must also believe in his bounty, because a man in all his endeavors is poised for some happiness and reward. Since the fall there are "many schemes" (Ecclesiastes 7:29). As the Sodomites, when they were struck with blindness, groped around Lot's door, so we grope here and there for a reward that may be adequate for our desires. The heathen were at a sad loss.

Augustine, following Varro, counted two hundred and eighty-eight opinions about the chief good. Some placed it in pleasures and such things as gratified sense. But this would make brutes of men, for it is the beast's happiness to enjoy pleasures without remorse. Cicero said, "He is not worthy of the name of a man who would spend one whole day in pleasures." "If only for this life we have hope in Christ, we are to be pitied more than all men" (1 Corinthians 15:19). But the Gospel gives eternal and happy enjoyment of God in Christ in the life to come, "eternal pleasures at your right hand" (Psalm 16:11), complete knowledge, perfect love, the soul filled with God. The Gospel outdoes all religions, propounding a most excellent reward for the holy life.

(2) Purity of precepts. In the Christian religion all moral duties are heightened to their greatest perfection. "Your commands are boundless" (Psalm 119:96), comprising every motion, thought, and circumstance. The precepts are exact, commanding love not only for friends but for enemies. The law is spiritual and good in all points: "The law of the Lord is perfect, reviving the soul" (Psalm 19:7)—that is, not only guiding the actions of the exterior man, but piercing his thoughts. We have a perfect law.

(3) The sureness of principles of trust. One of the most wonderful aspects of the creature's relationship to the Godhead is trust and dependence. And trust, being the rest and quiet of the soul, must have a sure foundation. Survey all the religions in the world, and you will find no basis for trust except in the Gospel—trusting in God for a common mercy, trusting in God for a saving mercy.

a. For a common mercy. There are no representations of God to the soul like those in the Gospel. The Gentiles had only vague and dark thoughts about God and therefore are generally described as "men, who have no hope" (1 Thessalonians 4:13). I remember that when our Saviour spoke against anxiety about outward needs he said: "So do not worry, saying, 'What shall we eat?' or 'What shall we drink?' or, 'What shall we wear?' For the pagans run after all these things" (Matthew 6:31-32), implying that such a way of life was only excusable in heathen who had no sure principles. But you who know providence and the care of a Heavenly Father should not be anxious in this way. It is true that the heathen had some sense of a deity; they had some understanding about the nature of God (see Romans 1:20). But the apostle says in the next verse that "their thinking became futile." When they came to represent God as an object of trust, they were vain and foolish. But now in the Gospel God is represented as a fit object of trust, and therefore the solemn and purest part of Christian worship is faith. Luther observed that "it is the design of the whole Scripture to bring the soul to a steady belief and trust." Therefore the psalmist, speaking about God's work in the world and in the church, when he comes to his work in the church says, "Your statutes stand firm" (Psalm 93:5). God deals with us according to sure principles.

b. For saving mercies. This is the test of all religions. The best is the one that gives the soul a sure hope of salvation. In Jeremiah 6:16 God says, "Stand at the crossroads and look; ask for the ancient paths, ask where the good way is, and walk in it, and you shall find rest for your souls." There are three things that trouble the soul: our distance from God, our fear of angry justice, and a despair of retaining comfort with a sense of duty. Therefore, before the conscience can have any rest and quiet, three couples must be brought together—God and man, justice and mercy, comfort and duty; all of them must embrace and kiss each other.

First, God and man must be brought together. Homer said that people would never be happy until the gods and mortal men came to live together. Certainly instinct makes us feel after an eternal good. "Men would seek him [God]" (Acts 17:27). Now, how can we have any link with God since there is such a distance between us and him? How can guilty creatures think of God without trembling, or approach him without being devoured and swallowed up by his glory? The heathen realized this to a certain extent and therefore held that the supreme gods were defiled by the unhallowed approaches of sinful and mortal men. Therefore they invented heroes and half-gods, a kind of middle powers, to be mediators, to convey their prayers to the gods and the blessings of the gods back again to them. So Plutarch said, "By these intermediate powers there was communion between the gods and men." To this teaching of the heathen the apostle alludes in 1 Corinthians 8:5; the heathens had "many 'gods' and many 'lords.'" They had many gods, many ultimate objects of worship; and many lords—that is, mediators. "Yet for us there is but one God, the Father" (1 Corinthians 8:6). There is one supreme essence and one mediator.

In this sure way the Scriptures lay down how we can have communion with God. The Godhead and manhood meet in one nature. The Son of God was made the Son of man, that the sons of men might become the sons of God. Therefore the apostle Peter explains that the great work of Christ was "to bring you to God" (1 Peter 3:18), to bring God and man together. So the apostle says in Hebrews 10:19-20 that we may "enter the Most Holy Place by . . . a new and living way opened for us through the curtain, that is, his body." This is an allusion to the Temple, where the curtain hid God's glory. Christ is the true Jacob's ladder (see John 1:51), the bottom of which touches the earth—there is his humanity, and the top of which reaches heaven—there is his divinity. So we may climb this ladder and have communion with God. As a Father said, "Climbing up in hope by the manhood of Christ, we have access to the Godhead."

Second, justice and mercy must be brought together. We want mercy and fear justice; guilt makes the spirit tremble, because we do not know how to redeem our souls out of the hands of angry justice. The heathen were under this bondage of the divine justice: "those who do such things deserve death" (Romans 1:32). So how can we appease angry justice and redeem our souls from this fear? You know the question in Micah 6:6-7, "With what shall I come before the Lord?" The heathen, in their blindness, tried to placate the Godhead by meritorious acts, either by costly sacrifices ("ten thousand rivers of oil") or by torturing themselves as Baal's priests who gashed themselves. In the Gospel, "love and faithfulness meet together, righteousness and peace kiss each other," as it says in Psalm 85:10. Justice, which terrifies the world, in Christ is made our friend and the chief ground of our hope and support; as 1 John 1:9 says, the Lord "is faithful and just and will forgive us our sins." One would have thought "faithful and gracious" a more proper term than "faithful and just," since pardon is an act of free grace. But justice is satisfied in Christ; so it does not detract from his righteousness to dispense a pardon. So the crown of glory is called "the crown of righteousness" (2 Timothy 4:8).

Many Scriptures teach that all the comfort and hope of a Christian hangs on God's righteousness. If you believe the apostle Paul, you will see that God's great purpose in appointing Christ, rather than any other Redeemer, was to show himself just in pardoning, so that he might be kind to sinners without damaging his righteousness. In short, justice is satisfied and mercy has the freer course. Listen to what the apostle says in Romans 3:25-26, "God presented him as a sacrifice of atonement, through faith in his blood. He did this to demonstrate his justice." And in case we should miss the emphatic word, he repeats it: "to demonstrate his justice at the present time, so as to be just and the one who justifies the man who has faith in Jesus." So in justification, where grace is most free, God makes his righteousness shine, having received satisfaction from Christ.

Third, comfort and duty are brought together. The end of all religion is that the soul may be quiet in itself and obedient to that which is supposed to be God. How shall we combine duty with comfort? Conscience cannot be stifled with loose principles. The heathen could not be quiet, and therefore when their reason was disturbed with sensual desires that they could not bridle they became violent. They plucked out their eyes because they could not look at a woman without lusting after her. And we who have the light of Christianity know how much more we cannot have comfort without duty. Although true peace of conscience is founded on Christ's satisfaction, yet it is found only in his service: "Come to me . . . and I will give you rest" (Matthew 11:28); but verse 29 says, "Take my yoke upon you . . . and you will find rest for your souls." As we must come to Christ for comfort, so we must remain under his discipline. See how wonderfully this is provided for in the Gospel. There is the power of the Spirit against weaknesses, and merit against failings, so that duty is provided for as well as comfort. You need not despair about weaknesses, as you have the help of a mighty Spirit. In short, when you have the greatest thoughts about duty, you may have the sweetest hopes of comfort and can say with David, "I would not be put to shame when I consider all your commands" (Psalm 119:6).

Note 6. God's children are his **firstfruits**. The word hints at two things—their dignity and their duty. These two considerations will show the meaning of the apostle's expression.

(1) It notes the dignity of the people of God in two ways. One is that they are "a people that are his very own" (Titus 2:14), the people God looks after. The world's people are his goods, but you are his treasure. **Firstfruits** is emphatic. Others are only his creatures, but you are his **firstfruits**. He delights to be called your God: "Blessed are the people whose God is the Lord" (Psalm 144:15). He is Lord of all, but he is your God. What a wonderful example this is of God's love for us, that he should reckon us as his **firstfruits**!

The other way is that they are a large proportion of the world. The **firstfruits** were offered for the blessing of all the rest: "Honor the Lord with . . . the firstfruits of all your crops; then your barns will be filled to overflowing, and your vats will brim over with new wine" (Proverbs 3:9-10). It is the same here with the children of God. These are the **firstfruits** that God takes in place of a whole nation, to convey a blessing on the rest.

(2) It hints at duty as, first, thankfulness in all their lives. **Firstfruits** were dedicated to God as a sign of thankfulness. Cain was implicitly branded for ingratitude because he did not offer the firstfruits. You who are God's **firstfruits** should live a life of love and praise, aware of his mercy. The apostle says the mercies of God should persuade us to offer ourselves "as living sacrifices" (Romans 12:1). Now, under the Gospel, there are no sin offerings; they are all thank offerings. So then, give your-selves up in spiritual worship. It is only reasonable that when God has given us life we should be his **firstfruits**. The motive for obedience under the Gospel is not fear but gratitude. ". . . to rescue us from the hand of our enemies, and to enable us to serve him without fear" (Luke 1:74). Your lives should show that you are **firstfruits**, yielded to God as a testimony of gratitude.

Second, this indicates holiness. The **firstfruits** were holy to the Lord. God's part must be holy; and therefore **firstfruits** that were in themselves an abomination, such as the firstborn of a dog or ass, were not to be offered to God—they were redeemed with money. God can brook no unclean thing. Sins in you are far more upsetting to God's Spirit than to other people. Jeremiah 32:30 says, "The people of Israel and Judah have done nothing but evil in my sight from their youth." The Septuagint reads, "they alone [or, they only] have been sinners before me," as if God did not take notice of the sins of other nations.

Third, this indicates consecration. Your time, energy, and concerns are all the Lord's. You cannot do with them as you please, but only what makes for the Lord's glory. You are not **firstfruits** when you seek your own things. You are not to live in your own ways, nor for your own ends. **Firstfruits** were handed over to God, and the owner had no rights over them. So then:

a. You are not to walk in your own ways; your desires and wills are not to guide you—only God's will is to guide you. "There is a way," says Solomon, "that seems right to a man" (Proverbs 16:25); a corrupt mind looks on it as a good way, and a corrupt will is ready to follow it. So the prophet Isaiah says, "We all, like sheep, have gone astray, each of us has turned to his own way" (Isaiah 53:6). Remember to study the mind and will of God. Your own ideas will seduce you, and your own affections will betray you.

b. Do not live for yourself: "Those who live should live no longer for themselves," for their own pleasure, profit, or honor (2 Corinthians 5:15). We have no rights over ourselves; everything is given up to God. All pleasures or honors are refused or received depending on how they can be used to the glory of God.

Commentary on Verse 19

My dear brothers, take note of this: Everyone should be quick to listen, slow to speak and slow to become angry.

My dear brothers. James has spoken about **the word of truth** being the instrument of conversion, and on that ground urges diligence in hearing and reverence in speaking about it. He is saying, you see what an honor God has given the Word; through it he bestows his new life. Therefore, **be quick to listen**—that is, have a teachable mind to wait on God's Word; be **slow to speak**—that is, do not rashly give your opinion about things concerning the faith; be **slow to become angry**—that is, do not be angry with those who differ from you. If we take these directions as being a specific reference to the matter in hand, the context is easy to understand. I agree that it is good to apply Scripture, and so this teaching extends to private conversation, when people are full of talk themselves and cannot bear to listen to others and seek private revenge in anger; these things are often found in Christian meetings and conventions. But the main aim of the apostle is to direct his readers to the solemn hearing of the Word.

Notes on Verse 19

Note 1. **Wherefore** [KJV]. It is a great encouragement to wait on God's ordinances when we consider the benefits God gives through them. Say this when you listen: I must listen so that my soul may live; I am going to the Word that is to give me life, to make my soul share in the divine nature.

Note 2. **Wherefore** [KJV]. Experience of God's ordinances makes us more eager to receive them. He has given you **birth by the word of truth; wherefore be quick to listen.** When God gives you success, he gives you a seal of his truth, a real experience of the comforts of his service. The Stancarists [the family of Stancaras, a professor at Königsberg and afterwards in Poland, where he died in 1574—*Ed. note*] think ordinances are useless for believers. But they are ignorant of the nature of grace, the state of their own hearts, and the purposes of the Word. Because this proud sect has revived in our own day, and because many people as soon as they have found the benefit of ordinances think they are above them, let us examine this a little more.

(1) They are ignorant of the nature of grace, which always leaves a longing for more: "My soul thirsts for you, my body longs for you" (Psalm 63:1). The apostle Peter says, "Now that you have tasted that the Lord is good . . . come to him, the living Stone" (1 Peter 2:3-4); that is, if you have had any experience of Christ in the Word (which is the case in the context), you will come to him for more. Grace is brought to life by previous experience, not blunted.

(2) They are ignorant of the purpose of the Word, which is not only to give us birth but to make the saints mature (see Ephesians 4:12-13). The apostles, when they had founded churches, returned to strengthen the disciples (Acts 14:22). We are to look after growth as well as truth. Now, in case you should think this only applies to newborn babies or to weaker Christians, you will see that mature Christians also need to exercise themselves in this way. The prophets "searched intently" into the writings of other prophets (1 Peter 1:10). Daniel himself, though a prophet and a prophet who had visions, studied the Scriptures: see Daniel 9:2. Even the greatest believers need to pray, meditate, read, and listen in order to preserve the work of grace that has started in their souls. Note in particular Luke 8:18, "Consider carefully how you listen. Whoever has will be given more; whoever does not have, even what he thinks he has will be taken from him."

(3) They are ignorant about the state of their own hearts. Are there no graces to be perfected and increased, no corruptions to be put to death, no good resolutions to be strengthened? Certainly no one needs ordinances more than those people who do not need them. The spirit is a tender thing. Things that are most delicate are most dependent. Brambles grow by

themselves, but the vine needs supports. Wolves and dogs scavenge, but sheep need a pastor. Those who look into their hearts will find two reasons for ordinances.

First, knowledge is imperfect. It is good to be aware of our own ignorance. No one is so proud and contented as those who know least; "the man who thinks he knows something does not yet know as he ought to know" (1 Corinthians 8:2). At first truths seem few and quickly learned. In any learning we are humbled with the imperfections of knowledge, and it is the same in divine matters. We see little in the world until we come to be more deeply acquainted with it. "Open my eyes that I may see wonderful things in your law" (Psalm 119:18). Then we discern depths and wisdom that we never thought of. The Word is an ocean without bottom or banks. A man may see an end of other things: "To all perfection I see a limit; but your commands are boundless" (Psalm 119:96). We can never exhaust all the treasure that is in the Word.

Second, affections need to be stirred. Commands need to be repeated to a dull servant, and our will is like that. Live coals need blowing. The apostle Paul says, "For you can all prophesy in turn so that everyone may be instructed and encouraged" (1 Corinthians 14:31). The apostle specifies the two purposes of prophesy—namely, that we may learn and be comforted.

Note 3. **Everyone**. This is a universal duty. No one is exempt from listening and patient learning. Those who know most learn more. Junius was converted through talking with a plowman. A simple layman turned the whole Council of Nicea against Arianism. God may use the meanest things to instruct the greatest. Paul, the great apostle, calls Priscilla and Persis, two women, his "fellow workers in Christ Jesus" (Romans 16:3, 12). Torches are lit many times by a candle, and the most glorious saints benefit from the lowest. Christ taught his disciples through a child: "He called a little child and had him stand among them" (Matthew 18:2). It is proud disdain to scorn the humblest gifts. There may be gold in an earthen jar. There is no one too old, no one too wise, no one too high to be taught. Let **everyone . . . be quick to listen**.

Note 4. **Be quick**. That is, ready. The commendation of duties involves the ready discharge of them. Swiftness includes two things:

First, freedom of spirit. Do it without being reluctant when you do it. No offerings are accepted by God except those that are freewill offerings: see Psalm 119:108.

Second, diligence in taking the next opportunity. Do not ignore an opportunity and say, "Another day." Delay is a sign of unwillingness. In Ezekiel 1 the beasts had four faces and four wings. They had four faces, waiting for the Spirit to come on them, and four wings, ready to fly wherever God sent them. This readiness is shown in three things:

a. In curbing all deliberations. "I did not consult any man" (Galatians 1:16). When the soul deliberates about duty, it neglects duty. Do not debate when God commands. The soul is half won over when it starts debating things. In Genesis 2:17 God says, "When you eat of it you will surely die." Eve repeats this in Genesis 3:3, "You must not eat . . . or you will die"; and Satan says, "You will not surely die" (verse 4). God affirms, the woman doubts, and Satan denies. It is not good to allow the devil the advantage in a discussion; when you pause over something, Satan works on your hesitancy.

b. In setting aside all excuses. Duty would never be done if we gave in to the soul's every doubt. Peter, as soon as he heard the voice of Christ, threw himself into the sea, while others came by boat (Matthew 14:29); he did not worry about the waves between him and Christ.

c. In yielding yourselves up to God's will without reservation, make no exceptions. The ear and heart must be open for every command. "Speak, Lord, for your servant is listening" (1 Samuel 3:9). He was ready to receive whatever God commanded. Alas, it is otherwise with us, though Christ offers himself to us, as he did to the blind man in Luke 18:41, "What do you want me to do for you?"

Note 5. **Quick to listen.** That is, to the Word of God, or else it would be good to be slow to listen. Various things are implied in this precept.

(1) It shows how we should value listening. Be glad for an opportunity. The ear means the sense of learning, and so it is of grace; it is that sense that is consecrated to receive the most spiritual dispensations. "How can they believe in the one of whom they have not heard?" (Romans 10:14). The Lord began his sermon with, "Hear, O Israel" (Deuteronomy 6:3). When Christ was solemnly declared to be the great prophet of the church, Matthew 17:5 records these words: "This is my Son, whom I love . . . Listen to him." Reading is useful, but the voice has a secret influence on the soul because of the link between the external word and inward reason. This is the way the authority and sovereign efficacy of the Spirit are conveyed. The apostle had spoken a great deal about the Word, and then he said, "This is the word that was preached to you" (1 Peter 1:25). It is not the Word read but the Word "preached." Reading is good in its place; but to neglect listening, pretending that you can read better sermons at home, is a sin.

(2) This shows how keen we should be to take every opportunity to hear the Word. If ministers should preach "in season and out of season," people should listen. People used to travel far for such an opportunity. Matthew 3:5 says, "People went out to hear him [John] from Jerusalem and all Judea and the whole region of the Jordan." Some of the places mentioned were thirty miles from Jerusalem.

(3) This shows readiness to listen to other people's understanding of the Word. We should not be puffed up with our own knowledge but must **be quick to listen** to what others say. It is a great evil to hold other people's

gifts in contempt. No one is so wise that he cannot receive some benefit from the different handling of what he already knows. It is beneficial to observe the breath of the Spirit of God in various instruments.

(4) This shows what we should do in Christian meetings. They often degenerate into noise and clamor; we are all quick to speak, but not to listen to one another, and so all our conferences end in confusion, and no good is gained by them. I recall that when a Manichee argued against Augustine and cried out, "Hear me, hear me," the Father modestly answered, "Neither hear me, nor I thee, but let us both hear the apostle." When someone cries, "Hear me!" and another, "Hear me!" let us both hear the apostle, and then we shall hear one another. James says, **Be quick to listen, slow to speak**.

Note 6. There are many occasions when we must be **slow to speak**. This clause must also be seen in the light of the context; that is, slow in speaking about the Word of God.

(1) This teaches people not to preach the Word until they are furnished with sufficient gifts. John was thirty years old when he first preached (see Luke 3:1); the fifteenth year of Tiberius' reign was John's thirtieth year. Everyone longs to be a teacher in Israel. Few wait until thirty years' experience equips them for so great a task. Tertullian observes that "men usually make much progress in the tents of heresy, and become teachers while they are only just Christians." He goes on: "they set up young men to teach, that they may win them by honor, when they cannot win them by truth." Certainly this is a bait that pride quickly swallows. Hasty births do not fill the house but the grave. Men who obtrude themselves too soon in a calling do not edify but destroy. It is good for a while to be **slow to speak**. Aquinas, when he heard Albertus, was called "the dumb ox" because for a long time he was completely silent.

(2) This shows that we should not be too quick in our judgments about doctrines. We should not rashly condemn or defend anything that is contrary to the Word of God. Be **slow to speak**; that is, do not speak until you have sure grounds for what you say.

(3) We should not be more keen to teach others than we are to learn ourselves. Many are **quick to speak** but slow to act. **Not many of you should presume to be teachers, my brothers** (3:1); that is, do not be keen to discipline others when you neglect your own soul.

(4) We do not talk about the things of God in an empty way. It is good to take every opportunity, but indiscreet speaking does more harm than silence. "When words are many, sin is not absent, but he who holds his tongue is wise" (Proverbs 10:19). "A man of knowledge uses words with restraint" (Proverbs 17:27). Empty vessels sound loudest.

(5) This teaches us not to be too quick to speak against the Word. It is good to be dumb at a reproof, though not deaf. Do not let every proud

thought be voiced. Guilt recoils against listening to the Word, and the mind is full of ungodly objections. Thoughts may be revised with further information, but words cannot be recalled. Thoughts only stain our own spirits; words taint others. Thoughts are less deliberate than words. With thoughts we sin with our mind only; with words, with our mind and tongue.

Note 7. Renewed men should be **slow to become angry**. You must understand this in the same way as the other clauses; so it implies that the Word must not be received or delivered with an angry heart. This concerns both listeners and teachers.

(1) The teachers. They must be slow to anger in delivering the Word.

a. Do not let the Word stem from private anger. Spiritual weapons must not be used in your own cause. The Word is not committed to you for advancing your own interests but Christ's.

b. Do not give yourselves over to your own passions and anger. People easily distinguish between this feigned thunder and divine threatenings.

(2) The people. This teaches them to sit patiently under the Word. Do not rise up in arms against a just reproof. This is natural to us, but be slow to do it. Do not yield to your nature. Anger only reveals your own guilt. The children of God are meekest when the Word hits their hearts directly. Bless God for meeting with you in the Word.

Note 8. Anger is curbed by delaying it. Be **slow to become angry**. Anger does not grow by degrees, like other desires, but at birth she is full grown. "A man's wisdom gives him patience" (Proverbs 19:11). Many men are like gunpowder. They ignite at the least offense. When people are quick to become angry, they dishonor God and wound their conscience. Later they are sad about the effects of their sudden anger. Athenodorus advised Augustus, when he was overtaken by anger, to repeat the alphabet. This advice was good, as it tended to cool a sudden rage, so that the mind, being distracted, might deliberate later on. Thus, after Theodosius the Great had rashly massacred the citizens of Thessalonica, Ambrose advised him to decree that all people sentenced to death should have their execution deferred until the thirtieth day, so that there might be time for showing mercy if it was necessary. It is a description of God that he is "slow to become angry"; certainly a hasty spirit is most unlike God. Solomon says, "Do not be quickly provoked in your spirit, for anger resides in the lap of fools" (Ecclesiastes 7:9).

Commentary on Verse 20

For man's anger does not bring about the righteous life that
God desires.

Here James gives a reason for the last clause. Men's anger stops them from attaining God's righteousness and from doing what God requires in his Word.

For man's anger. He emphasizes **man's**; he does not say **anger** in general, for there is always a righteousness in the wrath of God.

Does not bring about. That is, does not attain, does not bring about any righteous action. It prevents God from perfecting his work in us.

The righteous life that God desires. Some say this is justice mixed with mercy, which is the righteousness that the Scriptures ascribe to God, and anger will not let a man dispense it. But this sense seems too forced an interpretation. Others say that it means anger that does not execute God's just revenge but our own malice. However, the righteousness of God is the righteousness that God requires, approves, brings about. In this sense in Scripture things are said to be of God or of Christ when they are effected by his power or commanded in his Word. Thus faith is said to be the work of God (see John 6:29). It is clear that James is using a figure of speech here by which more is intended than said. The apostle means that human anger is so far from working righteousness that it brings all kinds of evil.

Notes on Verse 20

Note 1. From the context, note that the worst thing we can bring to a religious controversy is anger. The context speaks about anger occasioned by differences about the Word. Usually no passions are so outrageous as those that are engaged in quarrels about religion. However, this should not be the case. Christianity, of all religions, is the meekest and most humble. It is founded on the blood of Christ, who is a slain Lamb. It is sealed by the Spirit of Christ, who descended like a dove. Both are emblems of meek humility. Should a meek religion be defended by our anger, or the God of peace served with angry passions? Christ's warfare does not need such ungodly weapons. The devil's kingdom is often ruined by the rage of his own instruments. You cannot assist Satan more than when you wrong the truth by an unseemly defense of it. Use strong arguments but soft words.

Note 2. **Does not bring about the righteous life**. Anger is not to be trusted. It is not as just and righteous as it appears to be. Of all the passions, we most often justify anger. Anger, like a cloud, blinds the mind and then rules it. So do not believe anger. People give credit to their passion, and that increases it. Anger is full of mistakes; it seems to be just and righteous when it does nothing to promote **the righteous life that God desires**. Passion is blind and cannot judge; it is furious and has no leisure to debate and consider.

Note 3. **Man's anger . . . the righteous life that God desires.** Note the contrast, for the two words **man** and **God** are emphatic. The point is that an angry spirit is a spirit not welcomed by God. God is the God of peace and requires a quiet and composed spirit. Angry people are most unfit to act with grace or to receive grace. Angry people make room for Satan but grieve the Spirit (see Ephesians 4:26-27 and 30); they are more fit to receive sin than grace.

Note 4. This last note is more general and comes from the whole verse. Man's anger is usually evil and unrighteous. Anger and passion are sins that the people of God are often surprised by, and all too often they accept it without remorse, from conceit.

I shall therefore endeavor to show two things briefly:

(1) What anger is sinful.

(2) How sinful, and how great and evil it is.

It is necessary to state that all anger is not sinful. One type is allowed, another is commanded, another is reproved.

a. There are some reflex actions that are natural and not sinful. Anger in itself is only a natural response to what is offensive. So the apostle says, "In your anger do not sin" (Ephesians 4:26). He allows what is natural and forbids what is sinful.

b. There is a necessary holy anger, which is the whetstone of fortitude and zeal. So it is said, "Lot . . . was distressed by the filthy lives of lawless men" (2 Peter 2:7). Christ himself "looked around at them in anger" (Mark 3:5). Moses' anger grew hot (Exodus 11:8). This is only a reaction of the will, guided by the rules of reason. Certainly those who are angry at nothing but sin are angry and do not sin. However, this strong emotion must be used with great caution.

First, the principle must be right. God's interests and ours are often confused. We are more likely to be angry at affronts to ourselves than to God. Pride and self-love often rage at our own contempt and disgrace. Zeal is too good an affection to be sacrificed to the idol of our own esteem and interests.

Second, it must have a right object. The heat of indignation must be against the crime rather than against the person. Good anger is always accompanied with grief; it prompts us to pity and pray for the offending party. Christ "looked around at them in anger . . . deeply distressed at their stubborn hearts" (Mark 3:5). False zeal has malice in it and wants the offender rooted out. It seeks revenge rather than correction.

Third, the manner must be right. See that you are not tempted to any indecent speech. Moses had good reason to be angry, but "rash words came from Moses' lips" (Psalm 106:33). In religious contexts anger is often vented freely and lies unchecked under a pretense of zeal.

c. There is a sinful anger when it is either hasty and deliberate or excessive.

First, rash and sudden emotions are never without sin. Some fragile spirits are like fine glasses, broken as soon as they are touched, and all in a rage over a trifle. Some meek and grave spirits are like flints that do not spark unless there is a violent and great collision. Feeble minds are prone to anger. They are like broken bones, which flare up at the least touch. It argues much unmortifiedness to be so quickly moved.

Or, second, such anger is excessive when it exceeds what is merited. Anger should be like a spark that is quickly extinguished—like fire in straw rather than like fire in iron. Thoughts of revenge are sweet, but when they linger they are apt to turn sour. Aristotle reckoned there are three degrees of angry men, each worse than the former: some are hasty, others are bitter, others are implacable. Anger retained becomes revenge. This spirit is most unchristian. The rule of the Word is, "Do not let the sun go down while you are still angry" (Ephesians 4:26). If the sun leaves us angry, the next morning may find us malicious. Plutarch said of the Pythagoreans that if they had fallen out during the day they would before sunset mutually embrace one another and depart in love. There is a story about Patricius and John of Alexandria, between whom great anger had passed. At evening John sent him this message: "The sun is set." At this they were soon reconciled.

Third, anger without sufficient reason. "Anyone who is angry with his brother without cause will be subject to judgment" (Matthew 5:22, NIV footnote). But what is a sufficient reason for anger? Are injuries? I answer, no. Our religion forbids revenge as well as injury, for they differ only in degree.

Fourth, all anger must be aimed at correcting offenses, not executing one's own malice. The stirring of the spirit is not sinful until revenge mingles with it. So then, as there must be a good cause, there must be a good purpose. Cain was angry with Abel without cause, and therefore his anger was wicked and sinful (Genesis 4:5). But Esau had some reason to be angry with Jacob, and yet his anger was not excusable because there was revenge in it (Genesis 27:41).

My next task is to show you how sinful anger is.

a. Nothing gives room for Satan more than anger. Ephesians 4:26-27 says, "In your anger do not sin," and then, "Do not give the devil a foothold." It is as if the apostle had said that if you give room to anger, you will make room for Satan. When passions are neglected they grow into habits, and then the devil has a kind of hold on us. The world is full of the tragic effects of anger, and therefore when it is harbored you do not know what this may result in.

b. It greatly wounds your own peace. When the apostle spoke about the sad effects of anger, he added, "And do not grieve the Holy Spirit of God, with whom you were sealed for the day of redemption" (Ephesians 4:30).

The Holy Spirit loves a meek spirit; the clamor of passion drives him from us. It is only just for God to allow no peace of conscience to those who care so little for peace.

c. It disparages Christianity. The glory of our religion lies in the power that it has to sanctify the spirit. When people who profess Christ burst out in rude and indiscreet excesses, they stain their profession. Pagans are famous for their patience under provocation. When I find them passing over offenses with a meek spirit, without any intention of revenge, I cannot but wonder and be ashamed that I have less command of my own spirit than they had.

Commentary on Verse 21

Therefore, get rid of all moral filth and the evil that is prevalent, and humbly accept the word planted in you, which can save you.

The apostle, having spoken about the power of the Word, and that it should be heard willingly and without a contradicting spirit, and having shown the evil of anger, returns to his main exhortation. Lay aside all wrathful affections, he says, that you might be more fit to welcome the Word with an honest and meek heart, for your comfort and salvation. In the verse there is a duty to **accept the word**. To help you achieve this, **get rid of all moral filth**. This duty is to be performed **humbly**, with submission to **the word planted in you**. The motive is, **which can save you**.

Therefore. That is, because anger is such an obstacle to the righteousness that God requires; or it may refer to the whole context.

Get rid of. The word implies that we should put it off as an unclean garment. The same metaphor is used by the apostle Paul in Ephesians 4:22, "Put off your old self, which is being corrupted by its deceitful desires"; and in Colossians 3:8, in a similar case, "But now you must rid yourselves of . . . anger, rage, malice, slander, and filthy language."

All moral filth. The word is sometimes used for the filthiness of ulcers, and also for the nastiness and filth of the body through sweating. Here it is used to stir up greater abomination against sin, which is elsewhere called "dirt from the body" (1 Peter 3:21). Some suppose the apostle is referring to lusts that are most beastly. But either the sense must be more general to imply all sin, or more particularly restrained to filthy and evil speaking, or it does not fit the context.

The evil that is so prevalent. This may be translated "the overflowing of malice." It indicates scoffing. See 1 Peter 2:1, to which James might be alluding, as he wrote after him. Beza translates it, "the excrement of wickedness." Some think it alludes to the refuse from the sacrifices in the Kedron valley. Most take it generally for that abundance of evil and filthiness that is in the human heart.

Accept. This word is often used for the appropriation of the Word. **Accept** means to make more room for it in your hearts. Thus 2 Thessalonians 2:10 says, "they refused to love the truth." Faith is expressed in this way: "all who received him" (John 1:12).

Humbly. That is, with a teachable mind, with a modest, submissive spirit.

The word planted. Some refer this to reason, others to Christ, but this is absurd. This word shows the purpose and fruit of listening—that the Word may be **planted** in us. The apostle shows that by the industry of the apostles, the Word was not only propounded to them but rooted in them by faith. A similar metaphor is used elsewhere: "I planted . . . but God made it grow" (1 Corinthians 3:6). This metaphor is also used in Colossians 1:6, "this gospel is producing fruit and growing."

Which can save you. That is, as it is accompanied with divine grace; the Gospel is "the power of God for the salvation of everyone who believes" (Romans 1:16).

Your souls (KJV). That is, yourselves—souls and bodies. Salvation is attributed to the soul, as it is the principal part of the whole. In other passages the same manner of expression is used: "the goal of your faith, the salvation of your souls" (1 Peter 1:9). So Matthew 16:26 says, "forfeits his soul"—that is, himself. In such forms of speech the body is not excluded, because it always follows the state of the soul.

Notes on Verse 21

Note 1. **Get rid of**. Before we come to the Word there must be preparation. Instruments must be tuned before they can make melody. Solomon says, "Guard your steps when you go to the house of God" (Ecclesiastes 5:1). Christ says, "Consider carefully how you listen" (Luke 8:18). Come prepared. Let me say one word by way of caution and another by way of direction.

(1) By way of caution:

a. Do not exclude God from your preparations. The very dispositions of the spirit are from God.

b. Though you cannot get your hearts into the condition you desire, trust God: "Faith is being sure of what we hope for and certain of what we do not see" (Hebrews 11:1). The help that is absent to sense and feeling may be present to faith. You do not know how God may come to you.

The eunuch read and did not understand, and God sent him an interpreter (see Acts 8). It is not good to neglect duty out of discouragement; this is to commit one sin in order to excuse another: see Jeremiah 1:6 and Exodus 4:10-11.

(2) By way of direction: the heart must be purged, faith exercised, repentance renewed, weaknesses reviewed, God's glory considered, and the nature, grounds, and ends of the ordinances weighed in our thoughts. There must be enough preparation to make the heart reverent. God must be served with a joy mixed with trembling. The heart is never right in worship until it is gripped by awe of God: "How awesome is this place!" (Genesis 28:17). Such preparation will settle the spirit in a heavenward direction. David says, "My heart is steadfast, O God, my heart is steadfast" (Psalm 57:7)—that is, composed in a heavenly and holy frame. Engage in preparation that will make you humble and hungry. Grace is usually given to the hungry soul: "He has filled the hungry with good things" (Luke 1:53).

Note 2. Christian preparation mainly consists in getting rid of evil frames. Weeds must be rooted out before the ground is fit to receive the seed: see Jeremiah 4:3. A filthy spirit and the pure holy Word do not mix. Those who do not turn from their sins are unfit listeners. There is an extraordinary vanity in some people, who will lay aside their sins before some solemn duties but intend to return to them later. What can people who come in their sins expect from God? Their state denies their worship. God will have nothing to do with them.

Note 3. **Get rid of.** Take it off as a rotten and filthy garment. Sin must be left with utter detestation: "you will throw them away like a menstrual cloth and say to them, 'Away with you!'" (Isaiah 30:22). Sin is often expressed as an abomination. It is so to God; it should be so to us.

Note 4. **All.** We must not get rid of some sin, but **all** sin. So in Peter the particle is universal: "all malice" (1 Peter 2:1); and David says, "I hate every wrong path" (Psalm 119:104). When we hate sin as sin, we hate all sin. The heart is most sincere when the hatred is general. The least sin is dangerous and in its own nature deadly and destructive. We read of some who have been devoured by wild beasts, lions, and bears, but also of others who have been eaten up by vermin, mice, or lice. Pope Adrian choked on a gnat. The least sins may undo you. Christ speaks of a little leaven.

Note 5. **Moral filth.** Sin is **moral filth**; it sullies the glory and beauty of the soul and defaces God's image. This expression is often used. Consider "contaminates body and spirit" (2 Corinthians 7:1). Not only gross wickedness, such as comes from human lusts, is called **moral filth**, but such as is more spiritual—unbelief and heresy. Original corruption is given this name. "What is man, that he could be pure?" (Job 15:14). People are greatly mistaken when they think sin is an ornament, for the Spirit of God calls it dung and excrement. But more especially I find three sins called **moral filth** in Scripture:

(1) Covetousness, because it debases the spirit of man and makes him stoop to such indecencies as are beneath humanity.

(2) Lust, which in Scripture is called filthiness or the sin of uncleanness (see 1 Thessalonians 4:7), because it makes a man submit his desires to animal happiness, which is sensual pleasure.

(3) In this passage, **anger** and malice are called **moral filth**. We take pleasure in such, but it is only filthiness.

So, all that has been said encourages us to resist sin, to detest it as a defilement. It will darken the glory of our natures.

Note 6. **The evil that is so prevalent.** There is a great deal of wickedness to be purged from the human heart. As there is salt in every drop of the sea, so sin is in everything that is framed within the soul. In the understanding there are filthy thoughts and purposes; there sin begins. In the will are filthy tendencies, and the affections mingle with filthy objects. The memory retains nothing but mud and filthiness. The conscience is defiled and stained with the impurities of our lives. The whole body is an instrument of filthiness. Second Peter 2:14 says, "with eyes full of adultery" (the original says "full of the adulteress"). The tongue betrays the rottenness of the heart in filthy language. How we bless God that there is "a fountain . . . to cleanse them from sin and impurity" (Zechariah 13:1). Certainly conversion is not easy work—there is such a mass of corruption to be set aside.

Note 7. **Accept.** Our duty in listening to the Word is to receive it. In the Word there is the hand of God's bounty, reaching out comfort and counsel to us; and there must be the hand of faith to receive it. In receiving there is an act of the understanding, apprehending the truth and musing on it. So Christ says, "Listen carefully to what I am about to tell you" (Luke 9:44).

Note 8. **Humbly accept.** The Word must be received with all meekness. Christ was anointed to preach good news to the meek (see Isaiah 61:1). The main purpose now is to show what this meekness is. Consider its opposites. Since the fall graces are best known by their opposites. This meekness excludes three things:

(1) An angry fierceness, in which people rise in a rage against the Word. When they are admonished, they revile. Deep conviction often provokes fierce opposition: "The word of the Lord is offensive to them" (Jeremiah 6:10).

(2) A proud stubbornness. People scorn to set sail before the truth; and though they cannot maintain their opposition, yet they persist in it.

(3) A contentious wrangling. This is found in men who have undisciplined thoughts. The psalmist says, "He instructs sinners in his ways. He

will guide the humble in what is right and teaches them his way" (Psalm 25:8-9). Out of all sinners, God takes the meek sinner for his scholar. Camero observes that the Scriptures are so written that those who want to know can know, and those who have a mind to argue may take offense and perish through the rebellion of their own reason. For, says Camero, "God never intended to satisfy men of a stubborn and perverse wit." And Tertullian observed the same: "God has so disposed the Scriptures that those who will not be satisfied will be hardened." Our Saviour Christ says in Mark 4:11-12 that "To those on the outside everything is said in parables so that 'they may be ever seeing but never perceiving.'" As a just punishment for willful blindness and hardness, those who do not want to see will not see. When the heart is humble and obeys a truth, the mind is soon opened to accept it.

Secondly, I will show what meekness includes:

a. Humility and brokenness of spirit. There must be meekness before grafting. Gospel revivals are for the contrite heart: see Isaiah 57:15. The broken heart is not only a tamed heart but a tender heart, and then the least touch of the Word is felt.

b. A teachable spirit. "The wisdom that comes from heaven is first of all pure; then peace loving" (3:17). The servants of God come with a mind ready to obey; they wait to discover their duty: "Now we are all here in the presence of God to listen to everything the Lord has commanded you to tell us" (Acts 10:33). Perverse opposition will be your own ruin. Luke 7:30 says, "The Pharisees and experts in the law rejected God's purpose," but this was "for themselves"; that is, it was to their own loss. So Acts 13:46 says that you "do not consider yourselves worthy of eternal life." Disputing against the Word is a judgment on yourself. It is as if, in effect, you said, "I do not care for God or for all the grace and glory that he gives me."

Note 9. The Word must not only be understood by us but **planted** in us. This is God's promise: "I will put my law in their minds and write it on their hearts" (Jeremiah 31:33); that is, he will enlighten our minds to understand his will and will frame our hearts and affections to obey it. Then we shall not only know about our duty but have the inclination to do it. This is the true grafting. See, then, that the word is grafted in you. You will know it in this way:

(1) If it is grafted, it will be "producing fruit" (Colossians 1:6); it will spring up in your conversation.

(2) The graft draws all the sap from the stock to itself. All your affections, purposes, cares, thoughts will serve the Word: see Romans 6:17.

Note 10. The Word in God's hand is an instrument to save our souls. It is sometimes called "the word of truth," at other times "the word of life"; one notes its quality, the other its fruit. It is called "the power of God"

(Romans 1:16) and "the arm of the Lord": "Who has believed our message and to whom has the arm of the Lord been revealed?" (Isaiah 53:1). The Gospel is a saving Word; let us not despise its simplicity. Gospel truths should not be too plain for our mouths or too boring for our ears. "I am not ashamed of the gospel," says the apostle, "because it is the power of God for the salvation of everyone who believes" (Romans 1:16).

Note 11. The main preoccupation of a Christian should be to save his soul. This is put forward as an argument for listening to the Word. It will **save** your souls. Usually our greatest concern is to gratify the body. Man is part angel, so to speak, and part beast. Why should we please the beast in us rather than the angel? In short, your greatest fear should be for the soul, and your greatest concern should be for the soul. Your greatest fear: "Do not be afraid of those who kill the body . . . be afraid of the one who can destroy both soul and body in hell" (Matthew 10:28). So your greatest care—riches, and splendor in the world—these are the conveniences of the body; and what good will they do you when you come to be laid in the cold, silent grave? "What good will it be for a man if he gains the whole world, yet forfeits his soul?" (Matthew 16:26). It is only a sorry exchange to give the eternal welfare of the soul for a temporary reward from the world. "For what hope has the godless when he is cut off, when God takes away his life?" (Job 27:8). Many ungodly people rise early, go to bed late, and eat the bread of sorrows. Oh, that we were wise enough to consider these things, that we would make it our business to provide for the soul, to clothe the soul for another world, that we would wait on God in the Word, that our souls may be furnished with every spiritual and heavenly excellency, that we may not be "found naked," says the apostle in 2 Corinthians 5:3.

Note 12. Those who have received the Word must receive it again. Even if it was grafted in you, receive it so that it may save your souls. God has planned it to be a means not only of regeneration but of salvation. So until we come to heaven, we must have its help. Those who live above ordinances do not live at all, spiritually speaking. The Word, though it is an immortal seed, needs constant care and watering.

Commentary on Verse 22

Do not merely listen to the word, and so deceive yourselves. Do what it says.

This verse continues from the previous verse. He has spoken about the fruit of the Word and the salvation of the soul. In order that this may be obtained, he shows that we should not only hear it but practice it.

Do what it says. Here doing implies receiving the work of the Word into the heart and expressing the effect of it in life. There are three things that make people doers of the Word—faith, love, and obedience.

Do not merely listen. Some neither hear nor do; others hear, but they rest in it. Therefore the apostle does not discourage listening. **Listen,** he says, but **not merely.**

Deceive. The word implies a syllogism. It appears to be true, but it is false in matter or form. The apostle refers to those false discourses that are in men's consciences. Paul uses the same word to imply the deceit that people impose on others by plausible arguments: "I tell you this so that no one may deceive you by fine-sounding arguments" (Colossians 2:4).

Yourselves. The argument receives force from these words. If someone wants to baffle other people, he would not deceive himself in a matter of so great consequence. Or else it may be an admonition: you deceive yourselves, but you cannot deceive God.

Notes on Verse 22

Note 1. Listening is good, but it should not stop there. The apostle says, **Do not merely listen.** Many go from sermon to sermon and hear much, but do not digest it in their thoughts. The Jews were much given to turning over the leaves of the Scriptures but did not weigh them. Therefore our Saviour reproves them in John 5:39, "You diligently study the Scriptures." They thought it was enough to be concerned with the letter of the Scripture, and that mere reading would give them eternal life. There is a sad description of some foolish women in 2 Timothy 3:7, that they are "always learning but never able to acknowledge the truth."

Note 2. The doers of the Word are the best listeners. It is good when we hear things that are to be done and do things that are to be heard. That knowledge is best that is most practical, and that hearing is best that ends in practice. David says, "Your word is a lamp to my feet and a light for my path" (Psalm 119:105). It is light indeed that directs you in your paths and ways. Matthew 7:24 says, "Everyone who hears these words of mine and puts them into practice is like a wise man who built his house on the rock." That is wisdom, to go to the Word in order that we may leave it better people.

The true use of ordinances is to go to them so that we may profit from them. If you cannot find immediate benefit in what you hear, consider how it may be useful for you in the future. It is good to provide for Babylon while we are in Zion, and not to reject truths as being irrelevant to us but to store them up for future use.

Note 3. **Deceive yourselves**. Do not cheat yourselves with a false argument. Observe that self-deceit is founded on some false reasoning. You can help your conscience not to be deceived in the following ways:

(1) You may build on right principles. It is good to "hide the word in our hearts" and to fill the soul with sound knowledge. This will always rise up against vain hopes. If you want to destroy weeds, you must plant the ground with different seeds. "Bind them upon your heart forever . . . when you awake, they will speak to you" (Proverbs 6:21-22).

(2) If the witness of conscience is not to fail you, observe these rules: First, note the first sign of an aroused conscience. Sudden promptings through the Word or through prayer are the birth of conscience. The first voice of conscience is genuine. Therefore, whatever peace wicked people like to claim, their consciences truly witness to them. The artificial and second report of conscience is deceitful and partial, when it has been flattered or choked with some ungodly principles. But the first report, like a stitch in the side, is true and faithful.

Second, wait on the Word. One of its main uses is to help the conscience in witnessing and to bring us and our hearts to know each other: "The word of God is living and active. Sharper than any double-edged sword, it penetrates even to dividing soul and spirit, joints and marrow; it judges the thoughts and attitudes of the heart" (Hebrews 4:12). It reveals all those schemes through which we try to hide our actions from our own conscience.

Third, frequently call your conscience into the presence of God. First Peter 3:21 talks of "the pledge of a good conscience toward God." Will your conscience witness in this way to the all-seeing God? When Peter's sincerity was questioned, he appealed to Christ's omniscience: "Lord, you know all things; you know that I love you" (John 21:17). Can you appeal to God's omniscience and assure your hearts before him? "This then is how we know that we belong to the truth, and how we set our hearts at rest in his presence whenever our hearts condemn us. For God is greater than our hearts, and he knows everything" (1 John 3:19-20). God's omniscience is mentioned there because that is the attribute to which conscience appeals.

(3) For conscience to do its work as judge, you must do this: First, when conscience is silent, be suspicious of it; we are sometimes careless, and our heart grows senseless with pleasures. A dead sea is worse than a raging sea. This is not a calm but death. A tender conscience is always witnessing; so when it never asks, "What have I done?" that is a sign that it is seared. There is constant talk between a godly man and his conscience; it is either suggesting a duty or revealing defects. It is believers' daily exercise to judge themselves. Just as God, after every day's work, reviewed it and

"saw that it was good" (Genesis 1), so they review each day and judge its actions.

Second, if conscience does not speak to you, you must speak to your conscience. David told insolent men to "search your hearts and be silent" (Psalm 4:4). Take time to speak with yourself. The prophet complained, "No one repents of his wickedness, saying, 'What have I done?'" (Jeremiah 8:6). There should be a time to ask questions of your own souls.

Third, clarify every uncertainty. Conscience will sometimes lisp out half a word. Draw it out to full conviction. Nothing makes the work of grace so doubtful as when Christians content themselves with being half-persuaded. The Spirit delights in complete conviction: "He will convince the world of guilt in regard to sin and righteousness and judgment" (John 16:8). Conviction comes when things are laid down so clearly that we see it is impossible that it should be otherwise. The Spirit does this whether it is in a state of sin or righteousness. God says he will deal with his people so roundly that "you will remember and be ashamed and never again open your mouth because of your humiliation" (Ezekiel 16:63). They will be so convinced that they will not have a word to say except "Unclean! Unclean!"

Note 4. People are easily deceived into having a good opinion of themselves because of mere listening. We are prone to latch on to the good in any action and not to consider its evil: I listen to the Word, and therefore I am doing well. Watch out for this deceit. Such a weighty structure should not be raised on so sandy a foundation: see Matthew 7:26.

(1) Consider the danger of such a self-deception. Listening without action brings greater judgment on you. Uriah carried letters to Joab, and he thought the contents were for his preferment in the army, but it carried the message of his own destruction. We hear many sermons and think we will point something out to God; but from those sermons will God condemn us.

(2) Consider how far hypocrites go in this matter. They may stop following errors and listen to the Word constantly: see Luke 6:47. They may approve of the good way and applaud it: "Blessed is the mother who gave you birth and nursed you" (Luke 11:27-28). They may display a great deal of false affection: "Why do you call me 'Lord, Lord,' and do not do what I say?" (Luke 6:46). They may be endowed with gifts of prophecy and miracle-working; but see Matthew 7:22. Christ says, "Every tree that does not bear good fruit is cut down" (Matthew 7:19). There must be something positive. There may be some external conformity, but there is no effectual change; the tree is "a bad tree" (Matthew 7:18). So outward duties with partial reformation are no good.

(3) Consider how easily we are deceived: "The heart is deceitful above all things and beyond cure. Who can understand it?" (Jeremiah 17:9). Who can trace and unravel the mystery of iniquity that is in the soul? Since we

lost our uprightness, we have many schemes through which we avoid the voice of conscience (see Ecclesiastes 7:29).

Commentary on Verses 23-24

Anyone who listens to the word but does not do what it says is like a man who looks at his face in a mirror and, after looking at himself, goes away and immediately forgets what he looks like.

Here James enlarges on the previous argument about the vanity of superficial listening, with a simile taken from a man looking in a mirror.

Anyone who listens to the word but does not do what it says. That is, he is content with superficial listening and superficial knowledge about the Word of God and does not leave resolved to obey.

Is like a man. In the original the word for **man** is the word for the masculine sex. Some people criticize this. The apostle does not say, "like a woman"; women are more diligent. They look at themselves over and over again to remove every spot and deformity. But this is more clever than solid. The apostle uses the word **man** to mean both men and women, as in verse 12: **Blessed is the man who perseveres under trial**"—the man or woman.

Who looks at his face. "The face of his nativity." What is meant by that? Some say, the face as God made it at its birth, that he may behold God's work in it, and so they condemn makeup; or his natural face, on which men bestow least care. I think **face** means his own face, the mirror representing the very face that nature gave him.

After looking at himself, goes away and immediately forgets what he looks like. He forgets his facial blemishes. A careless soul ignores what the Word exposes and is not repentant.

Notes on Verses 23-24

Note 1. The Word of God is like **a mirror.** But what does it show us?

(1) God and Christ. "We, who with unveiled faces all reflect the Lord's glory, are being transformed into his likeness with ever-increasing glory" (2 Corinthians 3:18). A mirror implies the clearest representation that we are capable of here on earth. I admit that a mirror sometimes represents a dark vision, as in 1 Corinthians 13:12 ("Now we see but a poor reflection; then we shall see face to face"). Someday we shall see God himself: "We shall see him as he is" (1 John 3:2). But now we have his image and reflection in the

Word. Sometimes in Scripture the phrase "heart of flesh" stands for an earthly mind, and sometimes it stands for a tender heart. In contrast to "heart of stone," "heart of flesh" is taken in a good sense. Similarly, in contrast to the shadows of the law, seeing in a mirror implies clear discernment.

(2) The Word is **a mirror** to show us ourselves; it reveals the hidden things of the heart and all the deformities of the soul: "Whatever is hidden is meant to be disclosed" (Mark 4:22). The Word reveals everything. Our sins are the blemishes that the law reveals; Christ's blood is the water to wash them off and is revealed in the Gospel. The law reveals sins: "Once I was alive apart from the law; but when the commandment came, sin sprang to life and I died" (Romans 7:9).

Application. Here is a meditation for you. When you are looking into your mirror, think: the Word of God is a mirror; I must look after the complexion of my soul. Take part of the law and exercise yourself with it every day, and you will soon see the deformity of your own spirit. Do not look in a flattering mirror.

Note 2. The knowledge of formal professors is only slight and superficial. They are like people looking at their faces in a mirror, or like the glance of a sunbeam on a wave; it rushes into the thoughts and it is gone. Under the law, the beast that did not chew the cud was unclean. Meditation is very useful and sheds constant light. Some people know things but are loath to let their thoughts stay with them. Luke 2:19 tells us that "Mary treasured up all these things and pondered them in her heart." A slippery, vain mind will hardly hold on to truths.

Note 3. Proud men leave ordinances just as they go to them: they look and go away. Like the beasts in Noah's ark, they go in unclean and come out unclean. So many come unhumbled and unmortified and go away the same. Let this never be said of you.

Note 4. Poor understanding makes a very weak impression. Things work when the thoughts are serious and deep; musing makes the fire burn: see Psalm 39:3. And David, when he expressed his deep feelings, said, "My sin is always before me" (Psalm 51:3). Men thoroughly affected say, I shall remember that sermon all my life. David says, "I will never forget your precepts, for by them you have preserved my life" (Psalm 119:93). Others let good things slip because they never felt their power.

Commentary on Verse 25

But the man who looks intently into the perfect law that gives freedom, and continues to do this, not forgetting what he has heard, but doing it—he will be blessed in what he does.

In this verse you have the third reason why people should listen to the Word in order to practice it. The first was, they would only deceive themselves. The next, that mere listening would be of little benefit; no more than if a man glanced into a mirror and had a fleeting view of himself. And now, right listening correctly ends in blessedness.

But the man who looks. This metaphor comes from those who do not only glance at a thing but bend their body toward it, that they may pierce it with their eyes and pry into it. The same word is used for the disciples stooping down to look into Christ's sepulchre: see Luke 24:12 and John 20:4-5. It is also used about the search that the angels made to find out the mysteries of salvation: "angels long to look into these things" (1 Peter 1:12). The word implies three things:

(1) Deep meditation. He does not glance but **looks intently**.

(2) Diligent inquiry. They are not content with their first thoughts but pry into God's mind revealed in the Word.

(3) Openness. They look on it to find its virtue for their hearts: see 2 Corinthians 3:18.

Such a gaze brings the glory of the Lord into our hearts, just as Moses' face shone after he had talked with God. By conversing with the Word, we carry off its beauty and glory in our spirits.

Into the perfect law. Some people understand this to refer to the moral law, in contrast with the ceremonial law, which is not complete or able to justify. It is not perfect because it did not remain forever; "(for the law made nothing perfect), and a better hope is introduced, by which we draw near to God" (Hebrews 7:19). A man could not be sanctified, justified, and saved without Christ or through the dispensation of Moses. The soul could find no rest in the law without looking to Christ. Though this interpretation is possible, I apply it to all the Word of God, and in particular to the Gospel. The will of God in Scripture is called a law. So a godly man "meditates day and night" (Psalm 1:2) on God's law. Now this law is said to be **perfect** because it is so in itself, and those who look into it will see that they need no other word to make men of God perfect.

That gives freedom. It is called **freedom** because of the clearness of revelation; it is the counsel of God to his friends. Piscator says, "It spares no one, but deals with everyone freely. . . . It calls us into a state of freedom."

And continues to do this. That is, he perseveres in studying this holy doctrine and remains in its knowledge, belief, and obedience.

Not forgetting what he has heard. "A hearer of oblivion" is a Hebraism; this clause corresponds to the former simile about a man forgetting what he looks like (verse 24).

But doing it. That is, working hard to put everything into practice.

He will be blessed in what he does. That is, he will be **blessed** in all his ways; whatever he does will prosper. This may be an allusion to the words of Psalm 1:3, "Whatever he does prospers." There the psalmist speaks about obeying the law and meditating on the law, as James speaks here about looking at **the perfect law that gives freedom**. The Roman Catholics say, here is a clear example that we are blessed because of our deeds. But I answer, it is good to note the exact scriptural phrase. The apostle does not say *for* but *in* what he does. This is evidence of our blessedness, not grounds for it.

Notes on Verse 25

Note 1. **Who looks**. We should with complete earnestness apply ourselves to the knowledge of the Gospel. There should be deep meditation and diligent inquiry. Your first duty, Christians, is to accept the Word into your thinking: see Psalm 1:2. We should always be chewing this cud. Truths are ripened by meditation. Then there must be diligent inquiry: "The prophets . . . searched intently and with the greatest care" (1 Peter 1:10). "Search for it [wisdom] as for hidden treasure" (Proverbs 2:4). Precious stones do not lie on the surface; you must dig in the dark recesses of the earth for them. Truths do not lie on the surface. The beauty and glory of the Scriptures must be sought out with much study and prayer. A glance discovers nothing of any worth. So to know Christ in a general way is not the same as searching out the breadth and the depth and the length and the exact dimensions of his love for us.

Note 2. The Gospel is a law. It is often called by this name: "Through Christ Jesus the law of the Spirit of life set me free from the law of sin and death" (Romans 8:2). There the covenant of works is called "the law of sin and death" because it convicts fallen man of sin and hands him over to death. But the Gospel, or covenant of grace, is called "the law of the Spirit of the life" of Christ because it joins us to Christ, whose life we are enabled to live by the Spirit. It is called "the law of . . . life" because everything is found in the Gospel:

(1) Justice, without which law is only a tyranny. All the precepts of the Gospel are just. The Gospel is holy, good, and comforting.

(2) Proclamation, which is the life of the law. "Proclaim freedom for the captives" is how Isaiah refers to it (61:1).

(3) The author: God can prescribe to the creature.

(4) The end: public good, without which a law is a tyrannous exaction. The end is the salvation of our souls.

Well, then, look upon the Gospel as a law and rule, according to which:

(1) Your lives must be conformed: "Peace . . . to all who follow this

rule" (Galatians 6:16)—that is, who live according to the directions of the Gospel.

(2) All controversies and disputes must be decided by it: "To the law and to the testimony! If they do not speak according to this word, they have no light of dawn" (Isaiah 8:20).

(3) Your state is judged by it: "God will judge men's secrets through Jesus Christ, as my gospel declares" (Romans 2:16). The Gospel itself is a law, partly because it is a rule and partly because of the prevailing power it has over the heart. It is "the law of the Spirit of life"; so those who are in Christ have a law. The apostle says in 1 Corinthians 9:21, "I am not free from God's law but am under Christ's law"—that is, under the rule and direction of the moral law, as a part of the Gospel.

Note 3. The Word of God is a **perfect law**. It is perfect in various ways:

(1) Because it makes us perfect. The nearer we come to the Word, the greater is the perfection of our spirits. The goodness and excellency of the creature lies in conforming to God's will.

(2) It directs us to the greatest perfection, to God, to the righteousness of Christ, to perfect communion with God in glory.

(3) It concerns the whole man. It influences the conscience. Men go no further than outward obedience, but "the law of the Lord is perfect, reviving the soul" (Psalm 19:7). It is not a lame, defective rule; besides, outward observances are beneficial for the soul.

(4) It is a **perfect law** because of its changelessness; it does not need to be changed. A perfect rule needs no amendment.

(5) It is pure and free from error. No human laws are without some blemish in them. In Syrian law, virgins had to lose their virginity before marriage. So the laws of every country have some evidence of human frailty.

(6) It is a comprehensive rule. Whatever is necessary for knowledge, for regulating life and worship, for confirmation of true teaching, for refuting false teaching, it is all in the Word: "so that the man of God may be thoroughly equipped for every good work" (2 Timothy 3:17).

So then:

(1) Prize the Word. We love what is perfect.

(2) Allow nothing to be added to it: "Do not add to what I command you" (Deuteronomy 4:2). So the whole Bible concludes with the warning: "If anyone adds anything to them, God will add to him the plagues described in this book" (Revelation 22:18).

Note 4. The Gospel, or Word of God, is **the perfect law that gives freedom**. As it is **perfect**, so it **gives freedom**. It does so in various ways:

(1) It teaches the way to true freedom from sin, wrath, and death. By nature we are under the law of sin and death, entangled with the yoke of our own corruption, and bound over to eternal misery. But the Gospel

teaches liberty and deliverance. "If the Son sets you free, you will be free indeed" (John 8:36). There is no state so free as that which we enjoy through the Gospel.

(2) The bond of obedience laid on us is indeed a perfect freedom. For:

a. Our obedience is freedom. Duty is the greatest freedom, and sin the greatest slavery. You cannot have a worse restraint than to be left to walk in the ways of your own hearts. The angels who sinned are said to be "bound with everlasting chains" (Jude 6). A wicked man is in slavery here and hereafter. Sin itself is slavery, and hell a prison: see 1 Peter 3:19. If there were nothing in sin except the present slavery, that is enough to dissuade us. Who wants to be a slave to his own desires? But the present is nothing when compared with the future. Why should we think of Christ's service as a burden when it is the most happy liberty?

b. We do it because we are free. Whatever we do, we each do it as "the Lord's freedman" (1 Corinthians 7:22)—from motives of love and gratitude. God might rule us with a rod of iron, but he woos the soul with constraints of love. One passage says, "I urge you, brothers, in view of God's mercy" (Romans 12:1); another says, "The grace of God . . . teaches us" (Titus 2:11-12). The motives of the Gospel are mercy and grace; and the obedience of the Gospel is an obedience performed out of gratitude.

c. We have the assistance of a free Spirit, who helps us in the work of obedience. There is spirit and life in the commandments. Previously there was light in the commandment to guide our feet, but not fire to burn up our desires.

d. We do it in a free state and are God's children. "For you did not receive a spirit that makes you a slave again to fear, but you received the Spirit of sonship. And by him we cry, '*Abba*, Father'" (Romans 8:15).

Application. So, consider whether you are under a law of liberty or not. To this end:

(1) Ask your souls, what are you a slave to? Sin or duty? Do you delight in the law of the Lord in the inward man?

(2) When you perform a duty, what frame of mind are you in? Your motivation should spring from love.

Note 5. **And continues.** This commands us to continue in knowledge of and affection to the Word. "If you hold to my teaching, you are really my disciples" (John 8:31). "Anyone who runs ahead and does not continue in the teaching of Christ does not have God; whoever continues in the teaching has both the Father and the Son" (2 John 9).

Two things are opposed to us our abiding in the Word:

(1) Apostasy, when we abandon our previous profession and zeal for God. This is a sad case! "It would have been better for them not to have known the way of righteousness, than to have known it and then to turn

their backs on the sacred command that was passed on to them" (2 Peter 2:21). The less law, the less transgression.

(2) There are other gospels: "turning to a different gospel" (Galatians 1:6). "Command certain men not to teach false doctrines" (1 Timothy 1:3). People love to have something new and strange, which is usually the basis for heresy. "If anyone teaches false doctrines and does not agree to the sound instruction of our Lord Jesus Christ and to godly teaching, he is conceited and understands nothing" (1 Timothy 6:3-4). This desire to hear another gospel is very dangerous. New ways are the roads to an old error.

So then, if you are to abide in the Word:

(1) Be sure to cherish good thoughts if they come into your hearts. You should abide there. If the Spirit breaks in on your soul suddenly, do not let him go suddenly.

(2) Be careful to observe the first signs of decay in your spirits, that you may "strengthen what remains and is about to die" (Revelation 3:2).

Note 6. **Not forgetting what he has heard.** Hearers must take care that they do not forget the good things given to them. Here are some helps for the memory:

(1) Attention. People remember what they heed and regard. "Pay attention to what I say . . . keep them within your heart" (Proverbs 4:20-21)— that is, in a place where nothing can take them away. Where there is attention, there will be retention. The memory is the chest of divine truths, and a man should carefully lock them up. "Which of you will listen to this or pay close attention in time to come?" (Isaiah 42:23).

(2) Affection. This is a great friend to the memory. People remember what they care for. An old man will not forget where he has put his bag of gold. Delight and love are always renewing and reviving the object of our thoughts. David often asserts his delight in the law, and therefore it was always in his thoughts: "Oh, how I love your law! I meditate on it all day long" (Psalm 119:97).

(3) Application and appropriation of truths. We will remember what is relevant to us.

(4) Meditation, holy care to hold on to the Word, so that it is not snatched away from us by vain thoughts, and so the birds of the air do not gobble up the good seed (see Matthew 13:4). "Mary treasured up all these things and pondered them in her heart" (Luke 2:19); she "treasured" them because she "pondered" them.

(5) Observe what truths achieve. You will remember things that were spoken about a long time ago when you see them verified: see John 2:19-22. Things observed like this will make old truths come to mind again.

(6) Put into practice what you hear. You will remember the good you received from it: "I will never forget your precepts, for by them you have preserved my life" (Psalm 119:93).

(7) Commit it to the Spirit's keeping: "The Counselor . . . will remind you of everything" (John 14:26). Christ gave the Holy Spirit charge of his own sermons. The disciples' memories were too unreliable.

Note 7. **Not forgetting what he has heard, but doing it.** Sin comes for lack of memory. Forgetful hearers are negligent people; "those who keep his covenant . . . remember to obey his precepts" (Psalm 103:18). A godly man has a good memory; he remembers to act. Wicked people are often portrayed as having bad memories, as in Job 8:13, "who forget God," and Psalm 119:139, "my enemies ignore your word"—that is, they do not practice it. Yes, the sins of God's people are usually sins of forgetfulness. A bad memory causes a great deal of harm in the soul. "Do you have eyes but fail to see, and ears but fail to hear?" (Mark 8:18); the people did not consider the previous experience of the loaves and fishes and so distrusted Jesus. Hide the whole Word in your heart, that you may have a fresh truth to check sin in every temptation (see Psalm 119:11). Store up the mercies of God, that you may be thankful; forget not all his benefits (see Psalm 103:2).

Note 8. **But doing it.** The Word gives us work to do. It was not ordained for speculation. There is the work of faith (see John 6:29), the labor of love (see Hebrews 6:10), and fruits worthy of repentance (see Matthew 3:8). All this work the Gospel gives us to do—faith, love, and new obedience. Do not content yourselves, then, with a part of the truth. Faith is your work, repentance is your business, and the life of love and praise is your duty.

Note 9. **He will be blessed in what he does.** There is a blessedness linked to doing the work of the Word; not for the work's sake, but because of the mercy of God. So, see that you hear, so that you may come within the orbit of the blessing.

Commentary on Verse 26

If anyone considers himself religious and yet does not keep a tight rein on his tongue, he deceives himself and his religion is worthless.

The apostle, having shown the blessedness of those who are doers of the Word, now shows who are only listeners and do not put the Word into practice—people who allow themselves any known sin—and he gives as an example the evils of the tongue.

Question. Before I comment on the words any further, I will inquire why James places so much weight on this one thing. It seems so insignificant in itself and seems to have so little reference to the context.

Answer. (1) This is a main reason for our respect for our neighbor. True love for God will be manifested in love for our neighbor. God said, "You shall love God," and he also said, "You shall love your neighbor." The apostles often used this argument to unmask hypocritical arguments, as in 1 John 2:9, "Anyone who claims to be in the light but hates his brother is still in the darkness." See also 1 John 3:17-18, "If anyone has material possessions and sees his brother in need but has no pity on him, how can the love of God be in him? Dear children, let us not love with words or tongue but with actions and in truth." How can you imagine that those who are open to the love of God could be merciless towards other people? So 1 John 4:20 says, "Anyone who does not love his brother, whom he has seen, cannot love God, whom he has not seen."

(2) There is a natural inclination in us to cause offense with the tongue. Censuring is a pleasing sin that goes very well with our nature. The more natural corruptions are, the more care should be taken to suppress them: "I will watch my ways and keep my tongue from sin" (Psalm 39:1). As you watch, so you should pray and desire God to watch over your watching: "Set a guard over my mouth, O Lord; keep watch over the door of my lips" (Psalm 141:3). Being in awe of God is a great restraint.

(3) It was the sin of that age. This is apparent from the frequent references to it. See verse 19, all of chapter 3, 4:11, etc. It is a bad sign to be carried away by the evil of the times. Wicked people are described as following "the ways of this world" (Ephesians 2:2; the original Greek says "according to the age"). So also Romans 12:2 says: "Do not conform any longer to the pattern of this world"; this means, do not wear the clothes of the times.

(4) Because this seemed to be such a small sin, and having set aside bigger sins, they practiced it all the more. They were not adulterers or drunkards, and so they congratulated themselves on their apparent holiness. Note that indulgence in the smallest sin cannot coexist with grace. Your **religion is worthless** if you do not **keep a tight rein on [your] tongue**.

(5) This is usually the hypocrite's sin. Hypocrites, of all people, are least able to bridle their tongue. Those who seem to be religious are the most free in censuring others. They are aware of the guilt of their own spirits and so are most prone to suspect others. Censuring is a trick of the devil, which excuses indignation against their own sins. Gracious hearts reflect most on themselves. They do not look for things to reprove in others but things to lament in themselves. When a man is aware of his own failings, he is very sympathetic in reflecting on the weaknesses of others: "You who are spiritual should restore him gently" (Galatians 6:1).

(6) There is such a quick interchange between the tongue and the heart; that, says the apostle, is why their **religion is worthless**—they cannot **keep a tight rein on** their tongues. Seneca said, "Speech is the express image of

109

the heart," and someone greater than he said, "Out of the overflow of the heart the mouth speaks" (Matthew 12:34). The quality of many people's religion can be discerned by the intemperateness of their language. Words are the overflow of their wickedness.

With these reasons in mind, the opening of this verse is easier to understand.

If anyone considers himself religious—if he seems religious to himself or others, by the practice of a few things in worship.

Yet does not keep a tight rein on his tongue. That is, he does not abstain from the evils of the tongue, such as reviling and censuring.

He deceives himself. This may be understood in two ways:

(1) He has too good an opinion of himself. Self-love is the ground of hypocrisy. They do not search themselves or suspect themselves of any evil. Judas last of all asked, "Master, is it I?" They are too easy on themselves but too severe on others.

(2) The other sense may be that he comes at last to flatter himself, to deceive his own soul.

His religion is worthless. That is, either he makes the good things that are in him to be vain and unprofitable, or his religion is a pretense.

Notes on Verse 26

Note 1. **Considers himself religious.** Religion may be only a pretense. Consider "the man who thinks he knows something" (1 Corinthians 8:2)—that is, who flatters himself on his knowledge. "If anyone thinks he is something when he is nothing, he deceives himself" (Galatians 6:3).

Note 2. **Does not keep a tight rein on his tongue.** It is a major part of religion to bridle the tongue. There are several evils that must be restrained—lying, swearing, cursing, ribaldry. I will speak about these four.

(1) Lying. Beware of this in all its varieties. The devil—that is, the accuser—is called the liar too.

(2) Cursing. There is corruption at the heart when the tongue is so loose. There is seldom any blessing for those who are given over to cursing.

(3) Swearing. The righteous are afraid to take oaths (see Ecclesiastes 9:2).

(4) Ribaldry. This is "filthy language" (see Colossians 3:8) or "coarse joking" (Ephesians 5:4).

Note 3. **He deceives himself.** Hypocrites come at length to deceive themselves. A liar, by repeating his lies, begins to believe them.

Note 4. **His religion is worthless.** Pretended religion will be fruitless. Of all things, a man cannot endure his serious actions being in vain and to no purpose. This will be no small part of one's torment in hell, to think that all his profession has come to this.

Commentary on Verse 27

Religion that God our Father accepts as pure and faultless is this: to look after orphans and widows in their distress and to keep oneself from being polluted by the world.

Here the apostle comes to the positive part of the test. As a man must not take revenge in case his religion proves in vain, so he must do good, that it may be found to be pure and faultless.

Note from the context that negatives in religion are not enough. He must curb his tongue, but also he must look after the orphans. We should not be content with simply removing evil but must be concerned about what is good. There should not only be an abstinence from major sins but care taken to maintain communion with God. Descriptions in the Word are negative and positive: "does not walk in the counsel of the wicked . . . But his delight is in the law of the Lord" (Psalm 1:1-2). Some people are not drunkards, but are they godly? Is there any power in their religion? Are there any feelings of the spiritual life within their souls? God, who hates sin, delights in grace.

Now I come to the words of this verse. James urges them to do charitable deeds and engage in holy behavior, so that in this way they might show themselves to be truly religious.

Pure and faultless. James is not setting out the whole nature of religion but only some particular evidence of it. Religion also requires faith and worship, but the truth of these is seen in charity and a holy life. Therefore, those who oppose the Scripture in our day misinterpret this; they want to make the whole of religion consist in these outward acts. But the apostle is dealing with hypocrites, who feigned faith and worship and who also neglected charity.

Religion that God our Father accepts. That is, God who is the Father of Christ and the Father of us in him. The same phrase is used in many other passages: "Praise be to the God and Father of our Lord Jesus Christ" (2 Corinthians 1:3; see also Ephesians 1:3 and 5:20). Hypocrites may deceive men, who see the outside; but God the Father judges rightly. This is also mentioned to show the sincerity of such Christian acts. They should be carried out as in the presence of God.

To look after. This word embraces all duties of love. **To look after** them is to comfort them in their misery, to relieve them in their necessities. This one charitable act includes all duties to our neighbor.

Orphans and widows. These are specified, but others are not excluded. There are other objects of charity, such as the poor, the sick, the prisoners, the foreigners, who are also mentioned in the Scriptures. But orphans and widows most often need help and are most liable to neglect and oppression. They are often mentioned elsewhere in Scripture, as in Isaiah 1:17, "Defend the cause of the fatherless, plead the case of the widow." See also Psalm 146:9 and Proverbs 15:25 and 23:10.

In their distress. That is, in their oppression. This is added in case people should think they have performed their duty by visiting the rich and wealthy among the fatherless and widows.

To keep oneself from being polluted. This is linked to the previous duty. It shows the inseparable connection between charity and holiness and shows that religion is false when it does not teach holiness as well as charity. Roman Catholics separate them, praising charity as a merit to expiate the defect of unholiness.

By the world. The world, when it is taken in a negative sense, sometimes stands for the men of the world and sometimes for the desires of the world: "everything in the world—the cravings of sinful man, the lust of his eyes and the boasting of what he has and does" (1 John 2:16). **To keep oneself from being polluted by the world** is to keep ourselves from the infection of an evil example and the rule of worldly desires.

Notes on Verse 27

Note 1. Purity is the glory of religion. True Christianity is called a "holy faith" (Jude 20). So an impure life is incompatible with holy faith. "The deep truths of the faith" must be held "with a clear conscience" (1 Timothy 3:9). We live correctly when we have a pure heart. "Blessed are those whose ways are blameless" (Psalm 119:1). "Blessed are the pure in heart" (Matthew 5:8).

Note 2. Pure religion should be kept undefiled. A holy life and a generous heart adorn the Gospel. Religion is not adorned by ceremonies but by purity and charity. The apostle Paul speaks about making "the teaching about God our Saviour attractive" (Titus 2:10).

Note 3. A great fruit of piety is provision for the afflicted. In Matthew 25 you see acts of charity. Works of mercy become those who have received mercy from God. This is being like God. One of the chief glories in the Godhead is his tireless love and bounty. He looks after the orphans and widows; so should we.

Note 4. Charity singles out those in the greatest misery. The apostle says, **widows and orphans.** True generosity is when we give to those who are not able to reciprocate: "When you give a luncheon or dinner, do not invite your friends, your brothers or relatives . . ." (Luke 14:12-14).

Note 5. **God our Father.** We serve God best when we consider him as a **Father** in Christ. "Lord, Lord" is not half so sweet as **Our Father.** We are not servants but have received adoption as sons. Get an interest in God, that his work may be sweet to you. Mercies are sweeter when they come not only from a Creator but from a Father.

Note 6. Helping the afflicted and living a pure life go together. The apostle links them, and so does Christ: "Blessed are the merciful, for they will be shown mercy," and "Blessed are the pure in heart, for they will see God" (Matthew 5:7-8). Someone who is charitable and not pure is better for others than he is for himself. Goodness and righteousness are often linked in the Old Testament: see Micah 6:8 and Daniel 4:27. It is strange that people should separate what God has joined. So let the hand be open and the heart pure. You must **look after orphans and widows** and **keep [yourself] from being polluted by the world.**

Note 7. The world defiles. One can hardly walk here without defiling one's clothes.

(1) The things of the world taint our spirits. Through worldly objects we soon grow worldly. Christ prayed, "My prayer is not that you take them out of the world but that you protect them from the evil one" (John 17:15). Christ knew what a temptation it is to live amidst honors and pleasures. It was a happy thing that Paul could say, "The world has been crucified to me, and I to the world" (Galatians 6:14). The world is crucified to many, but they are not crucified to it.

(2) The desires of the world stain and deface your natures. The apostle Peter talks of "corruption in the world caused by evil desires" (2 Peter 1:4). Your affections were made for nobler purposes than to be wasted on your desires.

(3) The men of the world are dirty creatures. We cannot have anything to do with them without being defiled. The apostle says, "If a man cleanses himself from the latter, he will be an instrument for noble purposes, made holy, useful to the Master and prepared to do any good work" (2 Timothy 2:21). "From the latter"—that is, from the leprosy of evil examples, for the apostle is speaking of those vessels of dishonor that are in the great house of God, the world, which a man cannot touch without defilement. A man cannot hold any communion with them without being the worse. "These men are blemishes at your love feasts" (Jude 12); they defile the whole company.

So then:

(1) Let us become more and more weary of the world. In our heavenly home above, "nothing impure will ever enter it, nor will anyone who does what is shameful or deceitful" (Revelation 21:27). There are no devils in heaven; they were cast out long ago (see 2 Peter 2:4).

(2) While we live here, let us keep ourselves as undefiled as we can. "Yet you have a few people in Sardis who have not soiled their clothes. They will walk with me, dressed in white, for they are worthy" (Revelation 3:4). There are a few who escape the corruption of the world. You are kept by the power of God; yet, in some sense you must keep yourselves: "Blessed is he who stays awake" (Revelation 16:15). It is foolishness to think that because power is from God, we therefore have no responsibility.

James
Chapter 2

Commentary on Verse 1

My brothers, as believers in our glorious Lord Jesus Christ, don't show favoritism.

This chapter has two special admonitions, which were very necessary then. The first is against **favoritism** because of outward advantages, especially in church matters. The other is against ostentatious faith. He deals with the first admonition in verses 1-13, and with the second in verses 14-26. In this first verse he tells them to avoid showing **favoritism** because of some outward excellence that has no affinity at all with religion.

My brothers. A name used throughout the letter. Some people think he chiefly means the presbyters and deacons, who were responsible for allocating the seating. But I see no reason to restrict it to them, as it applies in all the other passages of the letter to all those to whom he wrote.

As believers. The word **believers** generally applies to the profession of the Christian religion or the manifestations of the grace of Christ in the souls of his people.

In our . . . Lord Jesus Christ. Christ is here called **our . . . Lord** because it is the correct term for him as mediator and head of the Church, and because of our interest in him: the head is dishonored through the disrespect of the members.

Glorious. Christianity is related to the Lord of glory. He gives honor to men, who otherwise would be poor and despised. If men believed Christ was **glorious,** they would not so easily despise those who have the least.

Show favoritism. Favoritism occurs when we give more respect to one person than to another for no good reason. The word signifies accepting someone's outside and respecting them for the external glory we find in them. The phrase, when it is used in the Old Testament, means wondering at a man's face, being overcome and dazzled at its beauty. Civility calls for outward respect and reverence to those who excel in the world. To give respect to a rich man is not evil. If all distinction between people were sinful, there would be no place for governments.

Notes on Verse 1

Note 1. Showing **favoritism** to people in religious matters is a sin. We may be guilty of it in many ways:

(1) By making external things, not religion, the ground of our respect and affection. The apostle says, "So from now on we regard no one from a worldly point of view. Though we once regarded Christ in this way, we do so no longer" (2 Corinthians 5:16). Viewing anyone from a worldly viewpoint is to love and esteem them from a secular motivation. Paul, when a Pharisee, looked for a Messiah coming in outward pomp and glory. Once converted, he set aside those worldly thoughts. Tertullian said, "We must not judge faith by people, but people by faith."

(2) When we do not give the proportion of affection according to the proportion of grace. Those who have the least worldly pomp, if they excel in Christ, should have the most Christian respect and honor.

(3) We can easily make greatness a cloak for baseness and excuse sin by honor. It is good to note how freely the Scriptures speak about wicked people being given the highest honor. The Turkish empire, great as it was, Luther said, was "only a morsel which the master of the house throws to dogs."

(4) When we give religious respect and serve men for base motives. "They . . . flatter others for their own advantage" (Jude 16).

(5) When church affairs are not carried on impartially toward the rich and the poor. Christ died for both rich and poor, and we must care for both (see Exodus 30:15). The poor and the rich had to give the same atonement for their souls; the souls of the poor were as precious to Christ as those who glitter most in outward pomp. The apostle Paul says, "I am obligated both to Greeks and non-Greeks" (Romans 1:14). The Pharisees gave Christ an excellent commendation in Mark 12:14—"Teacher, we know you are a man of integrity. You aren't swayed by men, because you pay no attention to who they are; but you teach the way of God in accordance with the truth." We should learn from our Lord and Master. We are never true ministers of Jesus Christ until we deal in the same way with people who are the same in themselves.

(6) When we hold the truths of God in contempt because of the people who bring them to us. Usually we pay attention to the man rather than the matter, and not the golden treasure so much as the clay pot. Out of prejudice it was said of Christ, "Is not this the carpenter's son?" Matheo Langi,

Archbishop of Salzburg, told everyone that the reformation of the mass was necessary, but that it was unendurable that a poor monk (referring to Luther) would make all these reforms. Similarly, in Christ's time a common question was, "Do any of the rulers believe in him?" Solomon says, "A man poor but wise . . . saved the city. . . . But nobody remembered that poor man" (Ecclesiastes 9:15-16). Erasmus observed that what was taken as orthodox in the Fathers was condemned as heretical in Luther.

Thus you see in how many ways we may be guilty of respect of people in religious matters.

Application. Consider these things. It is a heinous evil and a natural evil. We think that nothing counts but outward greatness. This is to devalue the members of Christ—indeed, to devalue Christ himself. "He who mocks the poor," even if they are only the common poor, "shows contempt for their maker" (Proverbs 17:5). But to despise poor Christians who have been renewed in the image of God is even worse. And it is worst of all when a Christian despises a Christian.

Note 2. Jesus Christ is a **glorious Lord** in his own person, which is "the radiance of God's glory" (Hebrews 1:3), and in regard to his present exaltation as he has a "name that is above every name" (Philippians 2:9). He will give you as much glory as your heart desires. If he does not make your enemies bow before you, he will still give you honor among his people, for he has promised to honor those who honor him (see 1 Samuel 2:30). So then, consider your thoughts about Christ. How do you consider him? Do you think of him as a Lord of glory? The apostle Peter says, "To you who believe, this stone [Christ] is precious" (1 Peter 2:7); the original Greek says, "honor." We account no honor like the honor of being related to Christ. You will know this disposition by two signs:

(1) All other excellencies will be as nothing. Not birth ("a Hebrew of Hebrews"), position ("a Pharisee"), moral accomplishments ("as for legalistic righteousness, faultless"), esteem in the world ("if anyone else thinks he has reasons to put confidence in the flesh, I have more"); "I consider everything a loss compared to the surpassing greatness of knowing Christ Jesus my Lord" (see Philippians 3:4-8).

(2) Being held in contempt will be nothing. **The brother in humble circumstances** may regard his humble position for Christ as a promotion; let him **take pride in his high position** (1:9). It is said of Moses that "he regarded disgrace for the sake of Christ as of greater value than the treasures of Egypt" (Hebrews 11:26). Note that he did not only endure the reproaches for Christ's sake but counted them as treasures, to be thought of as honors. Thuanus tells a story of Ludovicus Marsacus, a knight of France who was led to execution with other martyrs who were tied with cords. Out of respect for his position, he had not been bound; but he cried, "Give me my chains too; let me be a knight of the same order."

Note 3. Those who think Christ is **glorious** will think of Christianity and faith as glorious. A Christian is known by what he esteems. What, then, do you reckon as most excellent in yourselves and in others?

(1) In yourselves. What is your greatest honor and treasure? What do you desire for yourselves and for others? What would you part with first? Theodosius valued his Christianity above his empire. Luther said he would rather be "a Christian clown than a pagan emperor."

(2) In others. Who are most precious to you? Those in whom you see most clearly the image of Christ? Do not despise those jewels of Christ that lie in the dirt.

Commentary on Verses 2-4

Suppose a man comes into your meeting wearing a gold ring and fine clothes, and a poor man in shabby clothes also comes in. If you show special attention to the man wearing fine clothes and say, "Here's a good seat for you," but say to the poor man, "You stand there," or, "Sit on the floor by my feet," have you not discriminated among yourselves and become judges with evil thoughts?

I have put all these verses together because they are one sentence. The apostle reveals how guilty they were of the evil he warns them against by mentioning a normal practice of theirs in their church conventions.

Suppose a man comes into your meeting. In the original this is, "into your synagogue," by which some people understand their Christian assembly for worship. But that is not probable, because the Christian assembly is nowhere referred to as a "synagogue" but only as a "church." In the church-meeting there may be, without sin, several seats and places appointed for men of various ranks and dignities in the world; and it is a mistake to apply the censure of the apostle to such a practice. Others apply it to any meeting for deciding controversies, establishing public order, and allocating church offices; and by "synagogue" they understand the court where they judged all matters to do with themselves. Augustine seems to incline to this sense for one part of it—namely, for a meeting to allocate all church offices, which were not to be entrusted to men according to their outward quality but according to inward accomplishments. There was the same abuse in early times as is found, to our grief, among us—that people were called to office out of a respect to their worldly luster rather than their spiritual endowments. The gold ring was preferred to a rich faith, a practice wholly inconsistent with Christianity and with the dispensation of those times. God himself called fishermen and other despised people to the highest offices in the church.

The synagogue spoken of here is not the church assembly but the ecclesiastical court or convention for the settlement of disputes, where they were not to favor the cause of the rich against the poor.

Wearing a gold ring. "A gold-fingered man" is the force of the original word. The gold ring was a badge of honor and nobility. Therefore Judah had his signet (see Genesis 38:18-25); and Pharaoh, as a token that Joseph was promoted to an honorable position, "took his signet ring from his finger and put it on Joseph's finger" (Genesis 41:42). Ahasuerus treated Mordecai in the same way (see Esther 8:8).

Fine clothes. This too was a sign of honor: "Rebekah took the best clothes of Esau" (Genesis 27:15). Lightfoot says this refers to the priestly ornaments that belonged to him as his birthright. Similarly, when the prodigal returns, the father, to show him honor, calls for the best robe and a ring. It is said of the rich man in Luke 16:19 that he was "dressed in purple and fine linen and lived in luxury every day."

A poor man in shabby clothes. The original says, "filthy, sordid raiment." It is the same word that the Septuagint uses in Zechariah 3:3-4, where the high priest's "filthy clothes" are mentioned. This was a symbol of the calamitous state of the church.

If you show special attention to the man wearing fine clothes. The Greek word translated **special attention** means to gaze on and observe with some admiration and special reverence.

"Here's a good seat for you." The Greek means an honorable or worthy place. So it shows either rash allocation to them of the honors of the church or favoring them in their cause.

"You stand there," or, "Sit on the floor at my feet." These are expressions of contempt and disrespect. Standing or sitting at the feet was the posture of the younger disciples. Sometimes standing indicates those who stood on their defense; it is an allusion to the posture of men in courts. This different respect shown to the poor and the rich reminds me of a passage of Bernard who, when he happened to see a poor man poorly dressed, would say to himself, "Truly, Bernard, this man bears his cross more patiently than you do." But if he saw a rich man very well dressed, then he would say, "It may be that this man, under his fine clothing, has a better soul than you have under your religious habit." Here is an example of excellent charity, and far better than those in the text, who said to the man in the fine clothes, "Sit" and to the poor, "Stand." To the rich they assigned **a good seat,** but to the poor they assigned room **by my feet.**

Have you not discriminated among yourselves? This clause is translated in various ways. James asks, "Are you not partial?" It is an appeal to their consciences in making such a distinction between the rich and the poor. Does your conscience not tell you it is making a distinction that God never made?

And become judges with evil thoughts. From the order of the words in our translation, the meaning appears to be that they judge men's hearts by these outward appearances of meanness and greatness in the world. Here this is expressed by what is most inward in the heart—the thoughts. But this phrase **judges with evil thoughts** is to be taken in quite another sense. The meaning is, "You judge altogether perversely, according to the rule of your own corrupt thoughts and intentions." Their esteem and their ends were not right but were perverted by worldly desires. They esteemed outward pomp above spiritual graces, which was contrary to reason and religion.

Notes on Verses 2-4

Note 1. People honor worldly greatness. To a worldly eye nothing else is glorious. A corrupt judgment taints the practice of faith. A child of God may be guilty of much worldliness, but he does not have a worldly judgment. David's heart went astray; but his judgment was right, and this brought him back again (also Asaph; see Psalm 73; compare the whole psalm with the last verse, "As for me, it is good to be near God").

Note 2. **Have you not discriminated?** He poses them a question. To bring us to a sense of things, it is good to put questions to our consciences, because then we go straight to our own souls. Soliloquies and discourses with yourselves are of excellent value: "Search your hearts and be silent" (Psalm 4:4). It is a difficult task to bring a man and himself together, to get him to speak a word to himself. There are many who live in the world for a long time—some forty to fifty years—and all this while they cannot be brought to converse with their own hearts. This questioning of conscience will help you in humiliation, faith, and obedience.

In your work of humility, you will find yourself most awakened by asking these questions: "What have I done?" "Do I walk according to the holy law?" "Can I say, 'My heart is clean'?"

Note 3. **Judges with evil thoughts.** Evils start in the thoughts: "Out of the heart come evil thoughts" (Matthew 15:19). Affections pervert the thoughts, and thoughts stain the judgment. Therefore, when God spoke of the wickedness of the old world he said, "Every inclination of the thoughts of his [man's] heart was only evil all the time" (Genesis 6:5). The reason for atheism is blasphemous thoughts: "In all his thoughts there is no room for God" (Psalm 10:4). This is why you should go to God to cleanse your spirits from evil thoughts, why you should be humbled by them, why you should be on guard against them: "Let the wicked forsake his way and the evil man his thoughts. Let him turn to the Lord" (Isaiah 55:7). Note that it says not only *his way* but *his thoughts*.

Note 4. It is an **evil** thought that men are valued according to their outward excellency. This is against the dispensation of God, who puts the greatest glory on those who are of least account and esteem in the world. It is against the nature of grace, whose glory is not obvious to the senses but inward and hidden. A Christian's inside is best; all the world's glory is in show. Agrippa and Bernice "came with great pomp" (Acts 25:23). Christ often comes to us in disguise in his poor members.

Commentary on Verse 5

Listen, my dear brothers: Has not God chosen those who are poor in the eyes of the world to be rich in faith and to inherit the kingdom he promised those who love him?

In this verse the apostle gives another argument against showing favoritism: you will despise those whom God, out of his wise ordination, has called to the greatest honor. He gives an example in a threefold dignity that the Lord puts on the godly poor: they are **chosen** by God, **rich in faith,** and heirs of **the kingdom**.

Listen, my dear brothers. He attracts their attention and still gives them the loving name that he had used previously. It is usual in Scripture to preface all weighty matters with a call for attention: "He who has ears, let him hear" (Matthew 13:9). James says in the council of Jerusalem, "Brothers, listen to me" (Acts 15:13). Here the apostle uses this preface partly to stir them up to consider the dispensation of that age. So in 1 Corinthians 1:26 the apostle Paul says, "Brothers, think of what you were when you were called. Not many of you were wise by human standards"; that is, seriously consider the matter of God's calling in these times. James also uses this preface because he is about to warn against being perverse. When the matter concerns our case, it calls for our close attention.

Has not God chosen? That is, through the special gift of grace he singled out the poor to inherit life. This puts down the pride of great people, as if God should respect them for their outward dignity. The first choice that God made in the world was for poor men. Therefore we often read that the poor received the Gospel; not only the poor in spirit, but the poor in purse. God chose fishermen to preach the Gospel, and poor people to receive it. Few were won that were of any rank in the world, so that we might not think that the spread of the Gospel happens through the advantage of human power and props, but through divine grace.

Poor in the eyes of the world. That is, with regard to outward enjoyments. First Timothy 6:17 speaks about "those who are rich in this present world." There is another world that has its riches, but those who own land there are usually poor and despised. The saints are described as those who do not have their hopes in this world (see 1 Corinthians 15:19) or who are poor in this world; that is, in the opinion of the present world they are vile and abject.

Rich in faith. This may be taken in two ways. It may mean a high degree of faith, like the woman in Matthew 15:28 of whom Jesus said, "Woman, you have great faith." So when the apostle Paul urges believers on to an abundance of spiritual gifts and graces, he says, "Let the word of Christ dwell in you richly" (Colossians 3:16). Or **rich in faith** may be in contrast with worldly poverty. And note that God is said to have **chosen . . . to be rich in faith.** Such an expression is used in Romans 8:29—"predestined to be conformed to the likeness of his Son"; it is clearly taught by the apostle in Ephesians 1:4—"For he chose us in him . . . to be holy"—not *because* we are good, but *that we might be* good. This cannot be seen as the cause of faith; for as he chose us to be **rich in faith,** so he chose us to be heirs of glory. Therefore, this does not indicate the cause of God's choice but the purpose; not that they were so, but that they might be so.

To inherit the kingdom. Glory is often pictured as a kingdom.

He promised. Promises of this nature are everywhere: "I love those who love me" (Proverbs 8:17); "showing love to thousands who love me" (Exodus 20:6).

Those who love him. See the reasons why this grace is specified, given in the explanation and notes on 1:12. Note the order used by the apostle: he puts first *election*, then *faith*, then *love*.

Notes on Verse 5

Note 1. God often chooses the poor of this world. The lion and the eagle are passed by, and the lamb and the dove are chosen for sacrifice. The Gospel was "hidden . . . from the wise and learned, and revealed . . . to little children" (Matthew 11:25). God shows the glory of his power in preserving truth that is not supported by worldly arguments. Usually he shows his power by using weak means. Moses' hand became leprous before it performed miracles (Exodus 4). Jericho was blown down with rams' horns, and Goliath slain with a sling and a stone. God shows the riches of his goodness by choosing the poor. A thief was made the delight of paradise, and Lazarus was taken to Abraham's side. God reveals his wisdom by replacing people's outer defects with this inner glory. Levi, who had no inheritance among his brothers, had the Lord for his inheritance. So then:

(1) You who are poor, bless God; it is out of mercy that God should look on you. This comforts your poor state; rejected by the world, you are **chosen** by God. He who is happy in his own conscience should not be made miserable by other people's judgment. "Let not any eunuch complain, 'I am only a dry tree.' I will give them an everlasting name" (Isaiah 56:3, 5). Do not be discouraged though you are outwardly poor. The poor man is known to God by name. In Luke 16:19-31 he has a proper name, Lazarus; whereas the rich man is merely called "a rich man." However, we forget the poor and remember the rich man's name and title.

(2) You who are rich, do not consider this as the favor of God's people. Luther said, "profess that you will not be contented so; you will not be quiet till you have the tokens of God's special mercy."

Note 2. There are poor people in this world and poor people in the world to come. The rich man, who lived in luxury every day and was dressed in fine linen, wanted a drop of water to cool his tongue. Augustine says, "He wanted a drop, who would not give a crumb." You are left with your choice—to be rich in this world, but poor in the world to come; though here you wallow in a sea of pleasures, yet there you may want a drop of water to cool your tongue.

Note 3. The poor of this world may be spiritually rich. The apostle's riddle comes true: "having nothing, and yet possessing everything" (2 Corinthians 6:10); nothing in the world, but all in faith.

Note 4. Faith makes us truly rich; it is the open hand of the soul that receives all of God's bounteous supplies. If we are empty and poor, it is not because God's hand is closed, but because ours is not opened. A person may be poor despite abundance of wealth. It is grace alone that makes you excel forever. So then, you who are poor, do not envy other people's wealth; you who are rich, do not indulge yourselves in these pleasures. They are not true riches, nor can you always call them your own.

Note 5. The Lord only loves the godly poor. There are a wicked poor whose hearts are ignorantly stubborn, whose lives are viciously profane. Christ says, "Blessed are you who are poor, for yours is the kingdom of God" (Luke 6:20). This is explained by the evangelist Matthew: "Blessed are the poor in spirit" (Matthew 5:3).

Note 6. All God's people are heirs; they are the only heirs. They are heirs by virtue of their sonship. "If we are children, then we are heirs— heirs of God and co-heirs with Christ" (Romans 8:17). Jesus Christ was the natural son and the natural heir; and we, being adopted sons, are adopted heirs. In Hebrew 1:2 Christ is called "heir of all things," and he has invested us with his own privileges. Consider what an heir the child of God is, one who has received the same privileges as Christ; and therefore the apostle says he is a "co-heir." In a spiritual way, as we are able, we shall possess the same glory that Christ has. So then, you who have tasted the grapes of Eshcol and have experienced your adoption, you may be confident that God will never alter his purposes of love.

Again, they are heirs who not only look to inherit the goods of their Heavenly Father, but himself. God does not only make over heaven to you but himself: "I will be your God"; God is yours.

Note 7. The faithful are heirs of a **kingdom**. Heaven and glory are often pictured in this way. Kingdoms are for kings; and every saint is a spiritual king. Christ "has made us to be a kingdom and priests to serve his God and Father" (Revelation 1:6). First Peter 2:9 says that we are "a royal priesthood." These two dignities are joined together, because their kings were once priests; and the heads of the families were the priests. They are kings because of that spiritual power they have over themselves, sin, Satan, and the world; and because they are kings, therefore their glory must be a kingdom.

Again, Christ is a king; and therefore they are kings, and his kingdom is their kingdom. Being united to Christ, they possess his royalty. Again, there is a very great similarity between the glory we expect and a kingdom: "Do not be afraid, little flock, for your Father has been pleased to give you the kingdom" (Luke 12:32). It is called a kingdom because of its splendor and glory. The apostle gives a suitable exhortation in 1 Thessalonians 2:12, "Live lives worthy of God, who calls you into his kingdom and glory." Remember, you will one day be a king with God in glory.

Note 8. Heaven is a **kingdom** that is **promised**. It is not only good, thus attracting your desires, but certain, and so supporting your hopes. Look on it not only as a kingdom, but as a promised kingdom; and count him faithful who made the promise. Heaven is not only prepared but promised. You need not have just vague hopes but a steadfast confidence.

Note 9. The promise of **the kingdom** is made to those who **love** God. Love is the result of faith and the ground of all duty, and so the best indicator of a spiritual state. Those who do not believe do not love. They cannot obey if they do not love. Look, then, to this grace. Do you love God? When promises have conditions attached to them, we cannot take comfort in the promise until we have fulfilled the condition. As Christ asked Simon Peter, "Do you love me?" so ask your own soul, "Do you love God?" Confront the soul with it again: "Do you indeed love God?" The results of love are many. Those who love God love what belongs to God.

(1) They love his glory. Their great desire and delight is to honor him, so that they may in some way be useful to the glory of God. The sin mentioned in 2 Timothy 3:2, "lovers of themselves," is the opposite to this.

When all that people do is concerned with self-respect, they have little love for God.

(2) They love his commandments. "This is love for God: to obey his commands. And his commands are not burdensome" (1 John 5:3). Duty is their delight, and ordinances their solace.

(3) They love his friends. They love Christians as Christians, no matter how poor they may be. Love of the brothers is very important: see 1 John 3:14.

By these yardsticks you may judge yourselves.

Commentary on Verse 6

But you have insulted the poor. Is it not the rich who are exploiting you? Are they not the ones who are dragging you into court?

Here the apostle confronts them with their own misdeeds. For, having shown that favoritism is a sin, he appeals directly to their consciences. You have been guilty of it, you have despised the poor. And then, to show that their behavior was not only vain and evil, but mad and senseless, he presents a new argument: **Is it not the rich who are exploiting you?** In effect, he asks them whether they would show so much respect to their executioners and oppressors. But you may ask, is not the apostle here inciting them to revenge? Are we not to "love our enemies, and do good to those who hate us"? I answer:

(1) It is one thing to love enemies, but another to esteem them out of some perverse respect. There is a difference between fawning and ordinary human civility.

(2) Some people have acted so badly toward the church that they cannot command the least respect from the people of God: "Do not . . . welcome him" (2 John 10).

But you have insulted the poor. He shows how contrary their practice was to God's dispensation: God has honored the poor, but you dishonor them, as the word signifies. The prophet says the same: "You trample on the poor" (Amos 5:11).

Is it not the rich . . . ?. He may mean rich pagans and Jews who had not embraced Christianity. Persecution usually came from the scribes, Pharisees, and high priests: "the leading men of the city . . . stirred up persecution against Paul and Barnabas" (Acts 13:50). Or James may mean the pseudo-Christians who, being great and powerful, oppressed their brothers and used all kinds of violence against them. Or he may mean any kind of rich people.

Exploiting you. The word means to abuse their power against you, or to use a power over you that was never given to them. In this sense Solomon says, "The rich rule over the poor, and the borrower is servant to the lender" (Proverbs 22:7)—"rule" means, he exercises power that he has no authority to wield.

Dragging you into court. If this refers to the unconverted Jews, it means they helped the persecution. This is implied in Matthew 10:17, "They will hand you over to the local councils." Or if this refers to rich men in general, which I think is the case, it shows their violent practices toward the poor, dragging them to court as they used to do to debtors: "grabbed him and began to choke him" (Matthew 18:28).

Notes on Verse 6

Note 1. **You have insulted the poor.** Evil must be confronted. Nathan said to David, "You are the man!" (2 Samuel 12:7). When the practice is notorious, a weak accusation does no good. When a city is on fire, will a man come coolly and say, "There is a great fire over there; I pray God it will do no harm"? No; he will cry, "Fire! Fire! You are ruined if you do not put it out!" So, when the practice is public and clearly sinful, it is no good coming with a contemplative lecture or lame homily. You must confront the person. **You have insulted the poor.** "Sirs, this is your sin, and if you do not repent, it will be your ruin."

Note 2. **But you.** He says they are opposing God's dispensation. Insulting the poor is a sin not only against the Word, the written will of God, but against his mind and his dispensations. It is resisting God. It is against the mind of God as their Creator: "Rich and poor have this in common: the Lord is the Maker of them all" (Proverbs 22:2); that is, they have but one Maker. There is another meeting: they also meet in the grave (see Job 3:13-15). They meet in their death and in their Maker.

Note 3. Rich people are often persecutors or oppressors. Their wickedness takes advantage of the opportunity. Many have the will but have no power. The world would be a stage for all kinds of villainies were it not for the restraints of providence. Riches also exalt the mind. The rich have had little experience of misery, and so have little pity. God's intentions for Israel were these: do good to strangers, for you were a stranger; do good to the poor, for your father was a poor Syrian. Such arguments are frequent in Scripture. Jerome is harsh but too often true: "Every rich man is either an oppressor himself, or the heir of one." Certainly it is almost impossible to be rich and righteous. The rich are prone to moral evils, such as pride: "Command those who are rich in the present world not to be arrogant" (1 Timothy 6:17). They are prone to boasting, showing contempt of others: "Let not . . . the rich man boast of his riches" (Jeremiah 9:23). They are prone to injustice: "The rich rule over the poor" (Proverbs 22:7)—that is, by force and violence. The word may be read "domineer." Then there is the danger of luxury. But there are also spiritual evils, which are worse because they are less easily discerned. These are:

(1) Forgetting God, when he has remembered them most. People who live at ease have little or no sense of duty. Agur prays, "Give me [not] riches. . . . Otherwise, I may have too much and disown you" (Proverbs 30:9).

(2) Creature confidence. Hence these frequent cautions: "Command those who are rich . . . not . . . to put their hope in wealth" (1 Timothy 6:17); "though your riches increase, do not set your heart on them" (Psalm 62:10). Usually the creature comforts rival God.

(3) Worldliness. The more people have, the more sparing they are towards God. Solomon speaks of "wealth hoarded to the harm of its owner" (Ecclesiastes 5:13).

(4) Security. "You have plenty of good things laid up for many years" (Luke 12:19).

These are evils that cling to wealth, like rust to money.

Commentary on Verse 7

Are they not the ones who are slandering the noble name of him to whom you belong?

James proceeds to list the abuses of riches. Who are the enemies of God and of religion, the scorners of the worthy name of Christians, but the rich?

Are they not the ones who are slandering . . . ?. Some apply this to ungodly rich people who profess religion, as if their practices had brought shame on Christianity itself. They quote Romans 2:24, 2 Peter 2:2, 1 Timothy 6:1, and Titus 2:5 to support this view. Certainly religion is never dishonored more than by the lives of ungodly "religious" people. But it is a great mistake to apply what is said here to rich Christians. The apostle is only observing how rich people lived; they were usually bitter enemies of Christianity. So wealth was not a good criterion in the church when appointing people to leading positions.

The noble name. The Greek word translated **noble** means "honorable."

To whom you belong. In the original Greek this reads "who called you," and some people interpret it, "whom you call on." This describes

Christians: "all . . . who call on the name of our Lord Jesus Christ" (1 Corinthians 1:2); "everyone who confesses the name of the Lord" (2 Timothy 2:19).

Notes on Verse 7

Note 1. Wicked rich men, above all others, are most prone to blasphemy. "Because of your wealth your heart has grown proud," says Ezekiel 28:5. Riches breed pride, and pride ends in atheism. When men's hearts are inflamed with wine, they heap their malice on Christ's servants. The merry and well-fed Babylonians insisted on having a Hebrew song (Psalm 137). For many, no feast is complete unless John the Baptist's head is brought on a plate. Religion, or religious people, must be served to feed their mirth.

Note 2. Those who love Christ will hate blasphemers. Moses burned with a holy zeal when he heard that one had blasphemed God (see Leviticus 24:13-14). And David says, "They speak of you with evil intent; your adversaries misuse your name. Do I not hate those who hate you, O Lord? . . . I count them my enemies" (Psalm 139:20-22). Love is sensitive to the least wrong done to the one loved. It burns with a fiery zeal when such contempt as blasphemy is cast on Christ.

Note 3. Christ's name is a worthy name. Christianity will never be a disgrace for you, although you may be a disgrace to Christianity. "I am not ashamed," says the apostle Paul, "of the gospel of Christ" (Romans 1:16). Many are ashamed to be known as Christ's in ungodly company, as if there could be any disgrace in being Christ's servant. Oh, this is an honor for you! As Christianity is an honor for you, so you should honor it, that you may not stain a worthy name: "make the teaching about God our Savior attractive" (Titus 2:10).

Note 4. The people of Christ are named and called for Christ's name; "Christian" comes from "Christ." The apostle says, "From whom his whole family in heaven and on earth derives its name" (Ephesians 3:15). The name was given to them first of all at Antioch (Acts 11:26). They were called "disciples" before, but to distinguish them from false brethren, they gave them the name "Christians." They were called "Nazarites" and "Galileans" by their enemies; and about this time there was a sect of that name, composed half of Jews and half of Christians. This name, Christians, calls us to holiness. Remember what Christ did; you are called after his name: "Everyone who confesses the name of the Lord must turn away from wickedness" (2 Timothy 2:19). Alexander the Great said to one of his captains, also called Alexander, "see you do nothing unworthy of the name of Alexander." So, see you do nothing unworthy of the name of Christ.

Commentary on Verse 8

If you really keep the royal law found in Scripture, "Love your neighbor as yourself," you are doing right.

Now James reveals the ground on which they based their preposterous actions. It was not charity, as they claimed, but so they could be admired by people.

If you really keep—if you do obey the law, that part of it which governs outward things. The word **really** signifies, "if you accomplish perfectly." Sincerity is a kind of perfection. The Roman Catholics use this to show that a just man may fulfill the law of God. In this passage it only implies a sincere respect for the whole duty of the law.

The royal law. James may have called it this because God is the King of kings and Jesus Christ the King of saints (see Revelation 15:3). So the law, either in God's hands or in Christ's hands, is a **royal law**, the least deflection from which is rebellion. You would not lightly break kings' laws. God's laws are **royal** laws because of the dignity of their author. The Syriac interpreter favors this meaning, for he translates it, "the law of God." God's law may also be called this because of its own worth; what is excellent we call royal. Or it may be because of its great power on the conscience. God's **law** is **royal** and absolute. Or it may be called **the royal law** to show its plainness, like a "royal way" or, as we say, "the king's highway." So it is said, "We will travel along the king's highway" (Numbers 21:22). **The royal law** may imply the highway and road of duty.

Found in Scripture. That is, this duty to love others is set down in the Word. This is often repeated by our Lord (see Matthew 22:39) and by the apostles (see Romans 13:9; Galatians 5:14).

You are doing right. The same expression is used in Philippians 4:14 and implies that they were not blameworthy and might justly be acquitted from their guilt.

Notes on Verse 8

Note 1. The vilest wickedness has an attractive appearance. Sin loves to walk in disguise. Its real face is ugly and odious. Satan sometimes dresses up sins in the guise of duty and at other times represents duty as sin, as with Christ's healing on the Sabbath. Examine your own hearts. Is my motive right as well as my action? It is not enough to do what the law requires; it must be done in the way the law requires.

Note 2. Going to the law is the best way to discover self-deception. This is according to the law (says the apostle), and it is good. Paul died through the coming of the commandment (see Romans 7:9)—that is, through conviction on his heart; he saw himself in a dead and lost state. So Romans 3:20 says, "Through the law we become conscious of sin." So we should talk often with the commandment and consult it in all we do.

Note 3. The Lord's law is a **royal law.**

(1) It has a regal author. The solemn motive for obedience is, "I am the Lord." Marcion blasphemed in saying that the law came from an evil God. Many now speak so contemptuously about this, as if they had a Marcionite spirit. The same Lord Jesus who gave the Gospel also gave the law.

(2) It requires noble work, fit for kings. Service is an honor, and duty is a privilege. The brightest part of God's glory is his holiness; it is our calling to be holy.

(3) There are royal wages. This is nothing less than being made kings and princes for God: "There is in store for me the crown of righteousness" (2 Timothy 4:8). "I have served these eighty-six years," said Polycarp, "and he never did me harm." Reason with yourselves: will you sin against a royal Lord, such royal work, such a royal reward?

Note 4. The rule that God has left us is laid down in the Scriptures. There we discover his will, and from there it must be sought, "so that the man of God may be thoroughly equipped for every good work" (2 Timothy 3:17).

Note 5. The Scriptures require us to love our neighbors as ourselves. Paul says, "The entire law is summed up in a single command: 'Love your neighbor as yourself'" (Galatians 5:14). See also Matthew 7:12. Christ also says, "Love one another. As I have loved you, so you must love one another" (John 13:34). Christ's love was beyond understanding.

Note 6. To explain this, I shall first show you who your neighbor is and, secondly, what kind of love you should give him.

(1) Who is your neighbor? They asked Christ himself this question: "Who is my neighbor?" (Luke 10:29). The solution is found in Christ's answer. First, in general terms, everyone to whom I may be helpful. The word **neighbor** is used because our charity is exercised most to those who are near us. But it must not be limited to this, for Christ shows that a stranger may be a neighbor (Luke 10:36). All people are called "your own flesh" (Isaiah 58:7). Secondly, there are special neighbors, who live near us; as the apostle says, "If anyone does not provide for his relatives, and espe-

cially for his immediate family, he has denied the faith and is worse than an unbeliever" (1 Timothy 5:8). Thirdly, there are spiritual neighbors: "As we have opportunity, let us do good to all people, especially to those who belong to the family of believers" (Galatians 6:10).

(2) What kind of love is meant by this expression, "we are to love them as ourselves"? I answer: the expression shows the manner of our love, not its measure.

a. It stops self-love by urging us, first, to care for the good of others: "Nobody should seek his own good, but the good of others" (1 Corinthians 10:24). Ludolphus said, "The world was once destroyed with water because of the heat of lust; and it will be destroyed again with fire because of the coldness of love." Secondly, it urges us to care for their good really. John often speaks of "loving in truth." We must be as keen to promote their good as our own, without seeking any selfish advantage.

b. It also tells us to deal with others as we would have them deal with us. In all our actions it is good to make frequent appeals to our consciences.

Thus I have touched on the great rule for every action: **"Love your neighbor as yourself."** This prevents self-love by showing that we must do others good as well as ourselves; and it prevents injury, since we may do others no more evil than we do ourselves.

Commentary on Verse 9

But if you show favoritism, you sin and are convicted by the law as lawbreakers.

Here is the second part of the apostle's answer. In the former part there was the concession, you are doing right if you obey the law; but here is the correction: you are behaving contrary to the law, and so it is a sin.

If you show favoritism. That is, this is not a duty as you claim, but it is a sin; and whatever you think, the law, which is Christ's rule, will find you guilty.

And are convicted by the law. This may be understood either generally, that whatever they claim, the law would find them out; or else, more especially, it may be understood of the law that they urged: **"Love your neighbor as yourself"**—which required equal respect for the neighbor, whether rich or poor. Or else the apostle means the law against showing favoritism to people: "Do not pervert justice; do not show partiality to the poor or favoritism to the great, but judge your neighbor fairly" (Leviticus 19:15).

As lawbreakers. In the Greek the word for **as** implies reality, not just similarity; that is, you are indeed **lawbreakers.**

Notes on Verse 9

Note 1. The Word and rule reveal wickedness when our blind consciences do not. Conscience is but a weak light. "Look after yourself" is the language of corrupt nature. We need to attend upon the Word and consult with the law, not the crooked rule of our own consciences.

Note 2. It is only a crafty pretense when one part of the law is appealed to in order to excuse disobedience to another; for when we pick and choose, we do not fulfill God's will but our own. Conscience must be satisfied with something. So people usually please themselves by obeying what is least contrary to their interests and inclinations. Beware of such a partial obedience.

Commentary on Verse 10

For whoever keeps the whole law and yet stumbles at just one point is guilty of breaking all of it.

The connection between this verse and the previous one is this: they had pleaded that their respect of the rich was merely a necessary duty, a duty of the law; or at least that it was only a small offense, such as might be excused by their innocent intention and their obedience in other things, which was an opinion rife in those days. This conceit was common and appears in several passages. Our Saviour often accuses the Pharisees of it. Maimonides, in his treatise on repentance, has this passage: "Everyone has his merits and his sins. He whose merits are greater than his sins, he is *tzadoc*, the righteous man; he whose sins are greater than his merits, he is *rashang*, the wicked man; but where the sins and the merits are equal, he is the middle man, partly happy, and partly miserable." This was the sum of the Jewish doctrine in the more corrupt times; and some think the apostle might be opposing this error in this verse, by showing that the least breach rendered a man obnoxious to the danger of the violation of the whole law. But I think it means that they satisfied themselves with half a duty, giving too much care to the rich and nothing at all to the poor. God says, **"your neighbor"**; so I must not say, "my rich neighbor only." There must be an even-handed compliance with the whole will of God, or else it is not obedience, and you are in danger of breaking the law.

Whoever keeps the whole law. Suppose someone is exact in all other points of the law; this is impossible, but we can speculate about things that will never happen. Or else he is speaking according to their presumptions. They supposed they were not to be convicted as transgressors in any other matter.

Yet stumbles at just one point. Willingly, constantly, and in good conscience; with thought of merit and excuse because of his obedience in other matters.

Is guilty of breaking all of it. Liable to the same punishment, he has the same absence of hope and acceptance with God as if he had done nothing. A man may sin against the dignity and authority of the whole law, though he does not actually break every part of it. But you will ask, as the apostles did, "Who then can be saved?" (Matthew 19:25). Here is a terrible sentence that will greatly discourage God's little ones, who are conscious of their daily failings. I answer: the apostle aims to expose the hypocrites, not discourage the saints. I will now remove the false inferences:

(1) You cannot conclude that all sins are equal. They are all damning, but not all equally damning. Some guilt may be more heinous, but all is deadly. And that is what James asserts; he says, he **is guilty of breaking all of it,** but not equally guilty. So although all sins deserve death, there is still a difference between the various degrees of guilt and the curse.

(2) You cannot conclude that total rebellion is simply, in itself, better than formal profession. Christ loved the man for the good things that were in him from his youth and told him, "You are not far from the kingdom of God" (Mark 12:34). We read of greater sins and more intolerable judgment. Good moral pagans may have a cooler hell.

(3) You cannot apply this to those whose care for obedience is universal, though they do not count themselves perfect: "Then I would not be put to shame when I consider all your commands" (Psalm 119:6); not when I *have observed*, but when I *consider*. Gracious hearts look to all, though they cannot accomplish all; and on every known defect and failing they humble themselves and seek mercy. This does not exclude them, for then it would exclude everyone. But when people allow themselves partial obedience, without forethought, striving, or grief, they come under the terror of this sentence.

(4) You must not urge this sentence to the exclusion of the comforts of the Gospel and the hopes that we have by the grace of God in Christ. This sentence is in itself the rigor of the law, and such sayings brook the exceptions of repentance and grace. For the rigor of the law can only take place on those who are enslaved by it and are not freed by Christ. That this is the voice of the law is plain because it agrees with Deuteronomy 27:26,

"Cursed is the man who does not uphold the words of this law by carrying them out." Christ said, "Anyone who breaks one of the least of these commandments and teaches other to do the same will be called least in the kingdom of heaven" (Matthew 5:19); that is, he will not be acknowledged as a Gospel minister. Though there is a pardon, of course, for infirmities and failings, yet Christ has not relaxed the strictness of the law. The Pharisees thought that some commandments were arbitrary, and so the lawyer asked Christ, "Teacher, which is the greatest commandment in the Law?" (Matthew 22:36).

(5) You must not make this sentence pervert the order of the commandments; as if someone, in committing theft, committed adultery; and in committing adultery, he committed murder. Note that the apostle does not say, "He transgresses all"; but he **is guilty of breaking all of it.** The precepts are not to be taken separately but all together, as they make one entire law and rule of righteousness. Contempt reflects on the whole law when it is willfully violated in one part, just as he who wrongs one member wrongs the whole man or body of which it is a part.

Notes on Verse 10

Voluntary neglect of any part of the law makes us guilty of breaking the whole law. In God's sight, he who sincerely repents of one sin repents of all sins. So, one allowed sin is virtually a violation of the whole law; and therefore, when some people went to collect manna on the Sabbath God said, "How long will you refuse to keep my commands and my instructions?" (Exodus 16:28), implying that as they broke one they had broken all.

There are many uses of this note:

(1) It shows how sensitive we should be about every command. Willful violation amounts to a total neglect; therefore, as wisdom advises, "Guard my teachings as the apple of your eye" (Proverbs 7:2). The tiniest speck of dust irritates the eye, and in the same way the law is a tender thing and easily wronged. Lest you forfeit all your righteousness at once, it is good to be careful.

(2) Partial obedience is an argument motivated by insincerity. When we neglect duties that thwart ungodly desires, we do not please God but ourselves. We are to walk in all "the Lord's commandments" (Luke 1:6). David did everything God wanted him to (Acts 13:22).

(3) It is a vain deceit to excuse the defects in one duty by care for another duty. We see many people's hearts grow careless out of a vain conceit that excelling in some things will excuse disobedience in others.

(4) Whenever we fail we ought to renew our peace with God. I have

done what will make me guilty of the whole law; therefore, soul, run to your advocate: "If anybody does sin, we have one who speaks to the Father in our defense—Jesus Christ, the Righteous One" (1 John 2:1). Go to Christ that he may pardon you; your hearts are not right with God if you do not take this course. After daily transgressions, seek out a daily pardon. The children of God are like fountains; when mud is stirred up, they do not flow until they can become clear again. Particular sins must have particular applications of grace, for in themselves, in their own merit, they leave you under a curse.

(5) We must not only have regard for duty but all the circumstances around it. One point is dangerous. The Pharisees performed external duties and avoided the big sins but allowed themselves more hidden sins, which have dangerous consequences. Malice is murder; and therefore John says, "No murderer has eternal life in him" (1 John 3:15). And lust is adultery—see Matthew 5:28; a look, a glance, a thought, a desire is in itself damnable.

(6) Previous profession will do no good where there is total rebellion later. A little poison in a cup or one leak in a ship may ruin all. A man may ride in the right direction for a long time, but one turn at the end of the journey and he may lose his way. Gideon had seventy sons and only one illegitimate child, and yet that illegitimate child destroyed all the rest (Judges 8). Ecclesiastes 9:18 says, "One sinner destroys much good."

(7) The small size of the sin is a poor excuse; it is an aggravation rather than an excuse. It is sadder that we should fight against God for a trifle. In Luke 16:21 the rich man would not give a crumb, and this greatly displeased God; thus he did not receive a drop of water. God's judgments have been most remarkable when the occasion seemed the least significant. Adam was thrown out of paradise for eating fruit. God's command is still the same. "I merely tasted a little honey . . ." says Jonathan. "And now must I die?" (1 Samuel 14:43). It will be sad for you to go to hell for a small matter. One of the prophet's aggravations is that "they sell . . . the needy for a pair of sandals" (Amos 2:6). Would you oppose God for a small thing of little consequence? That is imprudent and unkind.

Commentary on Verse 11

For he who said, "Do not commit adultery," also said, "Do not murder." If you do not commit adultery but do commit murder, you have become a lawbreaker.

Here is support for the meaning of the previous sentence, that we are not to look to how it fits in with our desires and interests, but to the authority of the Lawgiver. James gives examples in the sixth and seventh commandments. God, who said one, said both; they are precepts of the same law and Law-giver. And therefore, in the violation of one of these laws the authority of the law is violated.

He who said, "Do not commit adultery." That is, the one who punished adultery with death (see Deuteronomy 22:22) also punished murder with death (see Leviticus 24:17 and Deuteronomy 19:13). The apostle uses the phrase **He who said** to allude to the preface of the law: "And God spoke all these words" (Exodus 20:1).

Notes on Verse 11

Note 1. We must not argue about the content of the command but look to the will of the Lawgiver. James shows that the whole law had an equal obligation on the conscience, because he who said the one said the other. God's will is motive enough for obedience: see 1 Peter 2:15; 1 Thessalonians 4:3 and 5:18. Every sin is an affront to God's sovereignty, as if his will were not reason enough, and to his wisdom, as if he did not know what was good for men. When your hearts balk at any duty, shame yourselves with these considerations. This is a trial of sincerity; duty is well done when it is done with a mere sight of God's will. It is a motive for universal obedience, as this duty is required as well as other duties and commanded by the same will.

Note 2. There are various duties and sins, according to the different laws of God. Do not be content, with Herod, to "hear many things" gladly but not to practice them. He who calls you to pray calls you to hear, to redeem the time for meditation and other holy purposes. All commands are equally commanded and must be equally observed. And do not be content that you are not guilty of the sins others are reproved of. The Pharisee could say, "I am no adulterer," but he could not say, "I am not proud."

Commentary on Verse 12

Speak and act as those who are going to be judged by the law that gives freedom.

Out of the whole discourse James infers a timely exhortation that they should order their speech and actions so as to endure the test and trial of **the law**, especially because this is commanded by an impartial law. This is the reason for this: those who want to be judged by **the law** should not forget the least part of it.

Speak and act. This links up with 1:27 and also with the topic of showing favoritism in this chapter. Not only actions but words fall under God's judgment and the law.

As those who are going to be judged. Some read this "as those that will judge" and apply it to the context. They give it the following sense: in the Old Testament, distinctions between people were not so expressly forbidden, but now they are taken away by the law of freedom; slave and free are all one in Christ (see Galatians 3:28). Therefore you are to judge without showing any favoritism. But I prefer the reading, **as those who are going to be judged**—that is, either in conscience here or at the judgment-seat of God hereafter.

By the law that gives freedom. The same expression is used in 1:25. But what does it mean here? The basic reason may link up with the servile attention they gave to rich people. The apostle agrees that there was freedom but not license; for there is still a law, though to the elect it is a **law** of **freedom**. To wicked people this is still a slavery and a hard yoke. Therefore, walk so that you may not be judged according to the law. Behave in a way that demonstrates you have come under the banner of love and the privileges of the Gospel; and then, when you come to be judged, you will be judged according to the Gospel. Otherwise there is no freedom for any who break the smallest law; they may expect **judgment without mercy** (verse 13).

Notes on Verse 12

Note 1. The law in the hands of Christ is a **law** of **freedom**.

It is a **law**: "I am not free from God's law but am under Christ's law" (1 Corinthians 9:21). There is a yoke, though not an insupportable burden. "He has showed you, O man, what is good" (Micah 6:8). The acceptable will of God is revealed in the law of ten rules, and the moral part of the Scripture is a commentary on that. This is also an imperative. It is not up to us whether we obey or not. Laws are obligatory. The Creator's will is seen in the law, and we are under its command. Morality is binding on us permanently: "The law is holy, and the commandment holy, righteous and good" (Romans 7:12). Our consciences would soon be offended at teaching that said murder, incest, or adultery were not sins. Only the pride of ungodly people thinks the Gospel frees us from the obligation of the law because it frees us from its curse.

Note 2. It is a **law that gives freedom**, for there is a great deal of freedom purchased by Christ.

(1) We are freed from the law as a covenant of works. We are not absolutely bound to such rigor on such strict terms. We should aim at complete obedience but not despair if we cannot reach it. A gracious heart cannot offend a good God without sadness. Sin is still damning in its own nature, still a violation of a righteous law, still an affront to God. You have more reason to be strict, because you have more help. We have more advantages, and therefore we should pay more attention to duty: see Philippians 3:1-11. People who are content with little grace have no grace. We must obey as children, not as servants: "I will spare them, just as in compassion a man spares his son" (Malachi 3:17).

(2) We are freed from being condemned. The law may condemn the *actions*, but it cannot condemn the *person*. So we have "died to the law" (Galatians 2:19) and the law to us (Romans 7:6), and therefore the apostle says, "Therefore, there is now no condemnation for those who are in Christ Jesus" (Romans 8:1).

(3) We are freed from the curse of the law. Ungodly hearts grow worse under restraint, just as water swells when the flow is stopped. A prohibition to a gracious heart is reason enough to carry out a duty, because God wills it.

(4) We are freed from slavery. By nature people carry out duties from slavish principles: "For you did not receive a spirit that makes you a slave again to fear" (Romans 8:15). The great principle in the Old Testament was fear. Therefore it was said, "The fear of the Lord is the beginning of wisdom" (Proverbs 9:10); and, "Fear God and keep his commandments, for this is the whole duty of man" (Ecclesiastes 12:13). Fear is represented as the great principle of duty and worship in the Old Testament and suited that dispensation. But in the New Testament we read that "love compels us" (2 Corinthians 5:14).

Application. This shows us the happiness of those who are in Christ. The law to a believer is a law of freedom; to someone else it is the law of slavery and death. We may "serve him without fear" (Luke 1:74)—that is, without slavish fear. Beasts are urged on with goads; but Christians are led by sanctified affections, motives of grace, and considerations of gratitude. Look to yourselves, then, to see whether you are in Christ or not. The same apostle who groaned under the body of death delighted in the law of the Lord in the inward man: see Romans 7. God's restraints do not enslave us; only our own corruptions enslave us.

Note 3. We shall be judged by **the law** on the last day; see Romans 2:12. The apostle argues that all who are not in Christ are under condemnation.

This was either a law written on tables of stone, as for the Jews, or on tables of the heart, as with Gentiles. All are judged according to the declarations of God's will. However their actions are scanned by a law, their faith will be judged and approved by their works, which, though they are not the causes of glory, yet are evidence for it. That works are brought into judgment is seen from Matthew 25:34-39. Also, Revelation 20:12 says, "The dead were judged according to what they had done." The Judge of the world will show that he acts rightly.

Again, if we are to be judged according to the measure of light and knowledge that we have of **the law**, we must bring forth fruits appropriate to God's dispensation. It is sad that after **the law** is written on the heart, it should be broken.

Note 4. It is a great help in our Christian life to think about the day of judgment. There are evangelical reflections that make the spirit strict but not servile. The apostle Paul makes the doctrine of judgment part of the Gospel: "God will judge men's secrets through Jesus Christ, as my gospel declares" (Romans 2:16)—that is, as I have taught in the dispensation of the Gospel. Christ's judgment is the highest act of his kingly office. It is most important to invite wicked people to repent, and therefore Paul chose this argument at Athens: "He commands all people everywhere to repent. For he has set a day when he will judge the world with justice" (Acts 17:30-31). There are three reasons why he used that motive. One is intimated in the text—because it is a pressing motive for repentance; and the other two may be easily derived from the context.

Secondly, Paul uses this argument to counter their plea that if they had been in the wrong they had found it a happy way, for no judgment or plague had struck them. The apostle anticipates this objection by telling them, "In the past God overlooked such ignorance" (Acts 17:30) but now takes notice. If they did not repent now, even if they escaped here, they would definitely meet with judgment later.

And, thirdly, Paul uses this argument because the pagans themselves had some kind of dread and expectation of such a day. Therefore, when Paul spoke about "the judgment to come, Felix was afraid," though he was a pagan (Acts 24:25). There cannot be a greater argument in favor of praise than when we consider our deliverance from wrath. We can look Christ in the face with comfort (see 1 John 2:28); and we may begin our triumph when others are overwhelmed with terror. So the apostle says, in effect, "In this way love is made complete among us, so that we will have confidence on the day of judgment." That is, here is the height of divine love, that when others call on mountains to cover them, we may lift up our heads with comfort and call the world's Judge our friend and father.

This awakens our souls to earnestly desire Christ's return. The good servant watches out for his master's coming (Matthew 24:44); and "the Spirit and the bride say, 'Come'" (Revelation 22:17). The day of judgment is the day of Christ's royalty and our marriage; here we are engaged, not married. When Christ left the world, there were mutual pledges of love and affection. He left us the pledge of his Spirit, just as Elijah ascending left his mantle; he took from us the pledge of our faithfulness. So everyone who has an interest in Christ must "long for his appearing" (2 Timothy 4:8).

Application. So then, reflect on this matter. Think of the Judge, of his majesty and the glory of his appearance. Think about when the graves are opened, rocks split, and Christ's unimaginable glory breaks forth with light like lightning through the heavens, when he comes riding on the clouds with flames of fire, attended with all the host of the elect angels, and the great shout and trump will summon all before the royal throne of Christ's judgment. Consider also his purity and holiness. When God revealed himself in a particular judgment, people said, "Who can stand in the presence of the Lord, this holy God?" (1 Samuel 6:20). But when Christ comes to judge all the world, with clothing "as white as snow" and the hair of his head "white like wool" (see Daniel 7:9), how will guilty creatures appear in his presence? No one can have confidence on that day except those who have unblemished innocence such as the angels or those who are washed in Christ's blood—the saints.

Consider his strict justice. Idle words weigh heavy in God's balance (Matthew 12:36). A man should never think of the severity of that day without crying out, "If you, O LORD, kept a record of sins, O Lord, who could stand?" (Psalm 130:3). "*Stand*"—that is, be able to make a strong defense on that day. Think about these things, so that you may trust in nothing but Christ's righteousness against Christ's judgment.

Note 5. **Speak and act.** Not only our actions, but our words, about which we are less careful, are judged by God and the Word: "But I tell you that men will have to give account on the day of judgment for every careless word they have spoken. For by your words you will be acquitted, and by your words you will be condemned" (Matthew 12:36-37). Usually we forget ourselves as we speak; but for careless words, not only evil but careless, we shall be judged on the last day. Evil words show a wicked heart, and careless words a vain mind. People think their *talking* should excuse their *walking*. Xenophon and Plato gave rules that men's speeches at meals should be written down so that they might be more serious. When Paul, in Romans 3:13-14, analyzes the natural man, he emphasizes the speech organs more than all the other parts: "'Their throats are open graves; their tongues practice deceit.' 'The poison of vipers is on their lips.' 'Their mouths are full of cursing and bitterness.'"

Commentary on Verse 13

*Because judgment without mercy will be shown to anyone who has
not been merciful. Mercy triumphs over judgment!*

James applies the previous directive to the matter: **Speak and act** as
those who would not come under the rigor of the covenant of works; for
if you allow yourselves to sin or do anything against **the royal law**, you
can expect nothing but **judgment without mercy**.

Because judgment without mercy. This expression shows the effect of
the covenant of works, which is **judgment** without any **mercy**.

Anyone who has not been merciful. It is as if he had said, mercy is not
only for those who honor rich men, but for those who are full of compassion for the poor; by **anyone who has not been merciful** he either means
showing no compassion for the needs of the poor or treating them
reproachfully. They were so far from giving due respect that they were
guilty of undue disrespect. Such a practice certainly will leave us ashamed
on the day of judgment.

Mercy triumphs over judgment! The word **triumphs** means
"boasts," "lifts up the head," as a person does when anything is accom-
plished with glory and success. Some take **mercy** here for God's mercy,
others for human mercy. Those who apply it to God expound it, "They
have a severe judgment; and if it is not so with everyone, it is the mercy of
God that has triumphed over his justice." But this is too forced. Others,
such as Gregory, say, with more probability, "Though unmerciful men are
severely dealt with, yet for others mercy triumphs over judgment." I
would agree with this, except that the apostle speaks here of that mercy
that man shows to man, for there seems to be a thesis and an antithesis in
the verse. The apostle asserts that the unmerciful will find no mercy. He
also says that mercy finds the judgment not only tempered but overcome;
that is, he who shows mercy is not in danger of damnation, for God will
not condemn those who imitate his own goodness, and therefore that man
may rejoice like a person who has escaped.

Now the orthodox, who apply this to human mercy, do not make this
a *cause* of our acceptance with God but an *evidence*. Mercy shown to people is a pledge of that mercy that we shall obtain with God. I confess all
this is rational; but look at the phrase in the text, and you will find that this
interpretation does not fit, for it would be harsh to say that our mercy
should rejoice against God's judgment. It is the mercy of God that rejoices
over his justice, and it is mercy in man that makes us rejoice in the mercy
of God. Mercy in God is expressed as triumph, and mercy in man is
understood as the evidence of it. The sum is: the merciful man may glory
as one who has received mercy, for the mercy of God rejoices over the jus-

tice of God on his behalf; he may rejoice over Satan, sin, death, hell, and his own conscience. In the court of heaven the mercy of God rejoices; in the court of conscience, the mercy of man. The one indicates a victory over the divine justice, the other a victory over our own fears.

Notes on Verse 13

Note 1. Man's condition under the covenant of works is very miserable. We meet with justice without being tempered by mercy. The Word speaks no comfort to such persons. Either exact duty or extreme misery are the terms of that covenant. "Do and live" and "do and die" is the only voice you will hear while you hold this view. God asked Adam, "What have you done?"—not, "Have you repented?" In the words of the prophet, "The soul who sins is the one who will die" (Ezekiel 18:20). The least breach is fatal. To fallen man the duty of that covenant is impossible, its penalty intolerable. Former sins cannot be expiated by subsequent duties. Paying new debts does not deal with the old score. Do you hope in God's mercy? One attribute is not exercised to the prejudice of another. In that covenant God intended to glorify justice, and you are accountable to a righteous law, and both law and justice must have satisfaction. As the Word speaks no comfort, so providence gives none.

All God's dispensations are judicial. The covenant of works was made with Adam and his seed, who were all natural men. The covenant of grace is with Christ and his seed, who are believers: see Isaiah 53:10. God has no interest in those who claim through Adam. Abraham's descendants came through Isaac, not through Ishmael; so God's children are in Christ. Others, who have only an average interest, cherish a vain hope: "their Maker has no compassion on them" (Isaiah 27:11).

But you will say, how can we know what we can claim? I answer:

(1) It is a reasonable deduction that you are under the old slavery if you cannot discern how your position has changed. The heirs of promise are described as those who "have fled to take hold of the hope offered to us" (Hebrews 6:18). God's children flee to Christ after considering the misery of their standing in Adam. The apostle cries out that he yearns to "gain Christ and be found in him" (Philippians 3:8-9).

(2) You may learn much from your heart's unsuitableness to the state of grace. For example:

a. If you live under the rule of any sin. James says that he who is guilty of one is guilty of all (see 2:10). Then the devil has an interest in you, not Christ. Habitual dispositions, good or bad, show who your father is. Note that "sin shall not be your master, because you are not under law, but under grace" (Romans 6:14). An interest in grace cannot coexist with a known sin.

b. If you abuse grace, you make grace an enemy, and then justice will take up the case of abused mercy. Usually people please themselves if they are right in doctrine but take no notice of that stain that is imperceptibly brought into their behavior. Beware when you use the Gospel as an excuse for neglecting your duty. There are Antinomians in life as well as doctrine.

Note 2. Unmerciful people find no mercy.

(1) This is a sin most unsuitable to grace. Kindness makes us pity misery: "You are to love those who are aliens, for you yourselves were aliens" (Deuteronomy 10:19). The man who was forgiven and grabbed his fellow-servant by the throat lost his pardon (Matthew 18:21-35). We pray, "Forgive us our debts, as we also have forgiven our debtors" (Matthew 6:12). God's love to us melts the soul and affects us not only with contrition toward God but compassion to our brothers. At Zurich, when the Gospel was first preached, they freed their prisoners, out of a sense of gratitude for their own deliverance by Christ.

(2) This attitude is unlike God; he gives and forgives. How will you look God in the face if you should be so opposed to him? Being unmerciful is twofold—when we neither give nor forgive. It shows:

a. A defect in giving. They ask, and your hearts are like flint. We are as much at fault when we do not do what we should do as when we do what we should not do. Covetousness and violence both weigh heavy in God's balance; and you may be as cruel in neglect as in injury.

b. Denying pardon to those who have wronged us. They have done you hurt, but you must be like your Heavenly Father. No one can do you as much harm as you have done to God.

Note 3. God usually retaliates and deals with people according to their wickedness. Asa, who put the prophet in the stocks, had diseased feet. Well, then, when it is so, know the sin by the judgment, and silence your complaining. Adoni-bezek, a heathen, observed, "God has paid me back for what I did to them" (Judges 1:7). So pray that God will not deal with you according to your iniquities.

Note 4. God acts mercifully with delight; his mercy triumphs over justice (see Micah 7:18; Jeremiah 32:41). God is infinitely just as well as merciful; this should encourage you as you approach God. Mercy is as acceptable to God as it is to you. Although the devil accuses the brothers, yet because mercy has triumphed over judgment, therefore we may triumph over Satan and go to heaven singing.

Note 5. Showing mercy is a sign of our interest in God's mercy: "Blessed are the merciful, for they will be shown mercy" (Matthew 5:7). "They will be shown": God will deal kindly with them, but it is mercy they receive, not a just reward. "A generous man will prosper" (Proverbs 11:25). I will show you what this mercy is. It is manifested:

(1) In showing compassion. Jesus had compassion on the multitude (Matthew 15:32); so should we. It is not mercy unless it springs from compassion. Heart and hand must go together. Generosity starts with compassion.

(2) In contributing to needy people. It is not enough to say, "Keep warm" (2:16).

(3) In forgiving offenses "seventy-seven times" (Matthew 18:22). Cicero said of Caesar, "He forgot nothing but injuries"; so should you.

Secondly, I shall show you when an act shows itself to be mercy:

(1) When it is done out of duty and the way God requires: "Do not forget to do good and to share with others, for with such sacrifices God is pleased" (Hebrews 13:16). Money must be given sacrificially, and given to people for God's sake.

(2) It must spring from good motives. The right motive is a sense of God's mercy; it is a thank-offering, not a sin-offering.

Commentary on Verse 14

What good is it, my brothers, if a man claims to have faith but has no deeds? Can such faith save him?

Here is the second exhortation against boasting about an idle faith. Some false hypocrites professed faith in Christ, and James proves the vanity of this conceit with several arguments.

What good is it, my brothers . . . ? That is, how will it further the purpose of religion? Similarly the apostle Paul, when he refutes other such presumptuous attacks, says, "I am nothing" (1 Corinthians 13:2); that is, he is of no esteem with God.

If a man claims to have faith. That is, he boasts about it to others or is proud and conceited. The apostle does not say, "If anyone has faith," but **if a man claims to have faith.** Faith, where it really exists, is profitable for salvation. He that *has* faith is certain of salvation, but this is not so with those who *claim* to have faith. In this whole discourse the apostle shows not *what justifies* but *who is justified*; not what faith *does*, but what faith *is*. The context does not show that faith without works does not justify, but that assent without works is not faith. The justification he speaks about has not so much to do with the person as with faith.

But has no deeds. That is, no fruit of holiness comes from it. The Roman Catholics foolishly restrict this to acts of charity. There are other products of faith, for it is a grace that has a universal influence in all the offices of the holy life.

Can such faith save him? That is, he is pretending to have faith; otherwise, faith saves. So Paul says in Ephesians 2:8-9, "For it is by grace you have been saved, through faith . . . not by works." Certainly our apostle here means pretending to have faith; otherwise this would be a direct contradiction.

Notes on Verse 14

Note 1. Fake graces are fruitless and unprofitable. Formal graces, as well as formal duties, do not help the spirit. It is a kind of blasphemy to disguise an impure life under a profession of faith. Less dishonor is brought to God by open opposition than by a Christian's profession that is used as a cover and excuse for profanity.

Note 2. Faked faith is easy and common. People are prone to say they have faith. When they see the uselessness of works and cannot stand before God by that claim, they pretend to have faith.

Note 3. **But has no deeds**. James shows that he means only saying that they have faith if there are no works and fruits derived from it. Where there is true faith, there will be deeds. There are three things that encourage the soul to carry out duty—a strong principle, a mighty aid, a high aim; all these exist where faith is. The strong principle is God's love, the mighty aid is God's Spirit, the high aim is God's glory.

(1) For the principle, where there is faith there will be love. Affection follows persuasion, and where there is love there will be work; therefore we often read about "the love you have shown" (Hebrews 6:10) and "your labor prompted by love" (1 Thessalonians 1:3).

(2) There is mighty aid received from the life-giving Spirit. Man's great excuse is lack of power. Faith plants us in Christ and so receives power from him. He lives in us by his Spirit, and we live in him by faith; and therefore we "bear much fruit" (John 15:5). It is noticeable that in verses 17 and 26 the apostle calls a faith without deeds a **dead** or lifeless faith, void of the life of the Spirit. Where there is life there will be action. Hypocrites are said to be "without fruit and uprooted—twice dead" (Jude 12). Twice dead—dead in their natural condition and dead in their profession of faith, and then uprooted; this is those who never had any vital influence from Christ.

(3) Where there is faith, there God will be glorified. Faith that receives grace gives back glory: ". . . glorify God on the day he visits us" (1 Peter 2:12). When God visits their souls in mercy, they will be thinking of how

they may glorify him, for faith is ingenuous and cannot take without giving. Well, then, use your faith. This is not an inactive assent; there will be deeds that you know will be good if they are done in Christ. "Apart from me you can do nothing" (John 15:5); but "I can do everything through him who gives me strength" (Philippians 4:13)—that is, by the influence of his grace and being done for Christ—that is, for his sake and glory: see Philippians 1:20. Paul's whole life was consecrated to Christ for the purpose of his glory. In short, those who work in Christ are united to him by faith.

Note 4. **Can such faith save him?** That is, will you come before God with these hopes of salvation? We should cherish no confidence that will not abide the day of the Lord. Will this be a sufficient plea, then, when all mankind is either to be damned or saved, to say you made profession (1 John 2:28)? The solemnity of Christ's coming is often used to expose groundless hopes: "Be always on the watch, and pray . . . that you may be able to stand before the Son of Man" (Luke 21:36)—that is, without shame and remorse at his coming; "that we will have confidence on the day of judgment" (1 John 4:17). People consider what will serve the present, what will quiet the heart, that they may follow their business or pleasures with the least trouble. But consider what will serve you for salvation, what will serve on the day of death or the day of judgment. No plea is sufficient but that which may be urged before the throne of the Lamb. So then, urge this on your souls: will this faith save me, so that I may be bold on the day of judgment? As Christ asked Peter three times, "Do you truly love me?" (John 21:16), so put the question again and again to your own soul: can I look Christ in the face with these desires? Sincere graces are called "things that accompany salvation" (Hebrews 6:9). This is the end of all self-examination: is it a saving grace? Nothing should satisfy me but what can save me.

Commentary on Verses 15-16

Suppose a brother or sister is without clothes and daily food. If one of you says to him, "Go, I wish you well; keep warm and well fed," but does nothing about his physical needs, what good is it? In the same way, faith by itself, if it is not accompanied by action, is dead.

Suppose a brother or sister. The apostle compares faith and good deeds and shows that phony faith avails no more than phony good deeds. By **brother or sister** he means Christians, united together by the bond of the same profession.

Is without clothes [naked, KJV]. That is, badly clothed; "nakedness" is often used in this way: see 1 Corinthians 4:11 (KJV).

And daily food. They have not enough to sustain life for a day. Christ calls this "daily bread" (Matthew 6:11). Under these two headings of nakedness and hunger James includes all the necessities of the human life, for these are the things absolutely necessary. Therefore Christ says, "Do not worry, saying, 'What shall we eat?' . . . or 'What shall we wear?'" (Matthew 6:31). "But if we have food and clothing, we will be content with that" (1 Timothy 6:8). And Jacob promised to worship if God gave him "food to eat and clothes to wear" (Genesis 28:20).

If one of you says to him. That is, someone who does not do them good in any way; otherwise good wishes are not to be despised, and some can only give a small amount of money, prayers, and advice.

"I wish you well." A solemn form of greeting. See Mark 5:34; Luke 7:50 and 8:48.

"Keep warm." That is, be clothed; this is in contrast with **without clothes.** Thus in Job 31:20 we read, "warming him with the fleece from my sheep."

"And well fed." Some translate this, "Be filled"; that is, may you have food to sustain your hunger.

But does nothing about his physical needs. That is, when you are able to; otherwise good wishes are acceptable. So "a cup of cold water" is welcome (Matthew 10:42). James's chief aim was to shame the rich, who tried to do their duty with a few cheap words and charitable wishes. This was a common offense, as is clear from 1 John 3:18, "Let us not love with words or tongue but with actions and in truth."

What good is it? That is, for the poor. The stomach is not filled with words, or the back clothed with wishes. This is like the mad person who tried to pay his debts with the noise of money and instead of opening his purse shook it. The poor will not thank you for good wishes, and neither will God for saying you have faith.

Notes on Verses 15-16

Note 1. An excellent way to discover our deceitful dealing with God is to compare it with our own dealings with one another. Christ made the Pharisees judge themselves (Matthew 21). Those who despised, abused, and persecuted the messengers killed the son; so Christ says to them, "What will he do to those tenants?" They reply, "He will bring those wretches to a wretched end . . . and he will rent the vineyard to other tenants" (verses 40-41). So will God do to you, says Christ (verse 43). God appealed to the Jews with a parable: "Judge between me and my vineyard" (Isaiah 5:3). We shall soon see the irrationality of our inferences in divine matters when we apply the case to human affairs. It is like saying, "My master is good; therefore I will offend him and displease him."

Note 2. **Suppose a brother or sister.** God's own people may be destitute of the necessities of life: "the world was not worthy of them" (Hebrews 11:38). It is true that David says, "I was young and now I am old; yet I have never seen the righteous forsaken or their children begging bread" (Psalm 37:25); but either he is speaking about his own experience, or else he is referring to the shameful trade of begging, which among the Jews was a token of God's curse (see Psalm 59:15). Certainly the Jews had more of the worldly and outward blessing of the covenant than believers did under the Gospel, as this was more appropriate for their dispensation.

Note 3. Mere words will not discharge duty. Good words are good in themselves and do become a Christian; but they are not enough. Words show that you know about your duty; mere words show that you lack a heart to carry out your duty.

Note 4. More particularly observe that a few charitable words are not enough. Words are cheap; compliments cost nothing. Will you serve God with what costs nothing? Words are but a cold kind of pity. The stomach is not filled with words but meat; nor is the back clothed with good wishes. Words are but a derision; you mock the poor when you bid them, **"keep warm and well fed"** and do not attend to their necessities. This is a kind of mocking of God. "Do not be deceived: God cannot be mocked" (Galatians 6:7). James is speaking about people who want to be thought charitable, but it was mere words.

Commentary on Verse 17

In the same way, faith by itself, if it is not accompanied by action, is dead.

Here James shows that mere profession of faith is no better than verbal charity. God looks on it as **dead,** cold, and useless.

In the same way, faith. James speaks according to their presumption: you call it faith; and it looks like faith, but it is dead in itself.

If it is not accompanied by action. He means not only good deeds but all other fruits of faith.

Is dead. The apostle alludes to a corpse or a dead plant, which only appears to be alive. It is dead with respect to root, and dead with respect to fruit. It is void of the life of Christ, and it is void of good fruits. Operation or motion is an argument for and an effect of life.

Not accompanied. The Greek means it is dead in itself; that is, no matter how great it is, it is all dead. The *King James Version* translates this **being alone,** denoting the emptiness, barrenness, and nakedness of such a profession; and so it ties in with that well known Protestant maxim, "faith alone justifies, but not faith that is alone."

Notes on Verse 17

False faith is a **dead** faith. It cannot act any more than a dead body can stand up and walk; it is dead, because it is not united to Christ. True faith plants us in Christ, and so we receive virtue and life from him: "I live by faith in the Son of God" (Galatians 2:20). Faith is the life that animates the whole body of obedience. So, here is a test for your faith: does it receive life from Christ? Does it act? If Christ is in you, he wants to live in you. Never think of living *with* Christ unless you live *in* Christ; and no one lives in Christ unless he bears "much fruit" (John 15:5).

Commentary on Verse 18

But someone will say, "You have faith; I have deeds." Show me your faith without deeds, and I will show you my faith by what I do.

The apostle amplifies this argument against an empty faith by imagining a dialogue between a believer and a boasting hypocrite. So the dispute does not lie so much between faith and deeds as between faith pretended and faith revealed by deeds. The apostle does not introduce them by saying, "You stand on your faith and I on my deeds," but says, **Show me your faith without deeds, and I will. . . ."** That is, show me a warrant for your faith, and I will soon prove my own.

But someone will say. That is, some true believer may come and argue like this with a boasting hypocrite.

"You have faith." Whatever you say, that is all you have—a mere profession of faith, or at best just some historical assent; the apostle grants that not only to them but to the demons (verse 19).

"I have deeds." He does not mean deeds without faith; that is contrary to what the text says: **I will show you my faith by what I do.** Deeds without faith are like a building without a foundation, mere acts of nature varnished with common grace. You boast with your tongue about faith; I shall not boast but will produce deeds that are a real commendation. Christ produces no other testimony but his deeds (Matthew 11:4-5).

Show me your faith without deeds. There are various readings of the original Greek. Some manuscripts read only, "Show me your faith"—and I will soon demonstrate mine. The best copies have **without deeds**, and the meaning is: you lack the truest testimony and demonstration of faith. Now show me such a faith; that is, make it good by any warrant from the principles of our religion.

And I will show you my faith by what I do. That is, soon demonstrate it to the world, or soon show it to be true faith out of the Word.

Notes on Verse 18

Note 1. A good way to convict hypocrites is to show how grace works in true Christians. The apostle begins a dialogue between them; in the same way Christ compares the two builders (Matthew 7:24ff.). Do we live as true Christians do—as those who through faith and patience inherit the promises?

Note 2. **Show me your faith without deeds.** In all our hopes and conceits of grace we should always look to the warrant we have for them. Can I show or prove this to be faith or love by any rational grounds or arguments from Scripture? Presumption is a rash trust, without any actual or clear ground. It is good to believe "as the Scripture has said" (John 7:38), to cherish no persuasion without seeing a clear warrant.

Note 3. Deeds are evidence of true faith. Graces are not dead, useless habits; they will have some results when they are weakest and in their infancy. As soon as Paul was born again, God said of him, "he is praying" (Acts 9:11). Newborn children will cry before they are able to walk.

(1) This is the evidence by which we must judge. Many Scriptures lay down evidence taken from sanctification and the holy life; they were written for this very purpose: see especially Psalm 119; 1 John 3:14, 19; 5:13. In many places promises are given, with descriptions taken from the meekness, piety, and good deeds of the saints: see Psalm 1:1-2; 32:1-9. Good deeds are the most obvious sign; all causes are known by their effects. Apples, leaves, and blossoms are evident when the life and sap are not seen.

(2) This is also the evidence by which Christ must judge: "judged according to what they had done" (Revelation 20:12). "Away from me, you evildoers!" (Matthew 7:23). They claimed to believe, but they had no deeds. See also Matthew 25:41-43.

Application. You must make use of this note to judge yourselves and to judge others.

(1) Yourselves. When the causes are hidden, the effects are obvious; therefore you can test graces by their results. Deeds are not the foundation of faith but evidence of it. Comfort may be increased by seeing good deeds, but it is not built upon them.

(2) Other people may be judged by their works. Where there is knowledge and a good life, it is not Christian to suspect the heart. Profession of faith may be counterfeited, but when it is honored with deeds you must leave the heart to God. To be **faultless** and **look after orphans and widows** is **pure religion** (1:27); that is what reveals it. Empty profession of faith may have more of fashion in it than power; but profession honored with deeds is love's rule to judge by.

Commentary on Verse 19

You believe that there is one God. Good! Even the demons believe that—and shudder.

This example shows what sort of faith he is arguing against—namely, the sort that consists in mere speculation—which can no more save anyone than looking at the sun can take you to the sun itself.

You believe. That is, you assent to this truth; the lowest act of faith is called believing.

There is one God. He gives this instance, without limiting the matter to this, partly because this was the first article of the creed, the fundamental truth in religion, and the critical difference between Christians and pagans. He means to include assent to other articles of faith.

Good! He approves of this assent as being good, though not sufficient; it is not saving, but it is good as a preparation and is required: "Hear, O Israel: The LORD our God, the LORD is one" (Deuteronomy 6:4; see also 1 John 4:2).

Even the demons believe that. That is, they assent to this truth and to other truths revealed in the Word.

And shudder. This word signifies extreme fear and horror of spirit; it comes from a word that implies the noise that is caused by the sea. Now, this clause is added not to imply (as some people suppose) that the demons do more than assent, having an experience of some type in their feelings, but to disprove this kind of faith and to show that it is not saving. The demons have an assent that causes horror and torment, but they do not have a faith that causes confidence and peace, the proper fruit of justifying faith (see Romans 5:1; Ephesians 3:12).

Notes on Verse 19

Note 1. Mere assent to the articles of religion does not imply true faith. True faith unites us to Christ; it knows his person. It is not only an assent to a Gospel proposition; you are not justified by that, but by being one with Christ. It was the mistake of former ages to make the promise rather than the person of Christ the formal object of faith. The promise is the warrant, Christ is the object; therefore, the way Scripture talks of this, faith terminates in him. There is not only *assent* in faith, but *consent*; not only an assent to the truth of the Word, but a consent to take Christ. There must be an act that is directly and formally about the person of Christ. A person may be right in opinion and judgment but of vile affections; and an ungodly "Christian" is in as great a danger as a pagan, idolater, or heretic, for even if his judgment is sound, his manners are heretical. True believing is not an act of the understanding only but a work of "all your heart" (Acts 8:37).

I admit that some expressions of Scripture seem to lay much weight on assent, such as 1 John 4:2 and 5:1, 1 Corinthians 12:3, and Matthew 16:16-17. But these passages either show that assent, where it is serious, comes from some special revelation, or else, if they give assent as evidence of grace, we must distinguish contexts. The wind that blows on our backs blew in their faces; and what draws many people to assent to the Gospel discouraged them. Therefore do not be satisfied with mere assent; this costs nothing and is worth nothing. There is an "embodiment of knowledge" (Romans 2:20) as well as "a form of godliness" (2 Timothy 3:5). An "embodiment of knowledge" is nothing but an idea of truth in the brain, when there is no power or goodness to change and transform the heart.

Note 2. **Good!** It is good to acknowledge the least appearance of good in people. So far so good, says the apostle. To commend what is good is the best way to mend the rest. This is a wonderful art of drawing people on further and further. So far as it is good, acknowledge it. "I praise you," says Paul, and later on, "I have no praise for you" (1 Corinthians 11:2, 17). Jesus loved a young man for his moral excellence (Mark 10:21). It was a hopeful step. The infant working of grace should be embraced on the lap of commendation or, like weak things, fostered with much gentleness and care.

Note 3. The demons assent to the articles of Christian religion. This comes about partly through the subtlety of their natures—they are intellectual essences, and partly because they have seen miracles of providence.

152

They are aware of the power of God in rescuing people from their paws; so they are forced to acknowledge that there is a God and to consent to many truths in the Scriptures. Many truths are acknowledged at the same time in Matthew 8:29,"Son of God . . . have you come here to torture us before the appointed time?" Paul commanded a spirit "in the name of Jesus Christ" (Acts 16:18). And an evil spirit answered the sons of Sceva, "Jesus I know and Paul I know about, but who are you?" (Acts 19:15). The spirit acknowledged that Jesus as the Master and Paul as the servant and messenger had mightily shaken his power and kingdom. So then, never rest content with the demons' faith. Can the demons be justified or saved? They believe there is a God, that there is a Christ, that Christ died for sinners. A Christian is to exceed and go beyond demons—indeed, beyond other people, beyond pagans, beyond hypocrites in the church.

Note 4. Horror is the effect of the demons' knowledge; the more they know of God, the more they shudder. They were terrified at a miracle or any glorious revelation of Christ's power on earth. So you may learn:

(1) Light that gives us no comfort is only darkness. The demons have knowledge but no comfort and so are said to be "kept in darkness" (Jude 6). The more they think about God, the more they shudder. It is miserable to have only enough light to awaken conscience and enough knowledge to be self-condemned, to know of God but not to enjoy him. The demons cannot choose but abominate their own thoughts of God. Do not rest until you have the sort of knowledge of God that gives comfort: "in your light we see light" (Psalm 36:9). There is light in this light; all other light is darkness.

(2) All knowledge of God apart from Christ is uncomfortable. That is the reason the demons shudder; they cannot know God as a Father but as a judge, not as a friend but as an enemy. Faith looking at God as Father and friend gives peace to the soul: see Romans 5:1. "Love drives out fear, because fear has to do with punishment" (1 John 4:18). This is the misery of demons and damned men and natural men, that they cannot think of God without horror; whereas this is the great solace and comfort of the saints, that there is a God: "your name is like perfume poured out," full of fragrance and refreshing (Song of Songs 1:3). Salt waters strained through the earth become sweet. God's attributes, which are in themselves terrible and dreadful to a sinner, bring us comfort and sweetness when they come to us through Christ.

Commentary on Verse 20

You foolish man, do you want evidence that faith without deeds is useless?

Here James reinforces the argument against an ungodly profession of faith. The dispute is not about the cause of justification but about what we should think about an empty faith.

You foolish man. He is an empty man, a metaphor taken from an empty container. It is the parallel word to "Raca," "fool," which is forbidden in Matthew 5:22. You will say, was it lawful for the apostle to use such words of contempt and disgrace? I answer:

(1) Christ does not forbid the word, but the word used in anger. We find "fool" used by Christ himself: "You blind fools!" (Matthew 23:17); "How foolish you are, and how slow of heart to believe" (Luke 24:25). Paul, too, says, "You foolish Galatians!" (Galatians 3:1). There is a difference between necessary correction and contemptuous speech.

(2) The apostle does not direct this to any one person but to a particular kind of people. Such a way of speaking to individuals savors of private anger, but being directed to a particular kind of people merely expresses a justified public reproof.

Do you want evidence . . . ? That is, do you want to understand the matter properly or to listen to what can be said against your faith? A similar form of words is used in Romans 13:3—"Do you want to be free from fear of the one in authority?"—that is, to be taught how not to fear him.

That faith without deeds is useless. Note that he does not say, "faith is useless without deeds," but **faith without deeds is useless.** There is a difference. If he had said that faith is useless without deeds, it would have argued that deeds are the cause that give life to faith, whereas they are effects that show there is life in faith. For instance, "a man without motion is dead" is correct, but "a man is dead without motion" is quite different. Briefly, in this argument the apostle presupposes several things:

(1) The way to know graces is by their results.

(2) Deeds are an effect of faith: **faith without deeds is useless,** and deeds are useless without faith. So deeds that are gracious are a proper, perpetual, and inseparable part of faith; they are effects that do not give life to faith but declare it, just as apples do not give life to the tree but demonstrate that life.

Notes on Verse 20

Note 1. **Do you want evidence . . . ?** False and mistaken faith usually means either that people do not understand what faith is, or that they are not thinking about what they are doing. Ignorance and lack of thought allow unwarrantable assumptions of faith to slip by without notice.

Note 2. **You foolish man.** People with shallow faith are vain, like empty containers, full of wind, and make the greatest sound; they are full of windy presumptions and boasting professions.

(1) Full of wind, they have a little airy knowledge, which puffs up: "ineffective and unproductive in your knowledge of our Lord Jesus Christ" (2 Peter 1:8). There is knowledge, but it is ineffective and unproductive—empty of any solid grace.

(2) They make a big noise; they can talk about grace, boast of knowledge, glory in their faith. Usually these presumptuous people are of a slight, frothy spirit and are all for tongue and an empty profession. A vain faith and a vain man often go together.

Note 3. Hypocrites must be roused with some sharpness. So the apostle says, **You foolish man.** John the Baptist called people, "You brood of vipers!" (Matthew 3:7). Hypocrites do not usually think and usually have a sleepy conscience, so that we must not whisper but cry out aloud. An open sinner has a constant torment and bondage on his spirit, which is soon felt and soon awakened; but a hypocrite is able to make defenses and replies. We must, by the warrant of these great examples, deal with him more roughly; mildness only soothes him in his error.

Note 4. An empty, barren faith is a dead faith.

(1) It may go with a natural state in which we are dead in trespasses and sins.

(2) It does not receive the life-giving influence of the Spirit.

(3) It lacks the effect of life. All life is the beginning of operation, tends to operation, and is increased by operation; so faith is dead, like the root of a tree in the ground, when it cannot produce the ordinary effects and fruits of faith.

(4) It is not available to eternal life and of no more use and service to you than a dead thing. Pluck it off! Who wants a dead plant in the garden? "Why should it use up the soil?" (Luke 13:7).

Commentary on Verse 21

Was not our ancestor Abraham considered righteous for what he did when he offered his son Isaac on the altar?

Here James puts forward something that might convince the vain man, taken from the example of Abraham—the believers of the Old and New Testaments being all justified the same way.

Was not our ancestor Abraham . . . ? James gives the example of Abraham because he was the prime example and idea of justification, and because many people were inclined to plead the example Paul puts forward in Romans 4:1-4, and because Abraham was specially revered among the Jews. James calls him **our ancestor** because he was so to the people James was writing to, the twelve dispersed tribes, and because he was ancestor to all the faithful, who are described as those who "walk in the footsteps of the faith that our father Abraham had" (Romans 4:12). And indeed this is the solemn name and title that is given to Abraham in the Scriptures—"our father Abraham": see John 8:53; Acts 7:2; Romans 4:1.

Considered righteous for what he did. That is, declared to be righteous because of what he did before God and the world. But you will say, is this not contrary to Scripture? Romans 3:20 says, "no one will be declared righteous in his sight by observing the law"; and particularly it is said of Abraham that he was not justified by works (Romans 4:2). How shall we reconcile this difference?

James speaks about some special justification that Abraham received when he offered Isaac; and you will find that from God he then received justification of his faith, though thirty years before that he had received justification of his person. When he was an idolater and ungodly (Joshua 24:2; Romans 4), God called him through his grace (Genesis 12:1-3) and justified him. "Abram believed the LORD, and he credited it to him as righteousness" (Genesis 15:6). He was justified by imputation and absolved from guilt and sin; so it could not damn him. But now, when he offered Isaac, his faith was justified to be true and right, for that command was meant to test it. Therefore, his obedience to God did two things: it renewed the promise of Christ to him (Genesis 22:16-18), and it gave him a testimony and declaration of his sincerity (verse 12).

It seems to me that as deeds are signs to us by which we may judge the quality of faith, so God judges according to what we have done, as is distinctly said in Revelation 22:12. God will demonstrate the faith of his saints to be right by producing their works and will reveal the ungrounded hopes of others by their works also, for great and small are all judged according to that rule. Not only hereafter but now also God judges according to works; that is, he looks upon them as testimonies and declarations of faith or of the lack of faith.

Diodati excellently comments that justification in Paul is opposite to the condemnation of a sinner in general, and justification in James is opposite to the condemnation of a hypocrite in particular. In Paul's sense a sinner is absolved; in James's sense a believer is approved. And so the apostles agree, as far as I can see, without exception.

When he offered his son Isaac on the altar. Note that though Abraham only offered him in purpose and vow, and not actually, James says **he offered**. Hebrews 11:17 also says, "By faith Abraham . . . offered Isaac"; he intended to do it and, if God had continued the command, would actually have done it. God counts as done what is about to be done and takes note of what is in the heart, even if it is not actually done.

Notes on Verse 21

Note 1. Those who want Abraham's privileges must see to it that they have Abraham's faith. You claim to be his descendants as believers. Two things are notable in Abraham's faith:

(1) He received the promises with all humility: "Abraham fell facedown" (Genesis 17:3), as mightily abashed and abased in himself to see God deal thus with him.

(2) By his faith he made good the promises, being upright before God and behaving in every way for his glory. There are two instances of his obedience on which the Holy Spirit has set a special note: one was leaving his father's house (Genesis 12:1), thus denying himself his possessions; the other was sacrificing his son (Genesis 22:1-2), thus denying himself his hopes. God calls every believer more or less to deny something that is near and dear.

Note 2. Believers must see that they honor and justify their faith by deeds. Never content yourselves with empty profession. Profession of faith shows what party we belong to, but holiness shows that we belong to God. I will give you a few directions about how to reflect on your graces as evidence of your state.

(1) You must be loyal to Christ. Many people seek all their happiness in the gracious dispositions of their own souls and so neglect Christ. This is putting the love token before the loved person. To rectify it:

a. Let there be a thorough going out of yourselves. Be sure to keep the heart righteous; and do not neglect the cornerstone on which to found your hopes. Assurance is usually given after the solemn and direct exercise of faith: "Having believed, you were marked in him with a seal" (Ephesians 1:13). Here the apostle shows the order of the Spirit's sealing, *after* believing or going to Christ, and the quality of the seal, as a Spirit of promise. He implies that when the thoughts have been freshly exercised in thinking about our own unworthiness and God's free grace and promises, then we are most fit to receive the witness and certification of the Spirit.

b. In viewing and enjoying your graces, still keep your heart on Christ. See what would become of you if it were not for free grace. God could find something for which to condemn you, not only in the worst sins but in the best duties; the most regenerate person dares not entrust his soul to the heavenliest thought he ever conceived. When Nehemiah had done something zealously, he added, "Remember me for this also, O my God, and show mercy to me according to your great love" (Nehemiah 13:22), intimating that God might find enough to ruin him even in this. So, in the face of the greatest evidence you should see free grace as the surest refuge. Jehoshaphat, when he had all the strength of Judah, numbered at 500,000, still went to God as if there were no other way: "We have no power to face this vast army that is attacking us. We do not know what to do, but our eyes are upon you" (2 Chronicles 20:12).

c. When all is said and done, you must the more earnestly renew your addresses to Christ and exercise faith with the more advantage and cheerfulness. You have much more encouragement to agree with him when you survey his bounty to your souls and consider those emanations of grace by which you are enabled to do good deeds. "I write these things to you who believe in the name of the Son of God so that you may know that you have eternal life" (1 John 5:13). He means that, having this assurance, they might renew the act of faith all the more cheerfully—as when Thomas felt Christ's wounds and had all the more reason to believe (John 20:27). Estius comments that this was "by a renewed and increased faith." So when you have felt Christ's bounty to you and by good deeds have cleared up your interest in eternal life, you have the greatest reason to cast yourselves on Christ again by faith and confidence. The whole business of our justification before God is carried on by a continual act of faith, from one act and degree to another.

(2) You must go to work with a spirit suiting the Gospel. Consider and understand your evidences and graces not in a legal perfection but as sprinkled with the blood of the covenant. If you look for love, fear, faith, hope in that perfection the law requires, the heart will still be kept unsettled; your business is to look to the truth rather than the measure. The man in Mark's Gospel could with confidence plead his faith though humbled with sad remains of unbelief: "I do believe; help me overcome my unbelief!" (9:24). We must not give false testimony against other people, much less against ourselves, and must therefore acknowledge a little good, even if it is in the midst of much evil.

(3) You must set to work prudently, understanding the nature of signs and the time to use them; everything is beautiful in its season. There are times when graces are not visible. In darkness we can see neither black nor white. In times of great dejection and discouragement the work of a Christian is not to *try* but to *believe*. "Who among you fears the LORD and obeys the word of his servant? Let him who walks in the dark, who has no light, trust in the name of the LORD and rely on his God" (Isaiah 50:10). It is most seasonable to encourage the soul to acts of faith and to reflect on the absolute promises, rather than on conditional ones. The absolute promises were intended by God as encouragements to such dis-

tressed souls. To a loose, ungodly spirit, an absolute promise is like poison; to a dejected spirit, like cheering wine. When the soul lies under fear and a sense of guilt, it is unable to judge; therefore, examination only increases the trouble. But again when the heart is drowsy and careless, trial is most appropriate; and it is best to reflect on the conditional promises, that we may think about the qualifications before we take comfort. When the heart grows rusty and secure, it is good to use Nazianzen's policy when his heart began to be corrupted with ease and pleasure: "I read the Lamentations of Jeremiah." In all spiritual cases it is good to deal prudently, lest we put ourselves into the hands of our enemies and help Satan's plans along.

(4) You must be humbly thankful, because everything comes from God. It is a vain spirit that is proud of what is borrowed or glories because he is more in debt than others: "Who makes you different from anyone else? What do you have that you did not receive?" (1 Corinthians 4:7). Whatever we find when we search, it must not be ascribed to free will but to free grace: "it is God who works in you to will and to act according to his good purpose" (Philippians 2:13). Free will establishes human merit; free grace checks it. The sun is not in debt to us because we borrow light from it, or the fountain because we draw water. Thus, lest pride taint the spirit by seeing our graces, it is good to reflect distinctly on God's bounty and our own vileness.

Note 3. **When he offered his son Isaac.** Isaac is counted as offered because that is what Abraham intended. Serious intention to obey is accepted as obedience. God has given pardon on our intent to return: "I said, 'I will confess my transgressions to the LORD'—and you forgave the guilt of my sin" (Psalm 32:5). But remember, your intentions must be like Abraham's.

(1) They must be serious and resolved, for he prepared himself to do what he was commanded. When people hope to do tomorrow what they should do today, these are fleeting intentions of which God takes no notice: "he knows the secrets of the heart" (Psalm 44:21).

(2) They must be the sort that end in action unless something stops us. When is that?

a. When we are hindered, as Abraham was, by heaven. In his case it was by divine command; in our case it will be by providence: "Because it was in your heart to build a temple for my Name, you did well to have this in your heart" (1 Kings 8:18). When providence diverts us from doing what we intended, God accepts our intention.

b. When we are hindered by weakness. "I have the desire to do what is good, but I cannot carry it out" (Romans 7:18). The apostle could not attain what he wanted to do; in such a case God looks to what is in the heart.

So then:

a. This serves to comfort God's people, who are very discouraged because they do not perform their duty as they want to. God notes your intention and judges you, as doctors do their patients—not by how much they eat, but by their appetite. Intentions and desires are works of God's own stirring up, the free offering and motions of grace. We may be over-ruled in practice, but earnest intentions that make you do what you can are usually serious and genuine. The children of God, who cannot justify what they do, plead the inner desires of their hearts: "You know all things; you know that I love you" (John 21:17); "your servants who delight in revering your name" (Nehemiah 1:11).

b. This warns us to be careful of our intentions. Many people would be more wicked if they were not restrained. God notes what is in their hearts: "Anyone who looks at a woman lustfully has already committed adultery with her in his heart" (Matthew 5:28). Seneca, too, says: "Purpose makes a man guilty, even if the act is restrained." God took note of the king of Babylon's intentions: "his purpose is to destroy, to put an end to many nations" (Isaiah 10:7). Inclinations should be watched over.

c. This shows God's readiness to receive returning sinners. As soon as the will lays down the weapons of defiance and moves toward God, the Lord runs to embrace such a poor soul, that he may satisfy it with some early comforts. "Before they call I will answer; while they are still speaking I will hear" (Isaiah 65:24). Acts of grace often anticipate acts of duty. As soon as you set your face toward God, he runs towards you.

d. This shows how we should entertain God's intentions and promises. Look on his promises with such certainty as if they were already fulfilled: "Fallen! Fallen is Babylon the Great" (Revelation 14:8). God can read duty in the intention; we have much more cause to read fulfillment in his promise. "Does he speak and then not act? Does he promise and not ful-fill?" (Numbers 23:19). His will is not changeable like ours, nor is his power restricted.

Note 4. **Offered his son Isaac on the altar.** This is his great argument of the truth of Abraham's faith. It is not an argument for faith producing every action, unless it produces actions like Abraham's. Actions that make you deny yourself are troublesome but right. David scorned any service that cost nothing. Actions fit to test believers are those where we must deny our own reason, affections, and interest. Let us see what we can in this action of Abraham's, so that we may go and do likewise.

(1) Note how great the temptation was. It was to offer his own son, the son of his love, his only son, a son longed for and obtained when "his body was as good as dead" and when "Sarah's womb was also dead" (Romans 4:19). Indeed, he was the promised son (see Romans 9:9). If Abraham had only been contending with natural affection, it would have

been a lot—love for one's children is always vehement; but there were special reasons and arguments for his love for Isaac. But Abraham was not only to conflict with natural affection but with reason, and not only with reason but with faith. He was, as it were, to execute all his hopes; and all this was to be done by himself. With his own hand he was at one stroke to cut off all his comforts; the execution of such a sentence was as harsh and bitter to flesh and blood as to be his own executioner. Go outside in shame, you who can deny yourselves so little for God, who attempt duties only when they are easy and obvious, who never care to recover them out of the hands of difficulty and inconvenience. Can you give up all that is near and dear to you? Can you offer up *your* Isaac? Can you offer up your ease and pleasure for duty? Not every action is a trial of faith, but only those that make us deny ourselves.

(2) Consider how willing he was to obey. As Abraham is the pattern of believing, so also he is the pattern of obeying. He received the promises as a picture of our faith; he offered up his son as a picture of our obedience: see Hebrews 11:17.

a. He obeyed readily and willingly: "Early the next morning Abraham got up" (Genesis 22:3). Some people would have delayed all they could, but he was up early. Usually we restrict our duty rather than restrict ourselves; we do not set about our duty early.

b. He obeyed resolutely. He concealed it from his wife and servants, and from Isaac himself, so that he might not be diverted from his purpose. Who nowadays is so wise as to arrange things so that he may not be hindered from his duty?

c. He denied worldly reason. In difficult cases we seek to avoid the command instead of seeking how we shall obey it. If we had been tested like this, we would have questioned the vision or looked for some other meaning. But Abraham did not do so, though he had occasion enough, for he was divided between believing the promise and obeying the command. God tested him in his faith; his faith was to conflict with his natural reason, as well as his obedience conflicting with his natural desire. But "Abraham reasoned that God could raise the dead" (Hebrews 11:19), and he reconciled the commandment with the promise. How easily we could have slipped out at this door and disobeyed with religious arguments. But Abraham offered Isaac.

Commentary on Verse 22

You see that his faith and his actions were working together, and his faith was made complete by what he did.

Having given the example, James now urges it upon the hypocrite who claims to have faith while cultivating an impure life.

You see. That is, it is clear. He tries to awaken the complacent worldly-liver by urging this example on his conscience.

That his faith and his actions were working together. This clause is given many senses. The Roman Catholics use it to prove that faith needs works for justification, as if works and faith were joint causes; but then the apostle would have said that actions worked together with his faith, and not faith with his actions. Among the orthodox it is expounded differently. The sense I prefer is that his faith did not rest in mere profession but was operative; it had efficacy and influence on his actions, working together with all other graces. It does not only exert itself in acts of believing but also in actions—deeds.

And his faith was made complete by what he did. This clause also has been twisted into several senses. The Roman Catholics deduce from it that in the work of justification faith receives its worth, value, and perfection from works—an idea prejudicial to the freeness of God's love and contrary to the constant teaching of the Scriptures. Faith gives value to works rather than works to faith (see Romans 14:23 and Hebrews 11:1-6); works are so far from being chief, and the more perfect cause of justification, that they are not respected as that at all.

(1) **Made complete** [KJV, **made perfect**—*Ed. note*]. That is, say some, "made known and revealed," as God's strength is said to be "made perfect in weakness" (2 Corinthians 12:9). No one will be so mad as to say that our strength adds anything to God's power, which cannot increase or decrease and has no need of any help from human weakness. Faith is **made complete** because it has the benefit of being revealed and more particularly shows itself; so faith is **made perfect**—that is, it is more fully known and apparent. The reason this expression is used, some say, is, first, because things that excel suffer a kind of imperfection while they are kept private; and second, because faith comes to maturity and perfection of growth when it can produce its own particular actions. This sense is probable. But:

(2) Others understand it to mean that faith or profession of faith is not complete until works are joined with it, faith and works being the two essential parts that make up a believer. This interpretation suits the apostle's intentions well enough.

(3) The exposition that I take to be most suitable is that faith working together with obedience is **made perfect**—that is, bettered and improved, just as our inner vigor is improved by physical exercise. In short, works do not complete faith by communicating their perfection to it but by stirring its own vigor.

Notes on Verse 22

Note 1. Faith influences all of a Christian's actions. In Hebrews 11 faith is made the great principle; actions are spoken of that strictly speaking belong to other graces. We say the general won the day, though the private soldiers acted worthily in the field, because it was under his direction. In the same way, because all other graces march and are marshaled to fight under the direction of faith, the honor of the day is ascribed to faith. Faith has great influence on all aspects of the heavenly life.

(1) Faith has the advantage of a sweet principle: "faith expressing itself through love" (Galatians 5:6). It represents the love of God and then uses its sweetness as an argument; it urges by such melting entreaties that the believer cannot say no. Paul says, "I live by faith in the Son of God, who loved me and gave himself for me" (Galatians 2:20). When the soul is hesitant faith says, "Christ loved you and gave himself for you; he was not hesitant in the work of salvation."

(2) Faith gives strong encouragement; it sees assistance in God's power, acceptance in God's grace, reward in God's bounty. When you are weakened with doubt and discouragement faith says, "Do your best, and God will accept you." When jealousy makes our heart faint and our hands feeble, faith shows the soul an angel standing at the altar with sweet incense (Revelation 8:3-4). Duty coming immediately out of our hands would smell bad; so Christ intercepts it, and it is perfumed at the hands of a mediator. Again, are you discouraged with weakness? Faith will reply, "You are weak, but God will enable you." It is an advantage, not a discouragement, to be weak in ourselves, that we may be "strong in the Lord and in his mighty power" (Ephesians 6:10). When the bucket is empty, it can be filled from the ocean more easily. Paul says, "when I am weak, then I am strong" (2 Corinthians 12:10). There is no heart too dead for God to bring to life, and he is willing. First Chronicles 15:26 says, "God had helped the Levites" when the work was physical; God helped them by taking away their weariness. And he will certainly give inner strength all the more—more love, joy, hope, which are the strength of the soul (see Nehemiah 8:10). Again, if the heart is lazy and reluctant or is content with ease and pleasure, faith can present the glory of the reward, the pleasures at God's right hand, etc.

(3) Faith breaks the power of the opposition. If the world stands in the way of duty, faith overcomes the world (see 1 John 5:4)—partly by bringing Christ into the combat, partly by spiritual replies and arguments. Reason tells us we must be for ourselves; faith tells us we must be for God. Reason says, "If I take this course, I shall be undone"; faith, by looking within the veil, sees that it is the only way to save all (2 Corinthians 3:15-17).

Well, then, from this we may infer:

(1) We need to get faith; there is as great a necessity of faith as of life. It is the life of our lives and the soul of our souls. God has arranged faith to be as necessary as Christ. What good will a deep well do us without a bucket? Whoever has a mind to work does not want to be without his tools; and who wants to be without faith if he is conscientious about his duty?

(2) Act it in all your works. No actions are good until faith works together with them; they are not acceptable, nor half so valuable: "By faith Abel offered" not only "a better sacrifice," as our translation reads (Hebrews 11:4), but "more sacrifice," as the Greek can be read. Faith is the best support you can have; worldly ends make us mangle duty, and doubts weaken us in duty.

Note 2. Faith is bettered and made more complete by acting. Neglect of our graces is why they decrease and decay; wells are the sweeter for draining. The apostle wishes Timothy to "fan into flame the gift of God" (2 Timothy 1:6). This is an allusion to the fire of the temple, which was always to be kept burning. Well, then, be much in duty, and draw out the actions of your graces. Many people are alive but not lively; decay imperceptibly leads to deadness.

Commentary on Verse 23

And the scripture was fulfilled that says, "Abraham believed God, and it was credited to him as righteousness," and he was called God's friend.

To strengthen the previous argument from the example of Abraham, James produces a testimony from Scripture to prove that Abraham had true faith and that Abraham was truly justified.

And the scripture was fulfilled. You will say, "How can this be, since that was said of Abraham long before?" Compare Genesis 15:6 with Genesis 22. And the apostle Paul says that Scripture was fulfilled in him before he was circumcised (Romans 4:10), which was before Isaac's birth, and certainly before he was offered. Luther rejects James's letter because of this, with some incivility of expression. The Roman Catholics seek to reconcile the matter by saying that though faith was credited to Abraham as righteousness before he offered Isaac, James proves that faith was not enough to justify him; he also needed actions, for, they say, his righteousness was not complete and full until it was made perfect by the addition of actions.

Note that a Scripture is said to be fulfilled in several senses—sometimes when the main point of the passage is urged; at other times when a similar case happens, and so a Scripture is quoted and said to be fulfilled not by way of argument but allusion (and a note is given by which the allusive sense may be distinguished from the main sense). When a text is quoted properly, the writer says, "that it might be fulfilled," thus noting the aim of the passage. When it is quoted by allusion or to give a parallel case, the writer says, "then it was fulfilled," implying that a parallel case occurred. So here it says, **the scripture was fulfilled**—that is, at this instance of his faith it might again be said that faith was credited to him as righteousness.

We may accept this exposition all the more because this sacrifice of his son (Genesis 22) was a greater demonstration of his faith than the sacrifice mentioned in Genesis 15. Things are said to be fulfilled when they are most clearly demonstrated, as in Acts 13:32-33 where the words "You are my Son; today I have become your Father" are said to be fulfilled at Christ's resurrection, because then he "was declared with power to be the Son of God" (Romans 1:4). So it is here; this being the evident demonstration of Abraham's faith, it appeared how truly it was said of him that he **"believed God, and it was credited to him as righteousness."** By that action he declared that he had a true, justifying faith, and therefore the Lord says after this trial, "Now I know that you fear God" (Genesis 22:12).

"Abraham believed God, and it was credited to him as righteousness." The original meaning of the phrase **it was credited to him as righteousness** is only to show that the thing was approved and accepted by God. It is often used in this way in the Old Testament, as when Phinehas' zeal is said to be "credited to him as righteousness" (Psalm 106:31). Therefore in this phrase the Scripture does not declare what the matter of our justification is, but only what value the Lord chooses to put upon acts of faith or obedience when they are performed in the face of difficulty and discouragement.

And he was called God's friend. The apostle says **he was called**—that is, he *was*; compare Isaiah 48:8, "you were called a rebel from birth"—that is, you were a rebel. So also in the New Testament: "that we should be called children of God" (1 John 3:1)—that is, that we should be children of God. Or else it alludes to the solemn name Abraham is given in Scripture, as in Isaiah 41:8, "you, O Israel . . . you descendants of Abraham my friend." See also 2 Chronicles 20:7. This title was given to Abraham because of his frequent communion with God—he often had visions—and because of his frequent covenanting with God—a great condescension, such as earthly kings offer only to their equals and friends. Therefore, in the passages where this title is given to Abraham, it has something to do with the covenant; and here it is said to be given to him for that testimony of his faith and obedience in offering Isaac, when the covenant was solemnly renewed and confirmed to him by oath.

Notes on Verse 23

Note 1. Actions ratify the Spirit's witness. The apostle says, **The scripture was fulfilled**—that is, it was seen that Abraham was indeed a believer, according to God's testimony. Sometimes the Spirit assures us by speaking to us through some inward whisper and voice, sometimes by implanting gracious dispositions, as it were writing his mind in us. It is good when we are aware of both. To look to works is the best way to prevent delusion. There is no deceit here, as in flashy joys. Fanatics are often deceived by sudden flashes of comfort. Actions, being a more palpable and constant pledge of the Spirit, bring a more solid joy: "This is how we know that we belong to the truth, and how we set our hearts at rest in his presence" (1 John 3:19)—that is, by real acts of love and charity. Flashes of comfort are only sweet and delightful while they are felt; but it is said of grace that "God's seed remains in him" (1 John 3:9), and "the anointing you received from him remains in you" (1 John 2:27). This is a lasting glory and the continual food of the soul, whereas those ravishings are like delicacies that God offers his people in times of festivity.

(1) Learn, then, that good works are not doubtful evidence. People of dark spirits will always be raising scruples, but the fault is in the people, not the evidence.

(2) Learn, too, to approve yourselves to God with all good conscience in times of trial; this will make good those imperfect whispers in your souls concerning your interest in Christ. Do as Abraham did: when called, he left his country; though he was childless, he believed the promise of numerous descendants; when God tested him, he offered Isaac. When God tries your faith or obedience with some difficulty, that especially is the time to gain assurance by being found faithful.

Note 2. Believers are God's friends. This was not just Abraham's title, but that of all the righteous. Thus Christ says, "Our friend Lazarus has fallen asleep" (John 11:11). More explicitly, he says, "I no longer call you servants. . . . Instead, I have called you friends" (John 15:15).

(1) We are God's friends because we are perfectly reconciled to him in Christ. We were enemies by nature, but God not only pardoned us but received us into friendship (Colossians 1:21-22). God not only spares converts—he delights in them. We would not have been saved if we had not been lost; the fall made way for the more glorious restoration, just as a broken bone, when it is well set, is strongest at the crack.

(2) All dispensations and duties that pass between Christ and his friends are passed in a friendly way.

a. Communication of goods. Plutarch's reasoning is good: "Friends have all things in common, but God is our friend, and therefore we cannot be in want"—a rare speech from a heathen. In the covenant God is ours, and we are his (Jeremiah 31:33 and 32:38-39; Zechariah 13:9). Great as he is, he makes himself over to us; and so by a complete resignation we are given up to him. The covenant is like a marriage contract and may be illustrated by that of the prophet Hosea: "You are to live with me . . . and I will live with you" (Hosea 3:3). God makes over himself and all his power and mercy to us, so that nothing happens to us without it being a blessing. If it is so common a mercy as rain, "there will be showers of blessing" (Ezekiel 34:26). In the same way we give ourselves up to God, even in the slightest matters of enjoyment: "HOLY TO THE LORD will be inscribed on the bells of the horses" (Zechariah 14:20); everything is consecrated.

b. Communication of secrets. "I no longer call you servants, because a servant does not know his master's business. Instead, I have called you friends, for everything that I learned from my Father I have made known to you" (John 15:15). Servants are only acquainted with what concerns their duty and work; the master commands but does not tell them the reason for the command. But now Christ had opened all the secrets of the Father concerning his own resurrection, the sending of the Holy Spirit, the calling of the Gentiles, the last judgment, eternal life, etc. And so you who lie close to Christ know his secrets: "Shall I hide from Abraham what I am about to do?" (Genesis 18:17). He will acquaint you with everything that concerns your salvation and peace. And on the other hand, believers open their secrets to God; they "have confidence to enter the Most Holy Place" (Hebrews 10:19; see also Ephesians 3:12). The word translated "with confidence" means "with liberty of speech" or, more strictly, liberty to speak all our mind. We may use some freedom with God and acquaint him with all our griefs and all our fears and all our wants and all our desires, as a friend would pour out his heart to another friend. As Exodus 33:11 says, "The LORD would speak to Moses face to face, as a man speaks with his friend."

c. Correspondence of will and desires. True friendship is built on similarity of will. God and the soul will the same thing—holiness as the means, and God's glory as the end: "You are my friends if you do what I command" (John 15:14).

d. Mutual delight. They delight in God, and God in them: "the LORD will take delight in you" (Isaiah 62:4)—in their persons, their graces, their duties. So also they delight in God, in their addresses to him, in his fellowship and presence. They cannot brook any distance, they cannot let a day pass without some communion with God.

e. God's special favor and respect to them. Others have only common mercies, but they have saving mercies. They have "hidden manna" (Revelation 2:17), joys of which others cannot conceive.

So, then:

(1) Here is comfort to the righteous, to those who have found any friend-like affection in themselves towards God. God is your friend. You were enemies, but you are made near through Christ. God delights in your persons, in your prayers, in your graces, in your outward welfare. It is a great honor to be the King's friend; you are favorites of heaven!

(2) Here is caution to you: your sins go nearest to God's heart. It was sad to Christ to be betrayed by his own disciples; it is a similar grief to his Spirit when his laws are made void by his own friends.

Commentary on Verse 24

You see that a person is justified by what he does and not by faith alone.

You see. This follows either from the whole discourse or from the particular example of Abraham. James alludes to Paul's manner of reasoning: "For we maintain that a man is justified by faith apart from observing the law" (Romans 3:28), and probably this discourse is intended to correct the abuse of that doctrine.

That a person is justified. That is, acquitted of hypocrisy; he is said to be **justified**, in our apostle's phrase, when his faith appears to be good and right, or when he is found just and righteous, just as it is said of Christ that "he appeared in a body, was vindicated by the Spirit" (1 Timothy 3:16)— that is, he was proved to be God.

By what he does. That is, by the parts and offices of the holy life.

And not by faith alone. Not by merely professing faith, just assenting—which is so far from justifying that it is not properly faith.

The main work in the discussion of this verse is to reconcile James with Paul. The conclusions seem directly opposite: see Romans 3:28 and Galatians 2:16. Paul also brings the example of Abraham against justification by works. There has been much ado to reconcile this apparent difference. Some, on this ground, deny the authority of James's letter; Luther did so, and many of the early Lutherans did. The apostles, activated by the same Spirit of truth, could not deliver contrary assertions; and though people usually out of extreme hatred of one error embrace another, yet this cannot be imagined, without blasphemy, of those who were guided by infallible assistance. It shows more reverence to the Scriptures to seek to reconcile both passages than to deny the authority of one.

(1) The Roman Catholics say that Paul speaks of the first justification, by which a man, if unjust, is made just, and that by works he understands works done without faith and grace, by the sole power and force of free will; whereas James speaks of the second justification, whereby a just person is made more just, and by works he understands those that are performed in faith and by the help of divine grace. To this I answer:

a. It confuses justification with sanctification.

b. The distinction is false and has no ground in Scripture. We can merit nothing after we are in a good state, and we are saved by grace all our lives: "in the gospel a righteousness from God is revealed, a righteousness that is by faith from first to last, just as it is written: 'The righteous will live by faith'" (Romans 1:17). If the righteousness by which a sinner is justified is wholly obtained by faith, there is no place for works at all. It is bad to associate nature with grace and to make man a co-worker in something in which God demands the sole glory.

c. It is little less than blasphemy to say that we are more just by our own works than by the merits of Christ received by faith, for they accept works to be the justification by which a person is made more just.

d. The phrase about being more just does not fit the apostle's purpose, for he is not showing how our righteousness is increased, but who has an interest in it. Nor will the adversaries grant that those against whom the apostle argues had a first and real righteousness. And besides, their view is contradicted by the example of Rahab who, according to their explanation, cannot be said to be justified in their second way of justification, and yet in our apostle's sense she is justified by works. Therefore, the Roman Catholic view will not remove the apparent contradiction between the apostles.

(2) The Arminians and Socinians go about it a different way. In order to deceive with a great appearance of fairness, they seem to ascribe everything to grace and to condemn the merit of all sorts of works because these are poor, weak, and imperfect. But they make new obedience the instrument of justification and say that God's free grace is only seen in the acceptance of our imperfect obedience. They say that Paul, when he denies justification by works, understands by works perfect obedience, such as the law required; and James only understands it as new obedience, which is the condition without which we are not justified. But to this I reply:

a. The apostle Paul does not only exclude the precise obedience of the law but the sincere obedience of the Gospel—all kinds of works—from the business of justification, as is seen in the frequent opposition of faith and works throughout the Scriptures. Take these for example: "For it is by grace you have been saved, through faith—and this not from yourselves, it is the gift of God—not by works, so that no one can boast" (Ephesians

2:8-9). "And if by grace, then it is no longer by works; if it were, grace would no longer be grace" (Romans 11:6). The two ways of grace and works are incompatible. It was the error of those against whom Paul deals in his letters to rest half upon Christ and half upon works; and that is why he is so zealous everywhere in this argument: "You who are trying to be justified by law have been alienated from Christ; you have fallen away from grace" (Galatians 5:4). For they went about to mix both the covenants and so wholly destroyed their own interest in that of grace.

b. It is a matter of dangerous consequence to set up works, under whatever pretense, as the matter or condition of our justification before God. It robs God of his glory and weakens the comfort of the creature. God's glory suffers because whatever we ascribe to ourselves is taken away from God. Now when we make our own obedience the matter of condition of our righteousness, we glory in ourselves, contrary to what is said in Romans 4:2-3; and the creature suffers loss of comfort when his righteousness before God is built on so frail a foundation as his own obedience. The examples of the children of God, who are always at a loss in themselves, show how dangerous it is to rely on ourselves. Take a few passages: "How can a mortal be righteous before God? Though one wished to dispute with him, he could not answer him one time out of a thousand. . . . Even if I were innocent, my mouth would condemn me; if I were blameless, it would pronounce me guilty. . . . Even if I washed myself with soap and my hands with washing soda, you would plunge me into a slime pit so that even my clothes would detest me" (Job 9:2-3, 20, 30-31). So also David shows that he was never able to use this plea of justifying himself by his own obedience (Psalm 143:2 and 130:3).

And in the New Testament the saints abundantly disown their obedience and righteousness, not daring to trust it—not even their new obedience on Gospel terms: "My conscience is clear, but that does not make me innocent. It is the Lord who judges me" (1 Corinthians 4:4). Paul did what he was able and was conscious of no crime or unfaithfulness in his ministry; yet all this will not justify. So he wanted to be "found in him, not having a righteousness of my own" (Philippians 3:9). He dared not trust the inquiry and search of justice with any holiness of his own.

To clear this point more fully, let me briefly state a few propositions:

First, whoever wants to be accepted by God must be righteous: "Your eyes are too pure to look on evil" (Habakkuk 1:13). God cannot give a sinner, as a sinner, a good look.

Second, not every righteousness will suffice; it must be such as will endure the pure eyes of God's glory. Hence those phrases righteous "in thy sight" (Psalm 143:2, KJV), "righteous in his sight" (Romans 3:20), and "something to boast about—but not before God" (Romans 4:2); see also Galatians 3:11 and elsewhere.

Third, such a righteousness can be found in no one. Our obedience is a covering that is too short: "What is man, that he could be pure, or one born of woman, that he could be righteous?" (Job 15:14). "Who can stand in the presence of the LORD, this holy God?" (1 Samuel 6:20). The least defect leaves us open to the challenge of the law and the plea of justice.

Fourth, this righteousness is only to be had in Christ. That is why he is called "The LORD Our Righteousness" (Jeremiah 23:6), and why Paul says he "has become for us . . . our righteousness" (1 Corinthians 1:30). Therefore, we are bidden to "seek first his kingdom and his righteousness" (Matthew 6:33). We must seek God's righteousness if we want to enter into God's kingdom.

Fifth, this righteousness is made ours by faith. Ours it must be, as in the first proposition, and ours it is only by faith: "a righteousness that is by faith from first to last" (Romans 1:17). Christ's righteousness is received by faith. It is the fittest and most self-denying grace; it is the grace that begins our union with Christ. And when we are made one with Christ, we possess his righteousness and merit, as our right, for our comfort and use.

Sixth, those who receive Christ's righteousness are also sanctified by him. New obedience is an inseparable companion of justification (see 1 Corinthians 1:30). By virtue of this union we have both: "if anyone is in Christ, he is a new creation" (2 Corinthians 5:17). So obedience is not the *condition* of justification but the *evidence*.

(3) The orthodox, though they differ somewhat in words and phrases, still agree in the same sense in reconciling James and Paul. Thus, some say Paul is arguing about the cause of justification and so excludes works, and James is arguing about the effects of justification and so enforces their presence. Others say Paul is arguing about how we are justified and James about how we shall give evidence that we are justified. One takes justification for acquittal from sin, the other for acquittal from hypocrisy; one takes it as the imputation of righteousness, the other as the declaration of righteousness. Other people say Paul is speaking about the role of faith and James about the quality of faith; Paul pleads for saving faith, and James pleads against mere assent. One speaks of justifying the person, the other of faith. All these answers are to the same effect, either subordinate to one another or differing only in expression.

Notes on Verse 24

Note 1. In the Scriptures there sometimes seems to be a difference, but there is no real conflict. The apparent difference is there for good reason.

God wants to forestall errors on every side, and the expressions of Scripture are ordered so that one may relieve another. For example, some people hold that Christ had only an imaginary body and was man only in appearance; therefore, to show the reality of his human nature you have the expression "the Word became flesh" (John 1:14). Others, straining that expression, held that the Godhead changed into humanity. To correct this excess, we have another expression: "He appeared in a body" (1 Timothy 3:16).

Note 2. A mere profession of faith is not enough to acquit us of hypocrisy. Christ would not own those who professed his name but worked iniquity (see Matthew 7:21-23); so also the church should not recognize believers for mere profession of faith. Sadly, in these times we look more for gifts and ability of speech than good works, and empty prattle weighs more than real charity.

Commentary on Verse 25

In the same way, was not even Rahab the prostitute considered righteous for what she did when she gave lodging to the spies and sent them off in a different direction?

Here James gives another example. But why does he mention Rahab?

(1) Because this act of hers is made an effect of faith: "By faith the prostitute Rahab, because she welcomed the spies, was not killed with those who were disobedient" (Hebrews 11:31). It was indeed a great act of faith for one who had lived among the heathen to be persuaded of the power of the God of Israel and of the right they had to that land. Her faith was brought about in her by divine instinct, in response to the report that was given of God and his works.

(2) Because this example can well be joined with the previous one. Some might object that not everyone could go as far as Abraham, the great pattern of all believers. But the least faith must produce works as well as the greatest, and so James gives Rahab as an example of the weakest faith.

a. As for her person, she was a woman, a prostitute, and a heathen when God worked on her. With so many disadvantages, it is to be presumed this was as low an example as could be given.

b. As for the act itself, it was accompanied by weakness, by a lie, which indeed is here suppressed, or at least not mentioned, lest it should deface the glory of her faith.

(3) Because there might be some doubt about this example. They might object that mere profession was accounted faith in Rahab, and she was a

prostitute. James replies that in Rahab the doctrine might be made good, for her faith, however weak, yielded some self-denying act or fruit.

But you will ask how this is pertinent to the purpose, to prove that pretense of faith without works is not enough to acquit us of hypocrisy. I answer that you must think of it like this: if she had only said to these messengers, "I believe the God of heaven and earth has given you this whole land to possess, yet I dare not show you any kindness in this city," it would have been only the dead, barren sort of faith James discusses here. But this belief prevailed so far with her that she did something helpful for them, though she incurred present danger and the tortures that the rage of her citizens would inflict on her for harboring spies.

Now I come to the words:

In the same way. This relates to the previous example of Abraham.

Even Rahab the prostitute. Lyranus thinks that the word for **prostitute** was her proper name; others think it only indicates that she was a hostess, a woman who kept a tavern. But the article—*the* **prostitute**—and the fact that this is repeated as a notable circumstance seem to imply that she was indeed a woman of disrepute; and it is mere folly to excuse what God wants to be made known for his own glory.

Was ... considered righteous for what she did. That is, she was shown to be sincere and honored by God before all the congregation. There was a special instruction to save her and her household when all her countrymen were slain, and afterwards she was joined in marriage with a prince of Israel.

When she gave lodging to the spies and sent them off in a different direction. The story is in Joshua 2. But is not this act questionable? Is it not treachery? Did she not sin against that love and faithfulness she owed to her country? She did not sin, because she had a warrant and a special revelation from God that the land of Canaan, and so her town, was given to the Israelites (Joshua 2:9-11). And being won to the faith, she was to leave her Gentile family and be incorporated in the people of Israel and so was bound to promote their interest, as Calvin points out. But you will say, "If there was no sin, why was her action so good? Was it no more than civility or necessary prudence and caution, since she was persuaded of this?" I answer:

(1) There was much faith in it, in believing what she had heard of God in the wilderness and the desert places of Arabia and magnifying his power and ability to destroy them. The people of her city were in great strength, they thought themselves safe within their walls; but God had revealed the truth to her by some special instinct, and she was confident of Israel's future success. And so, as Origen observes, she acknowledged what was past, believed what was present, and foretold what was to come.

(2) There was obedience in it, for whatever she did in this, she did out

of reverence and fear of God, whom she knew to be the author of this war; and though there was some weakness in the action, it was mostly a duty.

(3) There was self-denial in it. It was an action that might have had very dangerous consequences for her; but to demonstrate her fidelity to God she overlooked the threats and cruelties of her own people.

Notes on Verse 25

Note 1. God may often choose the worst of sinners. Faith is acceptable in a prostitute; those who set out late for heaven often make more way than someone who professes faith early on. The only women counted in Christ's genealogy are those who were stained with some infamy: idolatrous women, adulterous women, in Christ's own line—such as Rahab, Ruth, Bathsheba, Tamar. Chrysostom gives the reason: "he came to save sinners, and therefore wanted to be known to come from sinners according to the flesh." Manasses was received after witchcraft, Paul after blasphemy (1 Timothy 1:13), and all as precedents in which God would show mercy and long-suffering; so it is with Rahab here. So you will see that Matthew 21:31 says, "The tax collectors and the prostitutes are entering the kingdom of God ahead of you." The most odious and despised sinners, when they turn to God by repentance, find grace and a place in Christ's heart.

Note 2. The meanest faith must justify itself by works and gracious effects. Rahab, a Gentile convert, not only professed faith but preserved the spies. Do not let hypocrites plead that everyone is not like Abraham. Are you like Rahab? Can you produce any evidence of your faith? The meanest sort will show itself by some effect or other. The smallest faith, even if it is like a grain of mustard seed, will have some branches.

Note 3. Believers, even if they justify their profession, are still monuments of free grace. It is **Rahab the prostitute**, even though she was justified by works. The scars and marks of old sins remain not to our dishonor, but to God's glory.

Note 4. Ordinary acts are gracious when they flow from faith and are done in obedience, as when Rahab received the messengers. Entertainment in such a case is not civility but religion. Even "a cup of cold water . . . because he is my disciple" (Matthew 10:42) is not courtesy but duty and will not lose its reward. In Hebrews 11 many civil and secular acts are ascribed to faith, such as fighting battles, saving children, etc., because they were directed by faith to spiritual ends and were performed by supernatural strength.

Note 5. The great trial of faith is in acts of self-denial. Such was Rahab's, to prefer the will of God rather than the safety of her own country; and such was Abraham's in the previous example. Self-denial is the first thing that must be resolved in Christianity (Matthew 16:24). A person is not revealed when God's way and his own lie together. Your great inquiry should be, "In what way have I denied myself for God?"

Note 6. God hides his eyes from the evil that is in our good actions. Here mention is made of receiving the messengers, but no mention of the lie. The person who drew Alexander, who had a scar on his face, drew him with his finger on the scar. God puts the finger of mercy on our scars. See 5:11—**You have heard of Job's perseverance**; we have heard of his impatience, his cursing the day of his birth, etc., but no complaints are here mentioned.

Commentary on Verse 26

As the body without the spirit is dead, so faith without deeds is dead.

Here the apostle concludes the whole argument, showing how little is to be ascribed to an empty profession of faith without works. It is like the body without the spirit of life.

As the body without the spirit. In the [*King James*] margin we read **breath,** in the [NIV] text **spirit.** Many people prefer the marginal reading, because it is not "as the body without the soul," but **as the body without the spirit** or **breath.** Cajetan is of this opinion, and his words are notable because they fully accord with Protestant teaching. "By spirit," he says, "is not meant the soul, but the breath; for as the body of a beast is dead when it does not breathe, so faith without works is dead, breathing being the effect of life, as working is of living faith. So it is clear what the apostle means when he says that faith is dead without works, not that works are the soul of faith, but that works are the companions of faith, as breathing is inseparable from life." By this exposition, their doctrine that charity is the soul of faith and their distinction between unformed and formed faith fall to the ground. However, I think the Greek word in the text is not to be translated "breath" but **spirit** or "soul," the substance that gives life and movement to the body, for this is what the word means elsewhere: "Into your hands I commit my spirit" (Luke 23:46); "Lord Jesus, receive my spirit" (Acts 7:59).

The meaning is, then, that faith without works is like a body without a soul. And yet it does not follow that charity or works are the soul of faith, for the comparison does not hold in regard to animation but in regard to operation. As in the body without a soul there is only the outward shape but nothing to show life, so in empty profession of faith there is some appearance of faith, but no fruits to demonstrate its truth and life. It differs as much from faith as a carcass does from a living man.

Is dead. That is, it cannot perform the functions of life or of a man.

So faith without deeds. The Roman Catholics understand this to mean true, justifying faith. But dead faith cannot be true faith, just as a carcass is not a true man; and a true faith cannot be without works (see Galatians 5:6). We must understand this, then, to mean an external profession of belief, which because of some resemblance to what is true is called faith.

Is dead. That is, false or useless to all the ends and purposes of faith.

Notes on Verse 26

For practical notes, see verses 17 and 20. Here only note that mere profession, in respect to true faith, is only like a carcass. It is so in two respects:

(1) It is noisome like a rotten carcass, just as a worldly Christian is the carcass of a true Christian. When those who claim to be Christians but are worldly come near to Christ, he goes further off, as you would from what is offensive: "Away from me, you evildoers!" (Matthew 7:23). He cannot endure their presence.

(2) It is useless for all the purposes of faith. It cannot unite you to Christ so that you may possess his righteousness, nor give you a feeling of his Spirit. In short, it brings no glory to God and gives no comfort to the person who has it, nor any benefit to others; it is of no more use than a dead body when the spirit has gone.

James
Chapter 3

Commentary on Verse 1

Not many of you should presume to be teachers, my brothers, because you know that we who teach will be judged more strictly.

Here the apostle diverts to another matter, reinforcing what he had said in the first chapter about the evil of the tongue. However, this discourse is joined on to the previous one with good reason. People who vainly boast of their own faith are the most apt to censure others; and those who claim to be Christians are likely to take the greatest liberty in rigid and bitter reflections on the errors of their brothers.

Not many of you should presume to be teachers. The word translated **teachers** has various meanings. Sometimes it means absolute authority in the church. In this sense Christ alone is a teacher (Matthew 23:10); his word is law. Sometimes the word means a subordinate teaching and explanation of God's truth; and those who have this task are called "Israel's teacher[s]" (see John 3:10). Sometimes the word has the worst sense, that of a censorious reprover, one who occupies a chair of arrogance, magisterially inveighing against other people's practices; and this is what it means here. Why does the apostle choose this expression?

(1) It shows that he is not talking about authorized reproof. God has set some people in the church to be masters of manners—for example, the teacher and ecclesiastical magistrate. But because God has allowed a few, do not let everyone be a teacher or turn censurer: **Not many of you.** We are all inclined, but this itch must be killed.

(2) It shows that he is not forbidding private, brotherly admonitions, such as proceed from Christian care and love, but the censorious sort of reproving that was managed with as much sharpness as a man would use to his slave.

My brothers. Though the term is familiar and usual with James, it has a special emphasis here.

(1) Good men are often surprised and are too free with the failings of others.

(2) He does not want to be too rigid himself, and therefore he tempers his reproof with sweetness.

(3) The word has the force of an argument: **brothers** should not affect mastery over each other.

Because you know that we who teach will be judged more strictly. This is the first reason the apostle gives against the pride of criticizing, which is based on a consideration of the danger of sin or the severity of judgment following it, either from men—critics usually have their own measure used against them (see Matthew 7:1-2)—or from God. Who can expect pardon from someone who is severe to others? See Matthew 18:32-33. I understand this to mean chiefly judgment and condemnation from God, which is all the more severe to critics, for three reasons:

(1) The justice of retaliation. We condemn others, and God condemns us. We are severe on their failings; how can we expect God to be merciful to ours?

(2) Because God is the avenger of injuries (Romans 12:19), and among them the greatest is blasting the reputation of other people.

(3) A critic's sins are more aggravated because of the garb of indignation that he seems to put on against others: see Romans 2:1. In censuring others we only pronounce our own judgment, which the Scripture plainly represents to us in the well-known instances of David (2 Samuel 12), Ahab (1 Kings 20:39-42), etc.

Notes on Verse 1

Note 1. The best people need something to dissuade them from proud censuring. The apostle says, **Not many of you should presume to be teachers, my brothers,** and afterwards he includes himself in the number—*we who teach.* It is an attractive evil; it suits pride and self-love and feeds conceit. All these evils are in the best of God's children. In 1 John 2:16 "boasting of what he has and does" is mentioned last because it is the last to be mortified; it grows with the decrease of other sins and thrives on their decay. So "bear with my word of exhortation" (Hebrews 13:22). We sin and are not aware of censuring; pride rages when it is crossed. Hear such matters patiently; James is speaking to **brothers: Not many of you should presume to be teachers.**

Note 2. To censure other people is to assume the role of teacher over them. All teaching, especially reproof, is an act of power; that is why the apostle forbids it to women (1 Corinthians 14:34), because they cannot have power over a man. So when you are about to censure someone, check it with this thought: "Who are you to judge someone else's servant? To his own master he stands or falls" (Romans 14:4). It wrongs God if I put myself in his place; it wrongs my neighbor to claim a power over him that God never gave me.

Note 3. Christians should not affect this mastership over their brothers. You may admonish, reprove, warn, but it should not be in a masterly way. How is that?

(1) When we do it out of pride and self-conceit, as if we thought ourselves more just, holy, wise, etc. The Pharisee speaks as if he were above common weakness. Rather, "restore him gently. But watch yourself" (Galatians 6:1). We are all involved in the same state of frailty.

(2) When we do it as vaunting over their infirmities and frailties, to shame them rather than restore them. Ham laughed at Noah's drunkenness. This does not suggest a hatred of sin but envy or malice against the person. Paul's attitude was truly Christian: "I have often told you before and now say again even with tears, many live as enemies of the cross of Christ" (Philippians 3:18). Censures are full of *passion*, but Christian reproofs are full of *compassion*. This is the difference between reproving out of pride and out of love and charity.

(3) When the censure is unmerciful, and we remit nothing of extreme severity—when, indeed, we leave out extenuating circumstances. The censure should be extended no further than the facts. Jealousy collects more than is offered, but "love does not delight in evil" (1 Corinthians 13:6). It is against all law to be judge and accuser too and to hunt out an offense and then censure it.

(4) When we infringe Christian liberty and condemn others for things that do not matter. This indeed is to lay snares on the conscience and is a wrong not so much to our brothers as to God's own law, which we judge as if it were an imperfect rule (see 4:11). There is great latitude in habits and in food, and as long as rules of sobriety and modesty are not violated, we cannot censure but must leave the heart to God.

(5) When people do not consider what goes with charity as well as what will agree with truth. There may be censure where there is no slander. Many religious people think they are safe if they speak of others only what is true. But this is not all. Every evil must not be divulged; some must be covered with the cloak of love. There may be malice in reporting the truth. If there is no ill intention, such prattle will come under the heading of idle words, for which we are responsible.

(6) When we do it to get ourselves a better reputation by reporting their scandals. In the whole matter we are to be motivated by love and to aim at the Lord's glory. So, be careful that your reproofs are not censures; they must not be offered censoriously or magisterially, coming from pride

rather than love. Envy often goes under the guise of zeal; we need to be careful, especially in times of public disagreement.

For remedies:

(1) Cherish a humble sense of your own frailty. Other people fall sadly and foully, but what are we? We were as bad (see Titus 3:2-3); we may even be worse (see 1 Corinthians 10:12). Bernard tells of a man who, hearing of a fallen brother, fell into a bitter weeping, crying out, "He is fallen today, and I may tomorrow."

(2) Exchange a sin for a duty: "If anyone sees his brother commit a sin that does not lead to death, he should pray" (1 John 5:16). This will be a holy way to spend your zeal with the most profit.

Note 4. **You know that we.** A remedy for vain censure is to consider ourselves (see Galatians 6:1). How is it with us? Gracious hearts inquire most into themselves and are most severe against their own corruptions.

(1) They are most inquisitive into their own sins. The fool is always looking elsewhere; his eyes are like the windows of the temple, broad on the outside, narrow on the inside. He is curious to sift other people's lives but does not care to reform his own. But with good people it is different; they find enough deceit in their own hearts to use up all their care and thoughts.

(2) They are most severe against themselves. A good heart is ready to throw the first stone against itself (see John 8:4-5). Others can inveigh with much heat against other people's sins and indulgently cherish their own.

Note 5. Rash and undue judging of others, when we are guilty ourselves, makes us liable to greater judgment. The apostle works on this assumption. Sharp critics need to be careful or they will draw a hard law on themselves and in judging others will pronounce their own doom. Their sins are done knowingly, and the more they know, the more they will be punished. Ignorant people have the advantage that they have a cooler hell. So, do not carry on prescribing burdens for other people; that is a cheap zeal. The phrase about being **judged more strictly** is also applied to the Pharisees in Matthew 23:14, because of their hypocrisy. So those who criticize, whether because it is their job or out of love, need to look to themselves. Your first task should begin at your own hearts, and then you will carry on the duty more boldly and positively.

Commentary on Verse 2

We all stumble in many ways. If anyone is never at fault in what he says, he is a perfect man, able to keep his whole body in check.

James goes on to dissuade his readers from being censorious. In this verse he uses two arguments. The first is the frailty common to all of us, which may be thought of in two ways:

(1) Will you condemn them for something no one is exempt from? The excuse of weakness is the unhappy privilege of all mortal men.

(2) Will you not show them the tenderness that you need yourselves? You too may fail; **we all stumble in many ways.**

The next argument is the difficulty of not sinning with the tongue; anyone who can avoid that can do anything in Christianity.

We all stumble in many ways. He says **we**, including himself, even though he was an apostle of great holiness (Eusebius says he was surnamed "the Just" because of his great virtue). And indeed no one is exempt—not even the blessed Virgin, who is charged in Scripture for some slips (see Luke 2:49; John 2:3-4). It is useless to ask whether God can keep anyone totally free from sin in the bodily life; God's pleasure is declared the other way. And as for the question whether some transient action of a renewed person may not be without actual sin, I answer in these propositions:

(1) In our deliberate actions, especially those who are moral, there is some mixture of sin. Ecclesiastes 7:20 says, "There is not a righteous man on earth who does what is right and never sins." And Luther says the same, that the best works of the regenerate are sins if they are examined by God. And Gregory the Great says much the same, that man's merit is but sin and his righteousness unrighteousness if it is examined strictly. Indeed, before either of them the prophet Isaiah said that "all our righteous acts are like filthy rags" (Isaiah 64:6). Nothing we do is so pure that there is not some taint of sin clinging to it that in the rigor of the law, without a mediator, would be damnable. So even if the essence of the action is good, there is no way it can undergo the strictness of divine judgment because of worldly things sticking to it. Man is partly holy and partly worldly; the effect cannot be greater than the cause.

(2) I imagine there may be an action so quick that there is no room for corruption; for example, in a sudden glance or holy thought we may conceive a spiritual desire that, though not perfectly holy, is purely holy. Besides, in some actions the force and vigor of corrupt nature may be wholly suspended by the power of God—as it is in conversion, in which theologians say we are wholly passive. I cannot but justly condemn that unnecessary rigor in some who say that a renewed person actually sins in every action, be it but the walking of two or three steps. This is a silly notion that, under the guise of a deeper humility, destroys true humility. We need not make people more guilty. But the devil loves to cheat people of true humility by what is affected; and when the imagination invents supposed crimes, conscience is less troubled about those that are real.

(3) Such actions are not acceptable to God for their own sake. Partly

this is because though they are pure or free from sin, they are not perfect: they might be more holy yet. And partly it is because they are done by someone who has a corrupt nature and is stained with the guilt of other actual sins, the least of which renders him liable to the curse of the whole law (see 2:10). So these actions too need a mediator; as the apostle says, "my conscience is clear, but that does not make me innocent" (1 Corinthians 4:4). For one such innocent action, there are a thousand that are stained and polluted. Another question may be whether there are not some sins that in their own nature are so foul that a child of God cannot fall into them. I answer:

(1) There are some gross corruptions that are very contrary to grace, "the corruption of the world" (2 Peter 2:20). Therefore the apostle says, "The acts of the sinful nature are obvious" (Galatians 5:19)—that is, obvious to sense and reason, such as adultery, drunkenness, etc., acts that nature has branded with marks of shame and contempt. Into these a child of God may fall, though rarely and very seldom. We have instances of Noah's drunkenness, Lot's incest, and David's adultery. Therefore, we may conclude that the children of God do not only sin freely in thought, but sometimes foully in act—however, not usually, but only when specially tempted; they are not given to women or to wine. The usual practice is a note of God's hatred: "The mouth of an adulteress is a deep pit; he who is under the LORD's wrath will fall into it" (Proverbs 22:14). These sins, therefore, are not of usual incidence, as wrath and worldliness and pride are.

(2) There are other sins that are extremely contrary to nature itself, such as Sodom's bestiality, into which a renewed person cannot fall—partly for the great dishonor such a fact would reflect on religion, partly because it is a note of God's giving a person up to sin (Romans 1:26-27). These things are so far from being practiced by saints that they are not to be named among them (Ephesians 5:3).

If anyone is never at fault in what he says, he is a perfect man. Here is the second argument: bridling the tongue is a note of some perfection and effectual progress in grace. **Never at fault in what he says**—that is, he always says what is known to be true, and that charitably, without vanity or rash oaths, as Gregory of Nyssa fully expounds it. You may take the words as a supposition. If anyone avoids the evils of the tongue, I will make bold to call him a perfect man, such as is not found among mortals. We often say this sort of thing when we speak about an unlikely practice: "Anyone who could do this would indeed be a perfect man." Or you may take it positively, and in this case it is another argument against censoriousness: "If you do not offend in word, you are perfect"—that is, upright, sincere. People who are like this because they do not argue with God are expressed by the term **perfect**. Or else **perfect** is used here for some

182

growth in Christianity. In the Jewish discipline there were two sorts of people—*beginners*, who exercised themselves in virtuous actions and endeavors, and others, whom Philo calls *perfect*; they were those who had attained some progress in the matters learned. The same word is used in this sense in 1 Corinthians 2:6—"We . . . speak a message of wisdom among the mature." However much the weak like toys, grown Christians will discern wisdom in the plain preaching of Christ crucified. And this sense may be read in this passage: "Anyone who bridles his tongue is not a beginner or learner, one who is experimenting in religion, but a perfect person, one who has made some progress."

Able to keep his whole body in check. By **body** Grotius understands the church, which is called "the body" in 1 Corinthians 12:20 and Ephesians 4:12; and he makes the sense out thus: "Anyone who can keep himself in check in disputation is able to govern the church"—an intriguing exposition, but one alien to this context. By keeping his whole body in check is meant, then, governing all his other actions, which are here expressed by the term **body** because they are acted out by the members of the body—eyes, hands, feet, etc. Why he puts so much weight on this matter of governing the tongue, I shall show in the notes.

Notes on Verse 2

Note 1. No one is absolutely freed and exempted from sinning: "If we claim to be without sin, we deceive ourselves and the truth is not in us" (1 John 1:8). "Who can say, 'I have kept my heart pure; I am clean and without sin'?" (Proverbs 20:9). Solomon challenges all the world. Many may say this very thing boldly, but who can say so truly? All of us offend in many things, and many of us in all things. There is in everyone a cursed root of bitterness that God mortifies but does not nullify; it is cast down but not cast out. Like the ivy on the wall, cut off from the stump, body, and branches, some tendrils will sprout again, until the wall gets pulled down. God chooses that it will continue like this until we come to heaven. So then:

(1) Walk with more caution; you carry a sinning heart within you. As long as there is fuel for a temptation, we cannot be secure; the man who has gunpowder with him will be afraid of sparks.

(2) Censure with all the more tenderness; allow for human frailty in every action (Galatians 6:1). We all need forgiveness; without grace you might fall into the same sins.

(3) Be all the more earnest with God in asking for grace; God will still keep you dependent on and beholden to his power.

(4) Magnify the love of God with all the more praise. Paul groans under his corruptions (see the end of Romans 7) and then admires the happiness of those who are in Christ (Romans 8:1); they had so many sins, and yet none were damnable.

Note 2. The sins of the best people are many. The apostle says, **We all stumble.** God would not abolish and destroy all of those sins at once. There is a prayer against outward enemies: "Do not kill them, O Lord our shield, or my people will forget. In your might make them wander about, and bring them down" (Psalm 59:11). He does not want them utterly destroyed, but for some to be left as a memorial. This is the way God deals in respect to sin. It is brought down but not wholly slain; something is left as a monument of divine grace. Peter of Alexandria, when he destroyed the rest of the idols, left one that was most monstrous and misshapen to remind the people of their former idolatry. God will still honor free grace. The condition of his own people is mixed, light checkered with darkness; those who walk in the light may **stumble.** So then:

(1) Do not be altogether dismayed at the sight of failings. A godly person observed that Christians are usually to blame for three things: they seek in themselves what they can only find in Christ; they seek in the law what will only be found in the Gospel; and they seek on earth what will only be enjoyed in heaven. We complain of sin and ask, when will the earthly state be free? You should not complain but run to your Advocate. You complain, as do all those who have the firstfruits of the Spirit, that "your brothers throughout the world are undergoing the same kind of sufferings" (1 Peter 5:9). They are all troubled with a busy devil, a corrupt heart, and a wicked world.

(2) However, bewail these failings, the evils that abound in your hearts and in your duties, that you cannot serve God as entirely as you served Satan, that your evil works were merely evil, but your good works are not purely good.

Note 3. To be able to bridle the tongue shows that we have grown in grace. Not only James but the Scriptures everywhere make this a matter of great importance: "The tongue has the power of life and death" (Proverbs 18:21). A person's safety depends on using it aright. And lest you should think the Scripture only means temporal safety or ruin, see Matthew 12:37, "by your words you will be acquitted, and by your words you will be condemned." Your words are one of the prime things that will be brought to judgment. "He who guards his lips guards his soul [life], but he who speaks rashly will come to ruin" (Proverbs 13:3). Solomon implies that this is like a city besieged: opening the gates betrays its safety. In the same way, the tongue is the gate or door of the soul, as it goes out in conversation; keeping it open or loosely guarded lets the enemy in, which proves the death of the soul.

Similarly, in other passages this is the great sign of spiritual and holy prudence: "When words are many, sin is not absent, but he who holds his tongue is wise" (Proverbs 10:19). Empty vessels are full of sound; discreet silence, or a wise ordering of speech, is a token of grace. "A man of knowledge uses words with restraint, and a man of understanding is even-tempered" (Proverbs 17:27). The Spirit of God gives exhortation upon exhortation and devotes many Scriptures to this argument.

There were also special reasons why James should press this so much:

(1) This was the sin of that age, as appears from the frequent dissuasions from vain boasting of themselves and detracting from others in chapters 1 and 2. And it is a high point of grace not to be snared with the evils of our own times.

(2) This is the best revelation of the heart; speech is the express image of it: "out of the overflow of the heart the mouth speaks" (Matthew 12:34). When the heart is full, it overflows in speech. The story of blind Socrates is common, who said to a boy, "Speak, so that I can see you." We know metals by the sound they make. "The mouth of the righteous man utters wisdom, and his tongue speaks what is just. The law of his God is in his heart" (Psalm 37:30-31). Good people will always be revealing themselves and giving vent to the fullness of their hearts.

(3) This is the hypocrites' sin; they abstain from grosser actions but usually offend in their words, boasting professions, and proud censures: see 1:26.

(4) All of us are apt to offend with the tongue in many ways; most of a man's sins are in his words. One writer lists twenty-four sins of the tongue, and yet the number may be increased—lying, railing, swearing, ribaldry, scoffing, quarreling, deceiving, boasting, gossiping, etc. At first, indeed, there was no other sin in society but lying; but now how many evils does this one part of the body perpetrate? When the apostle gives us the anatomy of wickedness in all the parts of the body, he stays longest on the organs of speech and goes over them all: "'Their throats are open graves; their tongues practise deceit.' 'The poison of vipers is on their lips.' 'Their mouths are full of cursing and bitterness'" (Romans 3:13-14). You see, this part of the body needs much reforming and polishing. "An evil man is trapped by his sinful talk" (Proverbs 12:13); that is, not only does he trap others by it, but he himself is trapped, to his own ruin and destruction.

(5) This is a sin into which we fall commonly and easily, partly because of the close connection between the tongue and the heart—we sin in an instant, and partly because we sin in that way without noticing.

So then, take care not only of your actions but of your words. "I said, 'I will watch my ways and keep my tongue from sin'" (Psalm 39:1). He would take care with his whole life but would chiefly watch his tongue; it was in that way that iniquity and offense was likely to break out soonest. Next to keeping our hearts, Solomon tells us to keep our tongues: "Above all else, guard your heart"; then, "Put away perversity from your mouth" (Proverbs 4:23-24). First the heart, then the tongue, then the foot (verse 26). Consider:

(1) Your speeches are recorded (see 2:12). Xenophon recommended that all speech be written down, to make people more serious. Every idle word will be brought into judgment (see Matthew 12:36); light words weigh heavy in God's balance.

(2) They are punished: "He will turn their own tongues against them" (Psalm 64:8). Better that a mountain should fall upon you than the weight of your own tongue. "A fool's talk brings a rod to his back, but the lips of the wise protect them" (Proverbs 14:3). We boast and insult; God will make it a rod to scourge us. Our tongue is not a sword but a rod because God will punish contempt with contempt, both in this life and in that to come.

(3) Consider what a vile thing it is to abuse the tongue in strife, censure, or insult. God made the tongue to celebrate his own praise, to convey the holy conceptions of the soul to others. Human excellence should not be debased in this way; better be mute than speak wickedness.

(4) It is no small thing that God should show in nature that he has set bounds to the tongue: he has hedged it in with a row of teeth. Other organs are double; we have two eyes, two ears, but one tongue. Children cannot use their tongue naturally until they can reason; certainly, therefore, it was never intended to serve passion and pride and every idle humor.

For suitable remedies:

(1) Get a pure heart; there is the tongue's treasury and store. A good person is always ready to talk, not forced by the company, but because the law of God is in his heart: "The lips of the wise spread knowledge; not so the hearts of fools" (Proverbs 15:7). Because of the parallel clause, it should be understood as "not so the tongues of fools"; whatever is in the tongue comes from the heart. Out of the heart come slander and evil thoughts (see Matthew 15:19).

(2) Watch and guard your speech: "I said, 'I will watch my ways and keep my tongue from sin'" (Psalm 39:1). "I said" means, "I made a resolution." The tongue needs to be restrained with force and watchfulness, for it is ready to bring forth every wicked thought. You must not only watch over it but bridle it; it is good to break the force of these constraints within us and to suffocate and choke them as soon as they arise. "If you have played the fool and exalted yourself, or if you have planned evil, clap your hand over your mouth!" (Proverbs 30:32)—that is, bridle and stifle those angry thoughts. Do not deal too softly with unruly evils but strongly resist them. This rule should especially be observed in worship: see Ecclesiastes 5:1.

(3) All our endeavors are nothing. Go to God: "Set a guard over my mouth, O Lord; keep watch over the door of my lips" (Psalm 141:3).

David wants God to keep him from speaking amiss when he is in deep affliction. It is God alone who can tame the tongue: "From the LORD comes the reply of the tongue" (Proverbs 16:1). When the heart is not prepared, the tongue may falter. The saints sometimes desire God to open their mouth (see Ephesians 6:19; Psalm 51:15) and sometimes to shut it.

(4) So that you may not give offense with your words, use them in God's service. It is not enough to abstain from speaking evil. "Do not let any unwholesome talk come out of your mouths, but only what is helpful for building others up" (Ephesians 4:29). "Nor should there be obscenity, foolish talk or coarse joking, which are out of place, but rather thanksgiving" (Ephesians 5:4)—that is, thankfully remembering your sweet experiences. We must avoid the evil of the tongue, and we must talk with one another about God's blessings. "The tongue of the righteous is choice silver" (Proverbs 10:20)—not just because it is purged from vanity and lies, but because of its benefits. It is also called "a tree of life" (Proverbs 11:30) whose leaves are medicinal. So Proverbs 12:18 says, "The tongue of the wise brings healing." This should shame us, because we are so backward in holy conversation, into refreshing and healing one another. And so we may learn that Christianity does not make us silent in conversation but gracious.

Commentary on Verses 3-4

When we put bits into the mouths of horses to make them obey us, we can turn the whole animal. Or take ships as an example. Although they are so large and are driven by strong winds, they are steered by a very small rudder wherever the pilot wants to go.

In these two verses are comparisons that need less comment. They show that little things can guide great bodies, as in the case of a bridle and a rudder. In the same way, the guiding of the tongue, a little part, may be of just as great consequence in moral matters. By the bridle we keep the horse from stumbling, and by the rudder we keep the ship from the rocks. So Solomon says, "He who guards his mouth and his tongue keeps himself from calamity" (Proverbs 21:23).

Notes on Verses 3-4

Note 1. It is good to illustrate divine truths by earthly examples.

(1) Our knowledge comes through the senses. From things known we

understand better those that are unknown. From an earthly matter, with which we are acquainted, we get an idea of the worth of what is spiritual.

(2) In illustrations, the thing is portrayed twice over. If we use them more, we are more fit for occasional meditation, and we understand spiritual things more clearly.

Note 2. Nature, art, and religion show that the smallest things, wisely ordered, may be of great use. Do not neglect small things. He loses a great deal who "despises the day of small things" (Zechariah 4:10).

Note 3. God's wisdom is much in evidence since man is endowed with the ability to invent. A wild creature such as the horse is tamed with a bridle; things so bulky as ships are steered against the violent winds with a small helm. Aristotle says this is a matter worthy of consideration. These skills are all from the Lord: "See, it is I who created the blacksmith who fans the coals into flame and forges a weapon fit for its work" (Isaiah 54:16). God left these inventions to human work, but he gave men the abilities. In the case of embroidery, "I have filled [Bezalel] with the Spirit of God" (Exodus 31:3). For farming, see Isaiah 28:24-26; for war, Psalm 144:1. So then, bless God for his various gifts for mankind's welfare, and wait on him so that you may understand your calling: "Whoever gives heed to instruction prospers, and blessed is he who trusts in the LORD" (Proverbs 16:20). You must wait on the Lord for skill and for success. He teaches you how to tame the horse and how to steer the ship.

Note 4. From the first simile, note that men, because of their natural fierceness, are like wild animals. Man aspired to be God but became "like the beasts that perish" (Psalm 49:12). The psalmist says, "Do not be like the horse or the mule, which have no understanding but must be controlled by bit and bridle" (Psalm 32:9). To keep them from doing harm, men's tongues must be restrained. We possess a wantonness by which we kick against God's precepts (see Deuteronomy 32:15). It is by God's mercy that we are restrained. This natural fierceness is calmed through the control of the tongue.

Commentary on Verse 5

Likewise the tongue is but a small part of the body, but it makes great boasts. Consider what a great forest is set on fire by a small spark.

Likewise the tongue is but a small part of the body, but it makes great boasts. Here the simile is repeated; the tongue is like a bridle and rudder, small in size and yet very useful. **Makes great boasts** is indeed the proper meaning of the Greek word. From the context James could have said, "does great things," for what was shown was that someone who can control his tongue can control his whole body. To support such a proposition, James gives two illustrations that show that little things through good management may be very useful. From this he could have inferred that the small part of the body, the tongue, can do great things if it is under control. But James repeats the main proposition to support a different argument. It is as if he had said, "The tongue witnesses for itself; for by it people trumpet their presumptions and boast that they can do great things." He gives the example of boasting because:

(1) It is the usual sin of the tongue. This is the part of the body that most serves pride.

(2) It is usually the sin of those who have no control over their spirits and actions. Hypocrites and vain men are proud boasters. "Flattering lips" and "every boastful tongue" are linked together (Psalm 12:3). And in Proverbs 14:3 we read, "A fool's talk brings a rod to his back." True grace humbles; false grace puffs up.

Consider what a great forest is set on fire by a small spark. Another simile, showing that great disasters come from the abuse of so small a thing. You would think that words, which pass away with the breath in which they are uttered, would not have such a deadly influence; but, says the apostle, **a small spark** kindles much wood. Small things should not be neglected in nature, art, religion, or providence. In nature, important things grow from small beginnings. Nature loves to have the seed of everything small; a little yeast works through the whole batch of dough.

Notes on Verse 5

Note 1. A frequent sin of the tongue is boasting. Sometimes the pride of the heart comes from the eyes; therefore we read about "haughty eyes" (Proverbs 6:17). But usually it is displayed in our speech. The tongue trumpets it in these ways:

(1) In bold boasting. See Isaiah 14:13, where the king of Babylon threatens to fight against God himself, and then against his people. See also Hannah's resolve in 1 Samuel 2:3.

(2) In proud ostentation of our own worth. First we entertain our spirits with whispers of vanity and suppositions of applause; and then the rage of vainglory is so great that we trumpet out our own shame. It is wrong for a man to promote his own cause. In the Olympic Games the wrestlers did not put crowns on their own heads. What is justifiable praise on another's lips is boasting on our own.

(3) In contemptuous challenges of God and man. Of God: as Pharaoh

challenged in effect, "Who is the God of the Hebrews, that I should let you go?" Consider also Psalm 12:4, "We will triumph with our tongues; we own our lips—who is our master?" Of man: provocative speeches are recorded in the Word. Solomon says, "A fool's lips bring him strife" (Proverbs 18:6).

(4) In bragging promises, as if they could accomplish great matters beyond the reach of their gifts and strength: "I will pursue, I will overtake them. I will divide the spoils" (Exodus 15:9).

Note 2. Take notice of small things. We must not consider only their beginning but their end. A little sin does a great deal of harm, and a little grace has great efficacy: "At the beginning his words are folly; at the end they are wicked madness" (Ecclesiastes 10:13). At first people argue for fun but later break out into furious passion, and so from folly go on to madness. "Starting a quarrel is like breaching a dam; so drop the matter before a dispute breaks out" (Proverbs 17:14). It is easy to let out the water, but who can call the floods back? Strife is sometimes compared to fire, sometimes to water; both are treacherous elements once they are let loose. At first heresy is a small matter, but it spreads like gangrene from one place to another until it has destroyed the whole body. Arius, a small Alexandrian spark, kindled all the world in a flame. Providence too begins great matters in a small way. Luther's reformation was occasioned by opposing pardoners. Christ's kingdom was despised at first as a poor, tender branch. Later it "filled the whole earth" (Daniel 2:35).

So then:

(1) Learn not to neglect evils that are small in their inception; resist sin early on (see Ephesians 4:27); give no place to Satan. Look out for the first sign of error. "We did not give in to them for a moment," says the apostle (Galatians 2:5).

(2) Do not despise the humble beginnings of providence and deliverance; there is a "day of small things" (Zechariah 4:10). Philpot said the martyrs in England had kindled such a light in England as should not easily go out.

Commentary on Verse 6

The tongue also is a fire, a world of evil among the parts of the body. It corrupts the whole person, sets the whole course of his life on fire, and is itself set on fire by hell.

Here James applies the simile of a little fire to an evil tongue. I shall comment on the most difficult phrases.

A world of evil. "A world" is how we commonly express things that abound. It implies that the power of the tongue to hurt is very great; as the world is full of all kinds of things, so the tongue is full of all kinds of sin.

It corrupts the whole person. Ephraim Syrus thinks this is an allusion to the punishment of leprosy with which Miriam and Aaron were afflicted for the abuse of their tongues. But that does not fit the context. It means that it infects the whole man with sin and guilt. Sin, though it starts in the soul, is carried out by the body. One infected part of the body defiles another, and the tongue taints every part of the body.

Sets . . . on fire. James shows the effect of this tongue-fire: it not only blackens but devours and destroys. James uses the phrase **sets . . . on fire** because the effects of the tongue, which are usually unjust passion, anger, rage, and violence, are contrary to the "cool spirit" that Solomon says is in the prudent man. Be sure to watch over your spirit when it starts to be furious and inflamed.

The whole course of his life. Some translate this, "the wheel of our nativity," meaning the whole course of our lives. There is no action, no age, no state that can escape its influence. The Syriac interpreter has, "all our generations," as if the sense were that all ages of the world are conscious of the evils of the tongue and can produce instances of it. But the word means our natural course, or the wheel of human life.

Is itself set on fire in hell. James shows where the tongue gets all this malice and mischief: from hell, that is, from the devil, who is the father of lies, the author of malice, and by lies and slander sets the world on fire.

Notes on Verse 6

Note 1. There is a similarity between an evil tongue and fire:

(1) In its heat. It is the instrument of wrath and contention, which is the heat of a man—a boiling of the blood around the heart. Solomon says, "A man of understanding is even-tempered" (Proverbs 17:27). Hot water boils over, and passions in the heart overflow into words. Of the ungodly man it is said, "his speech is like a scorching fire" (Proverbs 16:27).

(2) In being dangerous. It kindles a great fire. The tongue is a powerful means to kindle divisions and strifes. You know we need to be careful with fire. It is a bad master and a good servant. Where it is let loose, it soon turns houses into a wilderness; and you have as great a need to watch the tongue. Solomon says, "Like a madman shooting firebrands or deadly arrows is a man who deceives his neighbor and says, 'I was only joking!'" (Proverbs 26:18-19). We spread fire, scalding words, and do not think about the danger.

(3) It burns. Reproaches penetrate like fire. David compares them to

"burning coals of the broom tree" (Psalm 120:4), which burn the hottest and the longest; they may be kept burning for a whole year. The Septuagint has, "desolating coals." Fire is a most active element and leaves a great pain. So do reproaches.

(4) It is kindled from **hell**, as the end of the verse says. Zeal is a holy fire that comes from heaven, but this fire is from hell. Isaiah's lips were touched "with a live coal . . . from the altar" (Isaiah 6:6); and the Holy Spirit descended in "tongues of fire" (Acts 2:3). But the fire in this verse is from below. So work for an even temper. A tongue that is **set on fire by hell** will be set on fire in hell. Hot words of wrath, strife, and censure come from Satan and lead to Satan. When you feel this heat on your spirit, remember from what hearth these coals were gathered. God's Word was like fire in Jeremiah's bones, and wrath is often like fire in ours. Even when wrath boils, keep anger from being a scorching fire in your tongues. See Psalm 39:3.

Note 2. There is a world of sin in the tongue. It is an instrument of many sins. By it we induce ourselves to evil; by it we seduce others.

Note 3. **It corrupts**. Sin is a defilement and a blot. Sin "contaminates [the] body" (2 Corinthians 7:1). Scandalous sinners are the stain of their society. When you hand yourselves over to sin, you defile yourself. It will be your own disgrace; it will be to your eternal disadvantage: "Nothing impure will ever enter [the heavenly city]" (Revelation 21:27). In short, sin is so impure that it is ashamed of itself. It seeks to hide itself from those who love it most, and it disguises itself as a virtue. No other argument is needed to make it odious but to see it in its own colors.

Note 4. Sins of the tongue defile greatly. We either spread evil to others by ungodly suggestions or provoke them to evil by our passion.

Note 5. **The whole person.** An evil tongue has great influence on other parts of the body. When someone speaks evil, he will commit it. When the tongue has the boldness to talk of sin, the rest of the body has the boldness to act it. First we think, then we speak, and then we act. People will say it is only talk. Do not be deceived; an evil tongue infects other parts of the body.

Note 6. **The whole course** (or "wheel") **of his life**. Man's life is like a wheel. It is always in motion; we are always turning and rolling to our graves. This also shows the uncertainty of any worldly state; the spokes are now up and then down, sometimes in the dirt and sometimes out of it. The bishops of Mentz have a wheel as their emblem. This is also the emblem of our lives; when you see a wheel, take the opportunity to meditate.

Note 7. The evils of the tongue have universal influence. There is no faculty that the tongue does not poison. No calling is exempt. The tradesman in his shop uses his tongue for gain: "A fortune made by a lying tongue is a fleeting vapor and a deadly snare" (Proverbs 21:6). Ministers in the pulpit often preach for gain (see Ecclesiastes 5:1). No one is so meek and humble that they may not be perverted. Holy Moses, the meekest man upon earth, was angry at the waters of Meribah and fell into a rage ("Rash words came from Moses' lips," Psalm 106:33). David prays well: "Set a guard over my mouth, O Lord" (Psalm 141:3). So, none of us should think these exhortations unnecessary.

Note 8. A wicked tongue originates in **hell**; the prophets' fires were kindled from heaven. The devil is "a liar" (John 8:44), and he accuses the brothers and loves to make others like himself. Learn, then, to abhor reviling, contention, and reproach, as you would hell-flames. These are just the eruptions of an infernal fire; slanderers are the devil's slaves and instruments. Again, if blasted with rude contempt, learn to slight it; who takes notice of the suggestions of the father of lies? The murderer is a liar. In short, what comes from hell will go back there: "Anyone who says, 'You fool!' will be in danger of the fire of hell" (Matthew 5:22). Wrath is here expressed in a word of reproach, and you see how deadly and grievous it is.

Commentary on Verses 7-8

All kinds of animals, birds, reptiles and creatures of the sea are being tamed and have been tamed by man, but no man can tame the tongue. It is a restless evil, full of deadly poison.

Having shown the cursed influence of the tongue, James shows how difficult the cure is. Wild beasts are more tractable and may be brought to hand sooner than an evil tongue; it is wilder than the wildest beast.

All kinds of animals, birds, reptiles and creatures of the sea. The list is long so that he can show how far human skill has reached. Stories abound of how lions have been tamed and used to hunt like dogs or draw a chariot like horses (see Pliny in his *Natural History*) and about how birds have been tamed and so on. In short, nothing is so wild in nature that human skill and hard work has not made it serve human use. This is a fruit of the dominion God gave man over the creatures in the beginning. Through an instinct in their nature everyone obeyed him and served him. But man rebelled and lost his command over himself and over the creatures. Even over his tongue, **a small part of his body**, he has no dominion. That is the purpose of this illustration.

Are being tamed and have been tamed by man. It is as if he said, "It not only has been done in ancient times, but we still see it done today." He uses this distinct expression to show that he not only means the subjection of the creatures before the fall, or some miracles such as the great fish not hurting Jonah (Jonah 2) or the lions and Daniel in their den (Daniel 6), but also what is ordinary and is frequently experienced.

But no man can tame the tongue. The old Pelagians read this as a question, as if the sense were: "Man can tame all other things; can he not then tame himself?"—implying that man can surely do this. This is quite contrary to the apostle's intention, which is to show how unruly the tongue is. Others, to avoid the apparent harshness of the sentence, say James is speaking about other men's tongues—who can stop them?—as if it were a saying similar to Psalm 120:3, "What will he do to you, and what more besides, O deceitful tongue?" That is, how shall I stop it? But this also does not agree with the apostle's intention; he does not say how we should bridle other men's tongues but our own. The meaning is, then, that no one can do it by himself.

It is a restless evil. Some take this causally: it is the cause of sedition and unruliness. But I think it means what was formerly expressed: it is an evil that cannot be controlled. It is a metaphor taken from animals that are kept in cages or chained. God has, in the structure of the mouth, made a double barrier of teeth and lips and through grace laid many restraints upon the tongue, and yet it breaks out.

Full of deadly poison. This is an allusion to poisonous creatures. The tongue is as deadly, and has as much need to be tamed, as venomous beasts. Besides, some beasts carry their poison in their tongues, as the asp does in a sac under the tongue, which, when they bite, is broken, and then the poison comes out. That is why it is said, "They make their tongues as sharp as a serpent's" (Psalm 140:3).

Notes on Verse 7

Note 1. Observe the tractableness of the animals to man, and the disobedience of man to God. Wild animals are tamed, snakes are charmed by our skill, but we are not charmed by all the enticements and allurements of heaven: "Their venom is like the venom of a snake, like that of a cobra that has stopped its ears, that will not heed the tune of the charmer, however skillful the enchanter may be" (Psalm 58:4-5). The ox, a creature of great strength, is obedient to man, a weaker creature; but we kick our heel against God, as the prophet says: "The ox knows his master, the donkey his owner's manger, but Israel does not know, my people do not understand" (Isaiah 1:3). Fallen man may learn mildness and obedience from the animals, and yet God has more power to subdue, and we have more reason to obey.

Note 2. Observe the greatness of man's folly and impotence in ruling his own soul. Though he tames other things, he does not tame himself. We seek to recover our loss of dominion over the creatures, but who seeks to recover the power that he once had over his own soul? How can we look to have our dominion over inferior creatures when through our wrong desires we make ourselves like one of them? We all want sovereignty but not holiness. Men seek to conquer others but not themselves. Solomon says, "Better . . . a man who controls his temper than one who takes a city" (Proverbs 16:32); that is the nobler conquest, but we do not achieve it. It was Augustine's complaint that we do not tame the beasts in our own hearts. The evil tongue is the worst snake.

Note 3. See the depth of human misery. Our own skill is able to tame the fiercest animals and make them useful—animals as strong as lions and elephants, as well as birds and snakes. But alas, there is more rebellion in our affections; sin is stronger, and our will cannot tame it. We may teach animals to do things contrary to their natural dispositions—elephants to crouch, horses to dance; but man is "a beast that will not easily come to hand," as Plato said.

Note 4. Skill in subduing creatures is a relic of our old superiority. The heathen discerned that we once had dominion, and the Scriptures plainly assert it: "Let us make man in our image, in our likeness, and let them rule over the fish of the sea and the birds of the air, over the livestock, over all the earth, and over all the creatures that move along the ground" (Genesis 1:26). Next to God's glory, they were ordained for man's service and benefit. All the animals were to come to Adam and receive their names, which was a kind of formal submission to his rule. To maintain this rule, God gave man wisdom, and instinct in the creatures through which they obeyed him. But ever since the fall this right was forfeited, and the creatures rebelled against obeying man. But the elect have a new right in Christ, which reinstates them to absolute rule over the creatures. Then the creation will be freed from the bondage of corruption and will be subject to the children of God (see Romans 8:19-22). But for the present this dominion is exercised in a much more inferior way than it was in innocency.

Notes on Verse 8

Note 1. The tongue is barely subdued for any good use. And in this life God does not give absolute grace to avoid every idle word. This refutes the idea of the power of free will alone; we cannot tame one part of the body. Consider the offenses of the tongue and you will see that you must walk humbly with God. If it cannot be tamed, what shall we do? Why do you tell us to bridle it? I answer:

(1) Though we have lost our power, God must not lose his right.

Weakness does not exempt us from duty; we must bridle the tongue, though we cannot do this ourselves.

(2) Even if we cannot bridle it, God can. "It is hard for a rich man to enter the kingdom of heaven . . . but with God all things are possible" (Matthew 19:23, 26). Difficulty and impossibility as to the creature's endeavors are established, that we may fly to God. The horse does not tame himself, nor the camel himself; man tames the beast, and God tames man. You tame a lion, and you did not make it; but God made you, and shall he not tame you?

(3) To those who attempt it and do what they are able, God will give grace; he never fails a diligent, waiting soul. Our first desires come from him, and so does their accomplishment; offer yourselves to do his work.

(4) Though we are not altogether without sin, we must not stop resisting sin. Sin *reigns* where it is not resisted; it only *remains* in you where it is opposed.

But you will say, what is our duty? I answer:

(1) Come before God humbly; bewail the depravity of your nature, manifested in this uncontrolled part of the body. This was one of the sins that Augustine confessed; he said his tongue was always an Etna throwing out fire. Tell God about it.

(2) Come earnestly. This was one of the occasions when Augustine in his *Confessions* sobbed, "Lord, give what you command, and command what you wish." He said this about lust and about the evils of the tongue. Cry for help—"Set a guard over my mouth, O Lord" (Psalm 141:3).

Note 2. **Restless evil**. There is an unbridled license in the tongue. When the mind is full of ideas, the tongue is keen to utter them. Therefore, we should use not only spiritual care but a holy restraint: "I will put a muzzle on my mouth" (Psalm 39:1). You need to look to the heart. Humble the heart into sweet submission.

Note 3. **Full of deadly poison**. A wicked tongue is venomous and hurtful. As Bernard observes, it kills three things at once: the person who is slandered (his reputation, from bad reports) and the person to whom it is told (he believes a lie) and himself (with the sin of defamation). Bless God when you escape those deadly bites; nothing but innocence will keep you safe. But if this is your lot, bear it with patience; there is a resurrection of reputations as well as of persons.

Commentary on Verse 9

With the tongue we praise our Lord and Father, and with it we curse men, who have been made in God's likeness.

Here James shows the good and bad use of the tongue: the good, to bless God; and the bad, to curse men—as well as the absurdity of doing both with the same tongue. You use the same part of your body for the best and worst purposes.

I will explain the phrases in the notes.

Notes on Verse 9

Note 1. The correct use of the tongue is to bless God: "O Lord, open my lips, and my mouth will declare your praise" (Psalm 51:15). Since God gives the gift of speech, he must have the glory; we owe it to him. This is the advantage we have over creatures, that we can be explicit in praising God. "All you have made will praise you, O LORD; your saints will extol you" (Psalm 145:10). The whole creation is like a well-tuned instrument, but man makes the music. Speech, being the most excellent faculty, should be consecrated to divine uses: "Nor should there be obscenity, foolish talk or coarse joking, which are out of place, but rather thanksgiving" (Ephesians 5:4). So then, go away and say, "I will extol the LORD at all times; his praise will always be on my lips" (Psalm 34:1). This brings heaven on earth. Some birds sing in winter as well as in spring. Stir up one another (Ephesians 5:19), just as one bird sets a whole flock singing.

Note 2. **Our Lord and Father.** That is, Christ (see 1:27). We bless God most cheerfully when we consider him as a father. Thoughts of God as a judge do not bring comfort. Our meditations on him are sweet when we look on him as a father in Christ. But not everyone can learn the Lamb's new song (Revelation 14:3). Wicked men can howl, though they cannot sing. Pharaoh in his misery could say, "The LORD is in the right" (Exodus 9:27).

Note 3. **And with it we curse men.** The same tongue should not bless God and **curse men**; this is hypocrisy. Acts of piety are empty when acts of charity are neglected: "God says, 'What right have you to recite my laws or take my covenant on your lips? . . . You use your mouth for evil and harness your tongue to deceit. You speak continually against your brother and slander your own mother's son'" (Psalm 50:16, 19-20). Hypocrites are the most censorious, but true piety makes people meek and humble. Some people can curse and bless at the same time: "With their mouths they bless, but in their hearts they curse" (Psalm 62:4); other people curse, pretending to be pious. The evils of the tongue, where they are not restrained, are inconsistent with true piety. With this tongue I have been speaking to God, and shall it presently be **set on fire by hell?**

Note 4. Man is made after God's own image: "Let us make man in our image, in our likeness" (Genesis 1:26). We may catch glimpses of God in his works, but in man we see God's very image and likeness. God's image in man consists in three things:

(1) In his nature, which was rational. God gave man a rational soul, simple, immortal, free in its choice; indeed, in the body there were some rays of divine glory and majesty.

(2) In those qualities of "knowledge" (Colossians 3:10), "upright[ness]" (Ecclesiastes 7:29), and "true righteousness and holiness" (Ephesians 4:24).

(3) In his state—all inward and outward blessings combined, as he enjoys God, exercises power over creatures, etc.

But this image is defaced and can only be restored in Christ. This was the great privilege of our creation—to be made like God; the more we resemble him, the more happy we are. Remember your original height. We urge people to walk worthy of their origins. Plutarch says of Alexander that he used to strengthen his courage by remembering that he came from the gods. Remember that you were made in the image of God; do not deface it in yourselves or make it open to contempt by giving others opportunity to revile you.

Note 5. We are dissuaded from slandering and speaking evil of others when we consider that they are made in God's image. I shall inquire how this can be a motive and wherein its force lies.

(1) How can this be a motive, since the image and likeness of God is defaced and lost by the fall? I answer:

a. He is speaking about new creatures especially, in whom Adam's loss is repaired and made up again in Christ: "[You] have put on the new self, which is being renewed in knowledge in the image of its Creator" (Colossians 3:10). "Put on the new self, created to be like God in true righteousness and holiness" (Ephesians 4:24). God is sensitive about his new creatures; intemperance of tongue against saints is dangerous. As the centurion asked, "What are you going to do? This man is a Roman citizen" (Acts 22:26), so take care what you say: these are Christians, created in God's image, choice pieces whom God has restored out of the common ruins.

b. He may be speaking about all people, for there are a few relics of God's image in everyone: "Whoever sheds the blood of man, by man shall his blood be shed; for in the image of God has God made man" (Genesis 9:6). There would be no force in this reason if there were nothing of God left in man after sin, though much deformed. So this saying in James argues that there still remains in people some resemblance to God, such as the simplicity and immortality of the soul; some moral inclinations instead of true holiness; ordinary evidences of the nature and will of God instead of saving knowledge. Although these cannot make us happy, they serve to leave us without excuse. There is also some preeminence over other creatures, as we have a mind to know God, being capable of divine illumination and grace.

(2) Wherein lies the force of the argument—cursing man made in God's image? I answer:

a. God has made man his deputy to receive love and common respect. Higher respect of trust and worship are to be reserved for God alone, but in other things Christians, even the poorest of them, are Christ's receivers. "He who rejects you rejects me" (Luke 10:16). "Whatever you did not do for one of the least of these, you did not do for me" (Matthew 25:45).

b. God himself is wronged by the injury done to his image, just as among men contempt and spite for the king's image or coin is done to the king himself. In Matthew 23:18 to swear by the altar, which was the symbol of God's presence, was to swear by God.

c. This is the fence God has placed against injury: "for in the image of God has God made man" (Genesis 9:6). This is referred not to the murderer, as if he had sinned against those common ideas of justice and right in his conscience, but to the victim, who is the image of God. God has honored this lump of flesh by stamping his own image on him; and who would dare to violate the image of the great King? To speak evil against him is to wrong the image of God. All God's works are to be looked on and spoken of with reverence, and much more his image.

So then, in your behavior toward people let this check any injury or impropriety of speech: this person is in God's image. Though images are not to be worshiped, yet the image of God is not to be splattered with reproaches, especially if they are new creations: these are vessels of honor. Consider who the sin is against: it is spiting God himself, because it is done to his work and image. Solomon says, "He who mocks the poor shows contempt for their Maker" (Proverbs 17:5).

Commentary on Verse 10

Out of the same mouth come praise and cursing. My brothers, this should not be.

James amplifies the absurdity by repeating it. Note his meekness: he might have reproved them sharply, but in dissuading them from the evils of the tongue he wants to give them a pattern of modesty and gentleness.

This should not be. That is, it should be quite different. This is a phrase savoring of apostolic meekness: see 1 Timothy 5:13 and Titus 1:11.

Notes on Verse 10

Note 1. Blessings and cursings do not suit the same mouth. This is like the person in Aesop who blew hot and cold with the same breath. A good person should be constant. The same heart cannot be occupied by God and the devil, nor the same tongue be used for such different purposes. The Pharisee prayed and censured at the same time (Luke 18:11). When the tongue is employed in prayer, it is as it were hallowed and consecrated, and therefore must not be used for vile purposes.

Note 2. **Should not be.** We must look not to what we desire to do but what ought to be done. Lust, or the bent of the spirit, is not the rule of duty. Many people advise with no other counselor but their own hearts; worldly constraints are a poor warrant. Animals are led by strength of instinct and natural impulse; man is to be governed by an outward rule. There is a higher Lord than your own will. Look, then, not at what you want to do, but at what you **should** do.

Commentary on Verses 11-12

Can both fresh water and salt water flow from the same spring? My brothers, can a fig tree bear olives, or a grapevine bear figs? Neither can a salt spring produce fresh water.

Here are several illustrations taken from the same aspect of nature, to show that one cause can give birth to only one sort of thing. He reasons from what is impossible in nature to what is absurd in manners.

Notes on Verses 11-12

Nature abhors hypocrisy; contrary effects from the same cause are against the way God orders matters in creation. It is true that a Christian has a double principle—flesh and spirit—but not a double heart. Hate the double-dealing that occurs when you profess religion and live in sin. See how contrary this is to the whole course of nature; say, "Surely this cannot come from a uniform and good heart." Especially use these illustrations to check the deformities of your speech. When you are inclined to both bless and curse, to pray and revile, say, "This would be monstrous in nature; is there anything else in the world with such different uses as the tongue?"

Commentary on Verse 13

Who is wise and understanding among you? Let him show it by his good life, by deeds done in the humility that comes from wisdom.

James now diverts to another matter, though it is closely related to the previous one—an exhortation to meekness as opposed to envy and strife.

Who is wise and understanding among you? He speaks about wisdom and **understanding** because all the former evils come from thinking that we have greater ability than others or because they affect the reputation of prudent Christians. Now, says the apostle, if you would indeed be like this, you must have a meek godliness.

Let him show it by his good life. The first requisite of true wisdom is to honor knowledge in practice, that being the point of all information; and the understanding person has a greater obligation to duty than do other people.

By deeds done in the humility that comes from wisdom. Here is the second requisite: prudent meekness in behavior, wisdom being most able to consider frailties and to bridle anger.

Notes on Verse 13

Note 1. Wisdom and **understanding** go well together; one informs, the other directs. Good apprehension and good judgment make a complete Christian. Where there is heavenly wisdom, there will also be prudence, a practical application of our light to the occurrences of life. So do not rest in "the embodiment of knowledge" (Romans 2:20); couple it with wisdom. A Christian is better known by his life than by his speech. Mere "knowledge puffs up" (1 Corinthians 8:1). People who speculate sublimely are just wise fools, like the lark that soars high and peers and peers but falls into the fowler's net. Knowledge without wisdom may soon be discerned; it is usually curious and censorious.

Note 2. True wisdom ends in good behavior. Surely the practical Christian is the most wise: in others, knowledge is only like a jewel in a toad's head. "Observe [God's laws] carefully, for this will show your wisdom" (Deuteronomy 4:6). This is saving knowledge; the other is mere curiosity. The point of all this is to examine those who please themselves with a false wisdom.

(1) The worldly wise. People are cunning and spin a web of vanity in achieving their worldly aims. Alas, this is the greatest folly! "Since they have rejected the word of the LORD, what kind of wisdom do they have?"

(Jeremiah 8:9). Who would dig for iron with picks of gold? Similarly, your spirits and your deepest concerns are worth more than vanity; they are tools that God uses for more than mere iron.

(2) Those who content themselves with human knowledge. Some can almost unravel nature but do not know God or themselves. Some of the heathen were well endowed with intelligence, but "although they claimed to be wise, they became fools" (Romans 1:22).

(3) People who hunt for ideas and sublime speculations, knowing only in order that they may know. A poor soul that looks to heaven has more true wisdom than all the great rabbis of the world: "The statutes of the LORD are trustworthy, making wise the simple" (Psalm 19:7).

(4) Those who are sinfully crafty have enough wit to brew wickedness. It is better to be a fool in that craft: "In regard to evil be infants, but in your thinking be adults" (1 Corinthians 14:20). Happy are those whose souls never enter into sin's secrets! "I want you to be wise about what is good, and innocent about what is evil" (Romans 16:19).

Note 3. The more true wisdom is, the more it is meek. Wise men are less angry and more humble.

(1) They are less angry. Much is spoken about a fool's wrath: "Stone is heavy and sand a burden, but provocation by a fool is heavier than both" (Proverbs 27:3). He lacks judgment to moderate its rage. The more wisdom a person has, the more he can check passion. "A man's wisdom gives him patience" (Proverbs 19:11).

(2) They are more humble. "With humility comes wisdom" (Proverbs 11:2). Pride and folly always go together, and so do humility and wisdom. The world often looks on meekness as folly, but it is heavenly wisdom. Moses is renowned in Scripture for wisdom and meekness. Those who are morally wise are the most humble. "The unfading beauty of a gentle and quiet spirit . . . is of great worth in God's sight" (1 Peter 3:4). The world counts this an effeminate softness; God counts it as beautiful. This is the best Christian temper. There are excellent fruits of meekness that reveal its use (see, for example, 2 Timothy 2:25 and Proverbs 15:1).

Note 4. **Let him show it.** A Christian must not only have a good heart but a good life, and must in his behavior show the graces of his spirit: see Matthew 5:16. We must study to honor God and honor our profession of faith. It is one thing to do works that can be seen and another to do them in order that they shall be seen.

Commentary on Verse 14

But if you harbor bitter envy and selfish ambition [strife, KJV] in your hearts, do not boast about it or deny the truth.

Having shown the effect of true wisdom, James infers that if the contrary were found in them, they would have little cause to glory; and he mentions two opposites to the double effect of wisdom: **envy** and **selfish ambition**.

But if you harbor. The apostle's modesty in reproving is noticeable. He does not positively indict them but speaks hypothetically, as he does in 1:25 and 2:15. In reproofs it is wiser to proceed hypothetically than by direct accusation.

Bitter envy. He notes the root of tongue-evils. We say it is zeal and justice, but the true cause is envy. He calls it **bitter envy** to distinguish it from holy emulation. It is **bitter** to ourselves and others. It makes us unpleasant to those with whom we have dealings.

And selfish ambition. This is the usual effect of envy. And he says **in your hearts** because although it is managed with the tongue or hand, it is first contrived in the heart, and because this aggravates the matter. There may be unintended breaches between Christians, but where they are cherished they are abominable.

Do not boast about it—that is, either your Christianity (allowing an evil so contrary to it) or your zeal (which is so culpable) or any special wisdom and ability, as if you were able to reprove others (this is the most probable meaning, for the main drift is against opinionated wisdom). You have no reason to boast of your intelligence and zeal in censuring or contention, as people often do in such cases, unless you want to glory in your own shame; rather, you have cause to be humbled, that you may get these vile affections mortified.

Or deny the truth. Some say this means by a worldly profession of faith. Hypocrisy is a practical lie. Some *speak* lies, others *do* them. But "he who does what is true comes to the light" (John 3:21, RSV). Beware of false pretenses of zeal and wisdom: see Romans 11:1 and 1 John 1:6.

Notes on Verse 14

Note 1. Envy is the mother of strife. They are often coupled. In Romans 1:29 "full of envy" is followed by "murder, strife . . ."; see also Romans 13:13; 1 Corinthians 3:3; 2 Corinthians 12:20; Galatians 5:20. There are two sins that were Christ's sorest enemies: covetousness and envy. Covetousness sold Christ, and envy delivered him. These two sins are still enemies to Christian profession. Covetousness makes us sell religion, and envy makes us persecute it. So "do nothing out of selfish ambition or vain conceit" (Philippians 2:3).

Note 2. **Selfish ambition in your hearts.** There is nothing in a person's life that was not first in his heart (see Matthew 15:19); that is the source of sin and the fountain of folly. So look to the heart; keep that clean if you want to have your life free from wrong. "Above all else, guard your heart, for it is the wellspring of life" (Proverbs 4:23). If you want to have a public life that is holy, let your heart be pure before God; especially cleanse your heart from **envy and selfish ambition**.

Note 3. Envious or contentious people have little reason to be proud. Envy suggests either an absence or poverty of grace. Where there is an absence of grace, envy reigns; and where envy is resisted but not overcome, grace is weak. "Those who belong to Christ Jesus have crucified the sinful nature with its passions and desires" (Galatians 5:24). "I saw," says Augustine, "a little child looking pale with envy." This is natural but odious; it is an attack on God and his dispensations, as if he had distributed his gifts unequally. It also hurts others; we malign the good that is in them, and so come hatred and persecution. This is also painful to ourselves, and so Proverbs 14:30 says that "envy rots the bones." In short, it arises from pride, is carried out in covetousness and evil desire, and ends in discontent. "Get rid of all bitterness, rage and anger" (Ephesians 4:31). It is hateful to God, prejudicial to others, troublesome to ourselves; it is its own punishment.

Envy reveals its presence:

(1) By grief at others' enjoyment. In Genesis 4 Cain was sad because Abel's sacrifice was accepted. Other people's having something does not cause our lack of it, but we envy it.

(2) In rejoicing at their evils, disgrace, and ruin: see Psalm 22:7.

(3) By lack of sharing. People want everything enclosed within their boundary and are vexed at the most common gifts of others, because they want to shine alone. Moses, on the contrary, said, "I wish that all the LORD's people were prophets" (Numbers 11:29). Consider these things, and how inappropriate they are to your professed faith. The same applies to strife: it does not become those who should be cemented with the same blood of Christ. All strife is bad; your heart is never better for it. But envious strife is worst of all. Paul said that some people preached the Gospel out of "envy" (Philippians 1:15), and in this way religion, which is the best thing, is made to serve the vilest desires.

Note 4. Envy and strife often go under the guise of zeal. It is easy to assume a pretense of religion. One faction at Corinth called their sect by the name of Christ: "I follow Christ" (1 Corinthians 1:12). They are listed among the rest of the factions; "I follow Christ," in the apostle's sense, is as bad as "I follow Paul," "I follow Apollos," and "I follow Cephas." So then, examine those desires that appear under the guise of religion; there may be zeal in the pretense, and bitter envy at the bottom.

There are two shrewd presumptions upon which, if you cannot

absolutely condemn this sort of thing, you may have cause to be suspicious. One is when it boils up into odd and peculiar actions. True zeal, though it may increase the stream, does not usually make it overflow the banks and break one rule to vindicate another. The other is when we are inclined to glory and boast, as in this passage. We usually boast of graces of our own making. "Come with me and see my zeal for the LORD" (2 Kings 10:16) was in effect simply, "Come and discern my pride and hypocrisy." Hypocrites have so little of the power of religion that they adore their own form.

Note 5. Hypocrisy is the worst kind of lie. The practical lie is worst of all. By other lies we *deny* the truth, but by this we *abuse* it; and sometimes it is worse to abuse an enemy than to destroy him. The practical lie is little better than blasphemy: "I know the slander [KJV, blasphemy—*Ed. note*] of those who say they are Jews and are not" (Revelation 2:9).

Commentary on Verse 15

Such "wisdom" does not come down from heaven but is earthly, unspiritual, of the devil.

To right the truth against whose glory they had lied, James adds these words, showing that though they had a pretense of zeal and wisdom, it was not heavenly wisdom but the sort that comes from the devil or the corrupt human heart. There is a great deal of difference between cunning and holy wisdom.

Such "wisdom" does not come down from heaven—that is, from God (as in 1:17), whose glory chiefly shines in the heavens; true wisdom comes from there. Some people see a criticism in the Greek word translated **come down**, which strictly speaking means "returns"; we lost it in Adam, and we receive it again **from heaven**. The sense, then, is that this is no wisdom of God's giving. But, you will say, all common knowledge comes from God, even that which concerns earthly matters. I answer: the apostle is not just speaking about skill but worldly wisdom and shows it is not the sort the Holy Spirit gives, but is inspired by the spirit of darkness.

But is earthly. Here he shows the properties of worldly wisdom; he lists three, matching the three sorts of lusts mentioned in 1 John 2:16. It is called **earthly** because it suits earthly minds and is used for earthly things, for a worldly or earthly purpose. In the same way Paul speaks about some people who are only wise for this world (1 Corinthians 3:18).

Unspiritual. The Greek word can be translated "animal." It is elsewhere rendered "natural"—"the natural man" (1 Corinthians 2:14, KJV;

the NIV has, "the man without the Spirit"—*Ed. note*), one guided by worldly reason; he is opposed to "the spiritual man" in 1 Corinthians 2:15, one who has divine illumination. This word is used again in Jude 19. The word strictly means those who have a soul or something that arises from the soul, and it is usually contrasted with the light and saving work of the Spirit. It is good to know on what grounds it was translated **sensual** [in the KJV]. I suppose the reason is partly the passage in 1 Thessalonians 5:23 where the apostle distinguishes "spirit, soul and body" as the three parts of the sanctifying work of the Holy Spirit. By "spirit" he understands the intellectual or rational part; by "soul," the mere animal part, which has the senses, the sensual appetite, what we have in common with animals; by "body" he means what we commonly understand by the word, the body as the organ and instrument of the soul. So as "spirit" is seen by James to mean our mere animal part, the translators render it **sensual** [KJV; **unspiritual** in the NIV—*Ed. note*].

Of the devil. This is the third characteristic of false wisdom. It is called this because:

(1) Satan is the author; worldly men are taught by hell. "The god of this age has blinded the minds of unbelievers" (2 Corinthians 4:4; see also Ephesians 2:2).

(2) It is the sort of wisdom that is in the devil; he is wise, so to speak, to do harm. He appeared in the form of the serpent, a subtle creature. Pride, ambition, envy, wrath, revenge—these are Satan's lusts. There are some sins that the Scripture calls "fleshly and beastly lusts," and there are other sins that are called "Satan's lusts" (see John 8:44). Man has something in common with the animals and something in common with the angels. Adultery, riot, etc., make a man brutish; envy, pride, malice, slander, etc., make a man devilish. The devil does not commit adultery, steal, etc., but he is proud, envious, and slanderous. Pride is his original sin, and so Paul says that a person "may become conceited and fall under the same judgment as the devil" (1 Timothy 3:6). Envy and slander are his actual sins. He envies lost man. He intelligently devises calumnies and reproaches; it is his work to be accusing and making public the sins and faults of others. This latter sense is the best.

Notes on Verse 15

Note 1. We should study the source of what we conceive to be wisdom. Is it from heaven or from the devil? The quality is often to be determined by reference to the source. True wisdom is inspired by God and taught out of the Word. See, for both, Job 32:8 and Proverbs 2:6; it is prayed for in 1

Kings 3:9 and Psalm 25:4-5. People have a natural ability to understand and discuss, but without the assistance and counsel and illumination of the Spirit we can do nothing in divine matters; we have this from God, from his Word and Spirit, after waiting and prayer. God's mind is revealed in Scripture, but we can see nothing without the spectacles of the Holy Spirit. The quickest, sharpest eye needs light: "He gives wisdom to the wise and knowledge to the discerning" (Daniel 2:21). So you who lay claim to wisdom in religion may know from this what sort it is, whether you were indeed wise. Prayer will be a great part of your duty, and the Word will be your rule and the Spirit your Counselor; and then there only needs to be one more thing, which is thankfulness to your Teacher. Wisdom, as it comes from God, will carry the soul to God, just as the rivers return to the sea from which they came.

Note 2. Human wisdom is corrupt. "Those who live according to the sinful nature have their minds set on what that nature desires" (Romans 8:5). All the discussions of the understanding, until it is sanctified, are only foolish. If wisdom is merely *natural*, it will soon be *devilish*. How vain are people without the Spirit of God in their worship! How wrongheaded in their conversations! The heathen, "although they claimed to be wise . . . became fools" (Romans 1:22). So do not rely on your own understanding. Soul-light is not enough; there must be spirit-light. The whole man is corrupted—head and heart and feet and all.

Note 3. Worldly wisdom is either **earthly** or **sensual** or devilish. It is a perfect distribution, like that in 1 John 2:16—"For everything in the world—the cravings of sinful man, the lust of his eyes and the boasting of what he has and does—comes not from the Father but from the world." The evils of the world may be reduced to these three heads— sensuality, covetousness, and pride, matching the treble bait that is in the world—pleasures, honors, profits, which pierce the hearts of all worldly people. Thus the devil assaulted our first ancestors (Genesis 3:6): it was for "fruit" (there is "the cravings of sinful man"); it was for the eyes (there is "the lust of his eyes"); it was for "wisdom" (there is "boasting"). Thus the devil assaulted Christ. He tempted him (Matthew 4) to turn stones into bread to satisfy his appetite; he showed him the glory of the world to tempt his eyes: "Throw yourself down"—there is presumption and indiscreet confidence. This is contrary to the three graces commended by the Gospel—being self-controlled, upright, and godly: "the grace of God . . . teaches us to . . . live self-controlled, upright and godly lives in this present age" (Titus 2:11-12). *Self-controlled* in contrast to the lusts of the flesh; *upright* in contrast to the lust of the eyes; and *godly* to check boasting. In short, the three great ends of our creation are our salvation, the good of others, and the glory of God. When people waste their days in pleasure, they neglect this great salvation. Covetousness is the bane of love, and pride and self-seeking turns us away from serving God's glory. All sins, you see, grow on these roots.

Note 4. **Earthly.** Wisdom that you find to be **earthly** should be suspect. A Christian should be wise for the kingdom of heaven: "The people of this world are more shrewd in dealing with their own kind than are the people of the light" (Luke 16:8). It is sad to be a fool for duty and wise for the world, to be serious in trifles and to trifle in serious matters. To the children of God it is said, "Set your minds on things above" (Colossians 3:2).

Note 5. **Sensual** wisdom, the sort that tends to gratify the senses and is spent on outward pleasures, is mere folly. Animals, which are not chosen by God, excel us in temperance; they are content with as much as natural instinct requires, and yet they enjoy pleasures without remorse. Vain men rack their wits and use their understandings to nurture their lusts; and they make provocation worse by sacrificing their time, care, and precious thoughts to so vain an interest as that of the stomach. Certainly our spite against the Lord is great; when we dethrone him we set up the basest things in his place: "their god is their stomach" (Philippians 3:19).

Note 6. **Of the devil.** Fallen man not only has something of the beast in him, but something of the devil. Christ had only twelve disciples, and one of those was a devil (see John 6:70). It was said of Judas when he plotted against Christ, "Then Satan entered Judas" (Luke 22:3); and then, says Luther, "there was a devil in a devil." All wicked people are Satan's slaves. Some are like devils themselves in contriving mischief, hatching wickedness, slandering the godly, envying the gracious state of their brothers, etc.

Commentary on Verse 16

For where you have envy and selfish ambition, there you find disorder and every evil practice.

James proves that such devilish wisdom as serves envy and selfish ambition cannot be good wisdom, for it brings about quite contrary effects— the one for holiness and meekness, the other for confusion and profanity. This sentence may be understood to apply either publicly or privately.

(1) If it is understood to refer to private individuals, the sense is that in whatever heart **envy and selfish ambition** reign, there is also great **disorder** and wickedness.

(2) If it is understood in a public sense, it means that in a society where **envy and selfish ambition** reign, there will be unrest and all licentiousness. Selfish ambition follows envy, and sedition follows selfish ambition, and all manner of wickedness is the fruit of sedition.

Notes on Verse 16

Note 1. If the verse refers to private individuals, then note that a spirit of **envy and selfish ambition** is an unquiet and wicked spirit.

(1) It is an unquiet and disorderly spirit; nothing unsettles the mind more. Other people's contentment and happiness proves our sorrow. An envious person "brings himself harm" (Proverbs 11:17).

(2) An envious spirit is a wicked spirit; there is no wickedness such a person will not undertake and carry out. The devil works on nothing so much as envy and discontent; such a spirit is fit for Satan's lure. So then, watch for the first stirrings of this, and check it as soon as the soul begins to look sour upon another person's happiness and betterment; you do not know how far the devil may carry you. The first instances that we have of sin are Adam's pride and Cain's envy; the first man was undone by pride, and the second debauched by envy. The whole world, even if there were no other people in it, could not contain two brothers when one was envied. Pride gave us the first *merit* of death and envy the first *instance* of it; the one was the mother, the other the midwife of human ruin. Adam was a sinner, but Cain a murderer; there envy tasted blood, and ever since it has been glutted with it. Cain's envy tasted the blood of Abel, but Saul's thirsted for David's, and Joab's gorged itself with that of Abner and Amasa. And still, if the severity of laws restrain envy from blood, it pines if it is not fed with injury.

Note 2. If this verse refers to society, then note that where there is **envy and selfish ambition**, there will be tumults and confusions. Disaffection divides as much as disagreement. Desire is the great breeder of strife. An envious and proud spirit may undo a commonwealth. Watch your hearts then. We also learn from this that religion is a friend to civil peace; it strikes not only at **disorder** in life but at desire in the heart, at envy and pride, the private roots of contention. Why should the world hate such religion? It represents a God who is "not a God of disorder but of peace" (1 Corinthians 14:33). It holds out a Gospel that is "the good news of peace" (Acts 10:36). It establishes a wisdom that prescribes the ways of peace (Hebrews 12:14; Romans 12:18). It increases the number of godly people, who are best in any community; mortified spirits are the most peaceable. Pride, envy, and self-seeking hustle other people into unrest, and they move all to serve their own desires and interests.

Note 3. Through unrest and contention every evil work abounds. Wickedness then takes heart and acts without restraint. Today this Scripture is fulfilled before our eyes; we need no other comment but our own experience. Envy makes us quarrel with one another, and quarreling gives opportunity for all loose behavior.

Commentary on Verse 17

But the wisdom that comes from heaven is first of all pure; then peace loving, considerate, submissive, full or mercy and good fruit, impartial and sincere.

James now comes to list the fruits of true wisdom. He calls it **the wisdom that comes from heaven** because all wisdom is known by where it comes from. He gives it several properties; they will be best explained in the notes.

Notes on Verse 17

Note 1. True wisdom is a pure and holy wisdom. The word that we translate **pure** means "chaste," "modest." There are two sorts of purity: that which excludes mixture (so we say wine is pure when it is not adulterated) and that which excludes dirt (so we say water is pure when it is not muddy). In the former sense purity is contrasted with hypocrisy, and in the latter it is contrasted with uncleanness, which is the correct meaning in this passage, since the word means "chaste." But you will say, "Who can say, 'I have kept my heart pure; I am clean and without sin'?" (Proverbs 20:9). The answer will be best given in looking at the meaning of the term. I will do it by six pairs:

(1) True wisdom is a cleanness in heart and life. Christ says, "Blessed are the pure in heart" (Matthew 5:8); and David says, "Blessed are they whose ways are blameless [undefiled, KJV]" (Psalm 119:1). The heart must be pure and the way undefiled. See also 4:8, **Wash your hands, you sinners, and purify your hearts, you double-minded**. Scandalous people (whom he means by **sinners**) must **wash** their *hands*; hypocrites (**double-minded**) must **purify** their *hearts*. The first care must be for the heart; a pure spirit will not brook filthy thoughts. Christ condemns the lustful glance (Matthew 5:28); and Peter speaks about some people who had "eyes full of adultery" (2 Peter 2:14), implying the impure rollings of the imagination. True Christians "abstain from sinful desires" (1 Peter 2:11) and also "put to death the misdeeds of the body" (Romans 8:13). Then after this we must look to the life and see that it is empty of scandals, so that as we do not incur blame from inward guilt, we do not give just cause for shame from outward behavior either. Then the good conscience may be a feast to give for a cheerful heart, and the good reputation will be an ointment to give a cheerful face. As in the soul there should not be "passionate lust," so

the body must be kept "in a way that is holy and honorable" (1 Thessalonians 4:4). This is the first pair: a pure spirit and a pure life.

(2) True wisdom will not brook filthiness either of error or of sin; error is a blot, as is sin. The way of God is called the holy commandment, and the way of the Gentiles is called "the corruption of the world" (2 Peter 2:20). Jude 8 says false teachers are "dreamers" who "pollute their own bodies." They are "dreamers" because of the folly and dotage which is found in error, and they "pollute" because of its defilement; therefore true wisdom must be made up of truth and holiness. It is said of deacons, "They must keep hold of the deep truths of the faith with a clear conscience" (1 Timothy 3:9). Precious wines are best kept in clean vessels. Some people are zealous against errors, yet are slaves to their own lusts. It is as great a judgment to be delivered up to vile affections as to a vain mind. Jerome speaks of some people who were "heathens not in opinion but in behavior." It is said of Julian the Apostate that he was a very just, temperate, strict man, but a bitter enemy to Christ. It is excellent when we can see truth and holiness matched. Sound in faith, fervent in love—how well these go together.

(3) In word and deed. We read of the pure life, "I will purify the lips" (Zephaniah 3:9). Many sin complacently with their tongues but do not want to be seen as bad as they appear in their talk. But the tongue **corrupts the whole person** (3:6). The apostle condemns "foolish talk" and "unwholesome talk" (Ephesians 5:4 and 4:29).

(4) There must be both an evangelical and a moral cleanness; that is, there must be not only an abstinence from grosser sins, but the heart must be washed in the blood of Christ, cleansed from unbelieving thoughts. The pure are principally those who believe (rightly) that their sins are pardoned in Christ and are renewed by the Holy Spirit. There is not only an abstinence from sin but a purging of their consciences and a washing of their hearts in the "fountain . . . opened . . . to cleanse them from sin and impurity" (Zechariah 13:1; see also 1 John 1:7). Many take little thought for this; they are civilly moral and lead a fair life in the world, but they are not "washed . . . sanctified . . . in the name of the Lord Jesus Christ and by the Spirit of our God" (1 Corinthians 6:11). Others look for salvation but not moral cleanness; they exalt justification to exclude sanctification. True purity is when the spirit is purged from both guilt and filth, the conscience being cleansed from "acts that lead to death" (Hebrews 9:14) and the heart from "a guilty conscience" (Hebrews 10:22).

(5) True wisdom must be in our interior life as well as in our behavior. People love to divide what God has joined; purity of heart and purity of ordinances must go together. Many people want pure behavior, and yet have an unclean spirit, as if outward reformation were enough. When the conscience is purged, then it is fit to "serve the living God" (Hebrews

9:14). Public care should not excuse private care; our first task is to attend to our own spirits. But there are other people who think all reform is confined to a person's own heart: look to yourself, and everything will be all right. Satan is busy everywhere. When external endeavor is perilous, then we think it is enough to watch ourselves. But as we are to watch ourselves, so we are also to watch others: "See to it, brothers, that none of you has a sinful, unbelieving heart" (Hebrews 3:12). "See to it that no one misses the grace of God and that no bitter root grows up to cause trouble and defile many" (Hebrews 12:15). The whole person is polluted not only by the infection and contagion, but by the guilt of the part that sins; scandalous sins are a blot on the body, until effectual remedies are used. True purity shows itself uniformly in public and private reformation.

(6) True wisdom avoids real defilement and apparent defilement: "Since we have these promises, dear friends, let us purify ourselves from everything that contaminates body and spirit" (2 Corinthians 7:1). What does this mean? To keep the body pure from the appearance of sin and to keep the heart pure from the guilt of sin. The case in question concerned being present at idol feasts, though they knew the idol to be nothing. The apostle dissuaded them by the promises of God's dwelling among them and then said, "Since we have these promises, let us purify ourselves from everything that contaminates body and spirit"—that is, from all that defiles the body with such an external presence, the idolatrous rites, as well as with "spirit-contamination"—that is, contaminating the soul with idolatry itself. So in Jude 23 we read: "hating even the clothing stained by corrupted flesh." This is a phrase taken from legal uncleanness, which was contracted by touching the houses, the vessels, or the garments of unclean people; they were to detest the appearance of sharing with people in their uncleanness. The true Christian avoids "every kind of evil" (1 Thessalonians 5:22). Bernard explains this as "whatever is of evil appearance: that he may wound neither conscience nor reputation; this is pure wisdom indeed."

All this is required of those who want to be truly pure; and "this will show your wisdom" (Deuteronomy 4:6), however troublesome it may be to the body and inconvenient in the world. The body may think it foolish, and the world may think this ridiculously scrupulous, but it is a high point of wisdom to be one of the world's fools (see 1 Corinthians 3:18). The wisdom required in the world is a holy innocence, not a Machiavellian guile (see Matthew 10:19). It is the glory of a man to be a fool in sin and wise in grace. Be careful, then, to pursue the great plan of holiness. This will make you conform to God, which is man's excellence; it will bring you to enjoy God, which is man's happiness (see Matthew 5:8 and Hebrews 12:14).

Note 2. True wisdom is **peace loving** and entirely lacking in contention. Solomon, the wisest king, got his name from *peace*; Christ, who is the wisdom of the Father, is also our peace. God is honored with the title "the Lord of peace" (2 Thessalonians 3:16; see also 1 Corinthians 14:33). Peace is the purchase of Christ and the work of the Spirit. Heaven's great plan was to make peace between two of the greatest enemies—God and sinful man. To be at peace with God is one of the great privileges of heaven. There is a sweet connection between peace and wisdom. Moses was renowned for wisdom and meekness—the wisest and yet the meekest man upon earth in his time. The cooler the spirit, the more freedom there is for wise debate. Holiness is a Christian's ornament, and loving peace is the ornament of holiness. Even the Qur'an says God created the angels of light and the devils of the flame; certainly God's children are children of the light, but Satan's instruments are furious, wrathful, all of a flame.

But you will say, in what ways must we be **peace loving**? I answer: we are to *practice* true peace and to *make* peace; to preserve it where it is, and to create it where it is lost; they are *peace lovers* and *peacemakers*.

(1) They are **peace loving**, neither offering wrong to others, nor avenging wrong when it is done to themselves—which indeed are the two things that preserve human societies in any quietness, whereas violence and rigorous austerities disturb them. This is your wisdom, then: to be harmless and innocent. The world may count this an effeminate softness, but it is the truest prudence, the ready way to a blessing. Matthew 5:5 says, "The meek . . . will inherit the earth." Others remain in a frenzy, invading other people's rights and property; yet when all is done, the meek have the earth. You would think they would lose their patrimony, and yet they hold it by the safest and surest tenure. Just as they offer no wrong, so they pardon it when it is done to them; people who see they need God's pardon so much will pardon others.

God is not inexorable. How often he overcomes evil with good! And truly since God is so ready to hear, men should be more generous and lenient. People think it is noble to keep up their anger; alas, it is a sorry weakness. Augustine calls this "the weakness of strength of pride." God, the injured party, loved us first (1 John 4:19); and Jesus Christ, "on the night he was betrayed" (1 Corinthians 11:23), instituted the Supper, consigning to man the highest mysteries when man did him the most spite. Similarly, when Christ was crucified, he prayed for his enemies. Christians have little reason to think of recompensing evil for evil. There is no spirit more inappropriate to your profession of faith than revenge; it is sweet to you but very odious to God.

And as the children of God take care over civil peace, so do they over church peace. True wisdom looks not only at what may be done, but what should be done in any given situation; it will do anything but sin, that we may not give ground for offense. Basil, when his adversaries were prevailing, abstained from offensive words in the doctrine of the Holy Spirit.

Rash spirits make the most of their liberty, and in things that do not matter one way or the other they take the course that will offend; there is little wisdom from heaven in such a spirit.

True wisdom, as it is careful not to offend Christ by a sin, also takes care not to offend the brothers by a scandal; just as it will not sin against faith by error, so it will not sin against love by schism. By faith we are united to Christ, and by love we are united to one another; we should take care not to break either bond. The question of separation is obscure, while the commands to love are clear and open. Withdrawal from the rest of the church is a very serious matter; so we should be careful about it. The modesty of Zanchy is well worth noticing; he wrote, "I, Jerome Zanchy, testify to the church of God to all eternity, that I separated from the Church of Rome with no other intention but to return to communion with it as soon as I may with a good conscience; and I pray to the Lord Jesus with all my heart that this may be possible."

(2) They are *peacemakers*, striving to bring about peace where it is lost. It is a thankless task to be a reconciler, but there is a blessing promised: "Blessed are the peacemakers, for they will be called sons of God" (Matthew 5:9). They have the greater encouragement from heaven because they meet with so much scorn on earth. Those who desire to repair breaches meet with the displeasure of both sides, just as those who interpose between two fencers receive the blows. So then, people who love to live in the fire and cherish contention are far from true wisdom.

Note 3. **First of all pure; then peace loving.** True wisdom demands that the greatest care be taken to be pure. In Matthew 5:8-9 we read first "Blessed are the pure in heart" and then "Blessed are the peacemakers." In 2 Kings 20:19 we read, "Will there not be peace and security [KJV, truth] in my lifetime?" That was the sum of Hezekiah's wish; truth must be in first place. Of all blessings, purity in religion is the best. As God is the best of beings, so religion is the best of blessings. A nation may be miserable in peace but not in purity. A wilderness with God is better than the plenty of Egypt with idols. Troubles and distractions far excel a sinful peace. When the devil possessed the nations they had great peace: "When a strong man, fully armed, guards his own house, his possessions are safe [are in peace, KJV]" (Luke 11:21). All true peace is founded on purity and holiness. It may be civil peace—"When a man's ways are pleasing to the LORD, he makes even his enemies live at peace with him" (Proverbs 16:7). The best way is to make peace with God, and then he can bend and dispose hearts to every purpose. It is the same with ecclesiastical peace: holiness makes the spirit meek, and the purest and surest agreement is in the truth. First there is pure language, and then you can serve God "shoulder to shoulder" (Zephaniah 3:9).

There are two corollaries:

(1) If the greatest care must be taken for purity, then peace may be broken in truth's quarrel. As Luther zealously said, "Heaven and earth should be blended together in confusion rather than one jot of truth perish." It is a sleepy zeal that lets errors slip away quietly without conviction.

(2) Truth must never be violated for the sake of peace, lest while we make peace with man we make a breach with God. The world wants its commotions ended, but the peace it desires does not stem from holiness. "Have salt in yourselves, and be at peace with each other" (Mark 9:50). Doctrine must be kept wholesome and truth retain its savor, and then we are to look after peace.

Note 4. We must have a high regard for peace—second only to purity. James does not just say, **first of all pure**, but **then peace loving**. Truth is to be given the first place; yet peace is not to be neglected. We are told to "make every effort to live in peace" (Hebrews 12:14). There are many commendations of such peace in Scripture; it is "good and pleasant" (Psalm 133:1). It is a sign of religion; by this "all men will know . . ." (John 13:35). The curtains of the tabernacle were to be looped together; Christians should be, too. Try your best to purchase this great blessing. See how it is pressed home: "If it is possible, as far as it depends on you, live at peace with everyone" (Romans 12:18). Deal with God; treat, yield, comply with men as much as you can with religion and a good conscience: "May the Lord of peace himself give you peace at all times and in every way" (2 Thessalonians 3:16). We must be earnest with the Lord and use all ways and means with men. You should not stick to your own interest. Usually we do stick here: "For everyone looks out for his own interests, not those of Jesus Christ" (Philippians 2:21). Remember that the Lord himself has given us a good pattern; one reason he abolished the ceremonial law was for the sake of peace (Ephesians 2:15-17).

Note 5. True wisdom is **considerate**. Beza renders this, "just with moderation" (compare Philippians 4:5, "Let your moderation be known unto all men" [KJV] and 1 Timothy 3:3, "gentle"). When people insist on every detail of their rights, it gives rise to contention, and all patience is lost. This gentleness, then, is opposite to strictness, to criticizing rigorously, and to intemperate argument. And so a truly wise Christian is moderate:

(1) In his criticism. He is not always making the worst of matters but judges charitably and favorably where things are capable of being interpreted without censure. People who examine everything by very strict rules and use harder terms than the nature of human actions requires may seem to be more wise and perceptive than others, but they show they lack this true wisdom that the apostle commends. Austerity is the sign of folly. Wise Christians, in weighing actions, always allow for human frailty.

(2) In his opinions. He does not urge his own too much or wrest those of his adversaries beyond what they intended to odious consequences that

they disclaim—a fault that has much disturbed the peace of Christendom. Charity should consider not what follows of itself from any other opinion, but what follows in the conscience of those who hold it. A person may err in logic without erring in faith; and though you may show him the consequences of his opinion, you must not make him responsible for them. To make anyone worse than he is, is the way to disgrace an adversary, not reclaim him.

(3) In his behavior. He gives up his own rights for the sake of peace. Otherwise, while we seek to get maximum rights for ourselves, we do ourselves the greatest wrong. Revenge proves our own trouble: "Do not be overrighteous, neither be overwise—why destroy yourself?" (Ecclesiastes 7:16). That rule applies widely in the affairs of human life. Among other things, it means forbidding complete innocence and strict prosecution. When magistrates go to extremes all the time, the name of justice becomes a cover for cruelty. The severity of the laws must be mitigated, not in an indulgence for sin, but for good reasons; and equity must still be preferred to the letter of the law. So also this applies to individual Christians when they stand upon their rights and will not give them up for anything, however conducive it may be to the glory of God and our peace with others. David says, "I am forced to restore what I did not steal" (Psalm 69:4), and our Lord paid tax to avoid scandal, though otherwise he would not have been obliged to do so (Matthew 17:25-27). We are not only to consider what is lawful but what is judicious.

Note 6. True wisdom is **easy to be entreated** (KJV; the NIV has **submissive**—*Ed. note*)—that is, of a generous readiness either to be persuaded to what is good or dissuaded from what is evil. People think it is a disgrace to change their mind and therefore are headstrong, willful, unpliable to all suggestions and applications that are made to them. But there is no greater piece of folly than not to give place to right reason. Being easily entreated must be shown:

(1) In giving in to all honest requests. If we find God's ear so ready to hear, it does not become us to be unmoved by other people's pleas. The crying of the poor is so like our addresses to God that I wonder how those who expect mercy can be so uncompassionate; the unjust judge was won by the widow's importunity (Luke 18:1-5).

(2) In yielding to the persuasions of the Word. This is what is meant by the promise of "a heart of flesh" (Ezekiel 36:26), a heart that is docile and tractable. Some people harden their hearts to the fear of God and will not be persuaded to good; the apostle calls such people "wicked and evil men" (2 Thessalonians 3:2).

(3) In yielding to the counsel of others when better arguments are advanced. Job would not deny the desires of the poor (Job 31:16). Naaman

allowed himself to be persuaded by his servants (2 Kings 5:12-14). David was persuaded by Abigail (1 Samuel 25:33).

(4) In matters of dispute, not being intemperately argumentative. Many people, out of pride, will hold fast to their first conclusion, even when it is clearly disproved: "The sluggard is wiser in his own eyes than seven men who answer discreetly" (Proverbs 26:16). Usually we find that people will not let go of their prejudices, and what is lacking in argument is made up in obstinacy, as if matters were to be decided by strength of will rather than by reason.

Note 7. The next qualification of wisdom is **full of mercy**, which is shown either to those who offend or to those who are in need.

(1) To those who offend: "it is to his glory to overlook an offense" (Proverbs 19:11). People think this is a disgrace, as if clemency were evidence of a lack of courage and spirit. But according to the judgment of the Word it is to your honor; there is more generosity in pardon than revenge.

(2) To those who are in need: "as God's chosen people . . . clothe yourselves with compassion" (Colossians 3:12). That is a good garment for a Christian, and without it he is naked and filthy before God.

Note 8. The next qualification is **full of . . . good fruit**, by which James understands all human actions that go with good nature and grace. Religion is not a barren tree. The godly are the best neighbors; everyday actions are done out of a spirit of grace. It the great fault of some people that when they begin to be *religious*, they leave off being *human*, as if the only tree that grew in Christ's garden was the crab apple.

Note 9. Another property of true wisdom is that it is **impartial**; in the KJV margin this is **without wrangling**, and the word can also mean "without suspicion" or "without judging." All these meanings fit the context well enough: "without partiality"—that is, not treating people differently because of outward things, which indeed is a high point of wisdom. Fools are dazzled by outward splendor and, like children, count nothing good unless it is flamboyant and showy. This is what the apostle calls regarding people "from a worldly point of view" (2 Corinthians 5:16). True wisdom does not weigh anything in worldly scales. If you render it "without wrangling," the sense is: true wisdom is an enemy to brawling disputes; passion lives at the fool's house. If you render it "without suspicion" it means: true wisdom does not suspiciously inquire about other people's faults; when we want to make others worse than they are, we make ourselves worse than they, for we show malice. "Do not pay attention to every word people say, or you may hear your servant cursing you" (Ecclesiastes 7:21). When people insist on listening to every word that is spoken, they often hear how nasty they are. Or you can render this, "without judging or censuring." Fools are the greatest censurers; what they lack in worth is made up in pride. And because they cannot raise themselves to an equality with

217

others, they try to bring others down by criticizing them, so that they become as low as themselves.

Note 10. The last characteristic is **sincere**. In true wisdom there is much light but no guile. The Christian must try most of all to be what he seems to be. The hypocrite is the greatest fool and in effect cheats himself most of all; all he gains is what hell pays: "He will . . . assign him a place with the hypocrites" (Matthew 24:51). So then, reckon sincerity as the highest point of wisdom: "Now this is our boast: Our conscience testifies that we have conducted ourselves in the world . . . in the holiness and sincerity that are from God. We have not done so according to worldly wisdom but according to God's grace" (2 Corinthians 1:12). Avoid hypocrisy in all the actions of life, not only in addressing God but in relation to other people. The Scriptures, which require "sincere faith" (1 Timothy 1:5; 2 Timothy 1:5), also require "sincere love" (1 Peter 1:22; 2 Corinthians 6:6). "Let us not love with words or tongue but with actions and in truth" (1 John 3:18). We should be as willing to *do* others good as to proffer it.

Commentary on Verse 18

Peacemakers who sow in peace raise a harvest of righteousness. [And the fruit of righteousness is sown in peace of them that make peace, KJV.]

These words are the conclusion of the whole discourse, suggesting the happiness of those who have the wisdom just described. The words have been expounded in different ways. Some people explain them as meaning that peace-loving people sow a seed that afterwards will yield sheaves of comfort in their hearts—as if by their attempts at peace they sowed the seeds of the everlasting reward that they will afterwards receive in heaven. Others explain these words as meaning that though these people bear many evils with a great deal of modesty and sweetness, they do not stop sowing the seed of righteousness. Which explanation is to be preferred? I think they may be combined; their sowing implies expectation of the reward, and their sowing **the fruit of righteousness** [KJV] shows the quality of their endeavors, which will appear as we explain the terms more fully.

Peacemakers. Christ says the same: "Blessed are the peacemakers" (Matthew 5:9). This implies not the successful outcome but the endeavor, for the notion of "making" in Bible phraseology means the bent of the soul—"he who does [or makes] what is right" (1 John 3:7), and "he who does [or makes] what is sinful" (1 John 3:8), showing the full inclination of the soul. So to "make peace" is to have strong and heartfelt desires for it.

Who sow. This implies either that they care about holiness—they have sown it—or the sureness of the reward of grace. It is not like water spilt on the ground but like seed cast into the ground. You do not lose your labor, but rather these efforts will yield an increase: see Isaiah 32:17. Or, lastly, it implies their non-enjoyment of the reward for the present; they do not reap but **sow** now; the **harvest of righteousness** is not realized so soon. It is common in Scripture to use the language of sowing and plowing for any consequences that do not follow immediately.

In peace. The meaning is either "in a peace-loving way" (but that seems to be expressed in the last clause [in the KJV, **that make peace**], or else "with much spiritual tranquillity and peace in their souls in the present." Compare Hebrews 12:11. Righteousness or sanctification brings peace with it.

A harvest of righteousness. This expression is used elsewhere—for example, "filled with the fruit of righteousness that comes through Jesus Christ—to the glory and praise of God" (Philippians 1:11); "fruit unto holiness" (Romans 6:22, KJV); and "discipline . . . later on . . . produces a harvest of righteousness" (Hebrews 12:11). In short, the **harvest of righteousness** is either the harvest that comes from righteousness—namely eternal life, which is the reward that God has promised for sanctification—or else it means sanctification itself, which is called "fruit" in Scripture in many respects:

(1) In respect of the root, Christ (John 15:5, 16).

(2) Because this is the free offspring of the Spirit in us, whereas sins are a servile drudgery. That is why the apostle uses such different expressions: "the *acts* of the sinful nature" (Galatians 5:19), but "the *fruit* of the Spirit" (verse 22).

(3) Because of the growth, as fruits gradually come to maturity and ripeness (compare Philippians 1:11).

(4) Because of its excellent and happy reward. It will be fruit, not an empty and dry tree; compare Romans 6:22 (KJV).

(5) In respect to the delay of this reward—it will be fruit, though now it is seed.

Those who combine care for righteousness with their attempts at making peace will have a multiple blessing and increased grace with peace in the present and will reap the crop of it all hereafter.

Notes on Verse 18

Note 1. Whatever we do in this life is seed; what we sow, we reap. (This metaphor is used of all moral actions, whether good or evil.) See how

Scripture follows this metaphor both regarding sin (see Galatians 6:8; Job 4:8; Hosea 8:7)—the crop may take a long time coming, but it will be according to the seed: "He who sows wickedness reaps trouble" (Proverbs 22:8)—and regarding duty or good actions ("Sow for yourselves righteousness, reap the fruit of unfailing love," Hosea 10:12)—that is, try to do good works and you will find God to be propitious. Such deeds are the *way*, not the *cause*. God shows mercy *according to* works, though not *for* works. In particular this is applied to loving giving: "Whoever sows sparingly will also reap sparingly" (2 Corinthians 9:6). So also with penitent tears: "Those who sow in tears will reap with songs of joy" (Psalm 126:5).

There is an intimate connection between our efforts and the Lord's rewards.

(1) Let this make us take care with our actions. They are seed; they fall on the ground, not to be lost, but to grow up again. We may taste the fruits of them long after they are committed; be sure you sow good seeds. To help you, think how the ground must be prepared (Hosea 10:12). If you want to reap mercy, plow up your fallow ground (see Jeremiah 4:3-4). The heart is like waste ground until it is prepared by breaking.

(2) Note the season: it is seed-time. Eternity depends on this moment. Take heed of sowing to the worldly nature; when others have their arms full of sheaves, you will be empty-handed. The foolish virgins made a great to-do when their lamps were empty.

(3) Note the ground of hope to God's children: their works are not lost; they are seed that will spring up again. "Cast your bread upon the waters, for after many days you will find it again" (Ecclesiastes 11:1). Think: whatever you do to God or for God is seed. The wicked regard it as lost, but you will find it again; you do not lose by serving God (see Malachi 3:4).

(4) This is a comfort to us. Here we are miserable. In our seed-time we are usually in tears; we must look forward to the harvest: "Light is shed upon the righteous" (Psalm 97:11). It is buried out of sight, but it will spring up again. The corn must first die in the ground; you cannot sow and reap in a day.

Note 2. Caring about **righteousness** brings **peace**. All good actions cause serenity in the mind. The kingdom of grace yields "inexpressible . . . joy" (1 Peter 1:8), even if it does not bring inexpressible glory. Joy enters into us before we enter into our Master's joy. First we get the morning star, then the sun. If there are songs in your pilgrimage, you will have hallelujahs in your heavenly country.

Note 3. It is the duty of God's children to **sow in peace**. The oil of grace and the oil of gladness go well together. So that you do not lose the comfort of grace, live socially with God and sweetly with men.

(1) Socially with God. Maintain a constant and intimate communion between you and heaven, so that your fellowship may indeed be "with the

Father and with his Son" (1 John 1:3). Neglecting God makes the conscience restless and clamorous: "Submit to God and be at peace with him" (Job 22:21).

(2) Sweetly with men. There is a holy amiableness, as well as a strict righteousness. "Jesus grew in . . . favor with God and men" (Luke 2:52). Athanasius was adamant and a magnet—having neither a loose easiness, nor an uncivil austerity. Do this and you will increase in comfort and grace; couple a sweet goodness with a severe righteousness.

Note 4. **Peacemakers.** True lovers of peace are and must be also lovers of **righteousness**. Peace without righteousness is just sordid compliance; righteousness without peace is just rough austerity.

Note 5. Righteous peacemaking is blessed with grace here and glory hereafter. This verse is a promise as well as an instruction. This is our comfort against all the difficulties and inconveniences that holy efforts at peace meet with in the world. Your reward is with God, and you have a pledge of it in your own souls. While conflict lessens grace in other people, you grow and thrive; and you shall reap in glory.

James
Chapter 4

Commentary on Verse 1

What causes fights and quarrels among you? Don't they come from your desires that battle within you?

In the previous chapter James had spoken against fights, since they proceed from envy, and pressed his readers to a holy wisdom. Here he speaks against fights and quarrels as proceeding from other worldly desires, such as ambition, covetousness, etc., which make them annoy one another and break out into unseemly brawlings. He proceeds by way of questions, appealing to their consciences.

What causes fights and quarrels among you? These words, **fights and quarrels**, are usually applied to private disagreements—either fights and arguments about riches, rank, and outward pomp, or else annoying lawsuits before unbelieving judges. And the reason given for this interpretation is that the Christians of those times did not dare openly attack one another in a hostile way; so they disturbed the peace of the places where they were scattered. However plausible this explanation may seem, to me it seems frivolous.

(1) It is harsh to render **fights and quarrels** as private differences, partly because these arguments the apostle is speaking about went as far as bloodshed—**You kill and covet, but you cannot have what you want. You quarrel and fight** (verse 2).

(2) Histories speak of wars and civil unrest between Jew and Jew (as in Acts 5:37), and probably many of the pseudo-Christians were engaged in these.

(3) The apostle in this letter is writing not only to the believers but to the whole nation of Israel, as appears from many passages in the letter.

Don't they come from your desires . . . ? [**From your pleasures**, KJV margin]. **Desires** and **pleasures** are often used interchangeably, and sometimes they are coupled, as in "enslaved by all kinds of passions and pleasures" (Titus 3:3). "Desire" strictly means the earnest motion of the soul after sin; "pleasure" means the contentment it finds in sin. Sin is a pleasure to the wicked; it takes up their desires or delights: "Their idea of pleasure is to carouse in broad daylight" (2 Peter 2:13); "delighted in wickedness" (2 Thessalonians 2:12). Pleasure is a sign of a habit that is difficult to give up. Beware of a delight in sin, when acts of uncleanness or thoughts of revenge are sweet to you, or when you take pleasure in proud reflections on your honor and greatness in the world. *Lord, if ever sin overcomes me, let it be a burden and not a pleasure.* It is sad to rejoice to do evil.

That battle within you. There are several sorts of battles in the human heart. In the heart of the wicked there may be battles:

(1) Between a man and his conscience. Aristotle said, "their soul is in mutiny," and elsewhere, speaking of a wicked man, "he is not friends with himself." A wicked man and his conscience are at odds.

(2) Between conviction and corruption. Sin storms at the light that reveals it.

(3) Between corruption and corruption. Worldly desires are contrary to one another and therefore jostle for the throne and usually take it in turn.

In a godly person the war is between sin and grace, between worldly counsel and enlightened reason. These battles are said to be **in your members** [KJV]. By **members** are understood both inward and outward faculties, which are employed as instruments of sin. James means the strong inclination of the will and affections against the knowledge of the truth. Similarly, Romans 6:13 reads, "Do not offer the parts of your body to sin"—that is, your faculties, which are exercised in and by the parts of the body, because of the relationship they have to the external parts, such as the eye to the understanding, the will to the hand, etc.

Notes on Verse 1

Note 1. Worldly desire is what causes trouble in a community. Covetousness, pride, and ambition make people overbearing and hurtful.

(1) Covetousness makes us argue with those who have anything that we covet, as Ahab did with Naboth. Hence those injuries and annoying lawsuits between neighbor and neighbor; hence public arguments.

(2) Pride is the viper's egg that breaks open to reveal the fiery cockatrice: "Pride only breeds quarrels" (Proverbs 13:10). Pride can endure no equals. Haman's thirst for blood came from his haughtiness; the disciples argued about who would be the greatest.

(3) Ambition. Diotrephes' love of preeminence disturbed the churches of Asia (see 3 John 9).

(4) Envy. Abraham and Lot's herdsmen fell out (Genesis 13:7). Two great ones cannot endure one another near them: "Let us not become conceited, provoking and envying each other" (Galatians 5:26).

Note 2. When evils abound in a place, it is good to look at their cause. People engage in an argument and do not know why. Usually worldly desire is at the bottom of it, and we will be ashamed when we see the cause. Is it not because I want to be greater than others? Grammarians talk of finding the root, and philosophers of finding the cause; and many Christians do this too. It is good to sift things to the bottom. Where does this come from? "Since there is jealousy and quarreling among you, are you not worldly?" (1 Corinthians 3:3).

Note 3. Worldly desire is a tyrant that battles *in* the soul and *against* the soul.

(1) It battles in the soul; it abuses your affections, to carry on the rebellion against heaven: "the sinful nature desires what is contrary to the Spirit" (Galatians 5:17). The Spirit no sooner presents a good idea than the flesh rises up in defiance against it; there is pride and passion and earthly-mindedness, envy, sensuality, unbelief, self-seeking, worldly policy. As soon as you decide to repent, believe, pray, these are ready to hinder you, to distract you, so that you cannot do the things you want to do.

(2) It battles against the soul: "abstain from sinful desires, which war against your soul" (1 Peter 2:11). You carry an enemy in your own hearts, which defaces the soul's beauty, disturbs its order, and keeps its liberty in check. Instead of God's image there is Satan's likeness.

Question. Do worldly desires battle in the heart of a godly man? The reason for asking is that James is writing to Christians and talks about **your desires that battle within you**. And Peter, also writing to Christians, says, "abstain from sinful desires" (1 Peter 2:11).

Answer. Yes; the life of a Christian is a wrestling, conflicting state. There is a double nature in the best people—"the sinful nature" and "the Spirit" (Galatians 5:17). We carry an enemy in our hearts; the Canaanite is not wholly cast out. *Lord, deliver me from one evil person and it will suffice* is a good prayer. The sinful nature and the Spirit, like the twins in Rebekah's womb, battle and struggle. Indeed, worldly desires stir and rage more in a godly heart than in a wicked one. Conviction may sometimes awaken drowsy desires, when without it all is still and quiet. But usually there is more trouble with sin after conversion, especially immediately after conversion. Since the fall it is an evidence of grace to find this opposition; since the admission of sin, grace is more concerned with the combat than with the absolute victory.

Commentary on Verse 2

*You want something but don't get it. You kill and covet, but you can-
not have what you want. You quarrel and fight. You do not have,
because you do not ask God.*

In the context the apostle is applying himself to the cure of worldly
desires. He has mentioned one effect in verse 1: inward and outward trouble, both in the world and within ourselves. He now comes to another
argument: the dissatisfaction of those efforts that come from worldly
desires. They distract the head with cares and engage the heart in sins, and
all to no purpose.

You want something. Usually this word is taken in a bad sense, to
mean inordinate and passionate desires; hence the [KJV] translation **lust.**

But don't get it. This may be taken two ways: either "you never
obtained," or "you have now lost." Trying to get things by wrong ways
seldom succeeds; or if it does, possession is soon lost.

You kill. Covetousness is as bad as murder—"Such is the end of all who
go after ill-gotten gain; it takes away the lives of those who get it"
(Proverbs 1:19).

And covet. "You emulate" or "you are given to envy." This word is
sometimes taken in a good sense: "eagerly desire spiritual gifts" (1
Corinthians 14:1). It is good when we try to imitate those who excel in
virtue or to go beyond them. But there is also a worldly emulation, which
has chiefly to do with external enjoyment and is a sign of being upset that
anyone should enjoy any external goodness equal to or better than ours
and a strong covetous desire to appropriate that goodness for ourselves. In
the first case there is malice, in the second covetousness; we take the word
here to mean chiefly the latter.

But you cannot have what you want. "You cannot arrive at happiness"; that is, either at the happiness of the people you emulate or at the
happiness you fancy. The language of desire is give, give, give; it is an
appetite without bound or measure. Given one world, we are not happy
but want another. Worldly people possess much but have nothing.

You quarrel and fight. You do not have. That is, though their worldly
desires had broken out so far as public rioting, still they were at a loss.

Because you do not ask God. That is, you do not use the lawful means
of prayer. But how can it be said **you do not ask** since in the next verse he
says, **When you ask, you do not receive, because you ask with wrong
motives?**

(1) Possibly he is taking to task one abuse here, another there—here,
that they hoped to help themselves by their own efforts without prayer;
and there, that their prayers were conceived for worldly ends.

(2) Because prayers not conceived in a humble way are not prayers; the prayers of worldly desire are not prayers.

Notes on Verse 2

Note 1. Worldly desires are usually disappointed: **You want something but don't get it**. God loves to deny desires when they are inordinate. Sometimes this is out of mercy. It is a blessing to be disappointed in the ways of sin; you cannot have a worse judgment than to have your worldly desires fulfilled. How unhappy people are when God leaves them to themselves without restraint! "The faithless will be fully repaid for their ways, and the good man rewarded for his" (Proverbs 14:14). The cursed apostate will have enough honors and pleasures. To check our desires, God in mercy fences our way with thorns (see Hosea 2:6). The blood heated by intemperance and the heart enlarged by desire are both sins that bring with them their own punishment, especially when they are disappointed. Amnon and Ahab were both sick, one with desire, the other with covetousness.

Application 1. When the heart is too much set on anything, it is the sure way to miss it. The fool talked of bigger barns, and that night his soul was taken away. Affections should rise according to the worth of the object: "Do not work for food that spoils, but for food that endures to eternal life, which the Son of Man will give you" (John 6:27). Your hard-working desires would suit a better object. Your strength should be spent on everlasting bread; that is, work without sin and without disappointment.

Application 2. Do not always be troubled when you cannot have what you want; you have reason to bless God. It is a mercy when worldly desires are disappointed. Say, with David, "Praise be to the LORD, the God of Israel, who has sent you today to meet me" (1 Samuel 25:32). Your hearts have been set on great things, and you thought, like the fool in the Gospel, that you would enlarge your barns and exalt your nest; and suddenly God came in and blasted all those worldly projects. Praise God for such providence. How complacent or sensual or worldly your spirit would have been! It was a mercy that the world was crucified to Paul, as well as Paul crucified to the world (Galatians 6:14).

Application 3. This teaches you what reflections to make upon yourselves in case of disappointment. When you miss any worldly thing that you have desired, say, "Have I not desired this? Did I not covet it too earnestly?" Absalom was the greater curse to David because David loved him too much. Inordinate longings make the affections miscarry. See how things that have too much of self seldom prove happy. We often find that people with much to worry about are unsuccessful; they turn this way and that and remain in the same place like a door on its hinges: "In vain you rise early and stay up late, toiling for food to eat" (Psalm 127:2). Success in human endeavors lies in God's blessing; it is a prerogative he has reserved to himself. Providence sometimes weans us from worldly desire and brings us to grace and shows us that a blessing is sooner gained by faith than by worldly care.

Note 2. Where there is covetousness, there is usually fighting, envy, and coveting. As graces go hand in hand, so also there is a link between sins; they seldom go alone. If someone is a drunkard, he will be wanton; if he is covetous, he will be envious. Christ cast seven devils out of Mary Magdalene, and another man was possessed by a legion. When the heart is brought under the power of any sin, it is equally at risk from all sin. Covetousness may be known by its companions—fighting and envy: "filled with every kind of wickedness, evil, greed and depravity" (Romans 1:29). Self-love is the root of all three; it makes us covet and desire what is good and excellent, and it makes us envy others for enjoying it, and then to break all bonds of duty and love so that we may snatch it from them.

Note 3. **You kill and covet. . . . You quarrel and fight.** It is desire and covetousness that is most apt to trouble neighborhoods. Solomon says, "A greedy man brings trouble to his family" (Proverbs 15:27); we may add, indeed, to all the homes near him. Covetousness is a base affection that will set you on the most unworthy practices. Those who are given to it trouble their families by exacting all their labors, and they trouble human societies by unjust arguments; they quarrel with those who possess what they covet. Ahab spilt Naboth's blood for the sake of his vineyard. Such persons work for social change so that they may feather their nests with the common spoils. Besides all this, they bring down God's judgment on their people; Achan's covetousness troubled the whole of Israel (Joshua 7). This is especially so if they are in high positions—as when magistrates build their own houses upon the ruins of other people's and obtain large revenues and estates with the public purse or by making poor people work for them; see Jeremiah 22:13.

Well, then, it is no wonder that covetous people meet with public hatred and detestation. They hurt not only God but human society; they are the sort of people who are moved neither by arguments of nature nor by those of grace. They neither fear God nor men (Luke 18:2). God has laid these two restraints on us—fear of himself to preserve religion, and the shame of the world to preserve human society. Some people are moved by neither. This was what the Jews were like: "They displease God and are hostile to all men" (1 Thessalonians 2:15); they agreed with nobody but themselves. Similarly, 2 Thessalonians 3:2 speaks of "wicked and evil men, for not everyone has faith"; nor does everyone have grace, good nature, or reason. Lactantius says of Lucian, "he spared neither God nor man." Covetousness makes people have this sort of sour disposition. Toward God it is idolatry; it is the bane of human society.

Note 4. Worldly desire will set people not only on dishonest endeavors but on unlawful means to accomplish their ends—killing and fighting and so on. Bad means go with base ends; they resolve to have it, and any means will serve to satisfy their thirst: "People who want to get rich fall into temptation and a trap" (1 Timothy 6:9); "one eager to get rich will not go unpunished" (Proverbs 28:20). If God will not enrich them, Satan will; and what they cannot get by honest labor, they make up by deceit and theft. That shows what a tyrant worldly desire is; if God does not bless us, it makes us go to the devil. And again, desire that makes you use dishonest means is rank desire.

Note 5. Whatever the wicked do, when God is against them their efforts are frustrated; whatever they try, they are disappointed: "he thwarts the purposes of the peoples" (Psalm 33:10). God will not let his creatures be too hard for him in all battles; he will overcome and have the best of it (Romans 3:4). But when does God set himself to frustrate the efforts of the creature? It is when the creature sets himself to frustrate God's counsels and plans. This may be done in several ways:

(1) When we want to do things in spite of providence. People are disappointed in some evil way once or twice, and yet they insist on trying again, as if they want to beat God. For example, the king of Israel risked the other fifty after two fifties were destroyed (2 Kings 1); Pharaoh hardened his heart after many plagues; Balaam beat his ass three times (Numbers 22:23-27), and after that built altar after altar to curse Israel.

(2) When people seek by worldly policies to avoid God's threats or promises. God had said, "I will cut off Ahab's posterity." To avoid this Ahab started to father children; he had seventy children, brought up in seventy strong cities, and yet all were beheaded by Jehu. Herod killed all the children of Bethlehem so that he might make sure of killing Christ, and some say he killed his own child who was being nursed there. About this Augustus said, "it is better to be Herod's swine than his son." Yet Christ was kept safe: "There is no wisdom, no insight, no plan that can succeed against the LORD" (Proverbs 21:30). He uses many words to show that the choicest abilities will not be able to win the contest against providence.

(3) When people crossed by providence seek happiness elsewhere by unlawful means, such as violence, extortion, or deceit—as if Satan would make them more prosperous than God would. See if these people's situation does not deteriorate and their families, whose state they try to improve in this way, become ruined. In ancient times they built a tower, as if there were more security in a tower than a promise (Genesis 11:4). There

are many devices in the human heart for bringing about their ends, but they are all marked with the curse of providence.

(4) When you say "I will" without God's permission: see Exodus 15:9 and 4:3. Confident intentions and presumptions that are not subjected to God's pleasure seldom prosper.

(5) By repeated efforts against the church: see Isaiah 8:9-10. They are still "shattered," even though they combine force with ingenuity and get together in most unholy leagues and renew their assaults with united strength; that is why the prophet so often repeats, "and be shattered."

Note 6. **Because you do not ask.** That is, you do not ask God's permission in humble and holy prayer. It is not good to engage in any undertaking without prayer. In prayer you ask God's permission and show that your action is not a contest with him. The families that do not call on God's name must be cursed; in their actions they say, in effect, that they will be happy without God. From this we learn that:

(1) It is a false argument against prayer to say that God knows our requests already, and that God's decrees are immutable and cannot be altered by our prayers. That was the argument of the old heathen philosopher Maximus Tyrus and of many Libertines in more recent times. But prayer is not for God's information but the creature's submission; we pray in order that we may have his permission. And again, God's decrees do not exclude the duty of creatures and the work of secondary causes: "I will yield to the plea of the house of Israel" (Ezekiel 36:37). "'I know the plans I have for you,' declares the LORD, 'plans to prosper you and not to harm you. . . . Then you will call upon me and come and pray to me, and I will listen to you'" (Jeremiah 29:11-12).

(2) No actions must be taken in hand except those we can commend to God in prayer. Any actions that we are ashamed to ask a blessing on must not be pursued; we must not engage in any enterprises that we dare not communicate to God in our supplications: "Woe to those who go to great depths to hide their plans from the LORD" (Isaiah 29:15)—that is, who plan their enterprises and never ask what God's will is or communicate their purpose to him in prayer.

Commentary on Verse 3

When you ask, you do not receive, because you ask with wrong motives, that you may spend what you get on your pleasures.

In this verse he anticipates an objection. They might say, "We do ask and go to God in daily prayers." The apostle answers, "You ask indeed;

but because of your wrong motive, you cannot complain of not being heard. Do you want to make God a servant to your desires?" To convince them, he shows what the aim of their prayers was: the convenience of a worldly life. **You ask . . . that you may spend what you get on your pleasures**.

There are several points to note in this verse; they may be reduced to the three below:

Notes on Verse 3

Note 1. We pray amiss when our ends and aims are not right in prayer. The purpose is a main element in every action and is the purest offspring of the soul. Practices and affections may be overruled; this is the genuine, immediate birth and issue of the human spirit. We may cite all sorts of actions here; we know their quality not by the matter, but the end. In things that are neutral in themselves, the nature of the action is altered by a wrong motive. To eat out of necessity is a duty we owe to nature; to eat out of wantonness is an effect of worldly desire. So in all things instituted and commanded, the end determines the action. When we make self the purpose of prayer, it is not worship of God but self-seeking. All our actions are to be referred and devoted to God; much more so with the acts that belong especially to the spiritual life, which is described in the words "live for God" (Galatians 2:19). That is the main difference between the worldly life and the spiritual; one is living for ourselves, the other is living for God. Especially, acts of worship are to be for God, for there the soul sets itself to glorify him. And as we address ourselves directly to him, we must not prostitute our addresses to a common use.

So then, consider your motives in prayer—not just the manner, not just what you are asking for, but the purpose. It is not enough to look for intensity of feeling; many people make that all their work, to raise themselves into some liveliness of spirit, but they do not consider their aim. It is true that it is good to come with full sails; fervent prayer is like an arrow drawn with all your strength, but it must be godly prayer. A worldly spring may send out high tides of feeling; our worldly desires are usually very earnest. It is not enough to look for fluency; worldly affections and imagination joined together may engage the wit and set it working. It is not enough to make God the object of the prayer—he must be its purpose too. Duty is sometimes called "serving God," *serving* denoting the object, and *seeking* denoting the end; in serving we must seek.

Note 2. Our ends and aims are wrong when we ask blessings for the use and encouragement of our worldly desires. There are several ways in which people sin with reference to the aim of prayer:

(1) When the end is grossly worldly and sinful. Some people seek God for their sins and want to engage the divine blessing on a revengeful and worldly enterprise, just as the thief lit his torch in order to steal by the lamps of the altar. Solomon says that the wicked offer sacrifice "with evil intent" (Proverbs 21:27).

(2) When people seek to gratify their worldly desires privately, they look on God as some great power who must serve them. They are like the man who came to Christ saying, "Teacher, tell my brother to divide the inheritance with me" (Luke 12:13). We want something from God in order to satisfy our desires: health and long life, that we may live pleasantly; wealth, that we may live in luxury every day; estates, so we can improve our name and family; victory and success, to excuse ourselves from glorifying God by suffering, or to wreak our malice on enemies. The divine grace, by a vile submission and diversion, is forced to serve our vainglory.

(3) When we pray for blessings with a selfish aim, and not with serious and actual designs of God's glory, as when someone prays for spiritual blessings thinking only of his own ease and comfort, such as praying for pardon, heaven, grace, faith, repentance only in order to escape wrath. This is merely a worldly aspect of our own good and welfare. God wants us to think of our own comfort, but not only that. His glory is the pure spiritual aim. Then we seek these things with the same mind that God offers them: "to the praise of his glorious grace, which he has freely given us in the One he loves" (Ephesians 1:6). Your desires in asking are only right when they suit God's purposes in giving. God's glory is a better thing, and beyond our welfare and salvation. So it is too in temporal matters, when people desire outward provision merely in order to live more comfortably, not to serve God more cheerfully.

So how shall I set about getting my motives right in prayer? This is a necessary question. Nothing makes us see the necessity of divine help for our prayers so much as this. To act for a holy purpose requires the presence of the Spirit of grace; supernatural acts need supernatural strength. It is true in these internal things that "flesh gives birth to flesh" (John 3:6). Water cannot rise higher than its fountain; nature by itself aims at its own welfare, ease, and preservation. Therefore, go to God; beg for uprightness—that is his gift as well as other graces. The help that we have from the Spirit is to make requests "in accordance with God's will" (Romans 8:27), or, as it is in the original, "in accordance with God"—that is, to make godly requests for God's sake. Besides, there should be much mortification; what lies uppermost will be expressed first: "out of the overflow of the heart the mouth speaks" (Matthew 12:34).

Note 3. Prayers framed out of worldly motives are usually unsuccessful. God's glory is the end of prayer and the beginning of hope, or else we can look for nothing. God never undertook to satisfy worldly desires. He will own no other voice in prayer but that of his own Spirit: "And he who searches our hearts knows the mind of the Spirit" (Romans 8:27). What is a worldly groan, and what is a spiritual groan? Expressing a worldly aim is merely a request met with a divine refutation; it is the best way to be denied. Spiritual sighs and breathings are heard rather than worldly roarings. If you cannot ask for mercy well, you will seldom be able to use it well; there is more enjoyment in the temptation. Usually our hearts are more devout when we want a blessing than when we enjoy it; and therefore when our prayers are not directed to God's glory, there is little hope that when we receive the talent we shall employ it for the Master's use.

Besides all this, prayers offered with a base motive greatly affront and dishonor God; you would make him a servant of his enemy: "Thou hast made me to serve with thy sins" (Isaiah 43:24, KJV; NIV, "You have burdened me with your sins"—*Ed. note*). We want to commit sin and want God to bless us in it. It is bad enough that you should be servants of sin, but that you should make God an accessory to your sin and yoke him with yourselves in the same service is not to be endured. So this teaches us what to do when our prayers are not granted. Let us not charge God foolishly but examine ourselves: were not our requests worldly? Suppose you prayed for life, and God left you to your own deadness; did your heart not fancy your own praise? If you prayed for safety, you wanted to live in ease, in pleasure; if you prayed for an estate, you were pleasing yourself in your ideas of greatness and esteem in the world. O brothers, as we care about success, let us not come to God with an evil mind! Holy desires are certainly answered (Psalm 10:17; 145:19).

Commentary on Verse 4

You adulterous people, don't you know that friendship with the world is hatred toward God? Anyone who chooses to be a friend of the world becomes an enemy of God.

Because they were so overcome with worldly lusts that their very prayers and devotions looked that way, James now shows the danger and heinousness of these desires. There are two arguments in this verse: first, such lusts will make you commit adultery; and second, they will make you enemies to God.

You adulterous people. This must be understood spiritually, as appears from the following words and the drift of the context, which is to inveigh against those desires and pleasures that entice the soul and withdraw it from God. These are spiritual adulterers whom the love of the world alienates and estranges from the Lord. This metaphor is also used elsewhere (see Matthew 12:39 and 16:4).

Don't you know ... ? He appeals to their consciences; this is a rousing question. Worldly people do not sin out of ignorance so much as not thinking.

That friendship with the world. By this he understands an emancipation of our affections to the pleasures, profits, and desires of the world. People try to please their friends, and they are friends of the world if they seek to gratify worldly people or worldly desires and if they court external vanities rather than renounce them—a practice that is inappropriate to religion. You may use the world but not seek friendship with it. People who want to be dandled on the world's knees lose Christ's friendship. "If I were still trying to please men, I would not be a servant of Christ" (Galatians 1:10). It is the same with gratifying worldly desires. We may use the comforts of the world but may not serve its desires and pleasures—a description of the worldly state (Titus 3:3).

Is hatred toward God. When you begin to please the world, you wage war against heaven and openly defy the Lord of hosts. The love of God and care to obey him is abated just so much as the world prevails in you. There is a similar expression in Romans 8:7, "the sinful mind is hostile to God." In this way the world not only withdraws the heart from God but opposes him. It is hard for someone to serve two masters, even if they think alike. But God and the world are opposite masters; they command contrary things: "If anyone loves the world, the love of the Father is not in him" (1 John 2:15); "you cannot serve both God and Money" (Matthew 6:24). People who match covetousness with Christianity seek to reconcile two of the most irreconcilable things in the world.

Anyone. General truths must be enforced by application, and so have a direct impact on the soul: "We have examined this, and it is true. So hear it and apply it to yourself" (Job 5:27).

Who chooses to be a friend of the world. Not everyone finds that the world favors them. Whatever they do, "the world has been crucified to" them; but they are not as Paul was, "crucified ... to the world" (Galatians 6:14). Therefore, the Scripture takes notice not merely of what is, but of the aim. Besides, a serious purpose and choice reveal the state of the soul; and whoever **chooses to be a friend of the world** is absolutely a worldly person. Similarly in 1 Timothy 6:9, "People who want to get rich fall into temptation." In heavenly matters deliberate choice and full purpose reveals grace: "to remain true to the Lord with all their hearts" (Acts 11:23). Therefore Christians should look to their purpose and aim. What is it? What do you give your minds to? When someone sets himself to become rich, to lay up treasures on earth, he is a worldly man; and when he gives his heart and whole mind to do what God requires, whatever comes of it, he is a true servant of the Lord. Solomon says the same thing: "Do not wear yourself out to get rich" (Proverbs 23:4); that is, do not give up your heart and endeavors to discover and follow every way to increase your wealth and situation. "One eager to get rich will not go unpunished" (Proverbs 28:20)—one who has set that up as his purpose. Now this purpose of the soul may be known partly by our resolutely pursuing the end without weighing the means and consequences, and partly by our diligence and earnestness of spirit. When the end is fixed, we put up with the hard work but are impatient with hindrances and disappointments.

Becomes an enemy of God. Actively and passively, worldliness makes a person hate God and be hated by God. Duty will either make us weary of the world, or the world will make us weary of duty. Obedient children of God experience the one, and hypocrites experience the other.

Notes on Verse 4

Note 1. Worldliness in Christians is spiritual adultery. It dissolves the spiritual marriage between God and the soul; of all sins it is the most inappropriate to the marriage covenant, the covenant of grace in which God declares himself to be "all sufficient" (Genesis 17:1 [Geneva Bible; NIV, "Almighty"—*Ed. note*]). We have enough in God, but we desire to make up our happiness in the creatures; this is plain whoring: "you [God] destroy all who are unfaithful to you" (Psalm 73:27)—that is, those who seek in the world what is only found in God. There are degrees in this whoredom. There may be adultery by desire when the body is not defiled; unclean glances are a degree of lust. The children of God may have some wandering and straggling thoughts; when the devil is at their elbows, the world may be increased in their esteem and imagination. But soon they correct themselves and return to God's arms: "Blessed are the people whose God is the LORD" (Psalm 144:15).

Note 2. Seeking the world's friendship is the quick way to be God's enemy. God and the world are contrary; he is all good, and the world lies in wickedness and commands contrary things. The world says, "Do not miss any opportunity for gain and pleasure; if you will be fussy in standing on conscience, you will do nothing but draw trouble on yourselves." But God says, "Deny yourselves, take up your cross, renounce the world," etc. The world says, "Why should I take my bread and water . . . and give it to men coming from who knows where?" (1 Samuel 25:11). But

God says, "Sell your possessions and give to the poor. Provide purses for yourselves that will not wear out" (Luke 12:33).

Commentary on Verse 5

Or do you think Scripture says without reason that the spirit he caused to live in us tends toward envy . . .

This verse has been twisted by the various expositions of the commentators, because it is not obvious which **Scripture** or what **spirit** the apostle is speaking about. Two opinions are worth looking at. Some people interpret it as the Spirit of God, others as the corrupt spirit of man. Those who think it refers to the Spirit of God read it as a double question: "Does the Scripture speak in vain? Does the Spirit who lives in us envy intensely?" And they interpret it thus: "Is it in vain that the Scriptures speak in the same way that I have spoken to you?" (meaning the last sentences spoken, which are scattered everywhere throughout the Word); "Does the Spirit who is in us envy intensely?" (that is, does the Spirit of God envy in such a worldly way?). They have three reasons:

(1) The sentence supposed to be in the latter part of the text is not found anywhere in Scripture, and therefore some people are forced to have recourse to some ancient book of piety now lost.

(2) The phrase **the spirit he caused to live in us** is most properly and usually applied to the Spirit of God, who is given so that he may dwell in us. It is not so appropriate to our corruption, which is not usually called a spirit, or at least not a spirit living in us.

(3) The word "he" in the first clause of the next verse, **But he gives us more grace**, must refer to the Spirit of God intended here.

The other opinion, that it refers to the wicked spirit of man, expounds the passage like this: "Does the Scripture say in vain?" (that is, it is not for nothing that the Scripture says . . .)—what does it say? That "the spirit living in us [that is, our corrupt nature; some say Satan, but it is more probably the former] envies intensely"? I incline to this opinion, and my reason is that the sense is straightforward. The other interpretation is more difficult, as is its appropriateness to the apostle's intention, which is to prove that worldly desires are natural to us but are inappropriate for someone who wants to be God's friend.

But how shall we answer the contrary arguments?

(1) To the argument that this saying is found nowhere in Scripture, I reply that the sense of it is found in Scripture, though not the exact words; and when Scripture is quoted generally, the sense is sufficient. The author

236

of Hebrews was writing to Jews who were versed in Scripture, and he was always quoting it generally, as also does Peter in many places, and also Paul: "In the Law it is written: 'Through men of strange tongues and through the lips of foreigners I will speak to this people'" (1 Corinthians 14:21). And in verse 34: "women . . . must be in submission, as the Law says." Now these precise words are to be found nowhere in the Old Testament, but they are the drift of many passages. Similarly, consider Ephesians 5:14, "That is why it is said: 'Wake up, O sleeper . . .'"—where there is a general citation. So here it is the drift of many Scriptures to speak of corrupt human nature and a wicked spirit living in us, though I imagine there is an allusion specifically to one place, as there is in all those other citations mentioned. The passage alluded to here is Genesis 8:21, "every inclination of his heart is evil from childhood." Though there is no mention of envy, yet the apostle might very reasonably apply a general passage to his particular purpose.

(2) The second argument is about the meaning of the words **spirit** and **live in us,** but this may very appropriately be applied to the corrupt, natural spirit that we now have. I notice that it is common for Scripture to call the soul's propensity to good or evil its "spirit," as in 1 Corinthians 2:12, "We have not received the spirit of the world." And the phrase "living in me" is used by the apostle, and applied to sin, in Romans 7:17. Nor is there any emphasis in the word to cause it to be peculiar to the gift of the Holy Spirit.

(3) To the argument concerning the beginning of the next verse, I reply that if you simply render it "*it* gives more grace," it refers to the Scriptures; if you render it "*he* gives more grace," it refers to God, who is mentioned in verse 4.

Notes on Verse 5

Note 1. Though sin is natural to us, it is not therefore less evil. It is the apostle's argument against envy and desire that "the spirit that is in us tends toward envy." Poison by nature is more than poison by accident. Similarly, David says, "Surely I have been a sinner from birth, sinful from the time my mother conceived me" (Psalm 51:5). *Lord, I have committed adultery, and I have an adulterous heart and nature!* We should fight all the more and be humbled with all the more grief over sins that are natural to us.

Note 2. **Do you think Scripture says.** Note, from the fact that these precise words are found nowhere, that Scripture says whatever may be inferred from the whole of it and from what follows from it. Immediate inferences are as valid as express words. Christ proves the Resurrection not by direct testimony but by argument (Matthew 22:32). What the Scripture implies, therefore, should be received as if it were expressed.

Note 3. **Without reason (in vain,** KJV). Worldly people make the Scriptures speak in vain to them: "we urge you not to receive God's grace in vain" (2 Corinthians 6:1)—that is, the offers of the Gospel. When God's Word has no corresponding effect, it is a vain and dead letter to us. Do not let the Scriptures, by way of comfort, counsel, or reproof, speak in vain to you. When you find a passage moving, ask yourselves, why was this spoken in God's Word? Was it spoken in vain, or shall I make it so?

Note 4. **The spirit he caused to live in us.** As we mentioned above, some people understand this to be said of Satan, "who is now at work in those who are disobedient" (Ephesians 2:2); but it is more correctly understood of our own spirit, the bent of our worldly hearts. We all by nature have a wicked spirit living in us. We commit sin, just as heavy objects move downward—not from outward forces, but from our own spirit and nature. Be all the more keen to share the divine nature, and be more watchful over yourselves! Your own spirit is the cause of sin; inner concupiscence is your worst enemy (1:14).

Note 5. **Tends toward envy.** A worldly spirit is strongly carried off in the ways of sin; it desires it. Be suspicious of any desires that are too strong; panting after earthly things comes from worldly desire.

Note 6. **Envy.** Natural corruption betrays itself most of all by envy. We have it as soon as we come into the world, and it is hard to leave it before we go out of the world again. The devil first envied us God's favor, and ever since we have envied one another. The children of God are often caught in this. So was Joshua (Numbers 11:28-29). Peter envied John as excelling him in the love of Christ (John 21:20-21). This is a sin that breaks both tablets of the law at once: it begins in discontent with God and ends in harm to man; it is the root of hatred against godliness.

Commentary on Verse 6

. . . but he gives us more grace? That is why Scripture says: "God opposes the proud but gives grace to the humble."

But he gives us more grace. Some read this as "it gives," applying it to Scripture. It gives grace because it offers it and is a means in God's hand of bringing it about. But I prefer to apply this to God, for it is said in contrast to **the spirit he caused to live in us tends toward envy;** and so it suits the context, which is to show that a worldly spirit is contrary to God. This clause, understood in this way, has been expounded in several ways; but the difference is mostly in the form of the expression, and the senses are all pious and subordinate to one another.

(1) You may refer it to the context thus: "Our spirit envies intensely, but he gives us more grace." That is, we are envious, but God is bountiful. It is common in Scripture to contrast God's liberality with our envy, his good hand with our evil eye (see Matthew 20:15). John Damascene calls God "one without envy" because he is most liberal or generous. Note that an envious disposition is very contrary to God. God wants sharing, but we want to keep things to ourselves. We want all blessings to be for us. We malign the good in others, but God delights in it. This may make envy odious to us; we all pretend to be like God. We want a cursed self-sufficiency; why can we not want holy conformity?

a. God has no need to give us his blessings; we need one another and the highest monarch. For us to want all good things fenced in, when our happiness is dependent and consists in mutual sharing, must be exceedingly vile.

b. This is not only unlike God but hurtful to him; we want him to be less good, and so we not only question the wisdom of his gifts but want to restrict the goodness of his nature.

Certainly, then, there is little of the Spirit of God where there is such an envious spirit. Grace lies in conformity to God; that is why it is described as participating in "the divine nature" (2 Peter 1:4). Grace is nothing but introducing the virtues of God into our soul. Now, God delights in giving us more grace, and so those who do not share their good with others or are all for keeping their blessings to themselves or cannot rejoice in the excellencies of other people have nothing at all, or very little, of the nature of God in them.

(2) Our spirit is strongly given to envy, but God gives us more grace. That is, there is enough in him to check the strongest sins; there is enough in God to help the creature in its sorest conflicts. "For a rich man to enter the kingdom of heaven . . . is impossible, but with God all things are possible" (Matthew 19:23, 26). Usually we judge God by our own standard, as if what is impossible to our own efforts is also impossible for divine grace: "'It may seem marvelous to the remnant of this people at that time, but will it seem marvelous to me?' declares the LORD Almighty" (Zechariah 8:6). There is more in God than there can be in nature, and Satan is not so able to destroy as Christ is to save. So then, when desires are strong, think of a strong God, a mighty Christ, upon whom help is laid. You cannot cure your spirits of envy, pride, self-confidence, or vainglory; but God **gives us more grace**. A sense of weakness should not be a discouragement but an advantage. So it was to Paul; when he was weak in himself, he was always most strong in Christ (2 Corinthians 12:9-10). The chief thing that

God requires of the creature is choice and will. All of God's aim is to bring us to our knees and for us to receive power from the hands of his mercy.

(3) Another consideration is this: though we are wicked and sinful, God will make his grace abound all the more; our spirit envies intensely, and **he gives us more grace**. Note that God often makes our sinfulness an occasion to reveal more grace. "Where sin increased, grace increased all the more" (Romans 5:20). What a wise God we serve, who can make our sins abound to his glory! And what a good God, who will make our wickedness the occasion of more grace! If Christ died for sinners, I am sure I can plead that "I am the worst" of them (1 Timothy 1:15). If you have no other plea, offer yourselves in this way to God and take hold of the promises.

(4) It is like this with us by nature, but **he gives us more grace**. When you are renewed and converted to faith in Christ, you have another manner of spirit; you are not carried by the old envious spirit that lives in you, but by a more gracious spirit that God has given you. Note that the old spirit and the new spirit are quite different. Through grace you will be different from what you were by nature. Conversion is revealed by a change. Oh, what a sad thing it is when Christians are what they always were! You should have **more grace**.

(5) But **he gives us more grace**; here **more** means better, as so often in the Scriptures. If you want to seek God in a humble manner, you want to be acquainted with richer things; you do not want to envy and contend with one another about external pleasures. What the world gives is not comparable with what God gives—**more grace**. "I do not give to you as the world gives" (John 14:27). More excellent blessings! Here we encumber ourselves with much serving, but God gives **more grace**. Faith will show us greater things than these. The main reason why people dote on the world is because they are not acquainted with a higher glory. People ate acorns until they were acquainted with the use of corn; a candle is very helpful until the sun rises. We do not have a right apprehension of grace until we can see that it yields us more than the world can. Created things give us temporary refreshment, and the world serves its time; but grace brings full and everlasting joy.

That is why Scripture says. What is the effect of this sentence? James applies it to his argument, which is to dissuade them from worldly pursuits and to urge them to address God humbly. Therefore it is no good leaving it out, as some people do—such as Erasmus, who thinks it started as a marginal note and was put into the text by some scribe.

Where does Scripture say this? There is some disagreement about the passage to which this refers. Some people think it was a holy proverb among the Jews. But this cannot be. The phrase seems to allude to some passage of **Scripture**. Some people think it is Psalm 18:27, "You save the humble but bring low those whose eyes are haughty." But humility here does not imply a low and abject condition, but a grace and disposition of mind; and the place cited speaks only of saving the afflicted people of God. Many people refer it to other general passages, but most probably it refers to Proverbs 3:34, "He mocks proud mockers but gives grace to the humble." Some people think James is alluding to 1 Peter 5:5-8, for this is simply a summary of that passage and was written after it, and so he may be asserting the divine authority of that letter. But I prefer to stay with the previous opinion.

"**God opposes the proud.**" That is, he stands in battle-array or in direct defiance and opposition against them. The proud man has his tactics, and God has his anti-tactics. The Word shows that there is a mutual opposition between God and the proud. And I note this particularly because in Proverbs it says, "He mocks proud mockers." They mock God, and God mocks them. God still counteracts the proud, as he did Pharaoh.

Mocking is a great sign of pride; disdain of others comes from overvaluing ourselves. God has made everyone an object of respect or pity; it is pride that makes them objects of contempt, and in them their Maker (Proverbs 17:5). Wicked men "sit in the seat of mockers" (Psalm 1:1). This is a sin so hateful to God that he takes notice of disdainful gestures—"the pointing finger and malicious talk" (Isaiah 58:9).

But gives grace. This is meant spiritually of the help and grace by which they may overcome their worldly desires; worldly desires cannot be overcome without the assistance of grace.

To the humble. This does not mean a vile and abject condition, but a holy brokenness and contrition, just as by "proud," in a spiritual sense, is meant stiff-necked and unhumbled sinners.

Notes on Verse 6

Note 1. God not only offers grace but reveals the way in which we may share it and defines the way in which we may give ourselves to him. God is in good earnest in the offers of grace; he not only offers but teaches and indeed draws us (see John 6:44-45). He is as willing to give faith as to give salvation.

Note 2. Those who want to have grace must go the right way to obtain it. They must not only consider what God gives but what he says. God, who has decreed the end, has decreed the means. That is why we not only have promises in Scripture but directions; it calls to account those who want to have the blessing but do not want to use the means. Most people content themselves with lazy wishes; they want to have grace but lie on their beds of ease and expect to be snatched up to heaven in a fiery chariot, or for grace to drop on them out of the clouds. God, who says he will give grace, says something else—that you must be humble in order to receive it.

Note 3. It is excellent to rank Scriptures in their order and know **why** everything is spoken in the Word, so that we may match absolute promises with conditional ones and put every truth in its proper place. James links the general offers of grace with another promise: God **gives grace to the humble**. It is good to know truth in its framework, in which all truths are joined in natural links and connections, just as the curtains of the tabernacle were looped to one another. Vague understanding only disposes us to error or looseness. Truths awe us most when we are aware of the relationship between them. "Mary treasured up all these things and pondered them in her heart" (Luke 2:19). The word translated "pondered" means "compared them with one another." A hint here and a hint there makes people loose and careless, as when absolute promises are not considered in the context of faith. Absolute promises may be our first encouragement, but conditional promises must be our direction; the former are a plank thrown out to save a sinking soul, but the latter show us the way to get into the ark. So then, do not be content with sermon hints until you have gotten a pattern of sound words and can discern God's intention in the various passages of Scripture, so that you may rank them in their order. The apostle here shows the reason why God said he **gives grace to the humble**.

Note 4. **God opposes the proud.** Of all sins God sets himself to punish the sin of pride. He abhors other sinners but professes open defiance and hostility against the proud. Someone asked a philosopher what God was doing; he answered that his whole work was to lift up the humble and cast down the proud. This is the very business of providence; the Bible is full of examples. This was the sin that turned angels into devils; they wanted to be above everyone, not under anyone, and therefore God tumbled them down to hell. As someone says, "God could not endure to have pride so near him." Then pride wrecked all mankind when it crept out of heaven into paradise on earth. You may trace the story of it all along by the ruins and falls of those who entertained it. Pharaoh, Herod, Haman, and Nebuchadnezzar are sad instances and loudly proclaim that all the world cannot keep up the person who does not keep his own spirit down. Herod merely endured the flatteries of others. He had on a suit of silver cloth, according to Josephus, and the sunbeams beat upon it, and the people cried, "This is the voice of a god, not of a man" because the angels used to appear in shining garments. Because he did not rebuke them, he was eaten up by worms (see Acts 12:21-23).

I notice too that God has punished this in his own people; there are terrible instances of his displeasure against their pride. Uzziah's pride led to his downfall (2 Chronicles 26:16); he was smitten with leprosy and died "out of grief and sorrow," says Josephus. David's numbering of the people and glorying in his own greatness cost the lives of seventy thousand. Under Hezekiah, "the anger of the LORD" fell "on Judah and Jerusalem" (2 Chronicles 29:8). These judgments on pride are sure and resolved. A man's pride will surely bring him down (Proverbs 29:23). If they do not visibly light upon the first person, they overtake their posterity: "The LORD tears down the proud man's house" (Proverbs 15:25). All their aim is to advance their house and family, but within two or three ages they are utterly wasted and ruined. And judgments on pride are very shameful, that God may pour the more contempt on them: "When pride comes, then comes disgrace" (Proverbs 11:2)—not only ruin, but "disgrace."

Why should God so expressly set himself against pride? Because of all sins, he hates this sin (Proverbs 16:5). Other sins are more hateful to men, because they bring disgrace and have more baseness in them, whereas pride seems to have a kind of bravery in it. But the Lord hates it because it is a sin that sets itself most against him. Other sins are against God's laws; this is against his being and sovereignty. Pride not only withdraws the heart from God but lifts it up against God. It is a direct contention as to who shall be acknowledged as the author of blessing and excellence: "Because you think you are wise, as wise as a god . . ." (Ezekiel 28:6). Babylon speaks in the name and style of God, and so does Nineveh: "I am, and there is none besides me" (Zephaniah 2:15). And as pride rises against his being, so it rises against his providence.

It is also the greatest enemy to God's law; there is pride in every sin. Sinning is a confronting of God and a despising of the Word of the Lord (2 Samuel 12:9). The will of the creature is set up against the Creator. But the sin of pride is much more against the law of God; it cannot endure the word that reproves it. Other sins disturb reason; this humors it. Drunkenness is more patient with reproof, the conscience consenting to the checks of the Word. But pride first blinds the mind, then arms the affections; it puts the judgment to sleep, and then awakens anger. Besides, pride is the cause of all other sins. Covetousness is the root of evil, and pride is the soul of it. Covetousness is just pride's purveyor. We pursue worldly pleasures so that we may puff ourselves up in the possession of them; and usually what is pursued in desire is enjoyed in pride. It is only the soul's complacency in an earthly excellence. "He is arrogant," and therefore "he is as greedy as the grave" (Habakkuk 2:5).

Application 1. The use of all this is, first, to caution us against pride. There are two sorts of pride, one in the mind and the other in the affections—self-conceit and an aspiring after worldly greatness. Both are natural to us, especially the former.

(1) We are amazingly apt to be puffed up with an idea of our own excellence, be it regarding riches, beauty, abilities, or grace. The apostle calls this

"boasting of what he has and does" (1 John 2:16), because it spreads throughout all the activities and comforts of life. Other desires are limited either by their end (such as lusts of the flesh, to content the body) or by their instruments (such as lusts of the eyes); but pride has a universal and unlimited influence. Only the whole of life is enough scope for pride. Those who have nothing excellent cannot excuse themselves from fearing it; we often find that people who have nothing to be proud of are the most conceited. We see this in our natures: man was never more proud than since he was wretched and miserable. Pride came in by the fall, and what should bring the spirit down has raised it. But those who excel have much more reason to be suspicious of themselves. Rich men, for example, are told, "Command those who are rich in this present world not to be arrogant" (1 Timothy 6:17).

Think about God's judgment on pride in abilities. Staupicius was proud of his memory, and God struck it. We find nothing causes madness so much as pride. Nebuchadnezzar lost his reason and turned into an animal when he grew proud. Many young men who were proud of their gifts have, by the just judgment of God, lost all their quickness and smartness and quenched their vigor in bodily and worldly delights. Remember, whatever we have was given by grace; and if we grow proud of it, it will soon be taken away by justice. Not only able men, but those of much grace and mortification may be tripped by pride; it once crept into heaven, then into paradise on earth. The best heart can have no security. Christians are not so much in danger of intemperance and sensual lusts as of pride; as other sins decrease, it grows. That is why pride is put last in 1 John 2:16, as being Satan's last device. Those who are set on the pinnacles of the temple are in danger of being thrown down in this way. Paul was apt to grow proud of his revelations (2 Corinthians 12:7). In heaven alone we are most high and most humble. A worm may breed in manna; strong comforts, raised affections, and strange euphoria may much puff up, and by gracious enjoyments we sometimes grow proud, secure, self-sufficient, and disdainful of other people (Romans 14:10). But this will cost you sharp decay.

(2) The other sort of pride is aspiring to worldly greatness. By such foolish pursuits you simply make God oppose you. Many people mistake ambition and think that desire for position is only unlawful when it is sought by unlawful means; but to feign greatness is contrary to the rules of the Gospel. We should leave our advancement to the sweet invitation of providence and stay where we are until the master of the feast asks us to sit higher. In our private choice we should be content with a reasonable supply of necessities: "everyone who exalts himself . . ." (Luke 14:11), not everyone who is exalted. In the Olympic games the wrestler never put on his own crown and garland; "Christ also did not take upon himself the glory of becoming a high priest" but was "called by God, just as Aaron

was" (Hebrews 5:4-5). When we do not wait for the call of providence, it is only an untimely desire for promotion, and either God prevents it or else it proves a curse and snare to us.

Application 2. We should not envy a proud person any more than we would someone on a gallows; they are only lifted up in order to be cast down forever. Chrysostom notes that we are apt to pity the drunkard but envy the proud. We need to pity them too, for they are near a fall: "Better to be lowly in spirit and among the oppressed than to share plunder with the proud" (Proverbs 16:19); that is, it is better to be of the beaten party than to form a confederacy with those who grow proud of their success.

Application 3. Note the instances of God's displeasure against pride on yourselves or those who are near you. Paul took notice of the thorn that was in his flesh, "to keep me from becoming conceited," he says (2 Corinthians 12:7). So you may often say, "This was an affliction to correct and abate my pride."

Note 5. God's grace is given to the humble. We lay up the richest wine in the lowest cellars; in the same way God's choicest mercies are laid in humble and lowly hearts. Christ did most for those who were most humble. There is enough excellence in God; he only requires a sense of emptiness in us. God loves to make all his works creations; and grace works most freely when it works upon nothing. It is not to God's honor that the creatures should receive nothing from mercy until they are brought to their knees; the condition that he lays down is, "Only acknowledge your guilt" (Jeremiah 3:13). The humble are vessels of a larger size, fit to receive what grace gives. From this you may learn why humble people are most gracious, and gracious people most humble. God delights to fill up such people.

Commentary and Notes on Verse 7

Submit yourselves, then, to God. Resist the devil, and he will flee from you.

Here James applies the promise and by inference emphasizes the duty specified in it: **Submit yourselves, then, to God**. But you will say, "What is the connection?"

(1) The reason may be inferred from the latter part of the sentence, thus: "God gives grace to the humble; therefore, submit yourselves." That is, come humbly, and seek the grace of God.

Note that general hints of duty must be faithfully applied to particulars in our own souls. Doctrine is like the drawing of a bow; application is hitting the mark. Many people are wise in generalities but vain when it comes to practicalities. Whenever you hear the Word, let the light of every truth be reflected on your own soul.

a. A sense of duty: "apply it to yourself" (Job 5:27). If God has required humility, I must submit to God; if the happiness and quiet of the creature consists in nearness to God, then "as for me, it is good to be near God" (Psalm 73:28). So you must take your share out of every truth; I must live by this rule. When sinners are invited to believe in Christ, they are to say, "I am the worst" (1 Timothy 1:15).

b. A resolution for duty, that your souls may conclude not only "I must," but "I will." "To you, O my heart, he has said, 'Seek my face!' Your face, LORD, I will seek" (Psalm 27:8, NIV footnote). The command is plural: "Seek"; and the answer is singular: "I will." This is the way the heart must respond to divine teachings.

(2) It may be inferred from the previous clause thus: "He opposes the proud; therefore submit yourselves." That is, let the Lord have a willing and spontaneous subjection from you.

Note, in this case, that the creature must be humbled either actively or passively. If you do not have a humble heart, God has a mighty hand: "Humble yourselves, therefore, under God's mighty hand" (1 Peter 5:6). He will either break the heart or break the bones. You must judge yourselves, or else God will judge you (1 Corinthians 11:32). God has made a righteous law: sin must be judged in one court or another, that the law may not seem to be made in vain. If at the last day, when the judgment is set and the books are opened and sinners stand trembling before the white throne of the Lamb and you are conscious of the whole process, Christ should then make you such an offer—"Judge yourselves, and you will not be judged"—with what thankfulness you would accept the suggestion!

And the next thing would be to inquire into your own hearts. Think: that is how it must be; we must judge or be judged, be humble or humbled. It would be better to anticipate acts of vengeance by acts of duty. Pharaoh and Nebuchadnezzar were humbled (Daniel 4:34), but to their cost. Passive humiliation is sore and deadly. It would be better for us to humble a proud heart than for God, in the threatening of Scripture, to humble our proud looks and make us feel what we would not otherwise. You will not judge yourselves? Ah, but how terrible it will be when the Lord comes to judge us for all our harsh words and ungodly acts (Jude 15)! When justice takes up the quarrel of despised mercy, it will be sad for us; and then we shall know the difference between God's inviting and God's inflicting.

Submit yourselves, then, to God. Note that anyone who wants to seek God's friendship must submit to him. James speaks about getting in with God, which must be in a humble way. There is an infinite distance between God and his creatures; we must come with reverence. But we are not only creatures, but guilty creatures; and therefore we must come with a holy awe and trembling.

(1) I shall inquire first what this subjection is. The word means placing ourselves under God, and so it denotes the whole duty of an inferior state.

a. There must be subjection to God's will—the whole man to the whole law of God. To submit to God is to give ourselves up to be governed by his will and pleasure; our thoughts, our counsels, our affections, our actions must be guided according to the strict rules of the Word. Usually the work of conversion stops here; we are loath to resign ourselves to God's will. Some of God's commands, such as those which are inward, are contrary to our affections; others, such as those which enforce external duties, are contrary to our interests. But we must "take [Christ's] yoke" (Matthew 11:29). A main thing to be looked at in our first supplication to God is this: are we willing to give ourselves up to his will without reservation? Can I subject everything, without any hesitation or reluctance, to the obedience of Christ (2 Corinthians 10:5)?

b. It implies a humble approach to God. **Submit yourselves, then, to God**; that is, lay aside your pride and stubbornness, humbly acknowledging your sins. Come as lost, undone creatures lying at the feet of mercy. How long it takes before our faces are buried in the dust (Lamentations 3:29), before we can come and say in truth of heart, "If we are damned, it is just; if we are saved, it is through much mercy."

c. It is handing ourselves over to the disposal of God's providence. "The Lord's will be done" (Acts 21:14) is a truly Christian way of speaking. Discontent is clearly rebellion; we want our will done, and not God's. When we complain, God and we contend; his will must be done to us as well as by us.

Thus you see there is a threefold submission: our worldly hearts to his holiness, our proud hearts to his mercy, our stormy minds to his sovereignty, that we may be obedient, humble, patient.

(2) Secondly, I shall inquire how this submission must be performed.

a. Sincerely. We must do his will because it is his will. God's will is both the rule and the reason of duty. So 1 Thessalonians 4:3 urges us, "It is God's will that you should be holy"; see also 1 Thessalonians 5:18 and 1 Peter 2:13. This is warrant enough and motive enough; God wants it to be so. Hypocrites do what they have to, but they have other motives. To do it sincerely is indeed to do a duty as duty, to do what is commanded because it is commanded.

b. Freely. Subjection is best when it is willing. If the beast came to the altar struggling and unwilling, men never offered it to their gods but counted it unlucky. Certainly the true God looks most of all for a ready mind: "I will hasten and not delay to obey your commands" (Psalm 119:60)—without doubting, disputing, or consulting with flesh and blood.

To offer Isaac was a hard duty, and yet that morning Abraham was up early (see Genesis 22:3).

c. Faithfully. To the Lord's glory, not our own ends. The Christian life must be for God (Galatians 2:19), according to God's will, for God's glory. The creatures' hardest task is to subject our ends to God's ends, as well as our ways to God's will.

(3) Thirdly, I shall inquire what considerations are necessary to urge this duty upon the soul. Man is a stout creature, and we are apt to break all cords and restraints. Our language is, "Who is lord over us?"

a. The necessity of the question. "Humble yourselves, therefore, under God's mighty hand" (1 Peter 5:6). It a madness to contend with One who can command legions. What are we to God? "Are we stronger than he?" (1 Corinthians 10:22). Who is so foolish as to stand against the Almighty? Men fawn upon those who have power; God can ruin us with a breath: "At the breath of God they are destroyed; at the blast of his anger they perish" (Job 4:9). We shall feel this power if we do not stoop to it. People who are not drawn by the power of God's Spirit are broken by the power of his providence. God has sworn: "'As surely as I live,' says the Lord, 'every knee will bow before me'" (Romans 14:11); that is, in effect, "do not regard me as a living God if I do not make the creature stoop." Listen to this, you who stand against the power of the Word: can you stand against the power of Christ when he comes in glory? "Will your courage endure or your hands be strong in the day I deal with you?" (Ezekiel 22:14).

b. The nobleness of surrender. Submission seems base, but to God it is noble. All other subjection is slavery, but this is the truest freedom. Vain men think it is a freedom to live at large, to gratify every worldly desire; this is the basest bondage that may be (2 Peter 2:18). Wicked men have as many lords as lusts. If conscience is awakened just a little, they are aware of the tyranny. They see they are in a bad way, and they cannot help it; they are drunkards, unclean people, worldly and do not know how to be anything else.

c. The utility and benefit of surrender. This will make almighty power the ground of your hope, not your fear: "Let them come to me for refuge; let them make peace with me" (Isaiah 27:5). This submission is the high way to exaltation (1 Peter 5:6). How men crouch for worldly ends and admire every base person for secular advantage, as Otho in Tacitus did: "kiss the people, even adore the basest, and all to make way for his own greatness." Should we not rather stoop and submit to the Lord? There is no baseness in the act, and there is much glory in the reward.

Resist the devil. What connection has this precept with the previous one? It may thought of in several ways:

(1) If you will humbly submit to God, you must expect to resist Satan. In this case, note that true obedience finds much opposition from the

devil. Since the fall, a godly life is not known by perfection of grace so much as by conflicts with sin. Satan is still busiest wherever he has least to do. Pirates do not set upon empty vessels, and beggars do not need to fear the thief. Those who have most grace feel most trouble from Satan. He envies them for enjoying the situation and interest in God that he himself has lost. The devil is loath to wake up those who are in his power: "When a strong man, fully armed, guards his own house, his possessions are safe" (Luke 11:21). But regarding the godly, he asks to sift them as wheat (Luke 22:31). Sometimes he buffets them with dreadful suggestions, at other times with worldly temptations. We cannot set upon a duty without Satan suggesting lazy thoughts and worldly advice. So then, you cannot judge yourselves forsaken by God because you are tempted by Satan; no brother in the flesh has not had his share (1 Peter 5:9). Such conflicts are not inconsistent with faith and piety. The devil tried this even with Christ himself after he had a testimony from heaven (Matthew 4). Paul was troubled with one of Satan's messengers (2 Corinthians 12:7). The best are exercised with the sorest conflicts. When the thief breaks into the house, it is not to take away coal but jewels.

(2) You may think of the connection like this: if you want to submit to God, you must beware of those proud suggestions with which Satan tries to puff up your spirits.

In this case, note that one of Satan's chief temptations is pride. Therefore, when the apostle speaks of submission, he immediately adds, **Resist the devil**. By pride Satan himself fell (1 Timothy 3:6). That is why the devil was cast out of heaven. He would like to have more company and draw us into his own snare. This is a bait soon swallowed; it is natural to us. He tried to tempt Christ himself to a vainglorious action. Certainly we all desire to be set on high pinnacles, though we run the hazard of a fall. We need, then, to be all the more watchful against such thoughts and insinuations. Places liable to assault usually have the strongest guard. And we may admire the wisdom of God, who can overcome Satan by Satan; Satan's messenger who buffeted Paul was meant to cure his pride (2 Corinthians 12:7).

(3) Having told them what submission is required, James also wants to tell them what resistance is lawful. You must submit to God, but not to Satan. The Scriptures, in order to speak distinctly and clearly, make contrasts of necessary duties like this. So in 1 Corinthians 14:20 we read, " In regard to evil be infants, but in your thinking be adults." Similarly in Romans 16:19, "I want you to be wise about what is good, and innocent about what is evil." These sayings match this one of the apostle: you must submit and yet resist.

Note that instead of worldly desires James mentions Satan. The apostle does not say, "resist sin," but "resist Satan." Note that Satan has a great hand in all sins. Survey the pedigree of sin, and you will see it may all call the devil father. Worldly desires are called his desires (John 8:44), and it is said that "anything beyond this comes from the evil one" (Matthew 5:37)—that is, from the devil. Giving way to anger is, in the apostle's language, giving the devil a foothold (Ephesians 4:26-27). Survey the iniquities of every age, and is not Satan's hand in it all? It is said of Judas' treason against Christ that the devil prompted him (John 13:2). So too with Ananias: "How is it that Satan has so filled your heart that you have lied?" (Acts 5:3). And in 1 Chronicles 21:1 we read, "Satan . . . incited David to take a census of Israel." And in Matthew 16:23, "Get thee behind me, Satan!" (KJV). The heathen, who did not understand the operations of the devil, thought all our conflicts were against internal passions. Now the apostle is clear that we fight not only against worldly desires, but "against the spiritual forces of evil in the heavenly realms" (Ephesians 6:12), which makes the fight all the fiercer.

Sometimes the devil begins the temptation, sometimes we do. He began with Judas; he prompted him by putting evil thoughts in his mind. At other times our own corruption works freely, but the devil may join in. So then, all sin involving the devil, let us defy him and his works and desires too. As followers of divine justice we defy Satan, though sadly we also honor him as head of the worldly state. We love his desires and so call him "father" and keep the crown on his head. Many people rail against him and yet honor him. As a proud spirit, all he aims for is homage and obedience; if he can get our spiritual respect, other things do not move him. As Christ does not love being flattered by us when we violate his laws, so Satan is not provoked by our speaking ill of him. His policy is to blind the mind and carry on his kingdom covertly in the darkness of this world. Every sinner is really the devil's drudge.

Note, too, from the nature of the duty urged, that it is the duty of Christians to resist Satan. This point is very useful in the Christian life, and a subject on which many eminent people in the church of God have taught. I shall try and explain four things:

(1) Satan has almost as great a power over wicked people as the Spirit of God has over holy people. The same words are used to describe the efficacy of Satan and the influence of the Spirit. God "works in" us (Philippians 2:13), and Satan "is now at work in those who are disobedient" (Ephesians 2:3). The Spirit of God gives "a new heart" (Ezekiel 36:26), but Satan operates strongly on people's will and understanding by their consent. Indeed, he works by way of imperious suggestion, but without any violation or forcing of people's will; on the godly he works by way of imposture and deceit, on the wicked by way of imperious command and sovereignty. Not only does he put into the heart fancies and ideas that stir up sensual and worldly desires, but also those that will blind

the spirit and understanding. Satan, who stirs some people to uncleanness, stirs others to error and blasphemy. That is why 2 Thessalonians 2:9-10 says, "The coming of the lawless one will be in accordance with the work of Satan displayed in . . . every sort of evil that deceives." We are not aware of the things spirits tell us. It is true we are most aware of Satan's force when we are tempted to bodily lusts, because they frighten conscience most of all, disturb reason, and oppress the body, and because between every temptation and sin there is an intervening explicit thought, of which the soul is conscious. But insinuations of error are more silent and plausible.

Scripture everywhere suggests the great understanding and craftiness of the devil. Hence we read of the devil's "trap" (2 Timothy 2:26) and "schemes" (Ephesians 6:11; 2 Corinthians 2:11)—words indicating great cunning and skill, which is much increased by experience and observation; he "considered" Job (Job 2:3). He observes and considers us and knows how to choose the right bait, partly by imagining by what corrupt aims most people live, partly by observing our prayers, talk, passions, etc. He can interpret the silent language of a blush, a smile, a frown, a look, the glance of a lustful eye, the gait and carriage of the body. To work upon us he sometimes uses men, including our nearest friends (in this way he used Peter to Christ, Matthew 16:22-23) or cursed deceivers (2 Corinthians 11:15). Sometimes he uses our own bodies; by upsetting our equilibrium he stirs us up to revenge, uncleanness, passion, and all sensual lusts. And therefore you need to keep the body in good shape, so that its moods are not armed against your souls. Sometimes he shows us the object, as he did with Christ, representing the world's glory to him in a map or landscape; in this way he stirs up desire through the eye: "With eyes full of adultery" (2 Peter 2:14; in the original it is, "of the adulteress"). First he shows us the objects, and then he makes us dwell on the idea until our heart is ensnared. Sometimes he puts thoughts in our minds through the help of our imagination; this must be one way, or how could he tempt us to despair or to spiritual sins, or how could he blind the mind by worldly imagination and ideas and by obstinate prejudices against the truth? And these thoughts, once they are put in our minds, may be continued in a conversation or argument, and the devil, guessing at the answer, may carry on with a reply. So we find that he attacks Christ with new temptations because he had received so full an answer.

(2) The next thing is to show what it is to resist him.

a. Negatively. We must not fear him; the devil has no power to force us, but only the skill to persuade us. Distrustful fear gives him the advantage. We are to "resist him, standing firm in the faith" (1 Peter 5:9). And again, we must not "give the devil a foothold" (Ephesians 4:27). Anger may make way for malice; and when the first thoughts of sin do not grieve us, the actual practice of them is not far off.

b. Positively. We must demonstrate our resistance, partly by refusing to commune with him. Sometimes he must be checked simply by a rebuke and abomination. When the temptation tends to a direct withdrawal from obedience, for example, it is enough to say, "Get behind me, Satan" and to chide the thought before it settles. Sometimes we must counter him with reasons and thoughts of grace. For example, when the temptation has taken any hold on the thoughts, and corruption rises up in defense of the suggestion, this is called "standing your ground" when the day of evil comes and extinguishing the flaming arrows of the evil one (Ephesians 6:13-18).

(3) The next thing is the way and means of maintaining this war by the graces of God's Holy Spirit. I will mention the chief ways:

a. Faith (1 Peter 5:9-10). You need faith, so that you may overcome mystically, by taking hold of the victory of Christ, and morally, so that you may reflect on the glorious rewards appointed for those who stand out in the course of trial and on the spiritual help that is at hand to encourage you in the fight. Faith is necessary in every way; it is called "the shield" (Ephesians 6:13). The shield covers the other parts of the armor; thus faith supports the other graces when they are assaulted—by getting help, by encouraging them, etc.

b. Prayer. Never cope with a temptation alone, but try to bring God into the combat: "pray in the Spirit on all occasions" (Ephesians 6:18). I believe "Spirit" [NIV] here means not the Holy Spirit, but the heart or soul; when you are assaulted, lift up your spirit in holy groans to God.

c. Self-control (1 Peter 5:8). We need to be watchful, to take heed of every worldly desire; and we need to be self-controlled too in the use of every support, every created thing, every activity. I think that by "self-controlled" the apostle means moderating our affections in worldly things, which is necessary for this purpose since all temptations are insinuated into our minds under the guise of pleasure, honor, profit, etc.; and so a heart drowned in the world is soon overcome.

d. Watchfulness. Those with gunpowder natures need to take care not only of burning arrows but of the least sparks. God is soon offended; therefore we must go about "with fear and trembling" (Philippians 2:12). Our hearts are soon overcome; so we need to watch what comes in, lest it proves itself a temptation, and what goes out, lest it proves itself corrupt. We should keep looking for victory in the fight and for the fight in the victory.

e. Sincerity. The apostle speaks of "the belt of truth" (Ephesians 6:14). A double-minded man is his own tempter, and unsettled souls simply invite Satan to make an alliance with their own doubts and anxieties. Such a mixture, like civil wars in a country, makes us prey.

(4) I shall only touch on the most persuasive arguments to engage us in the fight and warfare. Consider the necessity: either you must resist him or be taken captive by him; there is no middle course. If you make peace with him, it will only be to your own harm; to enter into league with Satan is to be overcome. Now he tempts; hereafter he will accuse (Matthew 4:1; Revelation 12:10). Satan flatters the creatures; but the snares of sin will at length prove chains of darkness. We look at the trouble of resisting him, but the sweetness of victory will abundantly compensate for it. Usually we make the mistake of seeing how delightful sin is and what a nuisance it is to resist it, and so we create a trap for ourselves. The right comparison is between the fruit of sin and the fruit of victory. We have often experienced what it is to be overcome; let us now see how delightful victory will be. Nothing reveals the power and support of Christianity so much as the spiritual conflict. If people give in to temptations and commit sins without remorse, it is no wonder they are so cold and dead in religion or that they have such dim and doubtful evidence of heaven; they never tried the truth and power of grace. The spiritual combat and the victories of Christ are riddles and dreams to them.

Besides all this, consider the hopes of prevailing. Satan is a foiled adversary; Christ has overcome him already. All that is required for victory is a strong "No." Do not give him any further reply. To resist him, not to yield to him, is the only way to be rid of him. You have a promise: **Resist the devil, and he will flee from you.** Christ has foiled the enemy, and he has put weapons into your hands so that *you* may foil him. He trod on this old serpent when his heel was struck on the cross (see Genesis 3:15). Now he wants you to set your feet on his neck; "the God of peace will soon crush Satan under your feet" (Romans 16:20). You need not doubt his help; though Satan is an "accuser," Christ is an "advocate." The Spirit of God strengthens us against the suggestions of the evil spirit, and the good angels wait on us (Hebrew 1:14), just as much as the bad angels molest us. Do not fear being deserted; when you are in Satan's hands, Satan is in God's hands.

Jesus Christ himself was tempted, and he knows what it is to be exposed to the rage of a cruel fiend; therefore "he is able to help those who are being tempted" (Hebrews 2:18; see also Hebrews 4:15). Those who have suffered with gallstones will sympathize with others who are wracked with pain and torture; Israel was a foreigner, so had to be kind to foreigners. Christ's heart is made more tender by his own experience; since he grappled with Satan, he is full of compassion for all who are attacked by him.

And he will flee from you. Here is the promise annexed to the duty as an encouragement. But you will ask how it is to be understood. Does

Satan always flee when he is resisted? God's children find in painful experience that the devil renews the battle and sometimes prevails at a second or third attempt.

(1) Every denial is a great discouragement to Satan; sin gives him a foothold (Ephesians 4:27). He is like a dog that stands looking and waving his tail ready to receive something from those who sit at the table; but if nothing is thrown to him, he goes away. Satan looks for an angry word, an unclean glance, gestures of wrath and discontent; but if he finds none of these, he is discouraged.

(2) After being denied, he may continue to trouble you. Jesus was assaulted again and again after a full answer. Indeed, in the end "he left him until an opportune time" (Luke 4:13). That is why Peter tells us we must always be alert (1 Peter 5:8).

(3) If we continue to resist, Satan will surely lose. A Christian has the best of it. Though Satan repeats his assaults a thousand times, he can never overcome you without your consent; and though the conflict may put you to some trouble, it brings you much spiritual gain, more obvious experiences of Christ's power, and a more earnest trust—just as dangers make children cling to their parent more firmly. Besides, it is honor enough to foil him in each individual attack, though usually a Christian not only comes off with the victory but with triumph, and Satan not only does not prevail but flees from us.

Commentary and Notes on Verse 8

Come near to God and he will come near to you. Wash your hands, you sinners, and purify your hearts, you double-minded.

James returns to the main thing in question—the success of humbly addressing God, showing we shall not lack divine help if we will just make way for it. God never lets us down until we first let ourselves down. We withdraw our hearts from God, and so it is no wonder if we do not feel the effects of his grace. All the world may judge whether God or sinners bear the blame for our wants and miseries. If "a man's own folly ruins his life," there is no reason why we should "rage against the LORD" (Proverbs 19:3).

Come near to God. You may look upon these words as spoken to sinners or to converts.

(1) If they are spoken to sinners, or people who have not been called, then the sense is, "Come near to God, seek him by faith and repentance, and he will come near to you"—that is, with his grace and blessing. In that

case, note that everyone by nature needs to come near to God. Coming near implies we have left; "even from birth the wicked go astray" (Psalm 58:3). As soon as we were able to go, we went astray. In Adam we lost three things—the image of God, the favor of God, and fellowship with God. All sins divide between God and the soul; "your iniquities have separated you from your God" (Isaiah 59:2). Sin makes us shy of his presence; guilt cannot endure the thought of the Judge, and it makes God offended with us. How can his holy nature delight in an impure creature?

And as sin in general does this, so there are some special sins that separate between God and the soul, such as pride (see Psalm 138:6). God stands at a distance and will have no communion with a proud spirit. So creature-confidence and self-satisfaction keep us from God; we stand at a distance, as if we had enough merit of our own: "Cursed is the one who trusts in man, who depends on flesh for his strength and whose heart turns away from the LORD" (Jeremiah 17:5). The closest union is brought about by faith, which makes the soul stay in him; and the greatest separation is when we go to other sources of confidence, for then we are simply leaving God. So then, consider your natural condition—aliens from God. So that you may resent it all the more, consider the cause and effects of this natural condition:

a. Its cause. The heart is set on sin and therefore estranged from God: "alienated from God" and "enemies in your minds because of your evil behavior" (Colossians 1:21)—that is, because the mind is set on sin. With such a distance between us and God, we do not delight in him. "Leave us alone!" Why? "We have no desire to know your ways" (Job 21:14). We do not love holiness, and therefore we do not love God. What madness this is, to part with God for sin!

b. Its effects. If you depart from God as a friend, you cannot escape him as an enemy. How beautifully Augustine puts it: "You that cannot endure the presence of God, or a thought of him, where will you go from him?" Or this: "Where can I go from your Spirit? Where can I flee from your presence? If I go up to the heavens, you are there; if I make my bed in the depths, you are there" (Psalm 139:7-8). Where will you go? "Am I only a God nearby, . . . and not a God far away?" (Jeremiah 23:23). God is here, there, and everywhere; you will find him wherever you go. Surely, then, it is better to draw near to him as a friend than to run from him as an enemy.

Note also that a great duty of the fallen creature is to come near to God. I do not mean to deal with this duty at length but will just look at three things:

First, how God and the creature may be said to be near one another, or to come near. Gods' special presence is in heaven, and we are on earth; and his general presence is with all the creatures, and so "he is not far from each one of us" (Acts 17:27). But James's statement is to be understood spiritually: we come near to him not by our physical feet, but by the soul. God's children are with him in their thoughts, in the affections and dispositions of their souls. Their heart and their treasure is there (see Matthew 6:20-21). Their desires are there; the world is only a large prison. But more especially it means their communion with God in duties in which their souls and prayers "come up" to him (Acts 10:4); and he is said to come down to meet them (Isaiah 64:5). This also indicates the continual relationship between God and them in all their ways. John's first letter was written so that his readers might have fellowship with the Father and the Son (1 John 1:3).

Second, how is this brought about, since we cannot endure the thought of God? The question is necessary. This was heaven's great purpose, to find a way of bringing us back into fellowship with our Maker. God has discovered a new and living way through Christ, which is why he is said to be "the way . . . to the Father" (John 14:6). And the main purpose of his incarnation and death was to bring us to God (1 Peter 3:18). To bring strangers and enemies together is a mighty work. But how does Christ effect it?

a. Partly by doing something *for* us—satisfying God's justice and bearing our sins in his body on the tree (1 Peter 2:24); otherwise guilt would have been able to have no dealings with wrath. Now Christ is a screen put between us; the divine glory would swallow us up, but Christ's flesh is a veil that takes off its edge and brightness (Hebrews 10:19-20).

b. Partly by doing something *in* us. Christ's work in bringing a soul to God has not ended with the cross; he gives us the graces of his Holy Spirit, which make us fit for communion with God. The principal ones are these:

Faith, which is nothing other than coming to God by Christ for grace, mercy, and salvation (Hebrews 10:22). Unbelief means going away from God (Hebrews 3:12; Zephaniah 3:2).

Then *love*, the grace of union. It makes us go out to God in desire; it keeps us there by delight. The one is the soul's thirst; the other is its satisfaction. Love runs out with the feet of desire and rests in the arms of delight.

Then *holiness*. God will show himself holy "among those who approach him" (Leviticus 10:3). Holy hearts are the fittest to deal with a holy God; otherwise, we would not endure God, nor he us.

Then *fear*, by which the soul walks with God and is near him. Where our thoughts are is where we are spiritually. It is said of the wicked that "in all his thoughts there is no room for God" (Psalm 10:4); but the godly always keep God in view: "I saw the Lord always before me" (Acts 2:25). Fear keeps them in his company.

Then *humility*. Because of our distance and guilt we cannot come to God unless we come humbly and on our knees: "Come, let us bow down in worship, let us kneel before the LORD our Maker" (Psalm 95:6). That is the most appropriate posture when we approach God; God will live with the lowly in spirit (Isaiah 57:15).

All these graces, exercised in our behavior with other people or in our religious duties (where we address God more directly), make the soul to be near him.

Thirdly, what special acts does the soul perform when it comes near to God? The answer may be given you from what we said before. There must be an act of faith in our needs; by faith we must see in God what we feel we need. Fear must be acted in all our ways, keeping us in God's eye; loose and careless people are far from God (Genesis 17:1). Then love and humility must be acted in religious duties. Coming near chiefly implies humbly and fervently addressing God—when you come to God naked, like coming to a rich man who will clothe you—when you come to God hungry, like coming to a generous man who will feed you—when you come to God sick, like coming to a physician who will cure you—when you come as servants of the Lord, as disciples to your master, as the blind to the light, as cold to the fire, etc. The best way for the creatures to approach is to begin and end in hope, when there is a rare mixture of humility and confidence; and there must be love in every act of devotion, for God must be sought as well as served.

So then, let us remember all this. Sin is departing from God; grace is returning. Come near to him, aim for the support of his presence; Christ is the way, but you must resolve upon it: *I must* and *I will*. "Your face, LORD, I will seek" (Psalm 27:8); there must be a concern to bring the soul to this resolve. Note what it says in Jeremiah 30:21, "'I will bring him near and he will come close to me, for who is he who will devote himself to be close to me?' declares the LORD." But will you devote yourselves? A practical commandment arises from conviction of the necessity and excellence of the duty; as David says, "It is good to be near God" (Psalm 73:28).

Objection. There is one doubtful point in the text that must be cleared up before we go any further, arising from the use of the phrase **come near to God**, as if it were in our own power. The old Pelagians misused this passage, and the Rhemists in their notes say that free will and human endeavor are necessary in coming to God and that man is a cause of making himself clean, though God's grace is the principal cause. Usually two things have been based on this passage: first, that the beginning of conversion is in man's power; and second, that this beginning merits or increases God's grace; for, they say, God will not come near to us unless we first come near to him and therefore, before special grace, the beginning of conversion must be in man, and upon this beginning God will come in.

Solution. First, this passage and similar ones show not what man *wants to* do but what he *ought* to do. We left God before he left us; we should be the first to return, as we were the first to leave. The wronged party may in justice wait for us to submit. Yet such is the Lord's kindness that he loves us first (1 John 4:19).

Second, commandments are not measures of our strength; it is not valid to argue from what ought to be done that it can or will be done. These things are expressed in this way for another purpose: to show God's right, to convince the creature of weakness, to show us our duty, to show us that we should do our utmost, and to convince us of the things we have failed to do.

Third, these precepts are not useless; they convey grace to those who are chosen. God fulfills what he commands, for, by means of the Spirit working with them, they are stirred up and made to **come near to God**. To other people the precepts are convincing, showing us our obstinacy; we will not come to God and lie at the foot of his sovereignty, saying, "O Lord, you have said, 'Restore me, and I will return'" (Jeremiah 31:18). People pretend they *cannot* come, but the truth is they *will not* come hungry to the table, thirsty to the fountain; they will not lie at God's feet for grace. So these precepts convince reprobates and leave them without excuse. I shall conclude with Bernard's wonderful saying: "We cannot seek God until we have found him; he wants to be sought in order that he may be found, and found in order that he may be sought: it is grace that must bring us to grace." The stray sheep cannot be brought home unless it is on Christ's shoulders.

(2) The other interpretation of these words is that they apply to Christians already converted and called; and in this case the sense is: "Come nearer to God every day in a holy communion, and you will have more grace from him."

In this case, note that gracious hearts should always be renewing their access to God through Christ—coming to Christ "like living stones" (1 Peter 2:5), always coming to him in everything we do and in every need. This maintains and increases grace and makes our life wonderful and strong. Coming near to God is not something we must do for an hour, it is not something appropriate merely when we are converted, but it is the work of our whole lives.

And he will come near to you. That is, he will make us find that he is near to us by his favor and blessing. We have a similar promise in Zechariah 1:3, "'Return to me,' declares the LORD Almighty, 'and I will return to you.'" It is the same in Malachi 3:7.

The way to have God turn to us in mercy is to turn to him in duty. This is the standing law of heaven, and God will not vary from it; it is the best way for God's glory and for the creatures' good. Mercies are most delightful and good to us when we are prepared for them by duty. Do not, then, separate mercy from duty. Expectations in God's way cannot be disappointed. Ephraim wanted blessings but could not endure the yoke of obedience. We are apt to lie upon the bed of ease and complacently look to see what God will do, but will not stir ourselves to do what we should do.

God will be near those who are careful to hold communion with him. "The LORD is near to all who call on him, to all who call on him in truth" (Psalm 145:18). Near to bless, to comfort, to give life, to guide, to support them. Let this encourage us to come to God—indeed, to run to him. The father ran to meet the returning prodigal (Luke 15:20). God will be first with loving-kindness: "You will call, and the LORD will answer; you will cry for help, and he will say: Here am I" (Isaiah 58:9). God says, in effect, "What have you to say to me? What do you want from me? Here am I to satisfy all your desires." Elsewhere it says, "Before they call I will answer" (Isaiah 65:24). When we apply ourselves to seeking God, he is near to counsel, to give life, to defend—ready with blessing before our imperfect desires can be formed into requests.

Wash your hands, you sinners. From the connection of this precept with the previous one, note that unclean people can have nothing to do with God. You must be holy before you can come near to him; conformity to his will is the ground of communion: "Blessed are the pure in heart, for they will see God" (Matthew 5:8). "You are not able to serve the LORD. He is a holy God" (Joshua 24:19). God cannot endure our presence if we are not holy; he "does not . . . strengthen the hands of evildoers" (Job 8:20). And we cannot endure his presence: "The sinners in Zion are terrified" (Isaiah 33:14). So then, if you want to be free with God, come with a holy heart; there is special purgation required before worship. The Israelites were to wash themselves when they heard the law (Exodus 19). And David says, "I wash my hands in innocence, and go about your altar, O LORD" (Psalm 26:6). He is referring to the solemn washing that God had appointed for those who came to the altar (Exodus 40). Again, if you want to be delightfully at ease with God in your ways, walk holily; the Spirit of God loves to live cleanly (see Psalm 24:3-4). Generally it was the custom of the eastern countries to wash before worship. Even the heathen gods would be served in white, the emblem of purity.

Wash your hands. This indicates good works—just as pureness of heart implies faith and holy affections. This is what it often means in Scripture, for example in Job 17:9—"The righteous who hold to their ways, and those with clean hands will grow stronger." Therefore, washing the hands was a sign of innocence, just as Pilate washed his hands in connection with Christ. The apostle Paul tells us to "lift up holy hands in prayer, without anger or disputing" (1 Timothy 2:8). Similarly, God tells the Israelites, "Your hands are full of blood; wash and make yourselves clean" (Isaiah 1:15-16). When we come empty to the fountain of goodness, we must not do it with impure hands. In all these passages "hands" mean the whole body and all the external organs of the soul, because they are principally used for accomplishing many sins such as bribes, lusts, and fights.

The Lord has required not only holy hearts but holy hands. The goodness of your hearts must appear in the integrity of your behavior. When people's actions are no good, they pretend their hearts are good. The heart must be pure and the way undefiled, so that we may neither incur blame from within nor shame from without; and once sin is committed, the hand must be cleansed as well as the heart. It is in vain to pretend repentance and washing the heart when the hand is full of bribes or ill-gotten goods and no restitution is made.

You sinners. In this first clause he is speaking to people who were openly sinful, tainted with the guilt of outward and manifest sins. "God does not listen to sinners" (John 9:31)—that is, to people living corrupt lives. Thus Mary Magdalene is called "a woman who had lived a sinful life" (Luke 7:37)—that is, openly profane; see also Luke 15:2. Now the chief thing open sinners must do is to cleanse their hands, or reform their live, so that by such acts they may avoid the foolish idea that the heart may be good while the life is scandalous.

Purify your hearts. James says this partly because in this clause he is dealing with hypocrites, whose life is plausible enough, but their main care should be about their hearts, and partly because everything comes from the heart.

If you want to have a holy life, you must get a clean heart. True conversion begins there; spiritual life, as well as natural life, is in the heart first. "Abstain from sinful desires . . . live . . . good lives" (1 Peter 2:11-12). First mortify the sinful desires, then the deeds of the body of sin. If you want to cure the disease, purge away the sick matter; otherwise sin may return and put salt in the spring: "Let the wicked forsake his way and the evil man his thoughts" (Isaiah 55:7). Notice that it is not only his "*way*," or course of life, but his "*thoughts*," the frame of his heart; the heart is the womb of thoughts, and thoughts are the first things that come from corruption (see Matthew 15:19). What God looks for and loves is "truth in the inner parts" (Psalm 51:6). Do not be concerned only for honor before people, but for your hearts before God; and let conscience be dearer to you than reputation. Many people are aware of failings in their behavior because they expose them to shame; we should be as aware of things that are not right in the heart. Sinful desires must not be digested without regret and remorse any more than acts of sin.

You double-minded. The word means "of two hearts" or "of two souls." A hypocrite has "a heart and a heart," which is odious to God; they dither between God and Baal and deny the religion that they profess.

Their thoughts are divided, and their affections are always hovering in a doubtful suspense between God and the world. See the notes on 1:8.

Commentary and Notes on Verse 9

Grieve, mourn and wail. Change your laughter to mourning and your joy to gloom.

He now prescribes another remedy against their worldly affections and practices; it is proposed with all the more earnestness because of the calamity then ready to fall on the Jewish nation.

Grieve [Be afflicted, KJV]. What is the meaning? Must we draw affliction and unnecessary troubles on ourselves? I answer:

(1) It must be understood to refer to afflicting ourselves in some commendable way. It may, therefore, imply that our bodily distresses ought to be borne patiently; that is, if God brings affliction on you, bear it, be content to be afflicted, for it is our duty to be what God would have us be; let your will be done when the Lord's is. Or else,

(2) Know your misery, be aware of it; it is some happiness to know our misery. Man, in proud obstinacy, chokes his grief and stifles conviction. Or else,

(3) It indicates compassion and fellow-feeling for other people's sorrows. A part of our body is capable of feeling pain as long as it is part of the body (see Hebrews 13:3). A wound in the arm affects the whole body; parts of the body must care for one another. Or else,

(4) Humbling and afflicting the soul for sin. This is most appropriate to the context. Sorrow seems to be made for that purpose.

If we do not want to be afflicted by God, we should afflict ourselves for sin. Voluntary humiliations are always the best; they please God the most, and they do us the most good. God is most pleased then. The angels rejoice at the creatures' repentance (Luke 15:7). Holy tears are the sponge of sin; a hard heart must be soaked, and a filthy heart must be washed in this water. We are most considerate when we are most pensive. Besides all this, the final outcome of it is very sweet. God will "revive the spirit of the lowly" and "revive the heart of the contrite" (Isaiah 57:15). So then, be afflicted; it is a hard duty but of great profit. Make your sorrow draw water for the sanctuary; affections, like the Gibeonites, must not be abolished but kept for temple use.

Mourn and wail. Why so many words to one purpose? The whole verse and the next say much the same. I answer: it is a hard duty and needs to be reinforced.

Note 1. Flesh and blood must be urged to acts of sorrow, for they are painful to the body and burdensome to the mind. Frothy spirits love their pleasure and ease. How many of the poor ministers of the Gospel go to God and say, as Moses did, "If the Israelites will not listen to me, why would Pharaoh listen to me?" (Exodus 6:12). *Lord, the people who claim to be Christians will not put up with this sort of teaching; so how shall we hope to prevail with the poor, blind world?* Certainly it is very sad that people adopt into their religion something that used to be a badge of profanity—namely, scoffing at doctrines of repentance and humiliation.

Note 2. It is a necessary duty; those who want to be Christians must expect to **mourn**. The Spirit descended in the form of a dove, to indicate both meekness and mourning. Christian affections will be tender. God's glory cannot be violated without your heart bleeding if it is right: "Streams of tears flow from my eyes, for your law is not obeyed" (Psalm 119:136). When sins are common, your souls will "weep in secret" (Jeremiah 13:17). If God's heirs are afflicted, you will have a fellow-feeling (Romans 12:15). Indeed, there will not only be occasions externally but internally—your own sins, your own lack. Your sins: "Woe to us, for we have sinned!" (Lamentations 5:16). Times will come when you will have occasion to mourn like the doves of the valleys. Oh, woe the time that ever I sinned against God! Your lack and your need: all supplies of grace are to be obtained this way. The disciple is not above his Lord. "He offered up prayers and petitions with loud cries and tears" (Hebrews 5:7). His requests were uttered with deep sighs. Christ, who shed his blood, also shed tears; and if he was "a man of sorrows," certainly we must not be men and women of pleasures.

Note 3. The next reason for this multiplicity of words is to show that we must continue and persevere in it. We would soon abandon our hard lesson, and we love to not dwell on sad thoughts; therefore the apostle brings us back again and again to our duty: **Grieve**, and then **mourn and wail**. Sorrow does not work until it is deep and constant, and the arrows stick fast in the soul. David says, "my sin is always before me" (Psalm 51:3). We must be held to it; slight sorrows are soon cured. Mourning is a holy exercise by which the soul is weaned from sin more and more every day and drawn out to reach for God. So it checks those who content themselves with a hasty sigh, dismissing the matter. Do you really think this is grieving and mourning and wailing? Call to account the heart that is so shallow it wants to run out into the house of mirth again straightaway. But you will say, "Would you have us to be weeping all the time?" I answer:

(1) It is true that sorrow befits this life rather than joy. Now we are "away from the Lord" (2 Corinthians 5:6), under the burden of "lowly bodies" (Philippians 3:21) and vicious affections. This is our pilgrimage;

we have only a few songs, God's "decrees" (Psalm 119:54). The communion we have with God in ordinances is only a little. Grace is mixed with sin, faith with doubts, knowledge with ignorance, and peace with troubles. Now we "groan" (Romans 8:23); we are waiting and groaning for a full and final deliverance.

(2) There are some special times for mourning—chiefly, for example, in times of God's absence: "when the bridegroom will be taken from them; then they will fast" (Matthew 9:15)—when we have not the support and refreshing of God's presence or the quickenings of his Spirit. The absence of the sun makes the earth languish; when you have lost the shine of his face, you should cry for him. The people to whom the apostle is speaking were envious, proud, covetous, ambitious, and he tells them to **mourn and wail**. Saltwater and bitter potions kill worms. In the same way weeping kills worldly desires; the exercises of repentance are the best way to mortify worldly desires. It is the same in times when judgments are threatened. Thunder usually causes rain; and threats should draw tears from us. So it should be, too, in times of calamity, when judgments are actually inflicted: "The Lord . . . called on you that day to weep and to wail, to tear out your hair and put on sackcloth" (Isaiah 22:12). So also times of great mercies are appropriate times to remember our unkindness. The warm sun melts things; she wept much who was pardoned much (see Luke 7:38, 47). When Christ had washed her soul with his blood, she washed his feet with her tears.

Change your laughter to mourning. He means their worldly rejoicing in their external comforts and possessions, which they had gotten by rapine and violence, as seen in the context.

Note 4. It is good to exchange fleshly joy for godly sorrow. In sorrow God will give us what the world cannot find in pleasure: serenity and contentment of mind. While worldly people repent of their joy, you will never repent of your sorrow (2 Corinthians 7:10). Worldly comforts grow burdensome in the end; but who was ever the sadder for the hours of repentance? Job cursed the day of his birth, but who ever cursed the day of his new birth? When we turn our laughter into mourning, God will turn our mourning into laughter: "You will grieve, but your grief will turn to joy" (John 16:20). Out of these saltwaters God brews the wine of spiritual consolation. So then, do not be prejudiced against godly sorrow. The saddest duties are sweeter than the greatest triumphs, and the worst and most afflicted part of godliness is better than all the joys and comforts of the world. It is better to have good things to come than to have them here. The man in Luke 16:23 had lived in jollity, but his good days were past. Do not measure things by the present sweetness but by the future profit. "Woe to you who laugh now, for you will mourn and weep" (Luke 6:25).

Note 5. An excellent way to moderate the excess of joy is to mix it with some weeping. He is speaking to men drunk with their present happiness, and his drift is to awaken them out of their senseless stupor. The way to lessen one passion is to let in the contrary one. There is danger in abundance; therefore in your jollity think of some mournful subjects. Nazianzen reports of himself that when his mind was likely to be corrupted with happiness it was his practice to read the Lamentations of Jeremiah and to inure his soul to the consideration of sad matters. It was God's own medicine for Belshazzar, in the midst of his cups, to bring him to think of his ruin by some handwriting on the wall. So then, when your mountain stands firmly, think of changes; evils come upon us unawares when we give up our hearts to joy.

And your joy to gloom. In this context he describes them as being worldly and as glorying in oppressing one another; he means here the sort of joy and laughter by which complacent sinners please themselves in their present success, putting off all thoughts of imminent judgment.

Note 6. Prosperous oppression is rather a matter of sorrow than joy to us. You laugh now, but God will laugh hereafter when your calamities and fears come (Proverbs 1:26; Psalm 37:12-13). Wicked people have never so much cause to be humbled as when they are prosperous; it is a sure pledge of their speedy ruin. Now you despise others and scoff at God's servants and ways; how you will hang your head when the scene is changed and you become objects of public scorn and contempt! Oh, that people would awaken their conscience and say, "I am laughing and triumphing; have I not cause to howl and mourn?"

Commentary and Notes on Verse 10

Humble yourselves before the Lord, and he will lift you up.

The apostle goes on inculcating and pressing the same duty upon them; and lest they should rest content with externals, he uses a word that particularly implies the internal acts of the soul.

Note from the context that it is not the outward expressions that God looks for in mourning, but the humble heart. God, who is a spirit, does not count bodily actions so much. Tears and wailing and beating the body may all be counterfeit, or else done without a principle of grace; and there may often be inward humiliation though an unemotional person does not yield tears. Godly sorrow does not always vent itself through the eyes. Roman Catholics place much importance on tears and afflicting the body. The spirit-work is the more difficult. Duties require much spirit, and soul-acts are too strong for weak people. I allude to Christ's expression concerning spiritual fasting in Matthew 9:15-16. Old worldly hearts cannot endure the rigor of such spiritual duties.

So then, in your first duties see that you not only mourn and weep but humble your souls. When you confess sins, it is not words and tears that God looks for, but a deep shame of the evil of your nature, your iniquities of life, and your defects in obedience. When you pray, look not so much at the outward heat and strength—agitated spirits and earnestness of speech; but see that the soul reaches for God by holy ardor and desires. In confessing public sins, it is not the exact enumeration but zeal for God's glory, compassion for others' good, and holy desires of promoting righteousness that the Lord looks for. Ashes and sackcloth are nothing to the work of the soul: "Is that what you call a fast, a day acceptable to the LORD?" (Isaiah 58:5).

Before the Lord. There is a similar passage in 1 Peter 5:6; but there it is, "Humble yourselves, therefore, under God's mighty hand." That expression implies a motive or consideration to enforce the duty, but James's words imply the sincerity of it.

Note 1. Duties are truly done when they are done as in God's sight. Fear and reverence of God make the heart more sincere (see 1:27 and 1 Peter 3:21). "I obey your precepts and your statutes, for all my ways are known to you" (Psalm 119:168); that was David's motive. So then, in all duties of worship remember that you are before God; there is a broad and pure eye of glory fixed on you. You are dealing with God, who tells people his thoughts and who discerns your spirits better than you do yourselves. The right way to speak of this is described in Acts 10:33, "We are all here in the presence of God to listen to everything the Lord has commanded you to tell us." We come to pray, to hear, to humble ourselves before God. The soul will have a double advantage from such thoughts: the work will be more spiritual, and more pure and upright. It will be more spiritual in that I am not to be humbled before man but before God. "Man looks at the outward appearance, but the LORD looks at the heart" (1 Samuel 16:7). Will this satisfy God? Is it the kind of fast he has chosen (Isaiah 58:5)? It will be more pure and upright in that whatever a person does to God, he will do it for God's sake; religious duties will be performed for reasons of religion, not because they are customary or to join in what other people are doing, but for God and to God.

Note 2. The sight of God is a special help to humiliation. The soul becomes humble by the true knowledge of God and ourselves: "my eyes have seen you. Therefore I despise myself and repent in dust and ashes" (Job 42:5-6). When Job had a glorious vision of God, he vanished into nothing in his own thoughts. The stars vanish when the sun rises, and our poor candle is so slight that it disappears when the glory of God rises in our thoughts. We see our lack in God's fullness; the ocean makes us ashamed of our own little drop. We see our vileness in God's majesty. What is the dust on the scales compared to a mountain, and our wickedness in comparison with God's holiness? Elijah pulled his cloak over his face when God's glory passed by him (1 Kings 19:13). Similarly, Isaiah cried out, "Woe to me! . . . I am ruined! For I am a man of unclean lips" when God showed him his glory (Isaiah 6:5). Whenever God appeared to the faithful, men were filled with fear because of their own weakness and corruption.

So then, this tells us how to be humble in our addresses to God: get as large and comprehensive an idea of him as you can; see his glory if you want to know your own baseness. People are feeble in duties because they have low thoughts of God. They offered the Lord a blemished animal because they did not consider he was a great King (Malachi 1:14). The elders who saw God in his glory "fell on their faces" (Revelation 11:16).

And he will lift you up. What does this promise imply? It means any kind of happiness, including deliverance out of trouble ("You hear, O LORD, the desire of the afflicted," Psalm 10:17) or promotion to worldly honor or dignity ("A man's pride brings him low, but a man of lowly spirit gains honor," Proverbs 29:23). Though promotion brings us to slippery places, the humble will be sustained and upheld. It is the same with advancement in grace or glory: "Whoever humbles himself like this child is the greatest in the kingdom of heaven" (Matthew 18:4); that is, he will have the most grace and glory.

Learn from this that submission and humility are the true way to exaltation. This is often repeated in the Gospel: "Everyone who exalts himself will be humbled, and he who humbles himself will be exalted" (Luke 14:11; see also Matthew 23:12). We are all by nature proud and want to be exalted; but the way to rise is to fall. God gave us a pattern in Jesus Christ: first, he "made himself nothing . . . he humbled himself and became obedient to death . . . on a cross! Therefore God exalted him . . . and gave him the name that is above every name" (see Philippians 2:5-11). So then, do you want deliverance? Humble yourself! Omnipotence will not be your terror but protection. Do you want grace? See more of God.

Lastly, we may be encouraged from all this to wait upon God with a holy humility and confidence in our lowly state: "When men are brought low and you say, 'Lift them up!' then he will save the downcast" (Job 22:29). When all your affairs go to decay, you may rely on these hopes. Peter says, "that he may lift you up in due time" (1 Peter 5:6). Wait for God, and the promise will surely be fulfilled; only be humble. Gracious humiliation is a deep sense of our misery and vileness, with a desire to be reconciled to God on any terms.

Commentary and Notes on Verse 11

Brothers, do not slander one another. Anyone who speaks against his brother or judges him speaks against the law and judges it.

Here the apostle comes to dissuade them from another sin, of which he had previously accused them, and that is detraction and speaking evil of one another.

Brothers, do not slander one another. This word implies any speaking that is prejudicial to someone else, whether it is true or false. Scripture requires our words to be appropriate to love as well as truth.

Speaking evil of one another is not appropriate for brothers and Christians. A citizen of Zion is described as one who "has no slander on his tongue, who does his neighbor no wrong and casts no slur on his fellow man" (Psalm 15:3). And there is an express law in Leviticus 19:16—"Do not go about spreading slander among your people." There are several kinds of evil-speaking. They may all be ranked under two heads—whispering and backbiting. Whispering is a private defamation of our brother among those who think well of him; backbiting is more public, in view of everyone without discrimination. Both may be done in many ways, not only by false accusations, but also by divulging others' secret evils, by extenuating their graces, by increasing or aggravating their faults, and by defrauding them of their necessary excuse and mitigation, by depraving their good actions by supposing they have sinister aims, by mentioning what is culpable, and by enviously suppressing their worth. So then, if all this is inappropriate for brothers, do not give way to it in yourselves or listen to it in other people.

(1) Do not give way to it yourselves. Nature is marvelously prone to offend in this way, and so you must restrain it all the more, especially when the people you seek to blemish are Christians: "Why then were you not afraid to speak against my servant Moses?" (Numbers 12:8). You should be afraid to speak against anyone, and much more against those whom God wants to honor. This is the devil's own sin; he is "the accuser of our brothers" (Revelation 12:10). He does not commit adultery or break the Sabbath—these are not laws to him; but he can bear false witness and accuse the brothers. And yet, what is more common among us? John the Baptist's head on a platter is a usual dish at our meals. When people's hearts are warm with food and good cheer, then God's children are brought in, like Samson among the Philistines, to amuse them. God will surely reward this in our hearts, either in this life ("Do not judge, or you too will be judged," Matthew 7:1) or else in the life to come, apart from repentance. It is said of the wicked that "He will turn their own tongues

against them" (Psalm 64:8). How insupportable is the weight of the sins of this one part of the body!

(2) Do not give way to it in others. Your ears may be as guilty as their tongues; therefore such whisperings should never be heard without some expression of dislike. Solomon commends a frown and a severe expression: "As a north wind brings rain, so a sly tongue brings angry looks" (Proverbs 25:23). Such persons are discouraged when they do not meet with acceptance. David would not have such people living in his house (Psalm 101:5). Certainly our countenancing them draws us into the guilty fellowship. Now if we must not receive these whispers against an ordinary brother, much less may we do so against a minister; there is express provision for the safety of their reputation (see 1 Timothy 5:19), partly because people are apt to hate anyone who reproves publicly, and partly because people in office are most closely watched (see Jeremiah 20:12 and Ezekiel 33:30), and partly because their reputation most concerns the honor of the Gospel.

Anyone who speaks against his brother or judges him. In that word **judges** the apostle shows what their criticism amounted to—usurping God's function and passing sentence on their brothers; and also what kind of evil-speaking he principally means—i.e., things that do not matter one way or the other, such as observing festivals, avoiding certain food, and so on (see Romans 14:3-4).

Censuring is judging; you arrogate to yourself an act of power that does not belong to you. When you are promoted to the chair of arrogance and censure, check yourself by this thought: "Who gave me this superiority?" The question put to Moses may well be asked of our souls, on behalf of our wronged brothers: "Who made you ruler and judge over us?" (Exodus 2:14). Paul uses the same sort of question: "Who are you to judge someone else's servant?" (Romans 14:4).

Speaks against the law and judges it. How can this be? There are several ways of making sense of this sentence. I will name the principal ones.

Firstly, every sin is a kind of affront to the law that forbids it; for by doing quite the contrary we in effect judge the law to be not fit or worthy of being obeyed. For instance, in the present case the law forbids rash judgment and speaking evil of one another; but the person who detracts from someone else approves what the law condemns, and so in effect judges that law to be not good.

Sin is judging the law. David was asked, "Why did you despise the word of the LORD by doing what is evil in his eyes?" (2 Samuel 12:9). In the heat of his desire, David looked on it as a slight law. Wherever you see it, you will find that in sinning there are some implicit evil thoughts by which the law of God is devalued and disapproved; we think it unworthy, hard, or unfair. And it is still Satan's great policy to represent God as a hard taskmaster and to make us think evil of the law. That is why Paul sought to prevent such thoughts when the law checked his lusts and brought him to a sense of misery: "The law is holy, and the commandment is holy, righteous and good" (Romans 7:12). But was it good even though it caused death to him? Yes, he says, I still look upon it as a rule of right; it is I who am worldly, my heart that is wicked, etc. So you see how to make sin odious. Sin is despising the law, speaking evil of the law; it slights the rule that it violates.

Secondly, they used at that time to condemn one another for things that did not matter, merely on their own will and sense, without any warrant from the Word (as you can see in Romans 14). Now this was a kind of condemning of the law, as if it were not full and exact enough but needed to be completed by human rules.

To make more sins than God has made is to judge the law. You imply that it is an imperfect rule; people want to be wiser than God and bind others in chains of their own making. It is true there is an "obedience of faith," by which the understanding must be captive to God but not to men; to the Word, not to every fancy. There is a double superstition, positive and negative: one is when people count holy something that God never made holy; the other is when they condemn what God never condemned. Both are equally faulty. We are not in the place of God; it is not in our power to make sins or duties. "Do not handle! Do not taste! Do not touch!" were the regulations of false teachers (Colossians 2:21). Three things are exempted from human jurisdiction: God's counsels, the holy Scripture, and the human heart. We should not dogmatize and subject people to ordinances of our own making, pressing our own austerities and rigorous observances as duties. Justice and wisdom are good, but to be "overrighteous" or "overwise" is quite wrong (Ecclesiastes 7:15-16). Man is a proud creature and would like to make his moroseness a law for other people and put forward his own private ideas as doctrine. It is usual to condemn everything that does not please us, as if our magisterial dictates were articles of faith. We must not come in our own name and judge as the world judges, or else we judge the Word. *Lord, grant that we will consider this in this dogmatizing age when everyone declares that his own ideas are law, and people* make sins *rather than* find *them!*

Thirdly, you may think of it like this: they might censure other people for things the Word allowed and approved, and in this way they condemned not private individuals so much as the law itself. If you think about it in this way, then:

To plead for sins, or to cast aspersions on grace, is to judge the Word itself. Thus you set the pride of corrupted wit against the wisdom of God in the Scriptures: "Woe to those who call evil good and good evil, who put darkness for light and light for darkness, who put bitter for sweet and sweet for bitter" (Isaiah 5:20). Usually it is like this in the world; grace meets with calumny and sin with flattery. Open and gross sins are all the more gently rebuked because they happen to go under a good name: drunkenness is good fellowship, censure is discussion, error is new light, rebellion is zeal for public welfare; but grace suffers because it looks bad. Just as in the early days they used to put Christians in bearskins and then bait them, so graces are called by other names and are misrepresented and then hooted at. The law says we are to be zealous, peace-loving, etc.; but in the world's reckoning zeal is fury, peace-loving and holy moderation is time-serving and servility, teaching humbling doctrine is legalism, etc. Many people deceive themselves with names like these, but do they not judge the law in all this? The law says that sitting drinking all day is drunkenness, but men call it good fellowship, and so on.

When you judge the law, you are not keeping it, but sitting in judgment on it. That is, when you exercise such a rash superiority over the law, you clearly exempt yourself from obedience and subjection to it.

It is no wonder if those who judge the Word are given over to disobedience. This is done grossly by those who either deny the divine authority of the Scriptures or accuse it of being an uncertain rule or examine all its teaching by their own private reason or by the writings and teachings of men, etc. And this is done less obviously by those who come to judge the Word rather than to be judged by it. It is true that we have liberty to examine, but we should not come intending to cavil and criticize. The pulpit, which in a sense is God's tribunal, should not be our bar. What we say must be examined by Scripture modestly and humbly; but we must not despise and slight God's ordinance and come merely to sit as judges of people's abilities or weaknesses. This is the best way to beget an irreverent and fearless spirit. And then when people lose their awe and reverence, their restraint is gone, and they become loose or desperately in error. God will punish their pride with some sudden fall.

Look to your ends, Christians; you will find a great deal of difference between coming to hear and coming to criticize. If you come with such a vain aim, see if you get anything by a sermon but something to carp at, and see if that does not bring you to looseness, and that to atheism. Usually this is the sad progress of proud spirits. First, preaching is criticized, not examined;, then the manners are tainted; then the Word itself is questioned; and then people lose all fear of God and man.

Commentary and Notes on Verse 12

There is only one Lawgiver and Judge, the one who is able to save and destroy. But you—who are you to judge your neighbor?

James persists in the same argument. God the **Lawgiver** is the only **Judge**; and who are you to invade or usurp his role?

There is only one Lawgiver. But you will say you can name many others—Lycurgus, Zaleucus, Solon, etc.—many who also had power of life and death, and many now who make and dispense laws. How can this sentence be true? I answer: Grotius thinks the apostle means Christ by this expression, in contrast to Moses, arguing against those who want to continue the ceremonial law and make distinctions between days and foods, etc. Now, James says, we in the Christian church have only one Lawgiver, Christ and not Moses. These two must not be yoked and coupled together. But this is too contentious and makes the text mean more than the context permits. More probably James means:

(1) There is only one absolute and supreme **Lawgiver**, whose will is the rule of justice. Others are directed by an external rule and prudent considerations of equity and safety, and in this they are simply God's deputies and substitutes, either in the church or in government: "You are not judging for man but for the LORD, who is with you whenever you give a verdict" (2 Chronicles 19:6).

(2) In spiritual things no one else can give laws to the conscience. In external policy human laws and edicts are to be observed. But he is speaking about the interior governing of the conscience, where God alone judges by the Word; for he is speaking against those who want to set up their own will as a rule of sin or duty in things that do not matter one way or the other.

God alone can give laws to the conscience. "The LORD is our judge; the LORD is our lawgiver; the LORD is our king, it is he who will save us" (Isaiah 33:22). Take them in a spiritual sense, and the words are exclusive: God, and no other, is our exclusive **Judge**, our only **Lawgiver**, etc. God knows the conscience, and therefore God only must judge it and give laws to it. God only can punish the conscience for sin, and therefore only he can declare an act to be a sin. It is the privilege of his Word to be "perfect, reviving the soul" (see Psalm 19:7).

Objection. An objection may be framed against this doctrine out of Romans 13:5, where it says, "Therefore, it is necessary to submit to the authorities, not only because of possible punishment but also because of conscience." So human commands seem to oblige the conscience.

Solution. I answer that they do so in a way, but not in the order and manner that God's do.

(1) Not directly and immediately, but by the intervention of God's command. As a Christian is bound to perform all civil duties for religious reasons, we are bound in conscience even though human laws do not bind conscience. "Submit yourselves for the Lord's sake to every authority instituted among men" (1 Peter 2:13). It is God's command that binds my

conscience to obey man's. "Obey the king's command, I say, because you took an oath before God" (Ecclesiastes 8:2)—that is, not only for fear of men, but chiefly to not wrong your conscience toward God.

(2) Not universally and unlimitedly. I must obey God on the mere sight of his will. But I must examine human laws to see if they are just and in accordance with love and public safety; and in many cases active obedience must be withheld. Peter and the apostles said, "We must obey God rather than men!" (Acts 5:29). There are many such cases. Conscience is bound toward God, even if we can see no reason for it, no good from it.

(3) Not absolutely. Whatever God commands, I am bound to do even in secret, even if it is contrary to my own thinking. But the principle of submission to man may be fulfilled by suffering a penalty because we forbear from obeying as required; and in some cases a person may do the opposite in private, where the thing does not matter and there is no danger of scandal or contempt for authority. So then, listen to no voice but God's in your conscience, no doctrines in the church but Christ's. When men brought in strange doctrines, they "lost connection with the Head" (Colossians 2:19). No offices, institutions, and worship must be allowed other than those he has appointed. Antiquity without Scripture is no sure rule to walk by. We must not look to what others did before us, but to what Christ did before them all. The authority of the church is not like this. She is "the pillar and foundation of the truth" (1 Timothy 3:15); that is, she is to display Christ's mind, as a post displays a king's proclamation.

The church has some power in rites of decency and expediency and order, by virtue of the general canon in 1 Corinthians 14:40 (though that text appears to be a restraint rather than an allowance and does not so much enlarge as moderate church power). But in the most important matters the church can only *declare* laws, not *make* them; and though she can indicate what is appropriate to order and decency in things that do not ultimately matter, those directions should still be managed so that they do not detract from the nature of the thing. And though Christian liberty may be restrained, it must not be infringed.

It is antichrist's harmful intent to usurp authority over the church of God, and this is the very spirit of antichristianism—to give laws to the conscience. Calvin says, "Men would have us more modest than to call the Pope Antichrist; but as long as he exercises a tyranny over the conscience, we shall never give up that term; indeed, we shall go further and call people members of Antichrist if they take such snares on their consciences." Setting up another lawgiver is truly antichristian, for then there is one head set against another, and human authority against the divine. Paul describes Antichrist in 2 Thessalonians 2:4: he "sets himself up in God's temple, proclaiming himself to be God"—that is, making himself absolute lord of consciences, bringing them to his obedience, working them to his advantage.

The one who is able to save and destroy. This indicates God's absolute power to do what he pleases with man either temporally or spiritually. This power is given to God everywhere: "See now that I myself am He! There is no god besides me. I put to death and I bring to life, I have wounded and I will heal, and no one can deliver from my hand" (Deuteronomy 32:39; see also 1 Samuel 2:6 and Isaiah 43:13).

Note 1. Absolute supremacy is only appropriate to one who has absolute power. The power of magistrates is limited by the will of God, because they depend on him and can do nothing except as they are enabled and authorized by him (John 19:11).

Note 2. God has absolute and supreme power over men and can do with them whatever he wants. And therefore we must:

(1) Keep close to his laws with fear and trembling; there is no escaping from this Judge (1 Corinthians 10:22). Eternal life and eternal death are at his disposal (Matthew 10:28).

(2) Observe his laws with encouragement; live according to Christ's laws, and he is able to protect you: "Our God is a God who saves; from the Sovereign LORD comes escape from death" (Psalm 68:20). He can save his people, and he has many ways to bring his enemies to ruin. Your friend is the most dreadful enemy of those who oppose him; he "holds the keys of death and Hades" (Revelation 1:18).

(3) Be all the more humbled if you break his laws. Oh, what will you do with this Lawgiver who rebukes you by a glance, turning you into hell? Have you enough courage and strength to withstand God? (See Ezekiel 22:14.) What will you do with him **who is able to save and destroy?** Wool overcomes the blows of iron by yielding to them. There is no way left but submission and humble prayers. God may be overcome by faith but not by power: "let them make peace with me" (Isaiah 27:5). By humble supplications you may struggle with God and "overcome" (Genesis 32:28).

But you—who are you to judge your neighbor? That is, what a distance there is between you and God! What a sorry judge you are compared with him! The same question comes in Romans 14:4.

It is good to shame pride with the consideration of God's glory and our own baseness. He is **able to save and destroy. But you—who are you. . . ?**

Commentary and Notes on Verse 13

Now listen, you who say, "Today or tomorrow we will go to this or that city, spend a year there, carry on business and make money."

Having spoken about people who held the law in contempt, he now speaks against those who hold providence in contempt, promising themselves a long time in the world and a happy ending to their worldly projects, without any sense or thought of frailty or the sudden strokes of God. In this verse he gives a most accurate representation of their thoughts.

Now listen. This is a phrase that provokes them to think, like awakening conscience or citing them before the presence and tribunal of God. The same words are used in 5:1.

If we want to know how evil our actions are, it is good to review and reflect. We sin and go on in sin because we do not stop to think. There should be wise consideration beforehand to prevent sin, and faithful recollection to prevent going on in sin. God complains, "No one repents of his wickedness, saying, 'What have I done?'" (Jeremiah 8:6). This recollection cites the soul before three bars: conscience, God's eye, and God's throne or tribunal. It rouses the light of conscience by comparing the action or speech with a principle of reason or the Word, as in the present case. Thus: Am I Lord of future events, that I determine them so confidently? Do things depend on my will? Are my life or actions in my own power? It draws the soul into God's presence, thus: do I want the jealous God, who disposes of human events and successes, to take notice of such speeches? And before God's judgment seat thus: would I defend such actions or speeches before God's tribunal? Will these worldly deliberations endure the severe search and trial of the great day?

You who say, "Today or tomorrow we will go to this or that city . . .". He imitates the way of speaking, or the thoughts, of the Jewish merchants. "Now we will go to Alexandria, or to Damascus, or to Antioch" (their usual trading places).

Note 1. Worldly hearts are all for worldly projects. Thoughts are the purest offspring of the soul and reveal its temper. People are what their desires are. "The noble man makes noble plans" (Isaiah 32:8). Worldly people are projecting how to spend their days and months buying and selling and making a profit. The fool in the Gospel is thinking of enlarging his barns and pulling down his houses and building bigger ones (Luke 12:17-18); this engrosses all his thoughts. One apostle describes such people in these words: "Their mind is on earthly things" (Philippians 3:19). Another says they are "experts in greed" (2 Peter 2:14); that is, they earnestly work out how to promote their gain and earthly aims. Gracious hearts are occupied with gracious projects and how they can be more thankful (Psalm 116:12)—how they can be more holy, more useful for God, more fruitful in every good work—what they must to do inherit eternal life. Think how much better this is, how much more appropriate to the purpose of our creation and the nature of our spirits. We were sent into the world not to grow great and pompous, but to enrich our souls with spiritual excellence.

Note 2. Worldly people think to enjoy their pleasures before they obtain them. People usually feed themselves with the pleasure of their hopes. Sisera's mother's ladies looked through the lattice, taking pleasure in the thought of a triumphant return (Judges 5:28-30). Thoughts are the spies and messengers of the soul; hope sends them out after the thing expected, and love after the thing beloved. When we look forward to something keenly, the thoughts spend themselves in creating images and suppositions of the happiness of enjoyment. If a poor man were adopted into the succession of a crown, he would take pleasure in thinking about the future honor and pleasure of the kingly state. Godly people, who are called to be "heirs together with Christ," are wont to preoccupy the bliss of their future state, and so in a way they only feel that to which they are looking forward.

Similarly, worldly people charm their souls with whispers of vanity and feed on the pleasant anticipation of that worldly delight to which they look forward. For example, young heirs spend on their hopes and riot away their estate before they possess it. So then, be careful—it is a sure sign of worldliness when the world is in your thoughts so often that you are always deflowering worldly pleasures by anticipating worldly desires and sin, and you have nothing to live on or to entertain your spirit with but these ideas of gain and pomp and the reversion of some external pleasure.

Note 3. Again, you may see their confidence in future events: **"We will go . . . spend a year there . . ."** Note that worldly affections are usually accompanied by worldly confidence and are certainly much encouraged by it. They are doubly confident: confident of the success of their efforts (**"We will . . . make money"**), and confident of their lives continuing (**"We will . . . spend a year there"**). Desire cannot be nourished without assuming success. When people multiply their efforts, they little think of God or of the changes of providence; it is enough to undo their desire if they think it could be disappointed. Besides, when the means exist, there is not much we ascribe to the highest cause. First the world steals away our affections, and then it intercepts our trust; there is not only adultery in this (4:4) but idolatry (Ephesians 5:5).

The world is not only our darling but our god; and that is the reason why worldly people are always represented as people who confidently assume things will happen. For example, in Luke 12:19, "I'll say to myself, 'You have plenty of good things laid up for many years. Take life easy; eat, drink and be merry.'" Or Job 29:18—"I will die in my own house, my days as numerous as the grains of sand." They think now they have enough to secure them against all chances. So then, be careful about your confidence and trust; when you are getting an estate, is your expectation founded on faith or desire? When you have gotten an estate, on what is your assurance of contentment based—the promises or your external welfare?

Note 4. Worldly people are confident not only of the present but of their future welfare, which shows that the heart is stupidly complacent and utterly unaware of the changes of providence. "Tomorrow will be like today, or even far better" (Isaiah 56:12). "In their thoughts their houses will remain forever" (Psalm 49:11 [see NIV footnote]). People love to enjoy their worldly comforts without interruption, thoughts of death, or change. Every day is like a new life and brings sufficient care with it; we need not look at such a long time. But worldly people, in their cares, provide not only for the next day but for the next year, being confident they have a next year; they do not want even to think about things changing.

"Spend a year there, carry on business and make money." He gives the chief example of carrying on business because too often these worldly thoughts and hopes and confidence are found in businessmen. But he means it of all sorts of people who undertake anything confident of their own wisdom and hard work, without the permission and blessing of providence.

Note 5. Businessmen are very liable to thinking and speaking that savors of worldly presumption and confidence. At the stock exchange and markets they are always talking about commodities and profit and trading, without any thought of God. "The merchant uses dishonest scales; he loves to defraud" (Hosea 12:7). Your ordinary business takes you from place to place; take God along with you wherever you go. Of all people you should be most astute; in your business be mindful of God and of yourselves—of God's providence and your own frailty—so that you are neither too much in the world, nor too confident in your own hard work.

Note 6. From the whole verse, note that it is a vain thing to promise ourselves great things without the permission of providence. To say, **"We will go"** or "we will do such and such" is vain, for we are not lords of our lives, nor lords of our own actions: "My times are in your hands" (Psalm 31:15). "Do not boast about tomorrow, for you do not know what a day may bring forth" (Proverbs 27:1). Today we are, and tomorrow we are gone; we cannot tell what may be in the womb of the next morning. It is the same with our actions: "what [the righteous and the wise] do" is "in God's hands" (Ecclesiastes 9:1). To get things done, and to do them successfully, we need counsel and a blessing. The prophet speaks of this: "I know, O LORD, that a man's life is not his own; it is not for man to direct his steps" (Jeremiah 10:23).

But when do people promise themselves great things without the leave of providence? In many ways. The main ones are these:

(1) When they undertake things without prayer. You may speak of success only when you have asked God's permission: "Submit to God and . . . what you decide on will be done" (Job 22:21, 28).

(2) When they are too confident of future contingencies and events without any submission to the will of God and boast merely on human likelihood (see Exodus 15:11 and Judges 5:28-30). "'May the gods deal with me, be it ever so severely, if enough dust remains in Samaria to give each of my men a handful.' The king of Israel answered, 'Tell him: "One who puts on his armor should not boast like one who takes it off"'" (1 Kings 20:10-11). Ben-Hadad wanted to strip Samaria so bare that he would not leave any dust there, but God disappointed him.

(3) When people's efforts are set up in the place of God, we think everything depends on mundane causes, and so we neglect God.

(4) When people promise themselves a time to repent later on. Many think to themselves, "I will pursue pleasure and profit, and then spend my old age devoutly and quietly; first build and trade and bustle in the world, and adjourn God to the aches and dull phlegm of old age." Foolish man decrees all future events as if they were all in his own control. So then, remember God all the time; this is a good idea for princes and for people who advise about public affairs. How often they prove unhappy because they do not seek God! The natural exercise of your faculties and the help of God's grace all depend upon God's good pleasure.

Commentary on Verse 14

Why, you do not even know what will happen tomorrow. What is your life? You are a mist that appears for a little while and then vanishes.

Having revealed their worldly presumption, he now disproves it by two arguments: first, the events of the next day; and second, the uncertainty of their own lives. Both give a notable check to such foolish confidence.

Why, you do not even know what will happen tomorrow. This is like saying, "You talk of a long time, and you do not even know what will happen the next day. Every day brings new providences and events with it." But you will say, "Is it unlawful to provide for the next day or for a time to come?" I answer: No. Solomon tells us to learn from the ant: "consider its ways and be wise! . . . it stores its provisions in summer and gathers its food at harvest" (Proverbs 6:6-8; see also Proverbs 30:25). It is simply wise foresight to prepare ourselves for foreseeable inconveniences. Joseph is commended for laying up food in the cities against the years of famine (Genesis 41:35). And it was the apostles' practice to provide stores for the brothers at Jerusalem ready for the famine foretold by Agabus (Acts

11:29). Just remember that this must be done with caution; such provision must not arise from distrust or from thought prejudicial to the care of providence (Matthew 6:30). It must not hinder us from the great care of our lives: provision for heaven (Matthew 6:33). It must be with submission to God.

What is your life? You are a mist. Many passages in Scripture show how brief our life is. It is compared to "the flowers of the field" (Isaiah 40:6-7), the "wind" (Job 7:7, KJV), a leaf before the wind (Job 13:25), and a "shadow" (Job 14:2). There is a heap of similes in Job 9:25-26—"My days are swifter than a runner; they fly away without a glimpse of joy. They skim past like boats of papyrus, like eagles swooping down on their prey." The Word uses all these similes so that we might be reminded of our own mortality by every fleeing and decaying object, and also to check those proud human desires for a place in eternity and lasting happiness in this life. In that passage of Job there is a monument of human frailty displayed in all the elements: on land, a runner; on water, papyrus boats; in the air, an eagle. The heathen poets are much given to deciphering the frail state of humanity. Aeschylus says that man's life is "the shadow of smoke"; Pindar calls it "the dream of a shadow." The simile used here is that of **a mist.** Showing how it resembles other things is not unimportant; it is done simply to show how quickly life passes, and because human life is just a little warm air breathed in and out by the nostrils—a narrow passage that is soon stopped up (Isaiah 2:22).

Notes on Verse 14

Note 1. We have no assurance of our lives and comforts or the events of the next day. This is a common argument; the heathen used it a lot. So then, let every day's care be enough for itself; live every day as the last day. Petrarch tells of someone who, when invited to dinner the next day, answered, "I have not had a tomorrow for many years." And Ludovicus Capellus tells us of one Rabbi Eleazer who advised people to repent only the day before their death—that is, right now (for it may be the last day before we die). It is a sad thing to promise ourselves many years and to have our souls taken away that night. Wicked people want to live longer in the body; their worldly projects are never at an end, but suddenly God comes and snatches away their souls.

Note 2. Human life is very short; it is a **mist that appears for a little while and then vanishes.** Though they toss to and fro, the whole of men's lives is just a fleeting shadow, a little spot of time between two eternities.

Augustine is not sure whether to call it a dying life or a living death (*Confessions*, Book 1).

(1) This checks people who pass their time rather than make the best use of it; they are prodigal of their precious time, as if they had too much of it. Our time is short, and we make it shorter. It is time for all of us to say, "you have spent enough time in the past doing what pagans choose to do" (1 Peter 4:3); or, as Romans 13:11 puts it, "The hour has come for you to wake up from your slumber" (this was the verse that converted Augustine).

(2) If life is short, then moderate your worldly care and projects; do not encumber yourselves with too much provision for a short voyage. A ship goes more swiftly if it is less burdened; people take in too much lading for a mere passage.

(3) Devote yourselves more to spiritual projects, so that you may lay up a foundation for a longer life than you have to live here; do a lot of work in a little time. Do we want to lose any part of what is so short? Do we want our short life to make way for a long misery? The apostle says, "I think it is right to refresh your memory as long as I live in the tent of this body" (2 Peter 1:13). We are all shortly to take off the outer garment of the body; let us do all the good that we can. Christ lived only thirty-two years or thereabouts; therefore he "went around doing good and healing all who were under the power of the devil" (Acts 10:38). Ministers pack a lot into their sermons when they only have a short time, and you should do the same; you have only a short time, so be all the more diligent.

Commentary on Verse 15

Instead, you ought to say, "If it is the Lord's will, we will live and do this or that."

Having shown how wrong their confidence is, James proceeds to put things right by urging them to remember with reverence God's providence and their own frailty.

Instead, you ought to say, "If it is the Lord's will." Here a doubt arises. Must we always of necessity use this form of speech, this explicit caveat?

(1) It is good to get in the habit of using holy forms of speech; this is a great help. The heart is best when such conditions are made explicit—"If the Lord please," "If the Lord wants," etc. Pure lips are appropriate for a Christian, who should be distinguished by holy forms of words just as other people are distinguished by their oaths and rotten speech. Besides,

this is useful for stirring up reverence in ourselves and for others' instruction. Such forms are confessions of divine providence and the uncertainty of human life.

(2) The children of God use these frequently: "I will come to you very soon, if the Lord is willing" (1 Corinthians 4:19); "I hope to spend some time with you, if the Lord permits" (1 Corinthians 16:7); "I pray that now at last by God's will the way may be opened for me to come to you" (Romans 1:10); "I hope in the Lord Jesus to send Timothy to you soon" (Philippians 2:19). The children of God know that all their goings are ordered by the Lord; therefore they often use these reservations of his will and power. See also Genesis 28:20 and Hebrews 6:3.

(3) Even the pagans, by the light of nature, would use these forms with some religion and would seldom speak of any purpose of theirs without this holy parenthesis. Plato in the *Timaeo* brings in Alcibiades' asking Socrates how he should speak, and he answers: "Before every work you must say, 'If God will.'"

(4) When we use these forms, the heart must go along with the tongue; common forms of words in which God's name is used are mere profanities if the heart is not reverent. Augustine cautions, "Do not learn to have in your hearts what everyone has in his tongue." The words are common, but the meaning is useful.

(5) It is not always necessary to be explicit, but there must always be submission to God's will whether implicit or explicit. The holy men of God have often expressed the intention to do things and yet not formally expressed such conditions—for example, in Romans 15:24, "I plan to do so when I go to Spain."

Notes on Verse 15

Note 1. All our undertakings must be referred to the will of God—not only religious ones, but secular actions. Our journeys must not be undertaken without asking his leave: "O LORD, God of my master Abraham, give me success today" (Genesis 24:12; see also Genesis 28:20). If this is neglected, it is no wonder you meet with so many setbacks; they do not come from your hard luck but your profane neglect. But what does is it mean to submit all our actions to the will of God?

(1) It is measuring all our actions by his revealed will; that is the rule of duty. We can look for no blessing except on actions that are consistent with it. We must submit to his secret will and conform to his revealed will. Worldly desire has its own will (see Ephesians 2:2), but we are to serve the will of God until we fall asleep (Acts 13:36).

(2) We must undertake any action with greater peace of mind when we see God in it—as in Acts 16:10, where Paul gathered that God had called him to Macedonia. When we see God guiding and leading us by means of his providence or by inward instinct, we may walk in the way he has opened to us with all the more encouragement.

(3) In our desires and requests we must seek God's advice: "not as I will, but as you will" (Matthew 26:39). In temporal things we must submit to God's will—for his mercy, for the means, and for time to achieve things. Creatures, who cannot ascribe anything to themselves, must not prescribe to God and give laws to providence, but must be content to want or have as the Lord pleases. If anything does not work out well, the Lord does not wish it; that is enough to silence all discontent.

(4) We must constantly ask his leave in prayer.

(5) We must still reserve the power of God's providence, saying, "If the Lord will," "If the Lord permit." God does not want us to be too confident in a worldly way; it is good to get the soul used to things changing. There are two things we should often consider in this connection, both of them in this text:

a. The sovereignty and dominion of providence. However wise and skillful you are in your enterprise, the Lord can nip it in the bud or stop it when it is actually happening. I have noticed that God is usually very sensitive about his honor in this point and usually frustrates proud people who boast of what they will do and have unlimited plans without any thought of the constraint they may receive in providence. It is a flower of the imperial crown of heaven, and the bridle that God puts on the rational creature, to arrange what will happen to human affairs. Therefore, God wants to be acknowledged in this: "In his heart a man plans his course, but the LORD determines his steps" (Proverbs 16:9). We make plans, but their execution depends wholly on God's will and providence. If we demand things, there is a contest between us and heaven about will and power; therefore, in such cases the answer of providence is more clearly and decisive to our loss, so that God may be acknowledged as Lord of the things that happen and the first mover in all causes and effects, without whom they have no efficacy.

b. Consider the frailty and uncertainty of your own lives; our being is as uncertain as the events of providence. In the passage, **If it is the Lord's will** implies that there must be an awareness of our own frailty as well as of the sovereignty of providence, so that the heart may submit to God the better. Psalm 146:4 says, "When their spirit departs, they return to the ground; on that very day their plans come to nothing." Certainly we will never be wise until we are able to number our days and sufficiently understand the uncertainty of our life in the world (Psalm 90:12).

Note 2. **"We will live and do this or that."** Notice that it is not enough if God allows us to live; he must also by the same will allow us to act. We may live and yet not be able to do anything to carry out our plans; for if God stops agreeing, the creatures cannot act, at least not with any success. This quite contradicts the teaching of the heathen philosophers. Seneca said, "It is by the gift of the gods that we live; that we live well is our own doing." And Cicero said: "It is the judgment of all mortals that prosperity is to be sought from God, but wisdom to be gotten by ourselves." But in the Scriptures we are taught otherwise—to seek from God not only success but also guidance; he gives us the ability to do things and a blessing when the action is finished. His will is both *efficacious* and *permissive*, and without both aspects we can do nothing; he must give us life and all things necessary to action. We must not only look up to him as the author of the success but as the director of the action. It is by his direction and blessing that everything happens. Even our will and wisdom are subject to divine control, and he can turn them as he pleases (Proverbs 21:1). Therefore, we must not only commit our ways to his providence but commend our hearts to the instruction of his Spirit. In short, all things are done by his will and must be ascribed to his praise.

Commentary on Verse 16

As it is, you boast and brag. All such boasting is evil.

Here the apostle comes to charge their consciences more particularly with arrogantly presuming on outward success, especially as we aggravate it by acknowledging it quite openly despite the threatenings of the Word.

As it is, you boast and brag. It is not easy to define what boasts the apostle means. The people he was writing to are charged in chapter 2 with glorying in their riches and afterwards with glorying in a mere profession of godliness; after that he charges them with glorying in their presumed wisdom, manifested in their crowing over other people's failings (chapter 3); now, last of all, he charges them with glorying in their worldly hopes or foolish predictions of their own successful efforts, as if their lives and actions were in their own power and exempted them from the rule of providence.

All such boasting is evil. That is, you think this is brave confidence, but actually it is worldly complacency. He says that it is **evil** because they defended it as good; it is evil because it comes from an evil cause—pride and wretched complacency; it is evil in its own nature, being a defiance of the world; it is evil in its effects, hindering you from good and setting you on ambitious projects when you should be attending to humbling duties and grieving, mourning, and wailing (as he said in verse 9). I see this as the apostle's thinking in this verse, which commentators usually pass over lightly without the necessary concern for the meaning of the context.

Notes on Verse 16

Note 1. Such is the degeneration of human nature that it not only practices sins but glories in them. Fallen man is inverted man, man turned upside-down. His love is where his hatred should be, and his hatred is where his love should be; his glory is where his shame should be, and his shame is where his glory should be. Many people count strictness a disgrace, and sin admirable. The apostle says, "their glory is in their shame" (Philippians 3:19). This sometimes happens through ignorance; people mistake evil for good, and so call revenge valor or resolution, and prosperity in an evil way the blessing of providence on their zealous efforts, and presumptuous carelessness a well-founded confidence. God charged his people with making great feasts of rejoicing when they had more cause to mourn: "Can consecrated meat avert your punishment? When you engage in your wickedness, then you rejoice" (Jeremiah 11:15). Usually by our foolish mistakes we bless and praise God like this when we have more reason to humble and afflict our souls. Sometimes this is because our conscience is numbed; when people have worn out all honest restraints, then they rejoice in evil and delight in their perversities (Proverbs 2:14). The drunkards think it is clever to drink so much wine and boast of how many cups they can drink; the confirmed adulterer boasts of so many acts of uncleanness; the swearer thinks it the beauty of his speech that he mixes it with oaths; and proud people think conceited clothing is their best ornament. *O good God, how man has fallen!* First we practice sin, then defend it, then boast of it. Sin is first our burden, then our custom, then our delight, then our excellence.

Note 2. We have no cause to rejoice or glory in our worldly confidence. It seems to come from a noble bravery, but actually it comes from lowness and baseness of spirit. It is just running away from evil, not mastering it. People dare not lay it to heart because they do not know how to fortify themselves against it. Faith (true confidence) always supposes and prepares for the worst but hopes for the best; it meets the adversary in the open and vanquishes it. The fool in the Gospel dared not think about his death that night (Luke 12:16-20). This is the baseness of worldly confidence, to put off trouble when it cannot put it away; and however it scorns the threat, it fears the judgment. Such people are so ill equipped to bear it that they dare not think about it.

Commentary on Verse 17

Anyone, then, who knows the good he ought to do and doesn't do it, sins.

In this verse the apostle deals with the prejudice by which people might evade his warning. People might reply, "We have no need to be taught such a plain lesson; we know that life is short and that God's providence rules everything." The apostle says, do you know all this? Then you are all the more obliged to subject your desires to his will and pleasure. James proves this by this general rule. There is nothing difficult in the words except for **sins** [KJV **to him it is sin**]—that is, "sin indeed." There is more revealed here of the nature of sin and the effects of sin, which one will find in his own conscience and in hell's torments and in God's sentences. You have similar sayings elsewhere; see John 9:41 and 15:22.

But you will say then, "Are people who sin out of ignorance wholly free from sin?" I answer no, for:

(1) Sins of ignorance are sins, though more forgivable (1 Timothy 1:13) and not punished so hard (Luke 12:47). God's law was once impressed on our natures, and we are bound to do all that was written on Adam's heart.

(2) Affected ignorance renders us highly culpable (2 Peter 3:5)—that is, when people shut the windows and resist the light, for then they could know but choose not to.

Notes on Verse 17

Note 1. It is not enough to know good; we must do it also. Often we find that people who know a lot are apt to be enslaved by their appetites, the lower and more brutish faculties; though they are orthodox, they are unmortified. They are keen against errors but indulgent to vices. Remember that you are to add to knowledge "self-control" (2 Peter 1:6); otherwise, what good will it do you? Others are ignorant of God in their minds and deny him in their lives. Others question the truth of religion and deny the power of it. We are apt to say, "I know this well enough already." Ah, but do I practice it? Is this not a new hint from God to convince me of my negligence? Surely God sees that I do not live up to this new knowledge, and therefore the same truth, this common truth, is brought back to my mind.

Note 2. Sins of knowledge are the most dangerous. They are more sins than other things are, because they have more malice and contempt in them. There is more contempt both of the law of God and of God's kindness; see Matthew 11:20. This is a sign that you love sin as sin, for when you know what it is you embark on it. Besides, sins against knowledge have more of the marks of God's vengeance on them. In the reprobate they are punished with great despair and horror of conscience (see Proverbs 5:11-14) or with hardness of heart. Iron that is frequently heated and cooled grows harder. It is fair of God to punish contempt for light with obduracy or with madness against the truth. The most moral heathens were the harshest persecutors, such as Severus, Antoninus, etc. This is clearly seen in apostates who carried on with most willful malice against the truths they once professed. People who were once the keenest believers turn into violent persecutors. They want to quench the light shining in their own hearts.

Alexander was once a disciple but "shipwrecked" his faith (1 Timothy 1:19-20); the same man is intended in Acts 19:33, for he lived at Ephesus, as we learn from both the letters to Timothy. The Jews set him up as the best accuser of Paul. He knew his doctrine and had to appear to turn all the blame for the uproar on the Christians. Once more we read of Alexander as a desperate enemy of the truth (2 Timothy 4:14). Certainly the rage and malice of such men is all the greater because of the abundance of the light they have renounced. No vinegar is so tart as that which is made from the sweetest wine. "Those who forsake the law praise the wicked" (Proverbs 28:4); that is, they not only commit sin but approve it in other people. Still, they are the most violent and forward men.

Sometimes God gives them up to sottishness; see Romans 1:21-32. It is very remarkable, and very much underlines the apostle's observation, that the most refined and civil heathens (who are presumed to have the most light) were given up to the most beastly errors about the nature of God. The Romans and Greeks worshiped fevers and human passions—every paltry thing instead of God; whereas the Scythians and more barbarous nations worshiped the thunder and the sun, things terrible in themselves, which plainly shows the justice of God's judgment in darkening their foolish heart because they were not thankful for the improvement of the light they had received. But God's greatest displeasure against sins of knowledge is declared hereafter in the torments of hell, where the proportions of everlasting horrors rise higher and higher, according to the various aggravations of sin (Luke 12:48). Thus God punishes sins of knowledge in the reprobate; but his own children also perceive the difference between these and other sins. Nothing breaks the bones and scourges the soul with such a sad remorse as sins against light. This broke David's heart: "you taught me wisdom in the inmost place" (Psalm 51:6, NIV footnote). He had committed adultery against the checks of conscience and the watchful light of the inmost place. I could say much more about this argument, if I did not want just to give hints.

Note 3. Sins of omission are aggravated by knowledge, as are sins of commission. The apostle says, **Anyone then, who knows the good he ought to do and doesn't do it.** Usually in sins of commission natural light is working more, because there is an actual disturbance by which the free contemplation of the mind is hindered, and because foul acts bring more shame and horror than mere neglect. Yet to omit a duty against knowledge may be as bad as to tell a lie against knowledge. The rule is positive, enforcing duty as well as forbidding sin; and because we know it, we are obligated by it. Oh, that we might be more conscientious in this matter and be as sensitive about omitting prayer in defiance of the light and neglecting to meditate and examine our conscience in defiance of the light as we are of committing adultery in defiance of the light!

James
Chapter 5

Commentary and Notes on Verse 1

Now listen, you rich people, weep and wail because of the misery that is coming upon you.

Before I come to the particular verses of this paragraph, it will be necessary to consider the people it refers to, for it seems strange that anyone going under the name of a Christian could be so vile as to oppress and persecute his brothers, even to death, condemning and killing innocent men (verse 6), dragging them into court (2:6), etc. Briefly, then, though the main part of the letter concerns the godly, and the principal purpose is their instruction and comfort, James often takes occasion to speak to the ungodly and unconverted among them. The ancient holy seed was now down to the dregs, guilty of oppression, injury, and all manner of profanity; and because these people lived dispersed and intermingled with the godly and those who had been won to the Christian faith, he takes the opportunity to speak to them in this diversion. To show you that this is no uncertain conjecture, let me produce my reasons:

(1) James addresses his whole letter **to the twelve tribes** (1:1) in general, without any express mention of their holy calling or faith, which is usual in the older apostolic letters.

(2) He uses the common form of greeting—just **Greetings**. When writing to Christians, the apostles solemnly wish them "grace and peace," etc.

(3) The style is more rousing and persuasive than usual, as if it were intended to awaken complacent sinners or worldly people.

(4) The last verses of the letter seem to intimate that much of his purpose was to convert unbelievers; see 5:19-20.

(5) Here he plainly speaks to rich, wicked men, though the truth is that it is not so much for their sakes as for the godly, to encourage them to patience. I like Calvin's assessment very much, that these six verses are not so much an admonition as a denunciation, in which the apostle is not so

287

much telling them what to do as foretelling what will be done to them, so that the godly may be encouraged to greater patience under their oppression. The apostle plainly implies this in verse 7.

I have spent a long time on this preface, but I hope you will judge it necessary, as it helps to explain not only this paragraph but also many other passages in the letter.

From the whole verse we may learn that we must not concern ourselves only with believers, but that we must give unbelievers their due—terror to those who deserve terror, as well as comfort to those who deserve comfort. Christ's sermon chiefly aimed at the disciples' benefit, but there were also many lessons for the crowds: "Now, when he saw the crowds, he went up on a mountainside . . . His disciples came to him, and he began to teach them" (Matthew 5:1-2)—the disciples listened within the people's hearing. And James intersperses many things that are of general usefulness.

Now listen. The phrase is a kind of call to the throne of God's judgment.

You rich people. He is not simply threatening rich people but those who are described afterwards—worldly rich people, drowned in pleasures, puffed up with pride—worldly, wicked, oppressive. And though he uses the word **rich**, the threat applies not only to those who abuse their wealth but also to those who abuse their greatness, public position, authority, power—such as princes, judges, magistrates, and their officers.

Because the apostle is speaking indefinitely, **you rich people**, it is notable that it is hard to possess riches without sin. Riches are called "worldly wealth" (Luke 16:9) because such wealth is usually possessed by wicked people, and because it is most adored and admired by wicked people, and because it is often gotten by unrighteous actions and hardly kept without sin. It is hard to have riches and not be hindered from heaven by them (Matthew 19:24), to not grow proud, sensual, injurious, and worldly. We see animals, such as boars and bulls, when they are full and in good condition, grow fierce and dangerous to man; in the same way, people get insolent when they enjoy abundance.

So then, do not covet riches so much or please yourselves in the enjoyment of them; but look to your hearts with all the more care. It is easy to offend in the midst of outward fullness. A long coat will soon get bedraggled and turn into a dirty rag, and a short one will not cover nakedness; something in between is best. Consider Agur's choice when he said, "Give me neither poverty nor riches. . . . Otherwise, I may have too much and disown you and say, 'Who is the LORD?'" (Proverbs 30:8-9). No state of life so begets contempt of God as a luxurious fullness.

But you will say, "What do you want us to do? Throw away our estates?" I answer no, but:

(1) Prize them less; when you possess them, do not let them possess

you. Shall I value unrighteous worldliness as the lot of God's people? No; let me rather seek the favor of God upon his people (see Psalm 106:4-5). You cannot know love and hatred by everything that is in front of you. Riches are given to the good in case they should be thought evil and to the bad in case we should think them the only and most important good.

(2) Do more good. Duties performed in the face of difficulty are all the more commendable: "Use worldly wealth to gain friends for yourselves" (Luke 16:9). Such wealth is usually the occasion of sin; make it the occasion of duty. The more liable we are to sin in any state, the more commendable in every way is the duty of that state.

(3) Seek God all the more earnestly for grace. When you are full, you need it much. It is not absolutely impossible for a rich person to go to heaven. Poor Lazarus rests there in the arms of Abraham, who had been rich in this world. God can loosen the heart from the world, so that riches will be no impediment to hinder you from heaven. Whatever difficulties we are told of on the way to heaven, they serve only to make us despair of our own strength and abilities (Matthew 19:26).

Weep and wail. This refers to the sorrow of man or or rational creatures and so indicates how dreadful the calamity would be—it would make them howl like wolves. Wailing is a sign of great grief—overburdened nature trying to give vent to its sorrow. Some people find an allusion here to their having lived like animals, like hounds and wolves, and here being told to howl like beasts; but this may be too strained. What we must ask is whether this is said here by way of advice or as threatening divine vengeance.

Some people think it is advice, as if James wants them to prevent their judgment by godly sorrow. The truth is, this is the way to escape judgments, by mourning for them before they come. After heavy showers the air is clear. It is better to **weep and wail** by way of duty than because of judgment. There will be weeping and wailing hereafter, but it will be of no use.

But I prefer to look on these words as a threatening and denunciation of judgment rather than as advice or an invitation to repent. This is partly because the prophets usually utter their threats in an imperative form, especially when they want to emphasize the sureness of judgment, as if it has already come, as in the words **weep and wail** here. The prophets do this to check the present complacency and jollity of the people they are speaking to: see Isaiah 15 and 16, Jeremiah 48:36, etc. Partly I prefer this interpretation because our apostle seems to cut off all hope from them: **because of the misery that is coming upon you,** he says—not "in case misery comes on you." And partly I prefer it because his main drift is to speak to the poor Christians, that they might be all the more patient under the oppression of these great men, showing that their prosperity would not last forever.

Note 1. Many people who frolic away their days have more cause to **weep and wail**. "Now listen . . ."; that is, you are merry and sensual and dream of nothing but golden days, without the least thought of the misery that is hastening upon you. After fine weather comes the storm, and when the wind is still heavy rain falls. Those who were to go into captivity first had their merry banquets (Amos 6:1-7). So then, learn that it is not those who have the least trouble who are in the happiest state but those who humanly have least cause.

Note 2. Riches and outward pleasures are a sorry ground for rejoicing. This is a joy that may end in sorrow; the rich are called to **wail**. When rich people are troubled, we ask what is wrong with them. But the judgment of God and of the world are contrary; his thoughts are not like your thoughts (see Isaiah 55:8). The world thinks no one has more cause to rejoice than the rich, and God thinks no one have more cause to mourn. So then, think about the reason for your rejoicing: "When anxiety was great within me, your consolation brought joy to my soul" (Psalm 94:19). Christians should expect their contentment to increase and can be sure their comforts are the sort that come from God. What a difference there is between David and the worldly fool in the Gospel! David tells his soul to "hope . . . in God" because of "the help of his countenance" (see Psalm 42:5, KJV). And the fool says to himself, "eat, drink and be merry." On what ground? "You have plenty of good things laid up for many years" (Luke 12:19).

Note 3. There is nothing but woe for them, as if they were past hope and counsel and only left to terror and threatening. James had said, **Now listen** before, to the ambitious businessmen (4:13). But he was *instructing* them, whereas here he is simply *threatening* the rich. Rich sinners are the most incurable. The reason is that prosperity gives rise to complacency. "Ephraim boasts, 'I am very rich; I have become wealthy. With all my wealth they will not find in me any iniquity or sin'" (Hosea 12:8). Because they were rich, they were not aware of their subtle wiles. Besides, these are seldom faithfully reproved; and when they are, such persons are most unwilling to bear the reproof. They storm at it, as if their greatness will get them off. "'I will go to the leaders and speak to them . . .' But with one accord they too had broken off the yoke and torn off the bonds" (Jeremiah 5:5). The meaning here is that they had thrown off all manner of respect and subjection to God's law. So then, you who have great estates, beware of these two things: complacency in sin, and storming at the reproofs of sin.

Because of the misery that is coming upon you. What is this? Partly great affliction in this life, partly hell-torment in the life to come; both may be understood.

(1) Christ foretold the temporal misery that happened to Jerusalem (Luke 19:43-44); this happened about forty years after his ascension. Then there were the calamities that happened to the Jews everywhere they were scattered, especially in Alexandria, a city where four out of ten Jews lived, and yet they were ransacked and by Flaccus' command forced into a small part of the city without food or fresh air, where they were not able to move for one another; and if any strayed out of that place, they were knocked down and killed. Many were choked to death in a fire when their oppressors lacked the fuel to burn them outright. Thirty-eight of their counselors and rich men were sent for, dragged through the streets, scourged to death, etc. This may be part of what James meant.

(2) Hell-torment, which is indeed misery to come. The others are just foretastes of what the rich man in the Gospel felt in the flames (see Luke 16:24).

Dreadful misery and judgment will come upon wicked rich people: **wail because of the misery. . .** You will not be miserable as a murderer or a fornicator (Salvian comments) but as a rich person, because you misused your wealth, or at least did not use it for God's glory. See what a list of threats there is against the rich: "Woe to you who are rich, for you have already received your comfort. Woe to you who are well fed now, for you will go hungry. Woe to you who laugh now, for you will mourn and weep . . ." (Luke 6:24-25). "Woe to you who add house to house and join field to field till no space is left and you live alone in the land" (Isaiah 5:8). It is notable that in both these passages words are used that merely imply riches, though it is the worldly man that is meant, who places all his delight, love, care, confidence, and glory in his riches.

Much is entrusted to the rich; they have more opportunities and obligations to do good than others, and yet usually they have the least heart and therefore are called to a more severe account in this world and the world to come. Sometimes God reckons with them in this world; in all change, rich people have the greatest proportion of calamity. The winds shake the tallest cedars most. God loves to tear down the strong oaks (Amos 2:9). But in the world to come they sadly come to know what it is to have wealth only in this world. God will not give you a double heaven. Who would risk eternal hell for temporal heaven? So if there is any worldly, wicked, rich man reading this today, **Listen . . . weep and wail because of the misery that is coming upon you.** You will say, "We do no harm with our wealth." No, but what good do you do? **Moths have eaten your clothes** (verse 2), and your wealth has rusted; you are wretched and worldly, negligent in religion, not bothering to devote what you have to good uses; and **anyone . . . who knows the good he ought to do and doesn't do it, sins.**

So also the poor may learn from this passage not to envy worldly pomp and glory. A little with righteousness is a greater blessing, and a pledge of more; all the great treasure of the rich brings only trouble and a curse (see Psalm 37:16; Proverbs 15:16). Your little may bring you more comfort than if all the stores of the wealthy were heaped together and given to you. These are principles that are only relished by people of a mortified and contented mind.

Commentary and Notes on Verses 2-3

Your wealth has rotted, and moths have eaten your clothes. Your gold and silver are corroded. Their corrosion will testify against you and eat your flesh like fire. You have hoarded wealth in the last days.

Here the apostle shows their particular sin and the reason for God's judgment. Note his method: first he threatens, and then he comes to convince in particular.

Every solemn threatening must be accompanied by sound conviction. This gives the arrow its head and makes it enter. Every "Woe" must have a "for" (Matthew 23, KJV); otherwise people will not take any notice of the terrible words. The success of our work depends on "a demonstration of the Spirit's power" (1 Corinthians 2:4).

Your wealth has rotted, and moths have eaten your clothes. Your gold and silver are corroded. Note that he speaks about all kinds of wealth. **Your wealth has rotted**—that is, corn and wine and oil, all things subject to rot. **Moths have eaten your clothes**—that is, silks, clothes, linen, and all such kinds of wares. By **Your gold and silver are corroded** he means the decay of all kinds of metals. By these details:

(1) He evinces their sin—that they want to hoard their goods and money and let them be eaten by moths and rust and so rot or perish without any profit at all, rather than put them to good use, such as supplying the poor and benefiting the community.

(2) He upbraids their folly—that they were such fools to place their confidence in what is so perishing and frail as to be eaten by rust and moths.

(3) He may be producing these circumstances as the first pledges of God's displeasure against them and the introduction to the curse on their hoards and treasures, in that they were defaced or destroyed by moths, wetness, or rust.

Note 1. Niggardliness is a sure sign of a worldly heart. Covetousness wants to keep everything; the fool in the Gospel talked of storing his goods in his barns (Luke 12:18). Those who are in love will not part with the pictures of their beloved or let their darling go out of their sight; what God wishes to have shared and spent, they are all for keeping and storing. God gave us wealth not to hoard but to spend. The noblest act of the creature is providing for others' needs. But a covetous person does not even spend on his own; a spiteful envy keeps him from supplying others.

Note 2. Keeping things from public use until they are corrupted or spoiled is niggardliness. When you do not spend them for God or for others or yourself, you are justly culpable. The Greek word for money indicates *use.* You abuse it when you make it *a possession*; then you might as well have so many stones as so many treasures. This is against God's plan and the good of human society. Scourge your souls with remorse for this baseness. Your meat rots while many a hungry stomach needs it; your clothes are eaten by moths when they could cover the nakedness of many a poor soul in the world; your money goes rusty when it should be spent for public defense. Musteatzem, the covetous caliph of Babylon, was such an idolater of his wealth and treasures that he would not spend anything for the necessary defense of his city, whereupon it was taken, and the caliph starved to death, and Haalon, the Tartar conqueror, filled the caliph's mouth with melted gold.

Note 3. Covetousness brings God's curse on our estates. He sends the rot and the rust and the moth. Nothing is gained by rapine or tenacity or greed or keeping things to ourselves. Not by greedy getting: when people will snatch an estate out of the hands of providence, it is no wonder if God snatches it away again. Ill gains are equivalent to losses: "Am I still to forget, O wicked house, your ill-gotten treasures . . . ?" (Micah 6:10); that is, have they still got them? Not by undue withholding: this makes people curse and God too: "People curse the man who hoards grain, but blessing crowns him who is willing to sell" (Proverbs 11:26). God can easily corrupt what we will not give and can cause a worm to breed in manna. Certainly there is a withholding that comes to poverty (Proverbs 11:24). So then, learn the meaning of the Gospel riddle, that whoever wants to save must lose, and the best way of bringing in is spending.

Note 4. There is corruption and decay on the face of all created glory—riches corrupted, garments moth-eaten, gold and silver corroded. It is madness to rest in perishing things: "Cast but a glance at riches, and they are gone" (Proverbs 23:5). Such a dependence is not only against grace but against reason; confidence should have a sure and stable ground. So then, take Christ's advice in Matthew 6:19-20, "Do not store up for yourselves treasures on earth, where moth and rust destroy. . . ." We are apt to seek treasures here, but the moth and the rust check our vanity; these riches are like treasures made of snow that melts in our fingers. Christ was saying in effect, "Provide purses for yourselves that will not wear out, a treasure in heaven that will not be exhausted, where no thief comes near and no moth destroys." You should look for a happiness that will last as long as your soul lasts. Why should we who have souls that will not perish look for things that perish with use? These things pass away, and the desire for them too (1 John 2:17).

Note 5. From the diversity of the terms **rotted, moths, corroded**, note that God has several ways in which to destroy our worldly comforts. Sometimes it is by moths, sometimes by thieves, sometimes by rust or robbery; they may either rot or be taken from us. So then, let us be all the more awed. Usually we look no further than the present likelihood. Sometimes God can use fire, sometimes a great wind, or the Sabeans; Job had messenger upon messenger (Job 1). Nothing keeps the heart so detached from earthly comforts as considering the various ways they may be taken from us. This evinces our close dependence on God and the absolute dominion of providence.

Their corrosion will testify against you. Scripture commonly speaks of inanimate things as testifying against the unthankful and wicked. As for the Gospel, Matthew 24:14 says, "as a testimony to all nations"; the preaching of the Word will be a witness that people had warning enough. So also with the dust of the apostles' feet: "shake the dust off your feet when you leave, as a testimony against them" (Mark 6:11). That is, it will be clear that you are free of their blood; if there is no other witness, this dust will witness to it. So it is with the rust here; it will be a witness. That is, for the present it is a convicting argument that you had enough, though you would not spend it; and hereafter it will be brought by the supreme Judge as circumstantial evidence for your condemnation. Your own consciences, remembering the moths and the rust, will bring to remembrance your covetous hoarding.

On the day of judgment the least circumstances of our sinful actions will be brought as arguments to convict us. God will not lack witnesses. The rusty iron, the corroded silver, the moth-eaten clothes will be produced; that is, our consciences will recognize them. "The stones of the wall will cry out, and the beams of the woodwork will echo it" (Habakkuk 2:11); that is, the materials of the house built up by oppression will come as joint witnesses. The stones of the wall will cry out, "Lord, we were built up by rapine and violence"; and the beams will answer, "True, Lord; that is exactly right." The stones will cry, "Vengeance, Lord, upon our ungodly owner"; and the beams will answer, "Woe to him, because he built his house with blood."

The circumstances of sin are like so many memorials to remind us of guilt and to remind God of vengeance. So then, think of these things for the present; this rust may be produced against me, this building, these musty clothes in the wardrobe. Conscience is a shrewd reminder; it writes when it does not speak. Often it is silent for the present and seems to take no notice of those circumstances of guilt; but they are all registered and will be produced at the last day. The very filth of your fingers in counting money will be evidence that you have defiled your soul with loving it.

And eat your flesh like fire. Some people interpret this as referring to those "harmful desires" (1 Timothy 6:9) with which the covetous encumber their lives and eat out the vigor of their own spirits; but this is hardly probable. It is much nearer to the apostle's meaning to interpret this eating as the means and cause of their ruin. Scripture often compares the wrath of God to fire, whether expressed by temporal judgment or eternal torment. "Your breath is a fire that consumes you" (Isaiah 33:11; see also Psalm 21:9; Isaiah 30:27); "their worm does not die, and the fire is not quenched" (Mark 9:44, NIV note). The effects of wrath are also ascribed to the cause that merits it, for what wrath is said to do, sin is said to do also, as in the passages cited; and here rust will eat like fire—that is, it will hasten the wrath of God, which will burn like fire, either in your temporal or your eternal ruin. Possibly there may be some hidden allusion here to the manner of Jerusalem's ruin, in which many thousands perished by fire, which was a pledge of the general judgment.

Note 6. In hell, the matter of our sin will become the matter of our punishment. The rust of hoarded treasure is not only the witness but executioner. As it has eaten away the silver, so it will eat a man's flesh and gnaw at his conscience. When one is burning in hell-flames, reflections upon the rust will be sad and horrible. The vexation and anger at one's past folly will heighten his present sufferings. Conscience and a sense of the wrath of God are a great part of the fire that burns souls; and the outward pains are much increased by remembering the past circumstances of sin. The revenging image and representation of them always runs in the thoughts, and their flesh is eaten but not consumed. Think about it! The rust that eats at the money is only a pledge of those devouring torments. It will be sad to think hereafter that all the money a man hoarded up became fire that he kept in his cupboards for his own eternal ruin. It is part of heaven's happiness to know as we are known—that is, to look back on the circumstances of our past lives and see what we were enabled to do by the care and help of grace. And in the same way it is part of hell's torment to review the course of a sinful life and look back with horror and despairing remorse on the known evidence and circumstances of one's own guilt. Present delights will prove future torments.

Note 7. Observe again the misery of covetousness here and hereafter. Now it burns the soul with desire and cares, and hereafter with despair and remorse of conscience. Here it is pierced with thorns, and there scorched with fire. What a hard time these drudges of Satan have! Worry now and horror hereafter! They labor and toil, and all so that they may go to hell with nothing. What do you gain by Satan? Every sinner is first caught in his traps and then bound in chains of darkness; but some, above all others, begin their hell by eating out all their quiet with burdensome care, so that they may eternally undo their souls with more trouble.

You have hoarded wealth in the last days. There is no cogent reason why we should take this metaphorically, especially since, with good warrant from the context and the purpose of the apostle and the state of those times, we may retain the literal meaning. I simply understand the words as an intimation of their approaching judgment; and so the apostle seems to me to censure their vanity in hoarding and heaping up wealth when those days when the Jewish nation was scattered and destroyed were just ready to overtake them. All the treasure that they had accumulated with such wrong to others and at such risk to their own contentment and with such violation of their own consciences was simply heaped up for the spoiler and the violence of the last days.

People are usually most complacent and worldly before their own judgment and ruin. What wretched people here had fallen upon the treasures of the last days! It is usually like this; people are most full of worldly projects when God is about to break down and pluck up. "Should you then seek great things for yourself? Seek them not. For I will bring disaster on all people, declares the LORD" (Jeremiah 45:5). Foolish people are like a colony of ants storing their nests when their hill is going to be plowed under; and there is never more general complacency than when judgment is at hand. A little before the Flood, "people were eating, drinking, marrying and being given in marriage. . . . Then the flood came and destroyed them all" (Luke 17:27). And the same is observed of Sodom: "buying and selling, planting and building" (verse 28). When people generally apply themselves to worldly business, it is a sad prognosis: they are simply producing for the murderer and heaping up for the plunderer. "While people are saying, 'Peace and safety,' destruction will come on them suddenly, as labor pains on a pregnant woman, and they will not escape" (1 Thessalonians 5:3). When complacency runs riot and is likely to degenerate into utter contempt of God, people are not likely to profit by the Word; so God takes the rod in hand, that he may teach them by the severity of discipline what they would not learn by kinder and milder persuasion.

Commentary on Verse 4

Look! The wages you failed to pay the workmen who mowed your fields are crying out against you. The cries of the harvesters have reached the ears of the Lord Almighty.

Here another argument of conviction is produced—namely, the oppression of their servants and laborers when they defrauded them of their reward. This sin is so harmful and heinous that it cries to God for vengeance. I will explain the phrases in the notes.

Notes on Verse 4

Note 1. Note from the context that there is no sin so heinous and base that covetousness may not be a mother or nurse to it. What could be more sordid than for a rich person to keep back the laborer's wages? It was base to hoard up their own treasures until they were corrupted with moth or rust; but it was a most accursed practice, after they had sucked out the strength and sweat of the laborer, to deprive him of his reward. Yet it is usually like this: people who do not part with their own right will not scruple to invade someone else's. First people are sparing and then harmful. Detest this sin with all the more aversion, for you do not know how far it will carry you; the apostle says it is "a root of all kinds of evil" (1 Timothy 6:10).

Note 2. **Crying out.** Some sins are **crying** and more especially require vengeance at the hands of God. This **crying** is applied to blood: "Your brother's blood cries out to me from the ground" (Genesis 4:10)—not his soul, but his blood. It is also applied to the wickedness of Sodom: "The outcry against Sodom and Gomorrah is so great and their sin so grievous . . ." (Genesis 18:20). It is also applied to the oppression of God's servants; they are dear to him: "God heard their groaning"; "the cry of the Israelites has reached me" (Exodus 2:24 and 3:9). It is also applied to the oppression of the widows and orphans: "Do not take advantage of a widow or an orphan. If you do and they cry out to me, I will certainly hear their cry" (Exodus 22:22-23). Similarly in verse 27 we have, "When he cries out to me, I will hear, for I am compassionate," concerning taking the neighbor's essential garment as a pledge. In short, all sins that disturb human society provoke divine justice to take notice of them. Besides, this crying in some cases shows the unwillingness of God to punish until he is solicited and urged to do so by the importunity and provocation of our own sins.

Note 3. As all oppression cries to God, so especially the oppression of poor servants and those who live by manual labor. This is twice repeated in the text—**who mowed your fields** and then again, **the cries of the harvesters.** And the reason is, this is their life, and so failing to pay them fairly is an act of the greatest unmercifulness; and besides, you cheat them of the solace of their labors. See Deuteronomy 24:15, "He is poor and is counting on it"; that is, he is relying on his wages at the end of the day.

But you will say, "How many ways may we oppress the poor laborer?" I answer:

(1) When through greatness you accept their labors without reward, as the gentry do with the peasants in many countries: "Woe to him . . . making his countrymen work for nothing" (Jeremiah 22:13), meaning Jehoiakim, who in his magnificent buildings used his subjects' labor without payment.

(2) When you do not give them a proportionate wage, taking advantage of their necessity, for then a great part of their labor is without reward. It is sheer covetousness to "exploit all your workers" (Isaiah 58:3), when your wages are scanty and short.

(3) When you defraud them of their reward by cunning, either through bad payment or crafty excuses. The Lord says, "I will be quick to testify against . . . those who defraud laborers of their wages" (Malachi 3:5). It is the same in James: **You failed to pay.** God knows what is oppression, even if it is veiled under clever pretense.

(4) When you reduce or change their wages. It is said of Laban that he changed Jacob's wages ten times (Genesis 31:41).

(5) When you delay payment. God commanded the Jews to do this before sunset: see Deuteronomy 24:14-15. It is a maxim of the law that not paying at the time is paying less, because of the advantage of interest; and in this text it says, **failed to pay [kept back by fraud,** KJV]. Though not wholly taken away, yet **kept back** was enough to be called sin. In contrast, the Lord rewards his servants before they have done their work; we have much of our wages beforehand.

Note 4. **The Lord Almighty.** That is, the Lord of hosts, a name often used in the prophetic books, but most commonly in Isaiah and Zechariah. It is not usual in the New Testament, God's titles there being more full of sweetness and grace. The reason it was used so much then was because the people of God were in great misery, needed much defense and protection, and were in danger of letting their hopes fall because of fear of men. It was a name of God so commonly known and used that the Septuagint retained the Hebrew term by which it was expressed: "the Lord of Sabaoth." And so also it is kept in the New Testament in Romans 9:29 and by James in this passage—not religiously, out of any mystery in the syllables, as Jerome supposes, but because this name for God was so familiar among the Jews and so familiar to the nations who had contact with them. The Lord is called the Lord Almighty, or Lord of hosts, because all his creatures are ranked in such order that they are always ready to serve and accomplish his will.

Note that the Lord is a Lord of hosts, commander-in-chief of all the creatures—angels, men, thunders, lightnings, storms, showers, lions, fevers, etc. They are all at his call, waiting for his Word: "Do you send the lightning bolts on their way? Do they report to you, 'Here we are'?" (Job 38:35); that is, "Lord, where shall we go? Here we are, ready to fulfill your Word." God's command reaches from the highest angel to the lowest creatures. The angels are principally called God's host: see 1 Kings 22:19 and Luke 2:13. And what power they have! One angel destroyed a hundred and eighty-five thousand people in one night (2 Kings 19:35).

This term can also mean the heavens: "all the stars of the heavens will be dissolved . . . all the starry host will fall" (Isaiah 34:4). What Peter calls the elements (2 Peter 3:10), the prophet calls the hosts. Judges 5:20 says, "From the heavens the stars fought, from their courses they fought against Sisera"—that is, by their influence and effect on the clouds and meteors. Do not argue with someone who can command legions and attack you with omnipotence: "Woe . . . to him who is but a potsherd among the potsherds on the ground" (Isaiah 45:9). How sad it is that while all the creatures serve God your heart should war against him and the Lord of hosts is not Lord of your soul!

Note 5. **The cries . . . have reached the ears of the Lord Almighty.** That is, he has noticed the wrongs done against them and will take care to avenge their quarrel. Note that the Lord of hosts is the avenger of the poor; the God of angels and thunders is the God who comforts the downcast. You may be high and rich in the world, able to take on poor creatures and crush them; but can you take on the Almighty? Take heed of wronging the poorest servants of God! Christ speaks of offending his little ones (Matthew 18:10); as little as they are, they have a great champion. The worm Jacob is looked after by the Lord Almighty. So the poor, the servant, the widow, the orphan—they are called his people, as belonging chiefly to his care; they "devour my people as men eat bread" (Psalm 14:4).

Take heed what you do; your poor servants have a Master in heaven who will call you to account. Jerusalem is threatened with captivity for her breach of covenant and unkindness to her slaves (Jeremiah 34:11-22); therefore do not defraud them, do not leave them without help. God will visit this sin upon many gentlemen who dismiss their old servants without help and care more about their dogs than about them. See what an avenger they have, one who is powerful enough! A good man should care for his beast (Proverbs 12:10); much more should he care for his servants.

Commentary and Notes on Verse 5

You have lived on earth in luxury and self-indulgence. You have fattened yourselves in the day of slaughter.

The apostle gives another example of how the wicked abuse their riches, and that is in sensual or refined living. They were reluctant in giving to the poor but easily and liberally spent their money on pleasures and gratifications of the flesh—like the epicure in the Gospel who lived in luxury every day but denied a crumb to Lazarus the beggar (Luke 16:19-21). Worldly desires, though they argue every inch with grace, easily give way to corruptions.

You have lived . . . in luxury. The word means indulging the senses in food, drink, and clothing.

Note 1. This sin is very natural to us. There were just two common fathers of the human race: Adam, the first created man, and Noah, the restorer. Both went wrong by appetite—one by eating, the other by drinking. We need to be careful. Christ told his own disciples to beware of dissipation and drunkenness (Luke 21:34).

Note 2. This sin is natural to all but chiefly occurs among the rich. There is, I confess, a difference in tempers. Wealth makes some people covetous and others prodigal; but the usual sin in the rich is luxury. Pride, idleness, and overeating are usually found in the houses of the great, who should be all the more wary.

Note 3. Though refined living is a sin of the wealthy, their abundance does not excuse it. God gave wealth for another purpose than to spend it on pleasures. It is bad enough in poor men to guzzle and drink away their days, which should be spent in honest labor, but it is inexcusable in the rich; God allows them to live more liberally according to their circumstances, yet not inordinately. Intemperance is odious to God in anybody, whoever they are.

Note 4. **Luxury** is living **in pleasure** (KJV). God allows us to use pleasures but not to live in them—to take delight, but not for them to take us. To live always at the full is mere wanton luxury.

On earth. This refers, say some, to vile beasts, which look toward the earth in the posture of their bodies; it is indeed their happiness to live in pleasure, to enjoy pleasures without remorse. But you cannot fitly interpret the apostle's words in this way. His meaning is that these persons placed all their happiness in this earthly life, and their spirits altogether ran after earthly comforts and earthly contentment, as though they had no higher life to live.

All the pleasure that the wicked have is on earth—here and nowhere else: "Remember that in your lifetime you received your good things" (Luke 16:25). It is sad to outlive our happiness, to come to lack our comforts and joys ("they have received their reward in full," Matthew 6:2), for one's heaven to be past. It is the folly of the worldly to be merry only in their place of banishment and pilgrimage; they live in pleasure here, where they are absent from God: "They spend their years in prosperity and go down to the grave in peace" (Job 21:13). Alas, their best days are past then! The earth is a place of labor and exercise; we were not put into it to take our fill of pleasure.

In . . . self-indulgence. The same word is used of the worldly widow in 1 Timothy 5:6, "the widow who lives for pleasure is dead even while she lives." The word implies such refinement as brings deadness to the spirit, and therefore the KJV translates it as **wanton.**

Note 5. Luxury is always accompanied by worldly complacency and contempt of God. In Deuteronomy 32:15 we read that Israel "grew fat and kicked"; in Hosea 13:6, "When I fed them, they were satisfied; when they were satisfied, they became proud; then they forgot me." Through too much plenty, the soul becomes self-indulgent and untamed.

Note 6. Abundance of pleasure brings us to **self-indulgence** and contempt for ordinary provisions. First we hold God in contempt and then his creatures. It is a great sign that sensuality has prevailed over you when the soul desires dainty food. Israel wanted quails. Our nature is not to be self-indulgent until it is made so by habit. It is strange to see how our nature degenerates by degrees and desires more and more with habit. At first we are pleased with what is plain and wholesome, but afterwards we must have unusual combinations. Sea and land will scarcely yield bits dainty enough for a gluttonous appetite.

You have fattened yourselves [nourished your hearts, KJV]. That is, to breed lust rather than satisfy nature. It is the same idea as Paul's "how to gratify the desires of the sinful nature" in Romans 13:14. The heart is the seat of desires; that is its chief meaning in theology. To nourish the heart is to fuel our desires, taking in excessive amounts in order to expend it in desire.

Pleasures nourish the heart and fatten it into a senseless stupidity. Nothing brings dullness to it like pleasures. Plutarch observes that the ass, the dullest of all creatures, has the fattest heart. Hence that expression in Scripture, "Make the heart of this people fat" (Isaiah 6:10, KJV). There is a fish that they call the ass-fish, which has its heart in its belly—a fit emblem of a sensual epicure. The heart is never more dull and unfit for the severities and heights of religion than when burdened with luxurious excess; therefore Christ uses the expression in Luke 21:34, "Be careful, or your hearts will be weighed down. . . ." Just consider how many reasons we have to be wary in our pleasures. Will the inconveniences they bring you move you away from God? "Drunkards and gluttons become poor" (Proverbs 23:21). How often has the stomach brought the back to rags? Or will the disasters they bring to the body move you?

Worldly desire, which is the final end and consummation of all pleasures, sucks the bones and, like a cannibal, eats your own flesh (Proverbs 5:11). But chiefly think of the inconvenience your precious soul sustains even while your heart is nourished and fattened. Pleasure infatuates the mind but quenches the radiance and vigor of the spirit; wine and women divert the heart (Hosea 4:11)—that is, the generous sprightliness of the affections. The apostle says of people given to pleasure that they are past feeling (Ephesians 4:18-19); they have lost all the smartness and tenderness of their spirits. Oh, that people would regard this and be careful to nourish their hearts while they nourish their bodies! You should starve desire when you feed nature; or as Augustine puts it in his *Confessions*: "regard your food as medicine, and use this outward refreshment as a remedy to cure infirmities, not to cause them." Or as Bernard puts it, you refresh the soul when you feed the body; and by Christian meditations on God's bounty, Christ's sweetness, and the fatness of God's house you keep carnal desire from being nourished.

In the day of slaughter. Some commentators, such as Brixianus, say that this means they fattened themselves for the slaughter, but that is forced. Beza renders it "as in a day of feast." Certainly there is an allusion to the solemn festivals of the Jews. Their thanksgiving days were called days of slaughter, when many animals were killed for sacrifices and food. In thank-offerings a large part was reserved for the use of the worshiper. Hence the expression in Proverbs 17:1, "Better a dry crust with peace and quiet than a house full of feasting, with strife"; that is, such a time should be cheerful, as was usual in the time of peace or thank-offerings. So also in Proverbs 7:14, "I have peace offerings at home"—that is, the meat of thank-offerings with which to feast and entertain others.

The fault these sensualists are charged with is double:

(1) They made every day a festival. It is a wanton luxury to make every day a day of slaughter; the rich man made his living "in luxury" worse because he did it "every day" (Luke 16:19). Some people do nothing but join pleasure to pleasure; their lives are nothing but a diversion from one worldly pleasure to another. There is a time to feast and a time to mourn (see Ecclesiastes 3:1-8). Such people disturb the order of seasons. Nature is relieved with changes but clogged with continuance. Frequency of pleasures becomes a habit; and besides, ordinary pleasures then become stale, and people start to look for new excitements. Pleasure itself must have pleasure to refresh it; accustomed delights become a burden.

(2) They gave to their desires what should only have been given to religion on special occasions. Usually it is human vanity to devote to one's desires what was intended for worship and a cursed sacrilege to serve the god of the stomach (Philippians 3:19); true zeal serves the great God of heaven and earth. In Amos 6:5 no music will serve the epicures but temple music: "You strum away on your harps like David and improvise on musical instruments." They wanted to be as excellent in their private feasts as David was in the service of the temple. "He gave orders to bring in the

gold and silver goblets that Nebuchadnezzar his father had taken from the temple in Jerusalem" (Daniel 5:2). Vain man thinks he can never honor his pleasures enough or scorn God and holy things enough.

Commentary and Notes on Verse 6

You have condemned and murdered innocent men, who were not opposing you.

The apostle now comes to another sin, and that is tyrannous and oppressive cruelty, which is also an effect of riches when there is no grace to sanctify their enjoyment.

From the context, note that plenty gives rise to harm; and when all things are possible, people think all things lawful. The rich and the great, if they are higher than others, do not think about him who is higher than they are: "If you see the poor oppressed in a district, and justice and rights denied, do not be surprised at such things; for one official is eyed by a higher one, and over them both are others higher still" (Ecclesiastes 5:8).

You have condemned. The apostle now gives the example of their cruelty and oppression, masked with a pretense of law. Before they killed, there was some form of legal process; they **condemned**.

God takes notice of the injuries done to his people under the form of a legal procedure—not only through open violence, but that which is done secretly: "Can a corrupt throne be allied with you—one that brings on misery by its decrees?" (Psalm 94:20). God regards it as more heinous when public authority, which should be defending the innocent, is used as a cover for oppression. Many people are careful to observe forms of law, even if they do not mind oppressing the godly. See Matthew 27:6, "It is against the law to put this into the treasury, since it is blood money"; yet it was lawful to spill the blood of Christ, according to them.

Again, the apostle says, **You have condemned** and also **murdered**; they used their authority and wealth to do this, corrupting judgment and using evil arts to destroy **innocent men**.

Any consent in the destruction of innocent people makes us guilty of their blood; and sins committed at our instigation become ours by being rightly imputed to us. Christ was put to death by authority of the Roman Empire and executed by the Roman soldiers; yet it is blamed on the Jews, the whole nation, because it was done at their instigation and with their connivance: "You, with the help of wicked men, put him to death" (Acts 2:23)—"this Jesus, whom you crucified" (verse 36)—"the Jews, who killed the Lord Jesus" (1 Thessalonians 2:14-15). Do not flatter yourself because you are not the immediate executioner. Beware how you provoke others to blood; the guilt will fall on your own consciences. God looks on the instigators as the principals. Ahab "sold himself to do evil in the eyes of the LORD, urged on by Jezebel his wife" (1 Kings 21:25). It was a sorry answer that the priests gave to Judas: "That's your responsibility" (Matthew 27:4); it was their responsibility too, since it was by their plot and conspiracy.

And murdered. This is added to show that oppression will go as far as death—wickedness knows no bounds and limits—and also to show why miseries were coming upon them.

Innocent men. This may refer generally to any just person, as in Isaiah 57:1 ("The righteous perish . . ."); but because the apostle speaks in the singular and with an article, some people understand it to refer to John the Baptist, and others (with more probability) to Stephen, whom the Jews stoned, and others (with most probability) to our Lord Jesus Christ. Because I strongly incline to this last, I shall produce my reasons:

(1) Jesus Christ is elsewhere called "the Righteous One" for emphasis (Acts 22:14).

(2) There seems to be a direct parallel to this passage in Acts 3:14, "You disowned the Holy and Righteous One and asked that a murderer be released to you."

(3) This was the great reason and cause of judgments on the Jews (see 1 Thessalonians 2:15-16), which is the point of this passage.

(4) The conclusion drawn by the next verse, persuading his readers to be **patient** in hope, arises very naturally from this thought. The former part of verse 6 shows the harm they have done and therefore the cause of their ruin; and the latter part deals with Christ's patience, the great example and pattern for ours.

I know the great prejudice against this interpretation is that all this is supposed to be spoken to Christian Jews; but we disproved that in the first verse. Brochman asks how this could be blamed on these sensual, rich people since those who condemned and killed Christ, and the main promoters of his sufferings, were the Pharisees and chief priests, dissembling hypocrites. But this is of no weight since the guilt lay on the whole nation, and they had taken the curse of his blood upon themselves and their children. The apostle is therefore quite in order to say to them, when he assigns the cause of the approaching judgment, **You have . . . murdered**.

Do not think it strange that the apostle does not call Christ Lord or Saviour, for he is speaking to unconverted Jews, and the best way he could convict them is to declare Christ's righteousness or innocence, as Peter and John also do: "the Holy and Righteous One" (Acts 3:14). Those who would not acknowledge him as Saviour by the plain evidence of his life might acknowledge him to have been a righteous person, as Pilate's wife did (Matthew 27:19). However, lest this interpretation should seem too doubtful, I shall make the notes apply either way.

Note 1. If you take the expression generally, as concerning any innocent person, you may observe that innocence itself cannot escape the pangs of oppression. The just are condemned and killed; thus the Scripture speaks of "the blood of righteous Abel" (Matthew 23:35). People hate what they refuse to imitate; and in the wisdom of God the worst judge their sufferings perversely: "they band together against the righteous and condemn the innocent to death" (Psalm 94:21). That is how it has been, is, and will be. Gregory says, "I would suspect him not to be Abel if he has no Cain."

Note 2. If you understand this particularly of Christ, note that Christ died not as a malefactor but as an innocent person. There were several circumstances that showed this: the disagreement of the witnesses, Pilate's wife's dream and testimony, Pilate's own acknowledgment, Judas' confession. Certainly he died not for his own sins but for ours, "the righteous for the unrighteous" (1 Peter 3:18). Our sacrifice was a lamb without spot or blemish. It is true he loved our justification better than his own reputation; and therefore when his innocence was questioned, he would not answer a word.

Who were not opposing you. The present tense (see KJV) is put for the past. If you understand this generally, it is to be understood of the weakness and meekness of innocent people.

(1) Their weakness. They are not able to withstand, and therefore you oppress them.

Weakness is usually oppressed. People are all the more bold with those who lack any way of resisting or defending themselves. But remember that the less outward defense people have, the more the Lord of hosts is engaged in their quarrel; he is the patron of the orphans and widows: "The victim commits himself to you; you are the helper of the fatherless" (Psalm 10:14). Weak innocence has a strong avenger.

(2) Their meekness. It is their duty not to be revengeful: "But I tell you, Do not resist an evil person" (Matthew 5:39). They must not satisfy or carry out their own private revenge.

Meekness invites injury but always at its own cost. What was said of Publius Mimus, though spoken for evil purposes, remains true: "by bearing an injury, you invite a second." Patience may be trampled on, but God will arrange a defense. Wicked people are mad without provocation. You have seen crows on a sheep's back picking wool; that is a picture of oppressed innocence. Wicked people do not consider who deserves the worst but who will suffer the most.

Note 3. If you understand this to refer to Christ, it is most true; he was condemned and slain without resistance. He came to suffer and therefore would not resist. He would declare his obedience to his Father by his patience before men; "he was led like a lamb to the slaughter, and as a sheep before her shearers is silent, so he did not open his mouth" (Isaiah 53:7). Pigs will howl, but the sheep is silent in the butcher's hands. "I offered my back to those who beat me, my cheeks to those who pulled out my beard; I did not hide my face from mocking and spitting" (Isaiah 50:6). Christ, as it were, offered himself to the affronts and indignities done to his person.

It is notable that Christ uses the same severity to check the devil's tempting him to idolatry and to Peter's dissuading him from suffering: "Away from me, Satan!" (Matthew 4:10); "Out of my sight, Satan!" (Matthew 16:23). When Christ was about to suffer, he told the pious women not to weep (Luke 23:28). About to wipe away all tears by the benefit of his cross, he wanted no shed tears to hinder him from it. Thus our Saviour did not resist; "all the injury he did was to himself," says Tertullian. He did not struggle when he was going to the cross; why do we struggle and find ourselves so reluctant when we are going to the throne of grace? Shall we be more unwilling to pray than Christ was to suffer?

Commentary and Notes on Verse 7

Be patient, then, brothers, until the Lord's coming. See how the farmer waits for the land to yield its valuable crop and how patient he is for the fall and spring rains.

He now turns from the rich oppressors to the poor, faithful brothers who were oppressed; by the word **then** we see that the previous paragraph was for their sakes. The rich will be punished for their wickedness and oppression, and therefore you must be patient.

Be patient, then, brothers. The word **patient** implies long-suffering, which is a further degree of patience. Patience is a sense of afflictions borne without complaining and of injuries accepted without revenge; long-suffering is patience extended until it finishes its work (as 1:4 puts it).

It is the duty of God's children to be patient under their sufferings, even if those trials are long and sharp. It is easier in a calm and sedate condition to talk about patience than to exercise it in time of trial. Philosophers have discussed patience and commended it; but Christians themselves have staggered when they have been exercised with a sharp sense of evil. When God gives his people up to the desires of their enemies, that is sad, and we are apt to complain; and yet the apostle says we should suffer with long patience.

I shall spare discussing motives and just show you what Christian patience is. It differs from complacency and stoical insensitivity; there can be no patience where there is no sense of evil. Christianity does not abrogate feelings but regulates them. Worldly people put off what they cannot put away and are not patient, but are stupid and careless. There are other remedies in Christianity than quenching our sorrows in the wine of pleasure. Christian patience presupposes a sense of evil and then takes the form of submission of the whole soul to the will of God.

(1) Note its nature. This is a submission of the whole soul. "The word of the LORD . . . is good" (Isaiah 39:8). Even if it is a terrible word to the unbeliever, the submission of a sanctified judgment can call it good. Then the will accepts it: "when . . . they pay for their sin" ("accept of the punishment," KJV—that is, take it kindly from God that it is no worse) (Leviticus 26:41). Then the affections are restrained, and anger and sorrow are brought under the commands of the Word. Then the tongue is bridled, lest discontent overflow; Aaron held his peace (Leviticus 10:3).

(2) Consider the grounds and proper considerations on which all this is carried on. Usually there is a progression such as this:

First, the soul sees God in it. "I was silent; I would not open my mouth, for you are the one who has done this" (Psalm 39:9).

Second, it sees God acting in sovereignty. "Who can say to him, 'What are you doing?'" (Job 9:12). "He answers none of man's words" (Job 33:13).

Third, lest this should make the heart storm, it sees sovereignty modified and mitigated in the dispensation of it with several attributes. With *justice*: in Deuteronomy 27:26, when every curse was pronounced they were to say "Amen"; if it comes about, it will only be just. With *mercy*: "you have punished us less than our sins have deserved" (Ezra 9:13). They were afflicted when they might have been destroyed; they were in Babylon when they might have been in hell. With *faithfulness*: they look upon afflictions as appendages of the covenant of grace: "It was good for me to be afflicted so that I might learn your decrees" (Psalm 119:71). When they are threshed, it is only so that they may lose their stalk and husk; God's faithfulness would not let them lack such help. With *wisdom*: "the LORD is a God of justice" (Isaiah 30:18) in his dispensations. God is too just to do us wrong and too kind and wise to do us harm.

Until the Lord's coming. Here is an argument to enforce the duty; God will come and put your injuries right. But what **coming** is he speaking about? Every manifestation of God's grace or judgment is called a **coming** of the Lord. It is pointless in such a well-known case to pile up passages. More especially his solemn judgments on a church or a people are expressed by that term, as with all the churches in Revelation: "I will come to you and remove your lampstand from its place" (2:5, to Ephesus); "Repent, therefore! Otherwise, I will soon come to you" (2:16, to Smyrna); "I will come like a thief" (3:3, to Sardis). Any solemn judicial procession of God is expressed by **coming**; but most of all it is applied to Christ's glorious appearing in the clouds, called his second coming. But you will reply again, "Which, then, is meant here? Any particular coming of Christ or his second coming for general judgment?" I answer: both may be intended. The early Christians thought both would happen together.

(1) It may mean Christ's particular coming to judge these wicked people. This letter was written about thirty years after Christ's death, and there was only a little time between that and the fall of Jerusalem, so **until the Lord's coming** could mean until the fall of Jerusalem, which is also expressed elsewhere by "coming" if we may believe Chrysostom and Ecumenius on John 21:22 ("If I want him to remain alive until I return, what is that to you?"), where they say "return" means coming back for Jerusalem's destruction. God often comes to his people in this way.

Christians, to assuage their griefs, should often think about Christ's coming to their rescue and deliverance. Have a little patience, and when your Master comes he will put an end to your afflictions. Long for the coming of Christ, but wait for it; do not bind the counsels of God. Usually his coming is when he is least looked for (see Luke 18:7-8 and Matthew 25:6-7). Who would expect the bridegroom at midnight? Usually because we are keen to see our hopes fulfilled we give up waiting. Our time is always present, and flesh and blood is soon tired; yet, long though it seems, it is only a short time: "He who is coming will come and will not delay" (Hebrews 10:37).

(2) It may mean the general day of judgment, which is the day of vengeance and reward. See both in 2 Thessalonians 1:6-8, "God is just. He will pay back trouble to those who trouble you and give relief to you who are troubled, and to us as well. This will happen when the Lord Jesus is revealed from heaven in blazing fire with his powerful angels." We are not to understand this as if they will not be punished nor we rewarded *before* that day. But then both will be more full and complete: the wicked who are now in chains of darkness waiting for a more terrible day, and glorified souls waiting for a fuller reward, their bodies remaining as yet under the dominion of death.

A spiritual argument for patience involves thinking of the day of judgment. Here we are beaten by enemies and fellow-servants, but then the Lord will come and all will be well (Matthew 24:51). It will be wonderful when we are hugged in Christ's arms and he says, "Well done, well suffered, my good and faithful servant!" and puts the crown on our heads with his own hands. So then, love the coming of Christ (2 Timothy 4:8) and hasten it (2 Peter 3:12).

See how the farmer waits. Here the apostle anticipates an objection: "Yes, but we are waiting a long time!" So does the farmer, says the apostle, for something that is not nearly as precious as your hopes. Clement's *Apostolic Constitutions* says that James and his brother Jude were farmers, and that is why they often used similes from their own calling, having to do with trees, plants, fruits of the earth, and so on.

For the land to yield its valuable crop. It is **valuable** because it costs hard labor and because it is a choice blessing of God for sustaining life. This term is used to show that though the fruit is dear to the farmer, just as deliverance is to you, yet he **waits** for it—**and how patient he is.**

For the fall and spring rains. That is, the **early** rains, which fall a little before sowing, and the **latter** rains (KJV), which fall a little before the ripening of the corn. These are phrases often used by the prophets. The meaning is that he waits until, in the ordinary course of providence, the crop ripens.

See how the farmer waits. We must look at external objects to see a heavenly purpose and should make use of every ordinary sight. This is what Christ does in his parables; elsewhere he bids us to learn from the lilies, just as James does with the farmer. Similarly, Job tells us to "ask the animals, and they will teach you . . . or let the fish of the sea inform you" (Job 12:7-8); that is, draw useful inferences from them in meditation. But you will say, "How shall we make use of common objects?" In two ways: by reasoning from them and by viewing the resemblance between them and spiritual matters, as in the present case in James.

(1) In meditation, argue like this: if a farmer using ordinary principles of reason can wait for the harvest, shall I not wait for the coming of the Lord, the day of refreshing? The corn is precious to him, and so is the coming of Christ to me; will he be so patient and endure so much for a little corn, and not I for the kingdom of heaven? He is willing to stay until everything has worked out and he has received the early and late rains; and shall I not wait until the divine decrees are carried out?

(2) In meditation, note the resemblance and say to yourselves, this is my seed-time, and heaven is the harvest; here I must labor and toil and there rest. I see that the farmer's life is a great labor; we can obtain nothing excellent without labor and an obstinate patience. I see that the seed must be hidden in the furrows and rot before it can spring up and grow; our hopes are hidden, and light is sown for the righteous (Psalm 92:12). All our comforts are buried under the ground, and after all this there must be a long wait. We cannot sow and reap in a day; effects cannot follow until all necessary causes have first worked out. It is not in the farmer's power to ripen fruits at will; our times are in the hands of God. Therefore it is good to wait; a long-suffering patience will reap the desired fruits.

Commentary and Notes on Verse 8

You too, be patient and stand firm, because the Lord's coming is near.

Here James applies the simile, again enforcing patience; it is a lesson that needs much pressing.

Stand firm. The Septuagint uses this term for the holding up of Moses' hands (Exodus 17:12). And here it denotes an immovableness in the faith and hope of Christianity, notwithstanding the many oppressions they had met with. In short, it implies two things—firmness of faith and constancy in grace.

(1) Firmness in faith, when, out of the encouragement of a sure trust, we can sit down under God's will and good pleasure.

(2) Constancy in grace, when we are not so bowed with our troubles as to depart from our innocence.

It is the duty of God's children in time of trouble to **stand firm** and to put on a holy courage. It is said of a good man that "his heart is secure, he will have no fear; in the end he will look in triumph on his foes" (Psalm 112:8); that is, he will neither be discouraged in respect to trust nor miscarry in respect to constancy and perseverance. Oh, that we would labor for this firmness! We lose hope, and therefore we lose patience; we are soft-hearted, and so we are overborne. There is a holy obstinacy and hardness of heart that is nothing but a firmness in our Christian purposes and resolutions. We need this in these times; there are persecutions and troubles. Soft and delicate spirits are soon tired due to errors and delusions; wanton and vain spirits are soon seduced due to scandals and offenses by false brothers going wrong. Weak and easy hearers are soon discouraged.

In Nehemiah's time there were troubles outside, delusions from the Samaritans and Tobiah, and oppression by false brothers (Nehemiah 5). To fortify you against all these, think of this: the Lord hates those who draw back. The crab is counted among the unclean creatures (Leviticus 11:10); the four beasts of prophecy each went straight forward (Ezekiel 1:9). If you do not know how to get this holy hardness or strength of spirit, go to God for it. Human strength is small and soon overborne: "Wait for the LORD; be strong and take heart and wait for the LORD" (Psalm 27:14). "God . . . after you have suffered a little while, will himself restore you and make you strong, firm and steadfast" (1 Peter 5:10). Ask him to give you courage and to strengthen and settle your faith against all temptations and dangers.

Because the Lord's coming is near. This may mean, first, **near** to them by a particular judgment, for there were only a few years before all was lost. This is probably what the apostles meant when they spoke so often about the nearness of Christ's coming (Philippians 4:5; Hebrews 10:25; compare 1 John 2:18). But you will say, "How could it be propounded as an argument for patience to the godly Hebrews that Christ would come and destroy the temple and city?" I answer:

(1) The time of Christ's solemn judiciary process against the Jews was the time when he acquitted himself with honor against his adversaries, and the scandal and reproach of his death was rolled away.

(2) The approach of his general judgment ended the persecution; and when the godly were provided for at Pella, the unbelievers perished by the Roman sword.

Secondly, this may mean the day of general judgment that, because of its certainty and the uncertainty of its particular approach, has always been represented to the church as near at hand. Or else this may mean that, in comparison with eternity, all the time between Christ's ascension and his second coming seems as nothing.

The world's duration, in comparison with eternity, is short. "With the Lord a day is like a thousand years, and a thousand years are like a day" (2 Peter 3:8). People count time long, because they measure it by the terms of their own duration; but God brings all ages into the indivisible point of his own eternity, and all is as nothing to him—just a moment, "like a watch in the night" (Psalm 90:4). Though there were more than two thousand years between the first separation and the calling of the Gentiles, God says, "For a brief moment I abandoned you" (Isaiah 54:7). The Word does not judge by sense and appearance. We, being impatient of delays, count moments long; but God does not judge these things "as some understand slowness" (2 Peter 3:9)—that is, as we conceive it. To short-lived creatures, a few years may seem an age; but Scripture, measuring all things by the existence of God, reckons otherwise. Human reason relies altogether on external sense and feeling; and therefore, just as man measures his happiness by incidents in time, so he measures his duration by temporal existence.

When will we look within the veil and learn to measure things by faith and not by sense? We count moments long; but God, who exists eternally, counts thousands of years as a brief moment. All external things have their periods, beyond which they cannot pass; but eternity is a day that is never overcast with the shadows of night. Certainly all time should be brief to those who know the greatness of eternity. And the whole globe of the earth is simply like a middle point to the vast circumference of the heavens. This life, too, is but a moment compared to eternity. If we valued everything as the Word does, it would not be so irksome to us to wait for Christ's coming. Too much softness cannot brook a little delay.

Commentary and Notes on Verse 9

Don't grumble against each other, brothers, or you will be judged. The Judge is standing at the door!

In this verse the apostle lays down the danger of evil groaning, using the same argument as before: the near and speedy approach of judgment. **Don't grumble against each other.** The word means, "don't groan against each other." Because it is not easy to determine the apostle's particular sense, the phrase has been interpreted in various ways. Some people explain it thus: "do not sigh in your grumbling to one another," as if God were unjust in punishing his children and letting the wicked be prosperous. But this cannot be the meaning. In the original it is **against** each other.

Others explain it as, "do not in a groaning manner require vengeance at the hand of God, but rather forgive, that God may forgive you." But certainly it is lawful to complain to God about our injuries, though not with a vengeful spirit. A lot of effort has gone into explaining the word "groan" or **grumble.** Groans in themselves are not unlawful. The apostle must mean the sort of groaning that arises from an evil cause, such as discontent at providence ("complaining groans") or despondency and weakness of mind ("distrustful groans") or revenge against their oppressors ("vindictive groans") or envy at those who suffered less than they did. If anyone's condition is more tolerable, we are apt to complain and to say there is no sorrow like our sorrow; and fretting against God makes us angry with men. Thus the apostle would understand envious groans; and this sense gives the KJV translators their **Grudge not**; that is, do not begrudge the happiness of those who are not faced with sufferings or with the same degree of sufferings that you face.

I would easily agree with this sense except that I can see no reason why we should not retain the proper sense of the word "groan." The apostle seems to me here to censure those mutual injuries and animosities with which the Christians of those times, having banded together under the names of Circumcision and Uncircumcision, grieved one another and gave each other cause to groan, so that they not only sighed under the oppressions of rich persecutors but under the injuries that they sustained from many of the brothers who, together with them, professed the holy faith. This exposition suits the state of those times and the present context. The apostle is persuading them to be patient now because the pressures arose not only from enemies but from brothers. He seeks to dissuade them from such a scandalous practice lest they should all be involved in a common ruin. Should brothers begrudge one another? Take heed; such practices seldom escape without a quick revenge. My thoughts are all the more confirmed in this interpretation because there seems to be a tacit allusion here to the story of Cain and Abel, where the blood of one brother cried out against the other, and God told Cain that sin lay at the door (Genesis 4:7), meaning the punishment of sin, just as the apostle tells these people that **the Judge** was **at the door**, meaning judgment was hanging over them.

Differences can often be so heightened among brothers that they groan against one another as much as against the common enemy. Paul, speaking of the state of the early days, shows how Christians were "biting and devouring each other" (Galatians 5:15). To show their rage, he uses words appropriate to the fights of animals. That is how it usually happens when conflicts arise in the church. Religious hatreds are most deadly. Thus Luther complains that he never had a worse enemy than Karlstadt, and Zwingli that the Roman Catholics were never so bitter to him as his friends. It is sad when we dispute against one another and tongue is armed against tongue and prayer is set against prayer and appeal is set against appeal—lambs acting the wolves' part.

Or you will be judged. That is, lest God punish you; or lest, by mutual allegations, you provoke a condemning sentence to pass against you both, and you also are involved in the common ruin.

Note 1. False brothers will also meet with their judgment. Not only the rich oppressors but you who groan against one another will be condemned; hell is the lot of the hypocrite: "He will . . . assign him a place with the hypocrites" (Matthew 24:51; in Luke 12:46 it is, "with the unbelievers"). Possibly our Saviour might use both expressions, hypocrites and unbelievers, to show that open enemies and secret ones will meet with the same judgment.

Note 2. Mutual groans and grudges between brothers are a usual forerunner of judgment; after biting and devouring, there follows consuming (Galatians 5:15). This comes about partly by the providence of God. Wanton conflicts are only cured by deep afflictions; and once spirits are so antagonistic to each other, there is no likelihood of agreement except in prison. The warm sun makes wood warp and split; in prosperity we grow wanton and divide; when the dog is let loose, the sheep run together. Usually in troubles there are not so many scatterings and secessions in Christ's flock. This is partly through ordinary causes. Our divisions give our enemies an advantage; we should be as wise about reconciling ourselves as they are about combining against us. Nazianzen used to call them "the common reconcilers." But party and faction makes people blind; such people will not reconsider until all is undone. A little before Diocletian's persecution there were sad divisions in the church; "they burned with mutual internal discord," says Eusebius.

The Judge is standing at the door! He had said before that **the Lord's coming is near**; now he adds that he is **at the door**, a phrase that not only

313

implies the sureness but the suddenness of judgment: see Matthew 24:33, "know that it is near, right at the door." This phrase too implies the speediness of the Jewish ruin.

Note 3. The nearness of the Judge should awe us into duty. To sin in calamitous times is to sin in the presence of the Judge—to strike, as it were, in the King's presence and to provoke justice when punishments hang over our heads. This is like King Ahaz, who trespassed all the more because of his wounds. When God holds up his hand, you are almost daring him to strike.

Note 4. If we are ready to sin, God is ready to judge: "If you do not do what is right, sin is crouching at your door" (Genesis 4:7); that is, the punishment, like a messenger of justice, is lying in wait to arrest us. It is often like this; while we are bustling and "beat[ing] our fellow-servants," our Lord is at the door, coming before we are ready for him (Matthew 24:48-51).

Commentary and Notes on Verse 10

Brothers, as an example of patience in the face of suffering, take the prophets who spoke in the name of the Lord.

Here the apostle urges us to patience by the example of the saints who, though they were dear to God and were employed in high and special services, still suffered various sharp afflictions.

They are an example to us in two ways: they are an example of sufferings, that we may not flinch from them or sink under them when we meet with them in the way of duty; and they are an example of patience, that we may copy their meek submission. Their sufferings are mentioned to reduce our discomfort, and Christ urges it in this way: "in the same way they persecuted the prophets who were before you" (Matthew 5:12). Their patience is mentioned to stir us to imitate them: "imitate those who through faith and patience inherit what has been promised" (Hebrews 6:12). Nobody ever yet went to heaven without these two graces being exercised first—faith in expectation of the future reward, and patience in sustaining the present inconveniences.

As an example. The word denotes the sort of example that is given for imitation. The same word is used when Christ commended his washing of the disciples' feet to their imitation (John 13:15).

The prophets. He mentions them as leaders of the church. Every purpose of life has its chieftains and princes. The Roman warriors can talk of their Camilli, Fabricii, Scipios, and the philosophers of their Aristotle, Plato and Pythagoras; but religion gives the example of the prophets.

Who spoke in the name of the Lord. That is, they were used by God and were authorized to speak to the people in his place, being specially gifted and supplied by his Spirit. Though they spoke by divine inspiration and were like God's mouth, they could not escape opposition but were molested and maligned in the world, even to the point of cruel death and sufferings, for faithfully passing on their message. Christ blames the Jews for this: "O Jerusalem, Jerusalem, you who kill the prophets and stone those sent to you . . ." (Matthew 23:37). So does Stephen: "Was there ever a prophet your fathers did not persecute? They even killed those who predicted the coming of the Righteous One" (Acts 7:52). Now if this was done to the prophets, who seemed to be sheltered under the shield of their special commission and the singular innocence and holiness of their lives, certainly private believers have less reason to promise themselves freedom and exemption.

Of patience in the face of suffering. That is, when God makes us like them in sufferings, we should be like them in patience. It is comfortable to come into their lot and to be bound up in the same bundle of honor with them. Their example is given partly to remove prejudice. This is nothing strange; it is not just *our* case. We are apt to say, "No one was ever in such a state as I am"—as in Lamentations 1:12, "Is any suffering like my suffering . . . ?" Yes, this was the lot of all the prophets. It is also partly to reduce the shame. We are not suffering with the common herd but with **the prophets.** Then it is partly to encourage us to imitate them. Example is particularly effective; people are apt to be led by the company they are in.

Note 1. The example of the saints encourages us to be patient. Man is a creature more easily led by the eye than the ear. We look on teaching as fanciful ideas; seeing it in practice confirms it greatly. The strictest and severest ways are not impossible nor untrodden; what has been done before may be done again. Besides, the example of the prophets is a check to expectations of an easy life; we may say with Elijah, "I am no better than my ancestors" (1 Kings 19:4). Can we expect more privileges than the prophets? Lesser people are ashamed when they cannot endure what people of a higher order have endured. Micah was in prison, Jeremiah in the dungeon, Isaiah sawn apart, and shall we balk at a little suffering? Our betters have endured far worse. Besides, good company is a great encouragement. "Since we are surrounded by such a cloud of witnesses . . ." says Hebrews 12:1, alluding in part to the pillar of cloud that guided the Israelites; having such a pillar going before us, we may travel to heaven more cheerfully.

Note 2. Afflictions come to all ranks of saints but especially to the prophets. Preaching is nothing but baiting the world. We are God's ambassadors, but we are often "ambassadors in chains" (Ephesians 6:20). What rewards did the prophets receive for all their pains and expenditure of spirit? Saws, swords, and dungeons. It is almost as necessary for a minister to be greatly afflicted as to be great in spirit and labors. God has reserved us, in these latter days, for all the contempt and scorn that villainy and outrage can heap on our persons. But it does not matter; it is the badge of our order, and we know where to get a better approval. No matter if the world counts us refuse when Jesus Christ counts us his own glory. The messengers of the churches are the filth of the world (1 Corinthians 4:13) but the glory of Christ (2 Corinthians 8:23); if we were dandled on the world's knees, it would be enough to make people suspect that we were not true to our Master.

Note 3. **Who spoke in the name of the Lord.** This denotes the cause of their sufferings: the faithful discharge of their office—speaking in God's name. Sufferings strengthen us when they overtake us in the way of duty. It is sad to be spat out of God's mouth and to be made contemptible for being partial in the law (Malachi 2:9), when the Lord makes us base before the people. Indeed, he usually does this with corrupt dispensers of holy mysteries; we then receive others' malice but God's judgment. But if this comes for faithfully performing your duty, for speaking boldly **in the name of the Lord**, you may bind it as a crown to your head. Why should we care about the scorn of an unthankful world when we have such a good Master? It is an honor for us to lose our name for God's, and it does not matter if we are nothing, so long as Christ is all in all. A minister should be like someone in a crowd lifting someone else up to be seen by everybody, though he himself is jostled and lost in the throng. If Christ is exalted, it does not matter if we suffer loss.

Commentary and Notes on Verse 11

As you know, we consider blessed those who have persevered. You have heard of Job's perseverance and have seen what the Lord finally brought about. The Lord is full of compassion and mercy.

The drift of the context is to persuade people to be patient. In this verse many things are offered for that purpose.

As you know, we consider blessed those who have persevered. We may imply, first of all, the judgment of all people; mere humans are inclined to have high thoughts of those who can bear the brunt of afflictions.

Note 1. Meek patience in afflictions is attractive even to human eyes. A double reason is implicit in the words **those who have persevered**—those who endure misery and show fortitude in misery. Misery works on pity, and fortitude calls for praises; miseries work on weak spirits, and constant miseries work on noble spirits. Those who are engaged in a good cause need not despair; we shall gain something with mere men. Resolute constancy and meek patience may recover those friends who have gone astray in prosperity; providence orders such things for good. But remember that you cannot take comfort from this unless it is in a good cause. Sometimes wicked ones are the oppressed party. They believe their sufferings entitle them to persecution, as the Donatists did in Augustine's time.

So although suffering is creditable, we must know that the persecuted cause is not always the best. Sarah was a type of the true church and Hagar of the false; Sarah corrected Hagar. There are people who when they suffer anything call it persecution when it is only just punishment. The Moabites, for example, when they saw the waters look red through the reflection of the morning sun thought they were mixed with blood. Many people claim persecution and martyrs' blood in this way when they are just being corrected and restrained a little.

Secondly, the word **we** may imply the judgment of the visible church. The whole Christian church acknowledges that the murdered prophets are happy, and we celebrate their memory. The word in the text (**blessed**) means to make or declare happy.

Note 2. God's people often live envied and persecuted but die sainted. We call the murdered prophets happy and celebrate the memory of those who endure; the scribes and Pharisees decorated the tombs of the dead prophets but killed the living (Matthew 23:29-30). They claimed to honor the departed saints but were harming the living saints. In John 5 the Jews claimed to love Moses but showed hatred to Christ. This comes about partly by the providence of God, who after death makes clears the innocence and holy behavior of his servants; posterity acknowledges those the former age destroyed. And this partly comes about because living saints are an eyesore; by the severity of their lives and reproofs they trouble and torment the world. Dead saints do not stand in the way of men's desires, for objects out of sight do not exasperate us.

This may comfort God's children today: "the Day will bring it to light" (1 Corinthians 3:13). When the heat of oppression is over, what is now called heresy will then be regarded as worship, and your sufferings will declare you not malefactors but martyrs. People cannot discern the present truth (2 Peter 2:12) because they are blinded with their own interests; but maybe truth itself will be the interest of the next age, and the bleak wind that now blows in our faces may then be on our backs. There are sometimes strange revolutions.

Again, this may serve to warn us. Let us not be content with fond affection for departed saints and worthies. The memory of Judas is not so accursed to us as Korah, Dathan, and Abiram were to the worldly Jews in Christ's time; Moses was dear to them, just as Christ and the apostles are to us. The best affection is that which is expressed by sincerity; dead saints are out of our envy, but how do we feel about the living who walk in their ways? It is good to examine what relationship there is between people who are hated today and the case of Christ and his apostles in the early days.

Thirdly, the word **we** may imply (and I think this is the chief implication) the judgment of the children of God, as opposed to the judgment of the world: **we consider blessed those who have persevered**—we who are enlightened by the Spirit of God. I prefer this interpretation because this sentence refers to a passage of Scripture: "Blessed is the one who waits" (Daniel 12:12).

Note 3. The judgment of the saints and the judgment of the world about afflictions are very different: they have different principles—the spirit of the world and the Spirit of God; they have different standards—that of faith and that of sense. A worldly person judges by appearance, but a spiritual person looks within the veil; the world judges afflictions miserable, but believers think them happiness. It is notable that all the beatitudes in Matthew 5 are connected to unlikely conditions, to show that the judgment of the Word and the judgment of the world are contrary to one another. So then, do not listen to the judgment of the world about affliction but to the judgment of the Spirit; not to what sense feels, but to what faith expects. The people of the world are miserable in their happiness, but the children of God are happy in their misery. But you will say, "How?" I answer:

(1) Suffering for righteousness' sake is a kind of grace that God gives us: "you are blessed" (1 Peter 3:14); "be glad" (Matthew 5:12); "rejoicing" (Acts 5:41). John Bradford said, "God forgive me this great unthankfulness for this exceeding great mercy, that he chooseth me for one in whom he will suffer."

(2) You gain by afflictions, experience, hope, and grace (Romans 5:3-4; Hebrews 12:11) and by the wonderful sense of divine consolation (2 Corinthians 1:5).

(3) God has promised to reward it bountifully; there is a blessing in hand but more in hope (see 1:12).

You have heard of Job's perseverance. James gives this example because Job was an eminent example of misery. From his giving this example we may learn that the book of Job was not a parable but a history of what really happened.

Note 4. **You have heard.** We would never have heard of Job if he had not been brought so low. Affliction makes saints eminent; Job's poverty made him rich in honor and esteem. Stars shine only in the night; the lower we are made by providence, the greater we are made. God's children never gain so much honor as in their troubles. Many people whose names now breathe out a fresh perfume in the churches would have lived and died obscurely, with their bones thrown into some unknown charnel, undistinguished from other relics of mortality, if God had not drawn them to public notice by their eminent sufferings.

Note 5. **Job's perseverance.** He showed much impatience and complaining, cursing the day of his birth, etc.; but here there is not a word of all this. Where the bent of the heart is right, the infirmities of God's people are not mentioned. Thus in Hebrews 11:31 there is no mention of Rahab's lie but only of her faith and her peaceable behavior towards the spies. Where God sees grace, he hides his eyes, as it were, from those circumstances that might seem to deface the glory of it. So in what Sarah says, though the whole sentence is full of distrust and unbelief, God takes notice of her reverence to her husband (see the notes on 2:25); she called Abraham "master" (1 Peter 3:6). Wicked people watch for our halting and feed their malice with our failings; they can overlook a great deal of good and fix only on what is evil. But the Lord pardons our defects when our heart is sincere. Job complained, but the Word says, **You have heard of Job's perseverance.** There was **perseverance** in the man. Job often submits to God, sometimes blesses God, dislikes the complaints extorted from him by the sense of his sufferings, and often corrects himself as soon as he has spoken any unbecoming word of God and providence; when he is reproved by God (chapters 38–41), he humbles himself (chapter 42).

Note 6. In our afflictions we should often think of Job's example. He was famous for miseries of various kinds—now Chaldeans, then Sabeans, now wind, then fire, etc. When afflictions come like waves, one on the heels of another, and you are put through various trials, think of Job. They hit all his comforts, his goods—a life is no life without a livelihood—and his children, those dear pledges of affection. You may lose one, but Job lost many; and if you lose all, it is only as Job did. Then on his own body, he was covered with sores. God's afflictions usually come closer and closer until they touch our very skins. You remember how Job's body was affected by sores, and even his soul was exasperated with the censures of his friends; this is getting closer and closer.

God's immediate hand silences the spirit. We take injuries from people very unkindly, especially injuries from friends; these are stabs to the very heart. Perils among false brothers was Paul's sorest trial; it is grievous to suffer from an enemy, but worse from a friend, and worst of all from godly friends. Yet this happened to Job; he complained that his friends were miserable comforters. Thus you see Job was famous for misery, but just as famous for perseverance. In all the expressions of this, two stand out, and they run through every vein of the whole book: his putting God forward and debasing himself; good thoughts of God and low thoughts of himself: "may the name of the LORD be praised" (Job 1:21) and "I have sinned" (Job 7:20, KJV). So then, in all your afflictions look to this example of misery and perseverance.

And have seen what the Lord finally brought about. This may be applied to Christ or to Job. Some people apply it to Christ for these reasons:

(1) Otherwise the main example of perseverance is left out.

(2) The change of the verb: "You have heard of Job, and you have seen what the Lord finally brought about in Christ." Adding this new word **seen** seems to be done by way of contrast with **heard.**

These reasons, when I first glanced at this text, inclined me to that opinion, especially when I afterwards saw the same reasons urged by the learned Paraeus. Many of the older commentators follow this line, such as Augustine, Beda, Lyra, and Aquinas, who makes more of it than I have seen anyone else do. Job and Christ, he says, the two famous examples, go well together: Job in the Old Testament, Christ in the New; in one we have a pledge of temporal reward, in the other a pledge of an eternal reward; you have heard of the one and seen the other; Job suffers but not to death; therefore, in order to give a complete pattern, James reminds them of the end of the Lord. That is what Aquinas says. If this were the sense, the point would be that Christ's death is the great spectacle and mirror of perseverance. But modern theologians take a different line, and with good reason:

(1) The drift of the context (verses 6-7) is not only to give a perfect pattern of miseries but a happy outcome. James had spoken about Job's perseverance, but if the previous sense were true he says nothing about his happy ending, which would be something very suitable to his purpose and most remarkable in the story.

(2) The apostle shows in the previous verse that he would give examples from some prophets and holy men of God, not in the Lord himself.

(3) The latter clause in the text cannot so easily be made to agree with the former sense—namely, that God has **compassion and mercy**; but it suits this latter sense well (**what the Lord finally brought about** with Job, because he is of great mercy, etc.).

The previous arguments may easily be answered:

(1) We must not teach the apostles how to reason or what examples to give. Possibly the example of Christ's patience is purposely omitted because the main thing in question, in which their constancy was assaulted, was their belief in Christ, and therefore it was not so necessary to give his example but rather the example of other holy people who were afflicted. Then people would not take offense at the cross and doubt the

faith they professed because of their great afflictions. To all this I may add that the sufferings of Christ are mentioned in verse 6, as we saw earlier.

(2) The words **heard** and **seen** both imply outward sense and mean knowing and understanding. The word **seen**, which is the clearer way of perception, is used in the latter clause because God's reward was so great and far more visible than **Job's perseverance**. And do not let the phrase seem too curt, for there is no special reason why the outcome of Job's afflictions should be called **what the Lord finally brought about**.

Note 7. We must not think about the nature and beginning of the afflictions of God's children, but rather of their outcome and end: "No discipline seems pleasant at the time, but painful" (Hebrews 12:11). There are two emphatic expressions: "at the time" and "seems"; our bodies find them "painful," but they are only painful "at the time." It is childish to judge afflictions by present sense; it is always worst with Christians in the present time: see Romans 8:18; 1 Corinthians 15:19; 2 Corinthians 4:16-18. So then, do not measure afflictions by the pain but by their outcome; besides our everlasting hopes, usually the obvious end is glorious. When Israel was sent out of Egypt, she went with gold and ear-rings (Exodus 11); the Jews were sent out of Babylon with gifts, jewels, and all necessary utensils (Ezra 1); and "the LORD made [Job] prosperous again and gave him twice as much as he had before . . . and everyone who had known him before . . . gave him a piece of silver and a gold ring" (Job 42:10-11). Wait for the end, then. The beginning is usually Satan's, but the end is the Lord's; at the beginning the power of darkness may have a time, but in the end the Lord will be seen.

Note 8. The Lord will give a happy end to all afflictions.

(1) A temporal end. Man may begin, but God must make an end. When man begins, the Lord will exercise his own dominion and sovereignty before the end comes.

(2) A gracious end: "this will be the full fruitage of the removal of his sin" (Isaiah 27:9). Now this is God's work. God's rod, as well as God's Word, does nothing without his blessing; otherwise they would both be poor, dead, and useless means. "I am the LORD your God, who teaches you what is best for you" (Isaiah 48:17)—by afflictions.

(3) A glorious end. It is the Lord's gift, not by our merit. Let us do our duty, then, and God will not fail; let us wait upon him with Job's perseverance, and he will give Job's end.

The Lord is full of compassion and mercy. This expresses partly the cause and partly the manner of God's appearance in Job's end.

(1) The reason Job had such a good end to his troubles was God's mercy, not his own merit; his root of happiness was that he had to do with a compassionate and merciful God.

(2) You will find God merciful and compassionate, whatever the world

says to the contrary. In the beginning you think him cruel, but in the end you find him merciful. Here are two expressions that express God's goodness: the first is **full of compassion**, and the next is **mercy**. This is the word that is opposite to the hard heart, and therefore the KJV renders it, **of tender mercy**. The one word has to do with our miseries, the other with our sins—compassion for our miseries, mercy in pardoning our sins. One denotes feeling and the other appropriate action—inward and outward mercy.

Note 9. **Full of compassion and mercy.** God's mercy is seldom spoken of without some addition such as "much" or "great" or "tender." Most commonly in the Old Testament it is found in the plural—"mercies" and "loving-kindnesses," and very often "much" or "great" is added: "his mercy is great" (2 Samuel 24:14); "with him is full redemption" (Psalm 130:7); "in his great mercy" (1 Peter 1:3); "the incomparable riches of his grace" (Ephesians 2:7). God delights to reveal this attribute in its royalty and magnificence. Certainly there is more in God's mercy than in our sins. Our container is full, but God's mercy is overflowing; and there is enough in God to supply all our needs. When you can exhaust overflowing mercy, then you may complain; there is enough in God to supply each and every believer. We all drink from the same fountain, and yet we cannot empty it. When will we learn from our Heavenly Father not only to do good works but to abound in them more and more? He is rich in mercy; when will we be rich in good works?

Note 10. God is very tender to his people in misery. Human reason only makes lies about God. When we listen to the voice of our own feelings, we are apt to say with Job, "You turn on me ruthlessly" (30:21); or at least like David, "I am cut off," though at that very time God was looking graciously on him: "yet you heard my cry for mercy" (Psalm 31:22). Israel was castigated for saying, "My way is hidden from the LORD; my cause is disregarded by my God" (Isaiah 40:27); that is, God has left me off the list of those whom he is to look after—he does not take any notice of me. Just wait a little while, and you will see that the Lord is very compassionate and tender. God's children have often at last been ashamed of their hasty words; and when providence has run its course, they can easily see that though the outside and bark was rough and harsh, yet it was lined with compassion and mercy.

Note 11. **Compassion and mercy.** God has provided for the comfort of his people in every way. He has compassion for their afflictions and pardon for their sins. He felt Job's misery and Job's weakness; his compassion might be discouraged by our complaints if he were not merciful as well as compassionate. Afflicted people may take comfort from this and answer the objections of their sad spirits; when you are harmed by other people, you will find compassion in God. You may say, "Yes, but I have sinned." I answer, there is mercy in him as well as pity.

Note 12. Note from the order of the words **compassion** and **mercy** that there is in God, first, compassion and then bounty; it is the same in Exodus 34:6, "compassionate and gracious." So let us learn from our Heavenly Father, when we do good, to do it with all our hearts; let the spring be within us. "Spend yourselves on behalf of the hungry" (Isaiah 58:10), and then satisfy the afflicted person.

Commentary and Notes on Verse 12

Above all, my brothers, do not swear—not by heaven or by earth or by anything else. Let your "Yes" be yes, and your "No," no, or you will be condemned.

As for the context, some people say this is what connects the previous matter and the present verse. People in affliction are usually impatient, and impatience betrays itself by oaths and curses—something very injudicious and no way complying with the apostle's meaning. We need not labor at method and connection; it is the usual practice of James and the other apostles to turn from one matter to another, according to the need of the times, without concerning themselves with the rules of method. In this verse there is an admonition not to swear, in which you may note:

(1) The vehemence of the warning—**above all**.

(2) An instruction:

a. Negatively: **do not swear**; and here some particular forms of swearing are specified: **not by heaven or by earth or by anything else**.

b. Positively: **Let your "Yes" be yes, and your "No," no**.

(3) He gives a reason: **or you will be condemned**.

Above all. The phrase has suffered various interpretations; it actually means "before all things." Lyra interprets the apostle like this: "Do not swear before all things; before every word or promise." This interpretation would be plausible if the order of the words were "My brother, do not swear before all things"; but it is "Before all things, my brothers . . ." Therefore, I prefer to take it as a form of emphasis and earnestness, which is frequent in the apostles' letters: "Above all, love each other deeply" (1 Peter 4:8). But you will say, "Why does he press this above all things?" The question is important. I will give some reasons, which will occasion a note in each case.

Note 1. Because it is a great sin to swear lightly and without thinking; this is specially forbidden in the Ten Commandments: "the LORD will not hold anyone guiltless who misuses his name" (Exodus 20:7). Of all things, God is sensitive about his own name.

(1) This is a great sin in respect to the subject: God's name ought to be sacred; every thought and mention should be accompanied with reverence. All sin is against God, but this is formally and directly against God. Even people are most sensitive about their reputation.

(2) It is a great sin in respect to the occasion: there is no temptation to do it except (the height of wickedness) choosing to sin because it is fun to do evil. Other sins have an external bait; here there is nothing but glorying in our own shame (Philippians 3:19). Or it may be an obstinate pride. It is a daring of God; they will sin because they want to. It is usually found in ruffians who have lost all sense of awe. Oh, let us beware of this sin of rash swearing, of every tendency that way, any irreverent use of the name of God in sudden outcries: "O God!" "O Lord!" etc., or any vain joking with oaths. Those who swear in jest will go to hell in earnest. The Jews were so sensitive about the name of God that they would not pronounce "Jehovah" in the law but read "Adonai," except for the high priest once every year.

Another reason why the apostle says **Above all . . . do not swear** is because it was a sin familiar to the Hebrews, as appears by various passages in Scripture; see Matthew 5:33-34 and 23:16-22. It was a sin very common among them.

Note 2. Common and well-known sins must be opposed with all earnestness. The apostle says, **Above all . . . do not swear**; such things are to be pressed more than any other. Usually the truths that concern the present age are disliked when we reflect on the guilt of the times. People would not have us preach Christ and the general doctrines of faith and repentance, which is nothing but a vain objection masked by a pretense of religion. When the preaching of Christ was the main truth proclaimed and the apostles applied themselves to it, the Corinthians cried for wisdom, meaning doctrines of civil prudence, and the softer strains of morality. That is why Paul said, "I resolved to know nothing while I was with you except Jesus Christ and him crucified" (1 Corinthians 2:2). This was the doctrine that most scandalized them, and so he resolved to take notice of no argument as much as that in his ministry.

The work of the ministry is not to contend with ghosts and outdated opinions but the errors and sins of the present time. It is the duty of Christians to exert their indignation on the main sin with which they are tempted: "I . . . have kept myself from sin" (Psalm 18:23). In the same way, ministers must concentrate their efforts against present guilt. If we were only providing for ourselves, we might read elegant lectures in divinity and entice others into a fool's paradise with words as soft as oil, never examining their wounds and sores. But our commission is, "Shout it aloud, do not hold back" (Isaiah 58:1).

Note 3. This is a custom that is abandoned with difficulty; therefore, **above all**, be careful about swearing. Augustine argues, "Why does the apostle say 'Above all'? Is it worse to swear than to steal? Worse to swear than to commit adultery? Worse to swear than to kill someone? No, but the apostle wants to strengthen us as much as he can against a pestilential custom." Certainly once we have got into this habit, it is hard to stop; any physical object that is often moved in the same way becomes easier to move in that direction, and the tongue is the same when it is used to swear. Habit has so great a power over us that the word is uttered before the mind can stop it. It takes longer to commit other sins such as murder, lust, or theft because other parts of our body are not as quick as the tongue. We can control our hand more easily than our tongue. So then, people who have learned to swear or use vain, idle expressions must watch with all the more care; a habit is soon acquired either by our own practice or by constantly being with people who have it. Be very careful; your habit will not excuse you. If it is your custom to sin, remember that it is God's custom to destroy sinners.

Do not swear—not by heaven or by earth or by anything else. About the opening of this passage, we may ask:

(1) Are all oaths forbidden? Many people have thought so. The Essenes thought all oaths as bad as perjury, as Josephus tells us. Jerome says the Pelagians held the same opinion. The Anabaptists have been uncertain on this point, sometimes being against all oaths and at other times saying they were only against rash oaths. Many modern writers of great note seem inclined to prohibit all oaths as inappropriate to the faith and simplicity that should be among Christians. However, oaths in themselves are lawful if taken "in a truthful, just and righteous way" (Jeremiah 4:2)—that is, without fraud, in a lawful matter, and on an important occasion. The apostle says an oath is "an end to all argument" (Hebrews 6:16). In the Old Testament any doubtful case that could not be settled in any other way was to be "settled by the taking of an oath before the LORD" (Exodus 22:11). The commandment itself allows some freedom: "You shall not misuse the name of the LORD your God" (Exodus 20:7), which implies there is a lawful use of God's name. In the New Testament, the apostle Paul in important matters often swore and called God to witness; see Romans 1:9 and 9:1; 2 Corinthians 1:23; Philippians 1:8 ("God can testify").

(2) What oaths are condemned? Our Saviour and the apostle James only counter that wicked custom introduced by the Pharisees, that a person might swear by the creatures if there was no mention of the name of God or things offered to God, as appears in Matthew 5 and 23. The Jewish nation was guilty of three things: frequent swearing; swearing by the crea-

tures; and breaking these oaths as not binding and valid. These sins were rife in the apostle's days, and the prohibition of the text must be chiefly applied to them. So **do not swear—not by heaven or by earth** must mean the forms that they had invented to evade the law; for the Jews thought they were safe if they omitted the great oath of *Chi Eloah*. Philo said that it was "a sin and a vanity" to "run to God, the Maker of all things, and to swear by him," but that it was "lawful to swear by our parents, by heaven and the stars." Similarly, it is said that some of the ancient Greeks did not readily swear by the gods but by the creatures and things before their eyes, and then that there was no harm and no solemn obligation in these oaths— vain pretenses and excuses, for though the name of God was not mentioned it was implied (Matthew 23:20-22 and 5:34-35), the creature being God's creature, and in an oath made by them God's name being implicitly called upon to be God's instrument of vengeance in case of perjury. The other clause, **or by anything else,** means other oaths of that kind.

Swearing by the creatures is unlawful; swearing is an act of worship, and therefore it must only be done in important matters by the name of God: "Fear the LORD your God . . . and take your oaths in his name" (Deuteronomy 6:13). The prophet reproved those who "swear by the shame of Samaria," meaning an idol (Amos 8:14). In such oaths we use the creature instead of God, whether by way of assertion as when we say, "as sure as there is light in heaven," or by way of execration as in "let heaven blast me or earth swallow me up," "the devil take me," etc. In all these coarse sayings there is a double evil—a rash oath, and an oath made by the creature instead of God. And yet what is more common than such forms among us?

Let your "Yes" be yes, and your "No," no. Some people think this is the same as what our Saviour says in Matthew 5:37, which implies that a Christian in his ordinary speech should content himself with simple affirmations or negations, that he may abstain from all appearance of an oath. "Yes" and "no" were the usual words. Now the apostle says, let your yes always be yes and your no always no; that is, let your affirmations and negations be plain and firmly grounded in simple truth. Paul said his preaching of the Gospel was not "Yes" and "No" but always "Yes" (2 Corinthians 1:18-19), and here we have **let your "Yes" be yes.** The first "Yes" refers to the promise, the second to the action; let there be "Yes" in the promise and "Yes" in the action. And in this the apostle seems to strike at the root, falsehood being the cause of wrong oaths.

An excellent way to prevent swearing is always to be truthful in our speech; then we need not introduce an oath. The trustworthiness of what we say will be enough. Oaths make us suspicious that a person is false and flippant. If people were serious and sincere in what they said, their word would be equivalent to an oath, and their very affirming would be swearing; whereas others in doubtful cases are hardly believed even if they swear ever so much, because they swear as a matter of course. They have prostituted the highest and most solemn way of assurance to every little thing and have nothing left with which to establish a controverted truth.

Or you will be condemned. This alludes to what the law says about swearing: "The LORD will not hold anyone guiltless who misuses his name" (Exodus 20:7). Here not only perjury but rash oaths are forbidden.

Rash and false swearing will bring sure judgment; because of oaths, people and nations mourn (Hosea 4). If duty does not move you, I think you would be startled at the danger and punishment. If you are not afraid to sin, it is strange you are not afraid to burn. All sins are threatened with death but this more explicitly. God has promised that he "will not hold anyone guiltless"; they are usually brought to trial quickly: "I will be quick to testify" (Malachi 3:5). Judgment marches against them swiftly— the "flying scroll" (Zechariah 5). Certainly there is no sin that more wearies God's patience, because there is no sin that banishes the fear of God out of our hearts as much as this one does.

Commentary and Notes on Verse 13

Is any one of you in trouble? He should pray. Is anyone happy? Let him sing songs of praise.

Here James turns to another matter, which is to tell us how to behave ourselves either in an afflicted or in a prosperous state. We are apt to fail or go astray in both.

Is any one of you in trouble? He should pray. James means those who are in the church, the flock of Christ. Christianity gives us no lease on temporal happiness, no exemption from the cross, but rather the contrary.

Is anyone happy? That is, is any of a good mind? The effect is used to imply the state, gladness implying prosperity, which usually makes the heart glad and happy. The word is translated "keep up your courage" in Acts 27:22.

Let him sing songs of praise. In the original there is just one word, meaning "let him sing"; but because the apostle is pressing them to put every state to a religious use, it is right to translate it, **let him sing songs of praise.** Certainly when the apostle tells them to sing, he does not mean songs to please the flesh but psalms to refresh the spirit.

Note 1. Our temporal state is diverse—now afflicted, then happy. It is the folly of our thoughts that we cannot be happy without thinking our nest is among the stars. "Each man's life is but a breath" (Psalm 39:5); our prosperity is like glass, brittle though shining. The complaint of the church may be the motto of all God's children: "you have taken me up and thrown me aside" (Psalm 102:10). The church is "afflicted . . . lashed by storms" (Isaiah 54:11).

Note 2. It is the perfection of Christianity to have a constant mind in changing states. Paul had learned to walk uphill and downhill with the same spirit and peace: "I have learned the secret of being content . . . whether living in plenty or in want" (Philippians 4:12). Most people are only fit for one condition. Some cannot carry a full cup without spilling; others cannot bear a full load without breaking. Sudden alterations perplex both body and mind. It is the mighty power of grace to keep the soul in an even temper.

Note 3. Different states require different duties. The Christian life is like a wheel, every spoke taking its turn. God has planted in us affections for every condition, grace for every affection, a duty for the exercise of every grace, and a time for every duty. The children of the Lord are like trees "planted by streams of water, which yield its fruit in season" (Psalm 1:3). There is no time when God does not invite us to himself. It is wisdom to do what is most in season. There is a time to encourage trust: "When I am afraid, I will trust in you" (Psalm 56:3); and there is a time to overthrow complacency. In misery the duty is prayer, in prosperity the giving of thanks. No providence exempts you from duty. It is our folly to betray our duties by our wishes. "If I were in such-and-such a state, I would serve God readily and cheerfully." But there is no state that grace cannot make use of for some religious purpose, for the advantage of some duty or other. Providence must not be blamed for your own neglect.

Note 4. It is excellent in religion to make use of present affliction—to use sadness to make us pray, or happiness to make us give thanks. The soul never works more sweetly than when it works with the force of some strong feeling. With what advantage may we strike while the iron is hot! When the feelings are stirred up because of something worldly, convert them to a religious use: "Do not weep for the dead . . . rather, weep bitterly for him who is exiled" (Jeremiah 22:10); that is, when sorrow is stirred up by your private loss, turn it into a public channel. So also with Christ's words in Luke 23:28, "Daughters of Jerusalem, do not weep for me; weep for yourselves and for your children." Christ did not want them to bewail his death in a worldly manner but to bemoan their own sins and their approaching ruin. So it is with joy and mirth: "Nor . . . coarse joking, . . . but rather thanksgiving" (Ephesians 5:4). Mentioning his wonderful experiences should be a Christian's mirth and joking. Oh, that we could learn this wisdom, to take the advantage of a worldly feeling, not to fulfill it but to use it for the purposes of the sanctuary. Once the feelings are aroused, give them a right object or they are likely to degenerate and offend, even though their original cause was legitimate.

Note 5. Prayer is the best remedy for sorrows. Griefs are eased by groans and by talking about them. This evaporation unburdens and cools the heart. It is helpful to pour out our complaints to a friend. Prayer is simply the exercise of our graces, and graces exercised will yield comfort. We have good reason in affliction to use the help of prayer:

(1) So that we may ask for patience. If God lays a great burden on you, cry out for a strong back.

(2) So that we may ask for constancy, in order not to use our hands to do evil (Psalm 125:3).

(3) So that we may ask for hope, then trust and wait on God for his fatherly love and care.

(4) So that we may ask for a gracious improvement. The benefit of the rod is a fruit of the divine grace as well as a benefit of the Word.

(5) So that we may ask for deliverance, with submission to God's will: "This poor man called, and the LORD heard him; he saved him out of all his troubles" (Psalm 34:6). Psalm 107 repeats four times, "Then they cried out to the LORD in their trouble, and he delivered ["saved, brought out"] them from their distress" (verses 6, 13, 19, 28).

Note 6. Thanksgiving, or singing God's praise, is the proper duty in time of mercies or comforts. It is God's plan and our promise that if he will "deliver" us we will "honor" him (Psalm 50:15). The spouse's eyes are dove's eyes (Song of Songs 4:1). Doves peck and look upward; for every grain of mercy, there is some return of praise. Mercies work one way or another. They become the fuel either of our desires or of our praises; they make us either thankful or wanton. Your condition is either a help or a hindrance in religion. Awaken yourselves to this service; every new mercy calls for a new song. It is sad to have a great farm by the divine bounty and pay no rent. You should proclaim his "love in the morning" and his "faithfulness at night" (Psalm 92:2). Our morning hopes are founded in God's mercy, and our evening returns of praise should take notice of his truth or faithfulness. We want mercy in the morning, but usually we forget to praise him at night.

Note 7. Singing songs of praise is a duty of the Gospel. Having such clear guidance from the text, it will be good to practice this holy ordinance. Most people do it from habit and in a formal, perfunctory manner and therefore are apt to stop once it is questioned. The devil usually takes advantage of that to draw people of uncertain faith to a type of atheism; when they do not know the reason for a duty, they are all the sooner won over to neglect it. This strengthening ordinance and spiritual recreation has been impugned in several ways:

Some people question the whole duty, as if it were legal worship, because we have no formal and solemn institution of it in the New Testament; but this response is without reason, for:

(1) Moral duties enjoined in the Old Testament need no other institution in the New. We can see that it is part of moral worship by the light of nature; even the heathens sang hymns to their gods. Also in the Old Testament it is always put with other duties of a perpetual and immutable obligation, such as in Psalm 95:1-2, where there is a complete list of all parts of public worship (the Word, prayer, etc.), and singing is included with them as equally necessary. Indeed, it is notable that all the psalms that prophesy about the worship of the Gentiles under the Gospel mention singing (see Psalm 108:2, Psalm 100, etc.).

(2) We have the example of Christ and his apostles: "When they had sung a hymn . . ." (Matthew 26:30). The same is recorded of Paul and Silas in Acts 16:25.

(3) We have exhortations in the New Testament—for example, in Colossians 3:16 and Ephesians 5:19, and here in 5:13.

(4) The churches agree. Pliny, in his letter to Trajan, mentions the Christians' "morning songs to Christ and God" as a usual practice in their solemn worship. Justin Martyr says, "We send up prayers and psalms to God."

Commentary on Verse 14

Is any one of you sick? He should call the elders of the church to pray over him and anoint him with oil in the name of the Lord.

Having given general directions, James now comes to particulars, giving the example of one special kind of affliction, sickness.

(1) He suggests the case as likely to be frequent among them: **Is any one of you sick?**

(2) He states the duty:

a. Of the sick Christian: **He should call the elders of the church.**

b. Of the elders, which is twofold: one ordinary and immutable: **to pray over him**, and the other temporary and appropriate to the gifts of those times: **and anoint him with oil in the name of the Lord.**

This verse has caused much controversy. I shall therefore first explain the phrases, then clear up the controversy, then give you the notes.

Is any one of you sick? The word means, "Is any weak?" or "without strength?" In the next verse the apostle changes the word: the prayer of faith will save **the sick person**—literally, "him that labors under a disease." From this change of the word the Roman Catholics conclude that extreme unction is not to be administered except to those who are mortally sick; but Cajetan, one of their cardinals, well replies that James does not say, "is any sick unto death?" but "is any sick?" It is true there is something in the change of word; it shows that the elders must not be sent for upon every light occasion but only in grievous cases where there is danger and great pain. It is an abuse by the Roman Catholics to interpret this as meaning extreme danger threatening certain death.

He should call. The initiative coming from from the sick person is a call we cannot withstand.

The elders of the church. The word "elders" is used in all sorts of ways. Sometimes it means our ancestors and those who lived before us, as in Matthew 15:2; but it cannot mean that here. Sometimes it is used for elders in years and wisdom, as in 1 Timothy 5:1. Thirdly, there are elders by office. The main meaning here is the order of elders who are elsewhere called "bishops," whether ruling or teaching elders, chiefly the latter. When we are sick we call in the best help, and presumably the best gifts are to be found in those who are called to teach in the church. To add the greater seal to their ministry and to supply the need for physicians, many of them were endued with the gift of healing.

Notice that James says **the elders**, in the plural, because, according to Grotius, in those eastern countries seven elders were usually called to serve in this role. Certainly in the early days there was great love in the different churches and societies of the faithful, and many elders would go to one sick person.

To pray over him. Here is the first duty of the elders. Some people say that **over him** means "for him," but the Greek does not easily bear that construction. It may imply the ancient rite of covering the diseased body with the body of the person praying, as Elijah did with one child (1 Kings 17:21) and Elisha with another (2 Kings 4:34). Paul did this with Eutychus: "Paul went down, threw himself on the young man," praying for life (Acts 20:10)—a rite that expressed great fervency and a desire that the dying person might, as it were, share his own life. Or it may mean laying hands on the sick, which was practiced by the apostles in curing the ill (see Mark 16:17-18). Thus Paul healed the father of Publius by laying hands on him.

And anoint him with oil. There is only one other place in the Scriptures that speaks of using oil in the healing and cure of diseases, and that is Mark 6:13, "They drove out many demons and anointed many sick people with oil and healed them." Among the Jews, oil was a common symbol of divine grace, and so it was appropriate to use it as a sign of the Spirit's power and grace revealed in miraculous healing. It was an extraordinary sign of an extraordinary and miraculous cure. Aretius was wrong to think the apostle meant some medicinal oil. Before him, Wycliffe believed the oils in Palestine were excellent and medicinal and that they were used for this purpose. But this, I say, is a mistake, for oil was not used as an instrument but as a symbol of the cure. The apostle does not mention what kind of oil it should be; it was probably olive oil.

In the name of the Lord. That is, either by his authority, calling on him to operate by his power according to the outward rite; or in his place, as his ministers; or to his glory, to the honor of Christ, who is meant by the term **Lord** here, for that is his proper title as mediator. All these miracles and cures were effected in his name: "In my name they will drive out demons" (Mark 16:17); "In the name of Jesus Christ of Nazareth, walk" (Acts 3:6); "It is Jesus' name and the faith that comes through him that has given this complete healing to him" (Acts 3:16).

Having explained the phrases, I now come to explain the controversy about whether this anointing with oil is a permanent ordinance in the church. The Roman Catholics make it a sacrament, which they call the sacrament of extreme unction. Others in our day want to revive it as a permanent ordinance for church members, expecting some miraculous cure. Therefore I must deal with both. I know that the intricacies of dispute are unpleasant to the ordinary person, so I shall not go over the whole argument but will briefly put forward some ideas that may prevent both the error of the Roman Catholics and the innovation of those who want to revive this rite today.

(1) In the apostles' time, when it was most in use, it was not absolutely necessary nor instituted by Christ. Some Protestants, I confess, say that it was instituted by Christ as a temporary rite, which is denied even by some of the Roman Catholics such as Lombard, Cajetan, and Hugo, who all base it on apostolic practice. For my part, I think it was only *approved* by Christ and not instituted, and that it was taken up as a normal practice among the Jews. As I recall, Grotius, in his commentary on the Gospels, proves that this was a normal rite among that people, for it was their custom to express everything inward and spiritual by some visible symbol; therefore God condescended to appoint various rites and symbols suited to the spirit of that nation. Therefore, when they prayed for the sick they would anoint them with oil as a token of the relief and joy they would obtain from God. This rite was initiated by the apostles and the early Christians with such precision and constancy that they would never give or take any medicine without anointing people with oil, so that I think in fact it was nothing but an imitation of a Jewish rite that Christ approved but never instituted. When Christ sent the apostles out and so solemnly conferred the power of healing on them, we hear of no such commands about anointing with oil. He told them to heal sicknesses but did not prescribe the manner.

You will at least grant that it never had the solemn ratification "till the Lord comes," which other permanent ordinances have. The apostles seldom used oil; they healed by touch, by shadow, by handkerchief, by laying on hands, by word of mouth, etc. So the rite the Lord approved was one that they might choose to use to reveal his power. Why then does James press the elders to anoint with oil? It was so that they might not neglect the grace of God, which in those times was usually dispensed together with this rite. As long as the gift remained in use, the customary rite and symbol might be used. But you will say that he couples it with a moral duty—with prayer, which is an act of perpetual worship. I answer, it is not unusual in Scripture to couple an ordinary duty with an extraordinary rite—for example, prayer and laying on of hands, or baptism and laying on of hands. Similarly, prayer here is linked with anointing with oil. But you will say, God honored it with a miraculous effect. But then, so he did with the water of Siloam to heal the blind (John 9:7), the pool of Bethesda to cure the diseased (John 5:2), Jordan for Naaman's leprosy, etc; and yet these cannot be set up as sacraments and permanent ordinances.

(2) In the apostles' time this was only used with great prudence and caution, for the apostles only anointed those they were assured by the Holy Spirit would recover. Here James seems to restrict it to cases where they could pray in faith. He who gave the faith always indicated when to use it; with the power, he gave discretion, so that they would not expose the gift to scorn by using it all the time. Our learned Whitaker was wrong to say that anointing was a symbol of health that had already been recovered and that the apostles anointed only those who were on the way to recovery. However, it is true that they anointed only those they were persuaded would recover; otherwise the apostle Paul would never have left Trophimus sick at Miletus (2 Timothy 4:20) or sorrowed so much for Epaphroditus' sickness (Philippians 2:27) if he could so easily have helped it by anointing with oil. But now among the Roman Catholics it is only given to those who are half dead or at the point of death.

(3) In its more common use afterwards, not all of those who were anointed were healed. God gave out his grace and power as he saw good, for the effect did not depend on anointing but on the prayer of faith. God worked then as he works now, by ordinary means—sometimes blessing them, sometimes leaving them ineffectual, all depending on his free pleasure and operation.

(4) When this ceased, we cannot tell; why it should cease we may easily judge if we will only understand its nature and purpose. The rite ceased when the gift ceased, which God has taken from the world after the early generations of believers. Gifts of healing are coupled with other miraculous gifts in Matthew 10:8, Mark 6:13, and 16:17-18; and healing ceased when the other gifts ceased. On the first mission of the apostles to win the world, Christ invested them with these gifts. Just as a newly planted tree needs watering but afterwards we stop watering it, these dispensations

ceased after a while. Miracles would not have been miracles if they continued; they would have been regarded as ordinary effects. He still provides for his own but not in that supernatural way; and he heals as he sees cause. When people can restore the effect, let them restore the rite; otherwise, why should we maintain a mere ceremony? Thus we see when it should cease; but when miracles did actually cease is not easy to define. If the story in Tertullian is true, they continued for some two hundred years after Christ, for he speaks of one Proclus, a Christian, who anointed Severus and healed him.

(5) Roman Catholic anointing, or extreme unction, is mere hypocritical pageantry. It must be prepared by a bishop, heated with so many breathings, enchanted by uttering so many words. The parts of the body anointed are the eyes, ears, nose, mouth, and, to be really complete, the kidneys and feet and, in women, the navel. The form of words is, "By this holy oil, and his tender mercy, God forgive you whatever you have sinned by sight, hearing, smell, touch." To make the blasphemy more ridiculous, Aegidius Conink, a schoolman, says the words "by his most tender mercy" may be left out. The administrator *must* be a priest and *may* be a bishop; the object must be a person believed to be at the point of death. The purpose of it, they say, is to expel the remains of sin, healing the soul and helping it against temptations and against Satan, in combat with the powers of the air. To state these things is to refute them, for even the most ignorant person must see the great difference between a miracle and a sacrament, between curing the body and the expulsion of sin.

Notes on Verse 14

Note 1. **Is any one of you sick?** Christ's worshipers are not exempt from sickness, any more than any other affliction. God may chasten those he loves. John 11:3 says, "Lord, the one you love is sick." Those who are dear to God have their share of miseries. Augustine asks, "If he were loved, how did he come to be sick?" In the externals of life God does not make any distinction. Usually those who have God's heart feel God's hand most heavy. I have noticed that God's children never question his love so much as in sickness; such thoughts come to us when the weakness of the body upsets the mind and deprives us of the free exercise of spiritual reason. Mind and body feel everything keenly. Besides, in sickness we do not have the explicit comfort from Christ's sufferings that we have in other troubles. It greatly helps our thoughts when we can see that Christ went through every miserable condition we are exposed to. Christ endured want, nakedness, trouble, reproach, injustice, etc., but not sickness. But he had such passions as hunger, thirst, and weariness, with which his body was afflicted. Christ knows from experience what it is to suffer pain and bodily inconvenience.

Even if we do not have the example of Christ, we have the example of all the saints. Paul had a wracking pain, which he expressed as "a thorn in my flesh" (2 Corinthians 12:7-9), and he was able to have no other answer but "My grace is sufficient for you." He alludes to the sort of punishment meted out to slaves for great offenses: they sharpened a stake and pointed it with iron and put it in at the slave's back until it came out at his mouth; and so with his face upward he died miserably. And so the apostle's expression means some bodily illness and wracking pain—maybe gout, internal ulcers, the stones, or some similar disease. Certainly Paul speaks about such infirmities in which he would glory because of the grace that is given with them and such as were likely to cure pride; so it cannot meant sin or some prevailing desire, as commentators usually say. Therefore comfort yourselves: God's dearest saints may experience the sorest sicknesses; and if God afflicts you with an aching head, you will have abundant reward if he gives you a better heart with it. If he makes your bones sore, bear it if he breaks the power of your corruptions by it.

Sicknesses are not tokens of God's displeasure. Job's friends were foolish to judge him by his calamity. People usually attack with the tongue when God has attacked with his hand. Alas, the children of God have bodies of the same make as others! Hezekiah, Job, David, and Epaphroditus were all corrected but not condemned. The Roman Catholics maliciously upbraided Calvin with his diseases. "You can see what he is," they said, "by his sicknesses and diseases." He was an indefatigable man but with a sickly, weak body. The same has happened to many of the Lord's precious servants.

Note 2. **He should call the elders**. Note that a sick person should chiefly be thinking about his soul. If anyone is sick, the apostle does not say, "He should call the physician" but **the elders**. Physicians are to be called in their place but not first, not chiefly. Asa made the mistake that "even in his illness he did not seek help from the LORD, but only from the physicians" (2 Chronicles 16:12). Sickness is God's messenger to call us to meet with him. Do not do as most people do and send for the bodily physician and then, when they are past all hope and cure, for the minister. Alas, how many people do this, and before a word of comfort can be administered to them, they are sent to their own place.

Note 3. **He should call**. The elders must be sent for. Someone who has continued in opposition is loath to submit at the last hour and to call the elders to his spiritual assistance. Aquinas says that this last office must only be performed for those who request it. Possidonius, in his biography of Augustine, says that Augustine used of his own accord to visit the poor, the orphans, and the widows, but he never visited the sick until he was called. It is indeed consistent with true religion to "look after orphans" (1:27), but the sick must call for the elders. Truly sometimes I have been afraid to prostitute the comforts of Christianity to people who foolishly neglect their own souls. We confess Christ sometimes where we know our company will not be unwelcome, and in some other cases we may go without being called, in order to learn from our Master and be "found by those who did not seek me" (Isaiah 65:1).

Note 4. **The elders.** For our comfort in sickness it is good to call in the help of the guides and officers of the church. They excel in gifts and are best able to instruct and pray. They can comfort and instruct authoritatively and officially; the prayers of prophets are especially effective. Thus God said to Abimelech, "he is a prophet, and he will pray for you and you will live" (Genesis 20:7). This was the special work of the prophets—to pray for the people, and they had more solemn promises of success: "If they are prophets and have the word of the LORD, let them plead with the LORD Almighty" (Jeremiah 27:18). Those who speak God's Word to you are the best people to commend your case to God. So then, do not despise this help.

Acts done officially have a more solemn assurance of blessing: "If you forgive anyone his sins, they are forgiven . . ." (John 20:23). They can give comfort authoritatively. It is not false theology to say that God will hear their prayers when he will not hear the prayers of other people: "My servant Job will pray for you, and I will accept his prayer and not deal with you according to your folly" (Job 42:8). Though Job's comforters were good men, God wanted to hear Job; therefore in Ezekiel Job is mentioned as a praying prophet. Use their help, then—it is help that has been ordained; and then you may expect a blessing all the more. When Hezekiah was sick, Isaiah the prophet came to give him faithful advice (2 Kings 20:1-2).

Note 5. **The elders.** Visiting the sick should be done jointly with the church officers; it is an important task and needs many workers. The diversity of gifts for prayer and discussion seems to call for this; it is the last office we can perform to those of whom the Lord has made us overseers.

Note 6. **To pray.** One necessary thing in visiting is commending sick people to God, and this prayer must be offered by them or over them, so that their sight may work on us better, and so our prayers may work on them.

Note 7. **And anoint him with oil.** The first preachers of the Gospel of Christ had power to do miracles. The doctrine itself, being so rational and satisfactory, deserved to be believed; but God wanted to give a visible confirmation, to encourage our faith all the more. When Christ had ended his sermon on the mount, he performed miracles; before, signs and wonders had been lacking. "We know you are a teacher who has come from God. For no one could perform the miraculous signs you are doing if God were not with him"

(John 3:2). This was the satisfaction God wanted to give the world concerning the person of the Messiah. Now these miracles have ceased, for Christ has demonstrated a fair claim to our belief, so that we might not be left in uncertainty. The devil can do remarkable things, though nothing that is truly miraculous; and therefore, lest we should be deceived, Christ has foretold that we can expect from Antichrist only "counterfeit miracles" (2 Thessalonians 2:9); "false Christs . . . will . . . perform great signs" (Matthew 24:24).

Note 8. **Anoint him with oil.** The miracles done in Christ's name were wrought by power but ended in mercy. In the very confirmation of the Gospel God wanted to show its benefit. The miracles tended to deliver people from miseries of soul and body, from blindness, and sickness and demons; and so they were most appropriate to the Gospel, which gives us promises of this life and that which is to come. These miracles were a fitting pursuance of Christ's doctrine—not only confirmations of faith, but instances of mercy and love; not miracles of pomp, merely to evince the glory of his person, but miracles of mercy and actions of relief, to show the sweetness of his doctrine, and also to teach us that in the Gospel God wants chiefly to reveal his power by showing mercy.

Note 9. **In the name of the Lord.** All the miracles were to be performed in Christ's name. The apostles and early Christians, though they had such an excellent trust, did not abuse it to serve their own name and interests but Christ's, teaching us that we should exercise all our gifts and abilities by Christ's power for Christ's glory: "O Lord, open my lips, and my mouth will declare your praise" (Psalm 51:15). That was a right aim. To desire life for our own glory is simply like the man who lit his candle at one of the lamps of the altar to steal by, or to beg heaven's aid for the service of hell. The name and form was used by the sons of Sceva but for their own ends, and therefore to their own ruin (Acts 19:13-16). To do things in Christ's name—that is, by abilities received from him—with a pretense of his glory when we intend our own will bring us ill success, as that attempt did to Sceva's sons. Christ wants to be honored with his own gifts and in dispensing every ability looks for our praise in return.

Commentary on Verse 15

And the prayer offered in faith will make the sick person well; the Lord will raise him up. If he has sinned, he will be forgiven.

Here James shows the effect of this anointing and praying, though it is notable that he ascribes it to the prayer rather than to the oil. The moral means is much more worthy than the ritual and ceremonial; and therefore he does not mention the anointing but the prayer of faith. He also shows that this is the normal spiritual means of cure, the other being only a rite they might choose to use in those times.

And the prayer offered in faith. That is, made out of or in faith. This is added to show that this remedy would only work when they had a special revelation or persuasion of its success. The miracle required faith both in the elders and in the person who was sick—faith in the person performing the miracle, and faith in the person upon whom it was performed. Otherwise it was not to be attempted, or it would not be successful. We see that unbelief hindered our Saviour's working: "He could not do any miracles there. . . . And he was amazed at their lack of faith" (Mark 6:5-6).

Will make the sick person well. The Greek word means "save." He is speaking about a bodily infirmity, and therefore it means a bodily salvation—that is, "will restore to health." Thus saving means healing; see Matthew 9:21 and Mark 6:56, "were saved" or "healed."

The Lord will raise him up. The word is used for resurrection from the dead and restoration to health out of sickness, not only here but elsewhere: see Matthew 8:15 and Mark 1:31. The reason the word is used is because sick people lie in bed, and when they recover we say they are "up again" or "on their feet again." **The Lord will raise him up** is added to show by whose power this is done. The value and efficacy of faith lie in its object; so strictly speaking it is not faith, but God called upon in faith, that saves the sick.

If he has sinned. Why does the apostle speak hypothetically? Who is there that can say, "my heart is clean" (compare Proverbs 20:9)? I suppose the apostle implies those special sins by which the disease was contracted and sent by God. Now in this matter he might speak by way of supposition, sicknesses being not always the fruit of sins, but sometimes laid on us as a means to reveal God's glory (John 9:3).

He will be forgiven. But how can another man's prayer of faith obtain the forgiveness of my sins? I answer, very well in God's way, and as they procure a means of conversion and repentance for me. It is not that they pray and believe, though I do whatever I want and then am forgiven; it is that they pray, and therefore God will give me a humble heart and, in the Gospel way, the comfort of a pardon. Certainly we are to ask spiritual things for other people, as well as temporal things. And if we ask, there must be some hope at least that God will grant them.

Notes on Verse 15

Note 1. Neither moral nor ritual means work any further than they are accompanied by faith. Anointing will not do it, prayer will not do it, but

the prayer offered in faith will make the sick person well. In the early days, when miracles were in their full force and vigor, the effect was always ascribed to faith: "your faith has healed you" (Matthew 9:22). Christ does not say, "your touching my garment" but "your faith." It is said in Mark 6:56 that all who touched his cloak were healed. Thus the woman thought the emanation was natural and not freely given. To instruct her, Christ shows it was not the rite but her faith. It is the same in Acts 3:16, "It is Jesus' name and the faith that comes through him that has given this complete healing." Note that this passage shows that the means cannot work without faith. The disciples were invested with great gifts, but they could not cure the boy with the demon because they lacked faith: "'I brought him to your disciples, but they could not heal him.' 'O unbelieving and perverse generation,' Jesus replied" (Matthew 17:16-17).

So then, learn that in all duties and means we should be careful to exercise faith, and we should strive to make the persuasion as express and particular as the promises will permit. Acts of trust are compelling, and the way to get God's power exercised is to glorify it in our own dependence.

Note 2. All our prayers must be made **in faith**; our apostle keeps repeating this argument: "when he asks, he must believe" (1:6), etc. Faith is the fountain of prayer, and prayer should be nothing other than faith exercised. No one can come to Christ aright unless he is persuaded to be the better through him. All worship is founded on good thoughts of God. We have no reason to doubt; we always find a better welcome with him than we can expect. Therefore, in all your addresses to God pray in faith— either declaring his power by counterbalancing the difficulty or declaring his love by acknowledging that the outcome is due to his pleasure.

Note 3. Prayers made **in faith** are usually heard and answered. Christ is so delighted with it that he can deny it nothing: "Woman, you have great faith! Your request is granted" (Matthew 15:28). Christ speaks there as if a believer obtains as much as he can wish for.

Note 4. Faith is effective when we use various means, not because of its own merits but because of God's power and grace. The apostle says, **faith will make the sick person well**, but adds, **the Lord will raise him up**. Faith is just the instrument; it is a grace that has no merit in itself. It is the empty hand of the soul and assigned to such high services because it looks for everything from God. The Roman Catholics look upon faith as an act in us; and because reason suggests that it is not worthy enough for such great effects, they put it together with works, which, they say, give it a value and a merit. They are mistaken.

Note 5. Sins are often the cause of sicknesses; we may thank ourselves for our diseases. The rabbis say that when Adam tasted the forbidden fruit his head ached. Certainly there was the rise and root of human misery: "That is why many among you are weak and sick" (1 Corinthians 11:30).

The body is often the instrument of sins and therefore the object of diseases; the plague and sore of the heart causes that of the body. It is very notable that Christ in all his cures points at the root of the disease: "Take heart, son; your sins are forgiven" (Matthew 9:2). It would have been an ineffective cure without a pardon; while sin remains, you carry the matter of the disease about with you. "Stop sinning or something worse may happen to you" (John 5:14). Obedience is the best medicine. While sin remains, the disease may be stopped but not cured; it will break out in a worse sore and scab. The prophet Isaiah says about Christ, "he took up our infirmities and carried our sorrows" (Isaiah 53:4), meaning the punishment of our sins. Peter applies it in this way in 1 Peter 2:24, "He himself bore our sins in his body on the tree"; but Matthew applies it to Christ's cure of sicknesses: "This was to fulfill what was spoken through the prophet Isaiah: 'He took up our infirmities and carried our diseases'" (Matthew 8:17).

How shall we reconcile these passages? I answer like this: in taking away sickness, which is the effect, Christ wanted to represent taking away sin, which is the cause. Christ's act in taking away sickness was a "type" of taking away sin. Matthew applies that to the sign, which actually applies to the truth itself or the thing signified. You may observe that just as the patriarchs, in their actions and in what they did, were "types" of Christ, so Christ's own actions were in a way "types" of what he himself was chiefly going to do. Thus casting out demons signified the spiritual dispossessing of Satan, and that is why demon-possession was so common in Christ's time. Similarly, the curing of blindness signified the giving of spiritual sight, and taking away sicknesses signified the pardoning of sins. So then, if sin is the cause of sickness, if we want to preserve or recover our health, let us avoid sin: "If you pay attention to his commands and keep all his decrees, I will not bring on you any of the diseases . . ." (Exodus 15:26). Otherwise you may, like one woman, spend all you possess on physicians, and still the cause will continue. In Deuteronomy 28:21-22 we see sin threatened with "wasting disease," "fever," "and inflammation"; usually the disease corresponds to the sin.

Note 6. The best cure is found in a pardon. The apostle says, **will make the sick person well; the Lord will raise him up. If he has sinned . . .** Oh, my brothers! It would be bad if any of us were cured without a pardon, if the wound remained on the conscience when the body is made sound and whole; therefore, first seek your pardon. The best medicine is one that deals with the cause. David says, "Praise the LORD. . . . He forgives all my sins and heals all my diseases" (Psalm 103:2-3). That is the right method; a sick person must first deal with God, and then with the physician. Asa went to the physician first, and therefore it did not work out well for him.

When God takes away the disease and does not take away the guilt, it is not a deliverance but a reprieve from immediate execution.

Commentary and Notes on Verse 16

Therefore confess your sins to each other and pray for each other so that you may be healed. The prayer of a righteous man is powerful and effective.

The word **Therefore** shows that this instruction is to be inferred from what was said before. There is a connection between the verses, for he wants the particular fault acknowledged so that they might pray more effectively for each other.

There is a connection between pardon and confession. The apostle says, **he will be forgiven,** and then **Therefore confess your sins.** See similar passages in Proverbs 28:13 ("whoever confesses and renounces [his sins] finds mercy") and 1 John 1:9 ("If we confess . . ."). This is the best way to find pardon; what is condemned in one court is pardoned in others. God has made a law against sin, and the law must be obeyed; sin must be judged in the court of heaven or in the court of conscience, by God or us. In confession the divine judgment is anticipated (1 Corinthians 11:31-32); this is the best way to honor mercy. When we are aware of many sins, mercy is all the more glorious. God wants pardon obtained in a way in which there is no merit; justice may be glorified by confession but not satisfied. We cannot make satisfaction to God, and therefore he requires acknowledgment. "I will not be angry forever. Only acknowledge your guilt" (Jeremiah 3:12-13).

This is the most rational way to settle our comfort; our griefs are best eased and mitigated if we express them. All passions are allayed by giving vent to them. David roared when he kept silence, but "I said, 'I will confess my transgressions to the LORD'—and you forgave the guilt of my sin" (Psalm 32:5). Besides, this is the best way to bring the soul to dislike sin. Confession is an act of mortification. It is as it were the vomit of the soul; it breeds a dislike of the sweetest morsels when they are found in what is loathsome. Sin is sweet when we commit it but bitter when we remember it. God's children find that their hatred is never more keen against sin than when confessing. So then, come and open your case to God without guile of spirit, and then you may seek your pardon. David makes this a reason for his confidence: "blot out my transgressions. . . . For I acknowledge my transgressions" (Psalm 51:1, 3 KJV).

Resolve to practice confession; it is irksome to the flesh but salutary and healthy to the spirit. Guilt is shy in God's presence; the Lord is dreadful to wounded consciences. But look at it this way: confession is the only way to seek your pardon. Gracious souls only want pardon God's way. "Lord, give me repentance, and then give me pardon," says Fulgentius.

But you will say, "We confess and find no comfort." I answer, it is because you are not as honest with God as you should be; you do not come with a necessary clarity and openness of mind. David says the only people who have the comfort of pardon are those "in whose spirit is no deceit" (Psalm 32:2). Usually there is some sin at the bottom that the soul is loath to disgorge, and then God brings trouble. David lay roaring as long as he followed Satan's advice. Moses had a secret sore that he would not disclose. He pled other things—inadequacy, lack of elocution; but worldly fear was the main reason for his reluctance. That is why God gently touched his secret sore: "Go back to Egypt, for all the men who wanted to kill you are dead" (Exodus 4:19). He had never pleaded concerning this, but God knew that was the interior problem. It is the same with Christians. Usually there is some sin at the bottom, and that is why God continues to trouble them. That is why it is best to take David's course: "I recounted my ways and you answered me" (Psalm 119:26). He told God everything, and then God gave him the light and comfort of grace.

Confess your sins to each other. This clause has been applied in various ways. The Roman Catholics make it the basis of auricular confession, but that is absurd, for then the priest must confess to the penitent as well as the penitent to the priest. James is speaking about reciprocal confession; therefore some of the more honest Roman Catholics have disclaimed this text.

Others apply it to hurts caused to other people; just as the sick person must reconcile himself to God so that he may recover, so he must reconcile himself to his neighbor whom he has wronged or offended. But **sins** covers more than just hurts caused to other people.

Some understand this to mean those sins in which we have offended by joint consent. For example, when a woman has consented to a man's lust she must confess her sin to him, and consequently and reciprocally he must acknowledge his sin to her, so that they may by mutual consent open themselves to repentance. But this interpretation and application of the words is too narrow.

I believe the apostle is speaking about those sins that most wound the conscience in sickness as its particular cause. That is why he speaks of this confession in connection with healing and prayer, for this is how we can most easily help other people move toward actions of spiritual relief, such as applying suitable advice and offering appropriate prayers. Things spoken at random are not usually so effective.

There is a time for confessing our sins not only to God, but to each other. I will not digress into controversy, but I shall briefly show the evils and inconveniences of the sort of confession that Roman Catholics require and the times when we must confess to each other.

(1) The Roman Catholic sacrament of penance obliges people, at least once a year, to confess to a priest all the sins they have committed since the last time, with all the details. No one is exempt from this law—neither prince nor king, not even the Pope himself. They place a great deal of merit and opinion on this. The truth is that this is the great device by which they keep the people loyal to them; knowing the people's secrets makes them feared all the more.

Now what we disprove in this is:

a. The absolute necessity of it. Confession to other people is only necessary in some cases; in others confession to God may be enough. That, indeed, is necessary: see 1 John 1:9.

b. Requiring such a precise and accurate enumeration of their sins, with all the details, makes it one of those insupportable burdens that neither we nor our fathers were able to bear. In short, this scrupulous enumeration is nothing but a rack to the conscience, invented and exercised without any reason. No one's memory is so happy as to answer what is required (Psalm 19:12).

c. Their making it part of a sacrament instituted by God. They argue this from this passage but wretchedly. One of the most modest of their own writers, Gregory of Valentia, lists many Roman Catholics who say the basis of it is only in universal tradition, though indeed it was instituted twelve hundred years after Christ, among other superstitions, by Innocent III.

d. The way it is practiced, and its consequences, rightly make it odious. It is tyrannical, dangerous to the security and peace of princes, betraying their advice, and hazardous to everyone. The practice is profane, as is clear from the filthy and immodest questions that the confessor is to ask, mentioned in Bucharadus, Sanchez, and others.

(2) We are not against all confession, as the Roman Catholics say we are. Besides confession to God, we hold that many sorts of confession to other people are necessary. For example:

a. Public confession. This may be by the church in ordinary or extraordinary humiliation. The congregation was to confess their sins over the head of the sacrifice (Leviticus 16:21). For one part of the day they read the law, and for another part of the day they confessed (Nehemiah 9:3). This is confession *by* the church. It is also necessary to have confession *to* the church.

This may be *before* admission to the church, when people solemnly disclaim the impurities of their former life, professing to walk in the future as befits members of the church: "Confessing their sins, they were baptized by him" (Matthew 3:6). The apostles, too, when they received members into the church, required the profession of faith and repentance, though there was not that scrupulous and narrow prying into their hearts and consciences that some people practice. John did not take a particular confession from every one of the multitude—it was impossible. So we read in Acts 19:18 that "many of those who believed now came and openly confessed their evil deeds"; that is, they solemnly disavowed their former life and practice.

Secondly, this public confession may come *after* admission to the church, when there are public scandals (for the church does not judge secret things). But those scandalous acts that are faults against the church cannot be remitted by the minister alone; the offense being public, the confession has to be public too. The apostle says of the incestuous Christian that his punishment was "inflicted on him by the majority" (2 Corinthians 2:6). And he tells Timothy that "those who sin are to be rebuked publicly" (1 Timothy 5:20), which Aquinas refers to as ecclesiastical discipline. Now this was to be done partly for the sinner's sake, that he might be brought to greater shame and conviction, and partly because of those outside, that the community of the faithful might not be represented as an ulcerous, filthy body, and the church not be thought to be a receptacle of sin but a school of holiness. And therefore, just as Paul shook off the viper, these were to be cast out and only received back when they solemnly acknowledged their sin. Thus Paul says, "a little yeast works through the whole batch of dough" (1 Corinthians 5:6; see also Hebrews 12:15, "that no bitter root grows up to cause trouble and defile many"). These passages mean not so much the contagion of their bad example as the taint of reproach and the guilt of the outward scandal by which the house and body of Christ was made infamous.

b. Private confession to other people. First, to a wronged neighbor, which is called turning to him again after giving offense (see Luke 17:4) and is prescribed by our Saviour in Matthew 5:24, "Leave your gift there in front of the altar. First go and be reconciled to your brother." God will accept no service or worship from us until we have confessed the wrong done to others. So in this passage we are told to **confess your sins to each other**. In disagreements there are offenses on both sides, and everyone will stiffly defend his own cause.

Secondly, this confession may be made to people with whom we have consented in sinning—for example in adultery, theft, etc. We must confess and pray for each other. It is necessary in love to invite those who have shared with us in sin to fellowship in repentance.

Thirdly, this confession may be made to a godly minister or wise Christian under deep wounds of conscience. It is foolish to hide our sores until they are incurable. When we have unburdened ourselves to a godly friend, conscience finds a great deal of ease. Certainly they are then more able to give us advice and can better apply the help of their counsel and prayers to our particular case and are thereby moved to more pity and commiseration. This will not only tell us generally how needy people are but will uncover their sores. It is indeed a fault in Christians not to disclose themselves and be more open with their spiritual friends when they are not able to extricate themselves out of their doubts and troubles. You may do this with any godly Christian, but especially to ministers who are solemnly entrusted with the power of the keys and may help you to apply the comforts of the Word when you cannot yourselves.

Fourthly, when in some special cases God's glory is concerned. For example, when some great judgment seizes upon us because of a previous provocation, which is made plain enough to us in gripes of conscience, it is good to make it known for God's glory. Thus David, when stung in conscience and smitten with a sudden conviction, said, "I have sinned against the LORD" (2 Samuel 12:13). When Achan was marked by lot, Joshua advised him, "My son, give glory to the LORD. . . . Tell me what you have done" (Joshua 7:19). Thus when divine revenge pursues us until we are brought to some fearful end and punishment, it is good to be open in acknowledging our sin, that God's justice may be cleared visibly; for in this God receives a great deal of glory, and people receive a wonderful confirmation and experience of the care and justice of providence.

And pray for each other. Note that it is the duty of Christians to relieve one another by their prayers. You will see that John, at the end of his first letter, gives the same charge: "If anyone sees his brother commit a sin that does not lead to death, he should pray and God will give him life" (5:16). That is, God will pardon him and thereby free him from everlasting death. Because particulars affect us more than general considerations, let me tell you:

(1) We must pray for the whole community of saints, every member of Christ's body—not only those we are familiar with, but those we are not acquainted with. "Keep on praying for all the saints" (Ephesians 6:18). This common stock of supplications is indeed the church's treasury. Paul prays for those who had never seen his face: "I am struggling . . . for all who have not met me personally" (Colossians 2:1). A Christian is a rich merchant who has his prayer partners in various countries, some in all places of the world, who deal for him at the throne of grace; and by this means the members of Christ's body have communion with one another, even though it is at a distance.

(2) It is our duty to pray especially for those to whom we are more closely related, as Paul in Romans 9:3 prays for his own countrymen. Similarly we should pray for our family and relations, that they may be

converted and be dear to us both humanly and in the Lord, as Onesimus was to Paul (Philemon 16). We should also pray for the particular assembly of the faithful we belong to. The minister should pray for his people, and the people for one another (see Ephesians 3:12). Certainly we do not do this as much as we should.

(3) More especially yet, we should pray for magistrates (see 1 Timothy 2:1-2) and officers of the church. As far as magistrates are concerned, this is the best tribute you can pay them. And with ministers, the importance of their work calls for this help from you. In praying for them you pray for yourselves. If the cow has a full udder, it is good for the owner. How passionately Paul calls for the prayers of the people: "I urge you, brothers, by our Lord Jesus Christ and by the love of the Spirit, to join me in my struggle by praying to God for me" (Romans 15:30). Let us not stand alone and strive alone! Therefore you should, as Tertullian says, "besiege heaven with a holy conspiracy."

(4) The weak must pray for the strong, and the strong for the weak. There is no one who should not do so. When there is a lot to do, you make your children do their share, as did even the busy idolaters in Jeremiah 7:18, "The children gather wood, the fathers light the fire, and the women knead the dough." All played a part. It is like that in the family of Christ. No one can be excepted: "The eye cannot say to the hand, 'I don't need you!'" (1 Corinthians 12:21). God delights to put us in debt to each other in the body of Christ, and therefore he will not bless us without the mutual mediation and intercession of one another's prayers, for this is the true intercession of saints. And so in a sense the living saints may be called mediators of intercession.

But chiefly the strong, and those who stand, are to pray for those who have fallen; that is what this passage means. Oh, that we would pay attention to this neglected duty! Not praying for others is unloving; not to expect it from others is pride. Do not stand alone; two, indeed many, are better than one. Joint striving mutually for the good of each other makes the work prosper. Especially, my brothers, pray for those in the ministry. Our labors are great; our corruptions are strong; our temptations and snares are many, possibly all the more for your sakes. Pray that our hearts may be made tender toward you and fitter to give your souls reproof, comfort, and counsel. Pray that we may have wisdom and faithfulness and speak the Word of the Lord boldly. So also pray for one another.

So that you may be healed. This word is a general one and implies freedom from the diseases of either soul or body, and both fit the context. He is speaking of sins and sickness indiscriminately. If you understand this of bodily healing, with respect to sickness, you may note:

Note 1. God wants a particular confession of the very sin for which he brought on the sickness before he heals you. But chiefly I understand this healing spiritually: confess, and the Lord will purge you from your sins and heal the wounds of your conscience. This is what healing means elsewhere in Scripture, such as in Psalm 41:4, "Heal me, for I have sinned against you"; or 1 Peter 2:24, "by his wounds you have been healed."

Note 2. Sin is the soul's sickness. There are many resemblances:

(1) The soul is disordered by sin, just as the body is put out of sorts by sickness.

(2) Deformity. Of all diseases mentioned in the law, sin was represented by leprosy, which most deforms the body.

(3) Sickness causes pain, and sin causes a sting in the conscience and horrors at the time of death (1 Corinthians 15:54-56).

(4) Weakness. The more sin there is, the more inability and feebleness for any work of grace. The apostle says, "we were still powerless" (Romans 5:6)—weak, sickly souls that could do no work; this is how we were in the state of nature. Indeed, after grace there is still daily feebleness; we never have perfect health until we reach heaven.

Hence you see there is a general resemblance between sin and sickness. **The prayer of a righteous man is powerful and effective.** This is added by way of encouragement. In this sentence there are three things:

(1) The prayer is described as **powerful.** The word in the original is so sublime and emphatic that translations cannot reach the height of it. It has been translated in various ways—for example, as ordinary, daily prayer (but without any reason), or as prayer wrought in us by the Holy Spirit. The KJV translators, not knowing what expression to use, translated it by two words, "effectual fervent." The phrase really means a prayer wrought and excited; and so it implies both the efficacy and influence of the Holy Spirit, and the force and vehemence of an earnest spirit and feeling.

A true prayer must be an earnest, fervent prayer. The ancient sign of acceptance was setting fire to the sacrifice. Success may be recognized by the heat and warmth of our spirits. Prayer was symbolized by wrestling. Compare Genesis 32:26 with Hosea 12:4; certainly that is the way to prevail. Thus it is likened to the man who would take no denial (Luke 11:8); what the KJV translates "importunity" [and the NIV "persistence"] is "impudence" in the original Greek. Acts 26:7 says that the tribes of Israel served God "earnestly"; the word means "to the utmost of their strength." Under the law the sweet perfumes in the censers were burnt before they ascended. Look to your feelings; get them fired by the Holy Spirit, that they may rise toward God in devout and religious flames. It is the usual sign of good that you will prevail with God like princes. Luther said, "Would to God I could always pray with such ardor, for then I would always have this answer: 'Your request is granted'" (see Matthew 15:28).

Be earnest and fervent, then, even if you cannot be eloquent. There is language in groans, and sighs are articulate. The child earnestly wants its mother's breast when it cannot ask for it in words. Only beware that your earnestness does not arise from worldly desires and concerns. The sacrifices and perfumes were not to be burned with strange fire. When your censers are fired, do not let the coal be taken from the kitchen but from the altar. God has undertaken to satisfy spiritual desires but not worldly desires.

In prayer we must be very diligent to work our hearts to the duty; thus the word indicates a prayer wrought and driven with much force and vehemence. It is said of the apostles that "they all joined together constantly in prayer" (Acts 1:14). The phrase means the sort of perseverance that is kept up with much labor and force. It is no easy thing to pray and to work a lazy, dead heart into a necessary height of affection. The weights in a clock always run downward, but they are wound up by force; "to you, O LORD, I lift up my soul" (Psalm 25:1). When our affections are raised, it is hard to keep them up; like Moses' hands, they soon flag and grow faint. A bird cannot stay in the air without continually flying and moving its wings. Neither can we persist in prayer without constant work and labor; our faith is so weak that we are kept there with difficulty. Affections flag, and then our thoughts are scattered; weariness leads to wandering. First our hearts are gone, and then our minds, so that we need much labor and diligence. All acts of duty are drawn from us by a holy force.

(2) The praying person is here described as **righteous**. This is not absolutely, as we see from the example of Elijah, who is said to be a man **just like us**; therefore, it means a man who is righteous in Christ, justified by faith.

In prayer we should not only look at the kind of duty, but also at the kind of person. God first accepts the person, and then the duty. Thus the apostle proves that Abel was accepted by God's testimony to his gifts (Hebrews 11:4); and the passage he alludes to, Genesis 4:4, plainly shows that God first looked to Abel, and then to his offering. I have read of a jewel that loses all its virtue when it is put into a dead man's mouth; prayer is such a jewel in a dead man's mouth—it has no power or efficacy: "The sacrifice of the wicked is detestable—how much more so when brought with evil intent!" (Proverbs 21:27). Balaam came with seven rams and seven altars, and all this would not do. John 9:31 says, this being a proverb and a known principle, "God does not listen to sinners."

So then, when you come to pray, it is yourself that matters. Otherwise, you will be in danger of a legal spirit, hoping to gratify God by your prayers and good intentions. There is not a surer sign of reliance on duties than when you look entirely to the quality of the duty and not to quality of the person, as if the person were to be accepted for the sake of the action and not the action for the person. This plainly takes you back to the old covenant and makes works the basis of your acceptance with God. Then again, you will be in danger of being refused. God will have nothing to do with the wicked; he will not "take the wicked by the hand" (Job 8:20 [Geneva version]). And God will ask what you have to do with him (Psalm 50:16ff.). Make sure of your interest in Christ; everything hangs upon that.

(3) The effect of the duty. It is **effective**. He does not tell you how effective—you will find that from trial and experience.

Prayers rightly managed cannot lack results. This is the means that God has consecrated for receiving the highest blessings. Prayer is the key by which the mighty ones of God can lock heaven and open it at will. The best of the graces is faith, and the best of the duties is prayer; these are the best because they are the most useful to our present state. It is wonderful to consider what Scripture ascribes to faith and prayer; prayer sues for blessings in the court of grace, and faith receives them. God himself speaks as if his hands are tied by prayer: "Now leave me alone . . ." (Exodus 32:10). Indeed, he bargains with Moses and offers to make him into a great nation if he will hold his peace. It is the same with the expression in Isaiah 45:11, "Do you question me about my children?" These expressions are to be wondered at in holy reverence but not strained, lest our thoughts degenerate into crude blasphemy. Certainly they are mighty condescensions in which the Lord wants to show us the fruit and efficacy of prayer as he is pleased to accept it in Christ.

So then, pray with this encouragement: God has said in an open place—that is, he has solemnly avowed before all the world—that no one will seek his face in vain (Isaiah 45:19).

Commentary on Verse 17

Elijah was a man just like us. He prayed earnestly that it would not rain, and it did not rain on the land for three and a half years.

James proves his general proposition by a particular instance—the example of Elijah. Before we come to examine the words, I shall discuss a doubt. How could he infer a general rule out of one single instance, especially from a man whose life was full of prodigy and wonder? I answer:

(1) When something is necessarily true, one instance is enough. Any proofs are more for illustration than confirmation.

(2) Even though the instance is particular, the command to pray is universal, as is the promise that we will be heard.

(3) His drift is to show that if Elijah obtained so much, our prayers will

not altogether be in vain; there may be less miracle in our answer, but there will be just as much grace.

(4) As for the special dignity of the person, the apostle himself anticipates that objection when he says Elijah was **just like us**. They might plead that Elijah was a special case—who can expect his experiences? The apostle anticipates this doubt by telling them that Elijah was subject to infirmities just like those of other people.

I come now to the words.

Elijah. He was an eminent prophet, and singular things are related of him in Scripture. He raised the widow's son (1 Kings 17:22); he obtained fire from heaven against the priests of Baal (1 Kings 18:38); he was fed by ravens (1 Kings 17); he went forty days and forty nights in the strength of one meal (1 Kings 19:8); he brought fire from heaven on the captains of two companies and their companions (2 Kings 1:10); he passed over Jordan dry-footed (2 Kings 2:8); he was snatched into heaven in a chariot of fire (2 Kings 2:11); he visibly appeared in the transfiguration of Christ (Matthew 17:3). And here our apostle instances another miracle—heaven itself seemed to be subject to his prayers and to be shut and opened at his pleasure.

Was a man just like us. Some people apply this to outward sufferings and afflictions, some to weaknesses of body and mental distress, some to moral infirmities and sins; all may be intended. The same word is used in Acts 14:15, when the people wanted to sacrifice to Paul and Barnabas: "We too," they said, "are only men, human like you." The word there means whatever distinguishes humans from the divine nature. Peter in a similar case said, "I am only a man myself" (Acts 10:26). Thus the Scripture shows that Elijah was hungry (1 Kings 17:11), that he feared death and therefore fled from Jezebel (1 Kings 19:3), and that he, in a fit of discontent, asked to die (1 Kings 19:4). All kinds of human weakness are ascribed to him.

He prayed earnestly. "He prayed in prayer"—a common Hebraism. Similarly Christ says, "With desire I have desired" (Luke 22:15, KJV)—that is, vehemently and earnestly. Because in Hebrew the form of expression always goes with the thing expressed, Aquinas' note is not altogether amiss: "it may note the agreement between tongue and heart"; the heart prayed, and the tongue prayed. This clause shows why Elijah was heard: he prayed with earnestness and faith, according to the will of God revealed to him.

That it would not rain. There is no such thing in the story, which you have in full in 1 Kings 17 and 18, where there is not a word about his praying that it would not rain. The Scripture there only shows that he foretold a drought. But it is more than probable that the worship of Baal, being accepted everywhere, did extort from this good man, so full of zeal for God, a prayer for drought as a punishment. Then, when the people had been corrected, he prayed for rain again. Because the apostle recorded the fact of his prayer, we cannot doubt its truth. It is common in Scripture for one passage to give us the gist of a story and another the details—for example, the story of Jannes and Jambres (see 2 Timothy 3:8). Also in Psalm 105:18 we read of Joseph that "they bruised his feet with shackles, his neck was put in irons"; no such thing is recorded in Genesis.

Notes on Verse 17

Note 1. God's eminent children are human, just as we are. "Your brothers throughout the world are undergoing the same kind of sufferings" (1 Peter 5:9). They are all troubled with a wicked heart, a busy devil, and a corrupt world. We are all tainted in our souls with Adam's leprosy. There are often notorious blemishes in the lives of the saints; they are of the same nature as other people and have not wholly divested themselves of the interests and concerns of flesh and blood. Rash words came from Moses' lips, and David turned aside to adultery; he gives the reason in Psalm 51:5—he had the same nature as other men. There are various dear children of God who fall foully like this. If they continued constantly in sin, it would mean they were not saints; and unfailing holiness would mean they were not men. So then, children of God who labor under the burden of infirmities may take heart. Such conflicts are not inconsistent with faith and piety; other believers are exercised like this. No one ever went to heaven without some work to develop "faith and patience" (Hebrews 6:12). When we share in the divine nature we do not get rid of the human nature; we ought to walk with care but still with comfort.

Note 2. It does no harm to the most holy people to look upon them as human like ourselves. There is a double fault. Some people canonize the servants of God, not considering them in their infirmities but making them half gods, exempted from the ordinary state of humanity. Thus they lose the benefit of their example, for in the Word they are presented as examples. Your prayers may be heard just as Elijah's were; your sins may be pardoned just as Paul's were (1 Timothy 1:16). God will strengthen and confirm the grace that is necessary in you, as he did with David (Zechariah 12:8). Other people reflect only on holy persons' infirmities, and instead of making them examples of mercy they make them patrons of sin. Thus every base spirit will plead Lot's incest, David's adultery, Noah's drunkenness. James here rehearses not only Elijah's weaknesses but his graces.

Note 3. In the lives of God's choicest servants there was some considerable weakness. Elijah, in the midst of his miracles, was encumbered with many afflictions. Paul had "surpassingly great revelations" but also "a thorn in the flesh." In the life of Jesus Christ himself there was an inter-mixture of power and weakness, of the divine glory and human frailty. At his birth a star shone, but he laid in a manger. Afterwards the devil tempted him in the wilderness, but there angels attended him. He was caught by the soldiers in the garden, but first he made them fall back. In the same way we note that the same disciples who were conscious of his glory on the mountain are afterwards called to be witnesses of his agony in the garden. Compare Matthew 17:1 with Matthew 26:37. All this shows that in the highest dispensations God will keep us humble, and in the lowest providences there is enough to support us.

Note 4. Grace is not without suffering or without passions and affections. The Stoics held that a man was only good if he had lost all natural feeling and affection. Elijah was a man with feelings like ours. Grace does not abrogate our affections but promotes them. It transplants them out of Egypt so that they may grow in Canaan; it does not destroy nature but directs it.

Note 5. All that God worked by and for his eminent servants was with respect to his own grace, not to their worth and dignity. God did much for Elijah, but he was a man **just like us**. Though his prayers were effective, he was, as every believer is, indebted to grace. When we have received great help, we are still unprofitable servants (Luke 17:10); when we reflect on the common frailty, we may say so in words of truth as well as in words of sobriety and humility. At first when God takes us to mercy we are like other people; was not Esau Jacob's brother (Malachi 1:2)? In their persons, in their humanity, there was no difference. God could not love anything in Jacob better than in Esau except for his own grace. So if we are promoted above other believers, it is out of mere grace; if from their shoulders upward some are higher than other saints, it is the Lord's choice, not their own worth. Elijah was **just like us**, and the widow was like other widows: "there were many widows in Israel. . . . Yet Elijah was not sent to any of them, but to a widow in Zarephath" (Luke 4:25-26). God has mercy on those he wants to; if you excel, who has made you different?

Note 6. Where the heart is upright, our infirmities will not hinder our prayers. Elijah was a man **just like us**, and yet he prayed, and it did not rain; imitate his faith and earnestness, and your infirmities will be no impediment: "May the LORD . . . pardon everyone who sets his heart on seeking God . . . even if he is not clean according to the rules of the sanctuary" (2 Chronicles 30:18-19). Christ, when he came into the garden, said he would eat the honey with the honeycomb (Song of Songs 5:1); he would accept their duties despite not being separated from the wax, from weakness and imperfection, and would drink his wine mingled with milk—that is, mixed with a milder and less noble beverage. Under the law the high priest was to bear the iniquity of their holy things (Exodus 28:38);

in the same way Jesus Christ does away with the weakness of our service. Those who do not justify their infirmities may pray with hope of success. God knows the voice of the Spirit; our worldly desires meet with his pardon and our spiritual desires with acceptance.

Note 7. **He prayed earnestly.** This is our duty—not only to say a prayer, but to pray a prayer: "The Spirit himself intercedes for us with groans that cannot express" (Romans 8:26); that is, we pray, and the Spirit prays in our prayers. When the tongue prays alone, it is just an empty ring. We often mistake lungs and sighs for grace, and the agitation of the bodily spirits for the impressions of the Holy Spirit; many people work themselves into a great heat and vehemence with argumentative speech, and that is all. The voice that is heard on high is the groaning of the soul. So then, pray earnestly; make all your prayers and supplications "in the Spirit" (Ephesians 6:18). Do not let the heart wander while the lips are praying; lip-labor does no more than a wind instrument—it makes a loud noise. But the essence of prayer lies in the raising of the mind.

Note 8. It is sometimes lawful to call down God's vengeance on the wicked. Elijah prayed that it might not rain, out of zeal for God's glory and detestation of the people's idolatry. I confess here that we must be cautious; imprecations in Scripture were often uttered with a prophetic spirit and by special impulse and intimation from God. Elijah's act must not be imitated without Elijah's spirit and warrant. The apostles, in a preposterous imitation of another act of Elijah's, suggested calling down fire from heaven (Luke 9:54), whereupon Christ checked them: "You do not know what kind of spirit you are of" (verse 55, NIV margin). There are fits of revenge or strange wildfire that was never kindled upon God's hearth.

I shall lay down some propositions to guide you in this matter of imprecation:

(1) There is a great deal of difference between public and private cases. In all private cases it is the glory of our religion to bless those who curse us, to pray for those who treat us spitefully. This is what we learn from the great author of our profession; he "was numbered with the transgressors" and he "made intercession for the transgressors" (Isaiah 53:12). This was a prophecy of the prayer that Christ uttered on the cross for his persecutors: "Father, forgive them, for they do not know what they are doing." His heart was full of love when theirs was full of spite. Truly the followers of the Lamb should not be of a wolfish spirit; we should be ready to forgive all private and personal wrongs. But in public cases, when divine or human right is transposed and disturbed, we may ask God to relieve oppressed innocence, to "crush the . . . hairy crowns of those who go on in their sins" (Psalm 68:21).

(2) In public cases we must not ask for revenge directly and formally. Thus our prayers must primarily respect the vindication of God's glory

and the avenging of our own case only incidentally: "Not to us, O LORD, not to us but to your name be the glory" (Psalm 115:1)—that is, not for our revenge or to satisfy our desires, but to restore the reputation of his mercy and truth. The main motive should be desire for the divine glory. The whole of Psalm 83 is full of imprecations, but it ends thus (verse 18): "Let them know that you, whose name is the LORD—that you alone are the Most High over all the earth." The vindication of God's honor was the main aim of their requests.

(3) God's people do not ask for vengeance against particular people as such, but in general against the enemies of the church, and expressly against such as are known to God to be perverse and implacable.

Note 9. God may allow judgments, especially that of unseasonable weather, to continue for a long time. In Elijah's time for three and a half years the heavens were like brass and the earth like iron. Perhaps this will calm our froward spirits, which are apt to complain against providence when we do not get the weather we like. Think how it was with Israel when it did not rain for three years and more. Fear him who can stop "the water jars of the heavens" (Job 38:37) and restrain the influence of the clouds; fruitful seasons are at his disposal: see Jeremiah 5:24. Secondary causes do not work by chance. This is the bridle that God has on the world; the ordering of the weather is one of the most visible testimonies of his power and goodness.

Note 10. It is sad for anyone to provoke the prophets of the Lord to pray against them. The grieving of Elijah's spirit cost Israel dearly. There is much in the prophets' messages, and there is as much in their solemn prayers. We may often observe in the history of the Old Testament that when God had a mind to destroy a people, he commanded his prophets to be silent. If their silence is a sad omen, what are their imprecations? When Zechariah's blood was shed, he said, "May the LORD see this and call you to account." This prayer cost them the miseries of Babylon, and the prophet's blood was not fully revenged until their utter ruin; compare 2 Chronicles 24:21-22 with Matthew 23:35-36. Certainly, even if there is little in prayers that are the effusions of revenge or fits of anger, yet when by your sin and insolence you give God's messengers cause to pray against you, their complaints are the sad presages of an ensuing judgment.

Commentary on Verse 18

Again he prayed, and the heavens gave rain, and the earth produced its crops.

Again he prayed. That is, in another strain, not by way of imprecation but supplication. This is recorded in 1 Kings 18:42, "Elijah . . . bent down to the ground and put his face between his knees," which was an action of the most humble and fervent prayer, by means of which God had determined to bestow a blessing.

And the heavens gave rain. "The heavens"—that is, the air and clouds, just as "the birds of heaven" is translated "the birds of the air" (Matthew 6:26). "The LORD's anger will burn against you, and he will shut the heavens so that it will not rain" (Deuteronomy 11:17)—"the heavens" meaning the clouds. It is the same in the climax of Hosea 2:21-22—"I will respond to the skies, and they will respond to the earth"; "the skies" means the clouds.

And the earth produced its crops. All causes depend on one another, and the highest on God; before this rain, there was a great famine because of the drought.

Notes on Verse 18

Note 1. When God means to bestow blessings, he stirs up the hearts of the people to pray for them. God, who decrees the end, decrees the means: "Once again I will yield to the plea of the house of Israel and do this for them" (Ezekiel 36:37); "Then you will call upon me and come and pray to me, and I will listen to you" (Jeremiah 29:12). When the time of deliverance came, God wanted them to seek it by prayer. So then, look upon the effusion of the spirit of supplication as a good sign; it is the first intimation and token for good of approaching mercy, like the chirping of birds before the spring.

Note 2. We may be sure that a blessing will be given, but we must not give up praying for it. Elijah had foretold rain, and yet when he seemed to hear the sound of it he started to pray. Daniel had understood from books that the day had arrived; so he was earnest in prayer (Daniel 9:1-3). When Christ intimates his coming ("Yes, I am coming soon!"), the church takes hold of that and prays, "Amen. Come, Lord Jesus" (Revelation 22:20). This shows that it is a bad sort of confidence that makes us neglect the means. God's children are never more diligent and free in their efforts than when they are confident of a blessing; hope is hard-working and leads to action.

Note 3. Prayer is a good remedy in the most desperate cases, and when you are lost to all other hopes you are not lost to the hopes of prayer. Though there had been three years' drought, Elijah prayed until he brought down sweet showers. Continue in prayer with some hope, even if the sky is like brass and the earth like iron. When the situation is desperate, the Lord comes in; he sent Moses when the quota of bricks was doubled.

Note 4. The efficacy of prayer is very great. Elijah seems to have the key of heaven, to open it and shut it at will. Nothing has such wonderful effects in the world as prayer. It made the sun stand still at Joshua's request (Joshua 10:12-13), and indeed to go backwards so many degrees when Hezekiah prayed (Isaiah 38:8). It brought fire out of heaven when Elijah prayed (2 Kings 1:10). It brought angels out of heaven when Elisha prayed (2 Kings 6:17). God himself will seem to yield to the importunity and force of prayer (Genesis 32:24-28); in this wrestling he will be overcome. Certainly those who neglect prayer not only neglect the *sweetest* way of conversing with God but the *most forcible* way of prevailing with him.

Note 5. **The heavens gave rain, and the earth produced its crops.** All secondary causes are interdependent. Created things help and supply one another. The earth is cherished by the heat of the stars and moistened by the water, and by the temperament of both is made fruitful, and so sends out innumerable plants for the comfort and use of living creatures; and living creatures then supply mankind. It is wonderful to think about the interdependence of all causes; the heavens work upon the elements, the elements upon the earth, and the earth yields crops for our use. The prophet notes this in Hosea 2:21-22, "I will respond to the skies, and they will respond to the earth; and the earth will respond to the grain, the new wine and oil, and they will respond to Jezreel." We look for the supplies of corn, wine, and oil; but they can do nothing without clouds, and the clouds can do nothing without stars, and the stars can do nothing without God. Created things depend on each other, and all depends on God. In the order of the world there is an excellent chain of causes by which all things hang together, so that they may lead the soul up to the Lord.

Commentary on Verses 19-20

My brothers, if one of you should wander from the truth and someone should bring him back, remember this: Whoever turns a sinner away from his error will save him from death and cover over a multitude of sins.

Here the apostle turns from prayer to another Christian task, and that is admonition—turning a sinner from the error of his way. A double fruit is attached: we shall be instruments both in their conversion and in their pardon. Some people think that this is a defense of the whole letter; rather, it may refer to the immediate context, for the apostle is dealing with those acts of Christian charity and relief that we owe to one another: visiting the sick, praying for the distressed, and now reclaiming those who have strayed.

If one of you. That is, of your nation, or rather congregation, for he imagines them to be already won to the knowledge of the truth.

Should wander from the truth. He understood errors both in faith and manners. The word chiefly means errors in the faith. But in the next verse he speaks about **a sinner** and of **cover[ing] over a multitude of sins**, and these phrases imply errors of life. So both must be understood. By **truth** he understands the rule of the Gospel, whether condemning errors in judgment or indirect practices. Thus, concerning the first it is said of Hymenaeus and Philetus in 2 Timothy 2:18 that they "have wandered away from the truth. They say that the resurrection has already taken place." And concerning the second, it is said of Peter in Galatians 2:14 that he was "not acting in line with the truth of the gospel." And the apostle John often speaks about "walking in the truth"—that is, according to that rule and order that the Gospel prescribes.

And someone should bring him back. To convert a sinner is strictly God's work. "We are God's workmanship, created in Christ Jesus to do good works" (Ephesians 2:10). Yet it is ascribed to man, to the ministers and instruments of conversion, as in Acts 26:18 ("to . . . turn them . . . from the power of Satan to God"), because they use the means by which God conveys a blessing. We may have planted and watered, but "God made it grow" (1 Corinthians 3:6). Note that James says **someone**—he does not limit it just to the minister; acts of spiritual love belong to the care of all believers. Wherever there is true grace it will be assimilating: "And when you have turned back, strengthen your brothers" (Luke 22:32).

Remember this: Whoever turns a sinner. That is, whoever is an instrument in God's hand by contributing the help and counsel of his prayers and efforts.

Will save him [shall save a soul, KJV]. Some people explain this as the soul of the admonisher—he will save his own soul; but it is more correctly understood of the soul of the person who is turned back.

Turns—that is, he is an instrument of the other's salvation. Thus Romans 11:14 says, "in the hope that I may somehow arouse my own people"; and 1 Timothy 4:16, "you will save both yourself and your hearers." **Will save him;** the KJV has **a soul.** The person—the principal part—is specified; and when this is saved, the body also is saved. So it is in 1 Peter 1:9, "You are receiving the goal of your faith, the salvation of your souls."

From death—eternal death, which has no power over the converted

(Revelation 20:6). This was Christ's work; to save souls from death, he himself died to procure salvation. Shall we not contribute a few endeavors to win others from death?

And cover over a multitude of sins. God's act is again ascribed to the instrument. The sense is, that person shall be a means of hiding the sins of an erring brother. I confess there is some difference about how to render the sense of this phrase. Brugensis applies it to the person converting: he will cover over a multitude of his own sins. His reason is taken from a parallel passage in 1 Peter 4:8, where it says, "love each other deeply, because love covers over a multitude of sins." He applies that passage, together with this one, to the merit of love before God. But to this I reply:

(1) The doctrine itself is false. Love is indeed a sign and argument of the forgiveness of sins, but not a cause. To pardon others gives us the greater confidence and assurance of our own pardon (Matthew 6:14).

(2) It is uncertain whether the expression in Peter, and this in James, have the same aim and purpose; indeed, there are strong reasons to the contrary.

(3) Even if we suppose that these passages are parallel, the one in Peter does not speak about covering sins before God but among men; and not of the covering of the sins of the loving person, but of the person being loved. That sentence is taken from Proverbs 10:12, "Hatred stirs up dissension, but love covers over all wrongs"—that is, it conceals and buries the faults of a neighbor. This can only be applied to the business of justification indirectly. I confess that some people apply this passage of James in the same way: **cover over a multitude of sins**; i.e., they say that by brotherly admonitions one will seek to prevent or hide others' infirmities, whereas those who hate their brothers do not desire to admonish them but to divulge their sins, to their discredit and infamy.

But to me the clause seems to serve another purpose, for it is ranked among spiritual benefits and is urged, not by way of duty, but motive; first **will save him** and then **cover**. Therefore, I believe it implies the act of justification, which is elsewhere called the covering of sins (Psalm 32:1). And he means the sins of the unconverted person, which we are said to cover when, as instruments, by our admonitions, we reclaim the erroneous person and bring him to repentance.

Note that it says, **a multitude of sins** for two reasons:

(1) To counter discouragement. Other persons may be very bad, but do not neglect to admonish and reclaim them. Admonition at the right time may be a means of covering over a multitude.

(2) To imply the contagion and spreading of this leaven. One error and sin gives rise to another, just as circles do in the water; and whoever begins to wander goes farther.

Notes on Verses 19-20

Note 1. Brothers may wander from the truth. The apostle says, **My broth-ers, if one of you should wander.** There is no saint portrayed in the Word of God whose failings and errors are not recorded. In the visible church there may be errors; no one doubts that God's children, the elect, may sometimes be led astray—not totally, not finally, and with great diffi-culty—into gross errors: "to deceive even the elect—if that were possible" (Matthew 24:24). It is not possible totally because of the infallible predes-tination and efficacious protection of God. Job 12:16 says, "both deceived and deceiver are his." He decides who will deceive and who will be deceived.

But it is true that brothers may die in a lesser error, one that is consis-tent with faith and salvation; but otherwise they cannot err, or at least not finally. So then, the best saints must be cautious. Christ says to his own disciples, "Watch out that no one deceives you" (Matthew 24:4). Error is contagious and goes along with our natural thoughts wonderfully; know-ing what is in us, we can soon go wrong. No wrong idea can be suggested to us without its seeds being in our own souls. Again, do not be scandal-ized when you see stars of the first magnitude leave their sphere and posi-tion and glorious lights fall from heaven like lightning. God's own children may err, and dangerously for a while.

Note 2. We are not only to watch out for our salvation, but for that of others. The apostle says, **If any one of you . . .** God has made us guardians of one another. It savored of rudeness and profanity when Cain said, "Am I my brother's keeper?" As God has set the conscience to watch over the inner person, so in regard to behavior he has set Christians to watch over one another. "See to it, brothers, that none of you has a sinful, unbelieving heart that turns away from the living God" (Hebrews 3:12)—not only in yourselves, but in any of you. "See to it that no one misses the grace of God and that no bitter root grows up to cause trouble and defile many" (Hebrews 12:15). There must be a constant watch kept not only over our own hearts but also over the congregations to which we belong. Members must take care of one another; this is the communion between saints.

(1) James reproves our neglect of this duty. Straying would have been largely prevented if we had been watchful or if we reasoned together in a Christian manner; what comfort and consolation we might receive from one another's faith and gifts! As no one is born for himself, so no one is born again for himself. We should "spur one another on" (Hebrews 10:24).

(2) This shows what a heinous sin is in those who are ready to seize on each person's hurt. Just as the dragon was waiting for the child in Revelation 12:4, or as angry Herod tried to destroy the babies in

Bethlehem, or as a March wind nips the early blossoms of spring, these persons nip and discourage the infancy and first buddings of grace by censure, reproach, and worldly suggestions and put stumbling-blocks in the way of young converts. It is usually like this when people begin to pay attention to the ways of God: profane men make them objects of scorn and contempt, and fanatical men lie in wait with crafty enterprise to deceive them. If it is a duty to save a soul, it is certainly a dangerous sin to seduce a soul. Such people are devilish; they are agents for the kingdom of darkness. Satan goes back and forth, and so do they. It is dangerous to share in other people's sins, to draw that guilt on your own head. You need to be established in the way that you promote with zeal; you need to have a high assurance of it. But usually in those who promote errors you may see either a blind and rash zeal or a corrupt aim. "These teachers will exploit you with stories they have made up" (2 Peter 2:3); they propagate their opinion with heat and earnestness, so that they promote their own gain.

Note 3. **If one of you should wander.** If there is just one—there is no one so base and contemptible in the church that the care of their safety does not belong to all. One root of bitterness defiles many. We are all concerned with infection and scandal; one spark may cause a great fire. It was so with Arius; a spark, hardly noticeable at first, kindled such a flame as burned in all parts of the world. "Catch . . . the little foxes" (Song of Songs 2:15). It is wise to watch the first appearances of sin and error in a congregation. It also presses us to take care of the most ordinary saint in our communion. Some people think they are too high in birth and abilities for the socializing there should be between members of the body of Christ. Andronicus and Junias, two poor prisoners, were of great note in the churches (Romans 16:7).

Note 4. **And someone should bring him back.** The expression is indefinite, and so not limited to the officers of the church, though it is chiefly their work. Besides the public exhortations of ministers, individual Christians should confer together for comfort and edification. I say not only they *may* but they *must* keep up Christian fellowship among themselves: "Encourage one another daily, as long as it called Today" (Hebrews 3:13). They are to stir one another up by speech that tends to show up sin and prevent hardness of heart and apostasy. God has dispensed his gifts in different ways, so that we might be indebted to each other. That is why the apostle calls it "God's grace in its various forms" (1 Peter 4:10). Everyone should throw in his lot according to his gifts and experience; as the wicked said to one another, "throw in your lot with us" (Proverbs 1:14).

Note 5. **Bring him back.** That is, bring him from his wandering. Among other acts of Christian fellowship, this is one of the most important. We must not only exhort but reclaim. This is a duty we owe even to our neighbor's beast: "If you see your brother's donkey or his ox fallen on the road, do not ignore it" (Deuteronomy 22:4). Exodus 23:4 even says, "If you come across your enemy's ox or donkey wandering off, be sure to take it back to him." Note in each passage that if the beasts were fallen or strayed, love commands us to help them and bring them back. Is God concerned for oxen and donkeys? If we can sin in regard to them, we can suffer for the sins of others. Bringing them back may be a thankless task, but it must not be neglected; usually we are swayed by worldly considerations, and we are loath to do what is unpleasant. So then, if it is our duty to admonish, it is another's duty to listen to the words of exhortation, to bear reproof patiently, or he will be opposing his own salvation. Error is touchy. Worldly affections are loath to have the judgment informed; they take away the light of reason and leave us only the pride of reason. There is no one as angry as those who are seduced or persuaded into an opinion; usually conviction and reproof give rise to hatred: "Have I now become your enemy by telling you the truth?" (Galatians 4:16). Truth is a good mother, but it often gives birth to a bad daughter: contempt and hatred. This should not be so! David regarded being struck by the righteous as "a kindness" (Psalm 141:5); faithful reproof and counsel are like a sword anointed with balsam—it wounds and heals at the same time.

Note 6. **Bring him back.** He does not say "destroy him"; the work of Christians is not to accuse and condemn, but to counsel and convert an erroneous person. To call down fire from heaven argues some hastiness and impatience of revenge; first burn them in the fire of love. Before any rigorous course is taken, we must use all due means of information. It is heretics who take "the way of Cain" (Jude 11). It is tyranny in the Roman Catholics to punish every scruple; if a doubt is suggested, even in confession, it can be expiated only with torments. Ambrose observed that "false religions brook no contradiction; and what is lacking in argument is made up in force; and therefore erroneous ways are cruel." No compulsive force should be used before care is taken to get better information and resolve the doubting conscience, as long as there is any desire to be informed. Paul calls for two or three admonitions before a church censure (Titus 3:10). They are cruel hangmen, not ministers, says Pareus, who do not care to save a soul from death but deliver it up straightaway to the devil, to the sword.

Note 7. **Remember this [let him know,** KJV]. To spur ourselves on to a good work, it is good for us actually to consider its dignity and benefits— to consider what a high honor it is to have a hand in such work. Thus the apostle presses us to patience for this reason: "we know that suffering produces perseverance" (Romans 5:3). And of sincerity he says, "working for the Lord, not for men, since you know that you will receive an inheritance from the Lord as a reward" (Colossians 3:23-24). So then, learn this wisdom in case of deadness and opposition of spirit; direct your thoughts to the worth and success of your duties. Human strength lies in discussion and reason, and there is no such relief to the soul as that which comes from thoughts at the right moment: whom do I serve? The Lord? Can any labor undertaken for his sake be in vain?

Note 8. **Whoever turns a sinner away from his error.** Previously this was called "wandering from the truth," and now "the error of his way." Note that errors in doctrine usually end in sins of life and practice; "these dreamers pollute their own bodies" (Jude 8). First people dream; then they defile themselves. We often see that impurity of religion is joined with uncleanness of body, and spiritual fornication is punished with bodily fornication. "A spirit of prostitution leads them astray; they are unfaithful to their God" (Hosea 4:12-13 [in the KJV it is, "They have gone a whoring from under their God . . . therefore your daughters shall commit whoredom"]). Augustine says that those who cannot be chaste go fornicating off from God. Truth awes the soul, and right belief guides the behavior; unbelief is the mother of sin, and wrong belief is its nurse. In error there is a sinful league between the rational and sensual parts, and thus worldly affections are gratified with worldly doctrines. The spirit or upper part of the soul gratifies the flesh or lower faculties, and therefore the convicting power of the Word is said to divide "soul and spirit" (Hebrews 4:12 [*Ed. note*—Manton says, "flesh and spirit"]), and also between worldly feelings and the crafty pretenses by which error is excused.

Note 9. **Will save.** Man under God has this honor. We are "God's fellow workers" (2 Corinthians 6:1). He is pleased to take us into fellowship in his own work and to give our efforts the glory of his grace. This is a high honor that the Lord gives us; we should learn to turn it back again to God, to whom alone it is due: "I worked harder than all of them—yet not I, but the grace of God that was with me" (1 Corinthians 15:10). "Your mina has earned ten more" (Luke 19:16)—not my hard work, but "your mina." "I no longer live, but Christ lives in me" (Galatians 2:20). When God puts the glory of his own work on the head of the creatures, they certainly have great cause to lay the crown of their excellence at the feet of the Lord; when the honor of the supreme cause is put upon the instrument, the instrument may well ascribe everything to the supreme cause. Such is the grace of God, that when you have used the means, he will count it as part of your spiritual success: "you have won your brother over" (Matthew 18:15).

We lose nothing by being employed in God's service. Let us strive and take pains in his work! Paul would be anything that he might win some (1 Corinthians 9:19-22). This also guides Christians. We must not neglect the means; God gives us the terms proper to the supreme cause. God says, "Spare him from going down to the pit" (Job 33:24). The ministers of the

Gospel who were to preach to Edom for the conversion of the elect there were called "deliverers" (Obadiah 21). It is remarkable that though the work of conversion is strictly speaking the Lord's, it is sometimes ascribed to ourselves, to show that we must not be negligent; sometimes to the ministers and instruments, to show that we must not hold their help in contempt; and sometimes to God, that we may not be self-confident or unthankful.

Note 10. **Soul** [KJV]. Salvation is principally of the soul. The body has its share: "our lowly bodies" will be "like his glorious body" (Philippians 3:21). But the soul is first possessed of glory and is the chief receptacle of free grace at present: see 1 Peter 1:9. So then, this teaches us not to look primarily for a physical heaven or a place of ease and pleasure. This is the heaven of heaven—that the soul will be filled up with God, understand God, love God, and be satisfied with his presence. Complete knowledge and complete love and union with Christ are the things that Christians should look for. And this teaches us to keep our souls pure; "sinful desires . . . war against your soul" (1 Peter 2:11)—not only against its present welfare, but against its future hopes. This also comforts the children of God; whatever their situation, it will be all right with their souls.

Note 11. **From death.** Errors are deadly to the spirit. The wages of every sin is death, especially of sin countenanced by error, for then there is a conspiracy of the whole soul against God. The apostle Peter calls heresies "destructive heresies." I confess some heresies are more destructive than others, but all of them have a destructive tendency. Only the way of truth is the way of life. There are some heresies that are totally inconsistent with salvation for eternal life, such as errors in fundamentals, joined with an obstinacy and reluctance against the light, which is the badge of a heretic who is in a state of damnation. So then, let us take heed how we dally with errors—there is death in them; would you play with your own damnation? Errors are dangerous; someone who embraces them embraces his own death. James here refutes those who say there is salvation in any way provided we live a good life. Some Libertines say this, and some of the Arminians in Holland. The Socinians also say that a man of any persuasion may be saved if he does not walk contrary to his light. At the Council of Trent, the salvation of the heathen by the power of nature without Christ was much discussed. The theologians of Collen published a book about *The Salvation of Aristotle the Heathen.* But the Scripture speaks only of one faith (Ephesians 4:5) and says that all nations will be brought to God by this Gospel (Matthew 24:14).

So that you may understand this matter more clearly, I will lay down a few propositions.

(1) No one can be saved without Christ. There is no other "foundation" (1 Corinthians 3:11). "Salvation is found in no one else, for there is

no other name under heaven given to men by which we must be saved" (Acts 4:12). "I am the way" (John 14:6).

(2) No one can be saved by Christ without knowing him and believing in him (John 17:3). Venator said that a person could be saved by Christ without so much as a historical knowledge of him, but in the Word we know of no salvation except by believing in Christ (John 3:17).

(3) We must believe in Christ according to the way the Scriptures show us—that is, the rule of faith (1 Corinthians 15:14; John 7:38). The apostle everywhere speaks against those who teach another doctrine (Galatians 1:6-8; 1 Timothy 1:3; 6:3). Therefore, if they are deceived they say Christ will not look at what you believe, but how you live, and will make everything depend on the good life.

(4) Lesser differences in and about the doctrine of the Scriptures, even if they are consistent with the main thrust of salvation, are damnable. Circumcision and uncircumcision is nothing to the new creature; yet to be of either of these against conscience is a matter of dreadful consequence, for then a lesser opinion is in the same rank as a known sin, being deliberately maintained against light. Consider, then, how much it concerns you to be right in judgment and profession, for though the error may not be damnable in itself, it may be so by circumstance, reluctance against the light being inconsistent with grace. There cannot be a greater argument of an unsubdued will than to stand out against conviction because of secular considerations; this is to love darkness instead of light (John 3:19) and to prefer present convenience before those glorious rewards that religion offers. How inconsistent that is with faith or true grace, Christ shows in John 5:44 and 12:43. I know people usually plead that there may be salvation as long as the error is not fundamental. Yes, but however small the error, there is great danger in going against the light (Philippians 3:15-16). Those who are mature must walk up to the height of their light and principles; and though in some cases profession may be unexpressed and we may keep what we believe between ourselves and God (Romans 14:22), yet we cannot do this in times of public contest and when we are solemnly called to give witness to truth. So do not be deceived with the pretense that there may be salvation in the way that you practice. As Despaigne argues, suppose you could be saved in the way you acknowledge to be erroneous; how can it be consistent with love to be guilty of such horrible contempt and ingratitude as to be content that God may be dishonored provided we may be saved?

(5) Gross negligence, or not taking the trouble to know better, is equivalent to standing against the light. There is deceit in laziness or affected ignorance; people will not know what they have a mind to hate. This is evidence of a secret fear and suspicion of the truth; people are loath to fol-

low it too closely, lest it oppose their desires and interests: "Everyone who does evil hates the light, and will not come into the light for fear that his deeds will be exposed" (John 3:20). "They deliberately forget" (2 Peter 3:5). Those who are pleased with ignorance of any truth err not only in their minds but in their hearts; it is the practice of God's people to be always searching (Psalm 1:2; Romans 12:2). We should not only do what we know, but search in order that we may know more.

(6) Those who live in a lesser error about faith or worship are saved with much difficulty (1 Corinthians 3:13). The apostle speaks about chaff and hay built on the golden foundation, and he says that anyone who does this will be saved as by fire; he loses much of his comfort and peace, is very scorched in spirit, and is kept in a darker, colder, and more doubtful way.

Note 12. **And cover over**. Justification consists in the covering of our sins. It is removed out of God's sight and the sight of our own consciences—chiefly out of God's sight. God cannot choose but see it since he is omniscient and cannot choose but hate it since he is holy, but he will not punish it, because he has received satisfaction in Christ. Sins are so hidden that they will not be brought to judgment; nor will they hurt us. God will cast them into the depths of the sea (see Micah 7:18). That which is in the depths of the sea is lost and forgotten forever; the ocean will never be drained or dried up. All these words the Lord uses to persuade us that once sins are pardoned it is as if they were never committed. Men *forgive* but do not easily *forget*; if the wound is cured, the scar remains. But God accepts us as if there were no breach.

Note 13. **A multitude of sins**. Many sins do not hinder our pardon or conversion. God's "gift followed many trespasses and brought justification" (Romans 5:16). "He will freely pardon" (Isaiah 55:7). All these thousands of years God has been multiplying pardons, and yet free grace is not tired out. The creature owes a great debt to justice, but we have an able surety. It is foolish to think that an emperor's revenue will not pay a beggar's debt. Christ has undertaken to satisfy, and he has enough money to pay. We are limited and therefore think too narrowly of the abundance of grace. But God is not like man (Hosea 11:9). Mercy is a treasure that cannot easily be spent. We have many sins, but God has many mercies: "according to your great compassion" (Psalm 51:1). Certainly mercy is an ocean that is always full and always flowing. Free grace can show you large accounts and a long bill, canceled by the blood of Christ.

May the Lord interest you in this abundant mercy, through the blood of Christ and the sanctification of the Spirit! Amen.